Critical Readings in the History of Christian Mission

Volume 1

Critical Readings in the History of Christian Mission

VOLUME 1

Edited by

Martha Frederiks
Dorottya Nagy

BRILL

LEIDEN | BOSTON

The Library of Congress Cataloging-in-Publication Data is available online at http://catalog.loc.gov
LC record available at http://lccn.loc.gov/2021937176

Typeface for the Latin, Greek, and Cyrillic scripts: "Brill". See and download: brill.com/brill-typeface.

ISBN 978-90-04-39552-7 (hardback, set)
ISBN 978-90-04-39543-5 (hardback, vol. 1)
ISBN 978-90-04-39544-2 (hardback, vol. 2)
ISBN 978-90-04-39545-9 (hardback, vol. 3)
ISBN 978-90-04-39546-6 (hardback, vol. 4)
ISBN 978-90-04-39958-7 (e-book, vol. 1)
ISBN 978-90-04-39959-4 (e-book, vol. 2)
ISBN 978-90-04-39960-0 (e-book, vol. 3)
ISBN 978-90-04-39961-7 (e-book, vol. 4)

Copyright 2021 by Koninklijke Brill NV, Leiden, The Netherlands.
Koninklijke Brill NV incorporates the imprints Brill, Brill Hes & De Graaf, Brill Nijhoff, Brill Rodopi, Brill Sense, Hotei Publishing, mentis Verlag, Verlag Ferdinand Schöningh and Wilhelm Fink Verlag.
All rights reserved. No part of this publication may be reproduced, translated, stored in a retrieval system, or transmitted in any form or by any means, electronic, mechanical, photocopying, recording or otherwise, without prior written permission from the publisher. Requests for re-use and/or translations must be addressed to Koninklijke Brill NV via brill.com or copyright.com.
Brill has made all reasonable efforts to trace all rights holders to any copyrighted material used in this work. In cases where these efforts have not been successful the publisher welcomes communications from copyright holders, so that the appropriate acknowledgements can be made in future editions, and to settle other permission matters.

This book is printed on acid-free paper and produced in a sustainable manner.

Contents

VOLUME 1

Introduction   1
Dorottya Nagy and Martha Frederiks

Methods

1   Recent Trends in the Historiography of Christianity in Southern
    Africa   39
    Norman Etherington

2   Writing of Past Times: An Interdisciplinary Approach to Mission
    History   67
    Andrea Schultze

3   'Trained to Tell the Truth': Missionaries, Converts, and Narration   76
    Gareth Griffiths

4   The Quest for Muted Black Voices in History: Some Pertinent Issues in
    (South) African Mission Historiography   95
    Tinyiko Sam Maluleke

5   Sources in Mission Archives   116
    Adam Jones

6   The Midwest China Oral History Collection   127
    Jane Baker Koons

7   From *Beyond Alpine Snow* and *Homes of the East*—A Journey
    Through Missionary Periodicals: The Missionary Periodicals Database
    Project   134
    Terry Barringer

8 Missionaries as Social Commentators: The Indian Case 145
   Geoffrey A. Oddie

9 Thinking Missiologically about the History of Mission 159
   Stanley H. Skreslet

10 Jesuit Scientific Activity in the Overseas Missions, 1540–1773 174
    Steven J. Harris

11 The Global 'Bookkeeping' of Souls: Quantification and
    Nineteenth-Century Evangelical Missions 186
    Martin Petzke

12 The Visual Embodiment of Women in the Korea Mission Field 222
    Hyaeweol Choi

13 On Using Historical Missionary Photographs in Modern
    Discussion 255
    Paul Jenkins

14 The Anthropology of Christianity: Unity, Diversity, New Directions.
    An Introduction to Supplement 10 270
    Joel Robbins

15 Expanding Mission Archaeology: A Landscape Approach to Indigenous
    Autonomy in Colonial California 302
    Lee M. Panich and Tsim D. Schneider

16 Schooling on the Missionary Frontier: The Hohi Mission Station,
    New Zealand 330
    Ian W. G. Smith

17 Objects of Expert Knowledge: On Time and the Materialities of
    Conversion to Christianity in the Southern New Hebrides 352
    Jean Mitchell

CONTENTS   VII

VOLUME 2

Approaches

18   Eusebius Tries Again: Reconceiving the Study of Christian History   375
     Andrew F. Walls

19   From Missions to Mission to Beyond Missions: The Historiography
     of American Protestant Foreign Missions Since World War II   388
     Dana L. Robert

20   The Overly Candid Missionary Historian: C. G. A. Oldendorp's
     Theological Ambivalence over Slavery in the Danish West Indies   421
     Anders Ahlbäck

21   The Colonization of Consciousness   447
     John and Jean Comaroff

22   Beyond Cultural Imperialism: Cultural Theory, Christian Missions,
     and Global Modernity   469
     Ryan Dunch

23   The Culture Concept and the Mission of the Roman Catholic
     Church   499
     Michael V. Angrosino

24   The Problem of Colonialism in the Western Historiography of Christian
     Missions   511
     Jane Samson

25   Theology and Mission between Neocolonialism and
     Postcolonialism   531
     Joerg Rieger

26   Translating the Word: Dialogism and Debate in Two Gikuyu
     Dictionaries   555
     Derek Peterson

CONTENTS

27 The Gospel, Language and Culture: The Theological Method in Cultural Analysis 579
Lamin Sanneh

28 Women and Cultural Exchanges 600
Patricia Grimshaw and Peter Sherlock

29 Understanding the World-Christian Turn in the History of Christianity and Theology 620
Paul Kollman

30 Transcontinental Links, Enlarged Maps, and Polycentric Structures in the History of World Christianity 635
Klaus Koschorke

31 World Christianity as a Theological Approach: A Reflection on Central and Eastern Europe 665
Dorottya Nagy

VOLUME 3

Themes I

Mission and Language

32 Bunyan in Africa: Text and Transition 689
Isabel Hofmeyr

33 Translation Teams: Missionaries, Islanders, and the Reduction of Language in the Pacific 704
Jane Samson

34 Christianizing Language and the Dis-placement of Culture in Bosavi, Papua New Guinea 722
Bambi B. Schieffelin

35 Exploring Nineteenth-Century Haida Translations of the New Testament 749
Marcus Tomalin

CONTENTS IX

Mission and Politics

36   Race, History, and the Australian Faith Missions   787
     Joanna Cruickshank

37   British Missions and Indian Nationalism, 1880–1908: Imitation and
     Autonomy in Calcutta and Madras   804
     Chandra Mallampalli

38   Medical Missionaries and Modernizing Emirs in Colonial Hausaland:
     Leprosy Control and Native Authority in the 1930s   828
     Shobana Shankar

Mission and Social Change

39   Christian Mind and Worldly Matters: Religion and Materiality in
     Nineteenth-Century Gold Coast   859
     Birgit Meyer

40   Mission or Empire, Word or Sword? The Human Capital Legacy in
     Postcolonial Democratic Development   887
     Tomila Lankina and Lullit Getachew

41   A Saturated History of Christianity and Cloth in Oceania   922
     Margaret Jolly

Missionaries

42   Christian Missionaries as Anticolonial Militants   951
     Karen E. Fields

43   Saint Apolo from Europe, or 'What's in a Luganda Name?'   966
     Emma Wild-Wood

44   'Culture' as a Tool and an Obstacle: Missionary Encounters in Post-Soviet
     Kyrgyzstan   990
     Mathijs Pelkmans

45 'It's Really Where Your Parents Were': Differentiating and Situating
    Protestant Missionary Children's Lives, c. 1900–1940   1016
      Hugh Morrison

Mission, Women, and Gender

46 'God and Nature Intended You for a Missionary's Wife': Mary Hill,
    Jane Eyre and Other Missionary Women in the 1840s   1049
      Valentine Cunningham

47 Female Emancipation in an Imperial Frame: English Women and the
    Campaign against Sati (Widow-Burning) in India, 1813–30   1070
      Clare Midgley

48 Married to the Mission Field: Gender, Christianity, and
    Professionalization in Britain and Colonial Africa, 1865–1914   1094
      Elizabeth Prevost

VOLUME 4

Themes II

Mission, Education, and Science

49 From Heathen Kraal to Christian Home: Anglican Mission Education
    and African Christian Girls, 1850–1900   1137
      Modupe Labode

50 From Transformation to Negotiation: A Female Mission in a
    'City of Schools'   1154
      Julia Hauser

51 Some Reflections on Anthropology's Missionary Positions   1178
      John W. Burton with Orsolya Arva Burton

CONTENTS

52 Natural Science and *Naturvölker*: Missionary Entomology and
    Botany   1190
       Patrick Harries

Mission, Health, and Healing

53 The Medical Mission Strategy of the Maryknoll Sisters   1233
       Suzanne R. Thurman

54 Converting the Hospital: British Missionaries and Medicine in
    Nineteenth-Century Madagascar   1249
       Thomas Anderson

55 Chinese Perspectives on Medical Missionaries in the 19th Century:
    The Chinese Medical Missionary Journal   1268
       Gao Xi

56 Language, Medical Auxiliaries, and the Re-interpretation of Missionary
    Medicine in Colonial Mwinilunga, Zambia, 1922–51   1290
       Walima T. Kalusa

Mission and Other Faith Traditions

57 Towards a Missionary Theory of Polytheism: The Franciscans in the Face
    of the Indigenous Religions of New Spain   1323
       Sergio Botta

58 Some Hindu Perspectives on Christian Missionaries in the Indic World
    of the Mid Nineteenth Century   1346
       Richard Fox Young

59 Methodists and Muslims in the Gambia   1370
       Martha T. Frederiks

60 Evangelicalism, Islam, and Millennial Expectation in the Nineteenth
    Century   1386
       Andrew Porter

XII

Mission and Art

61   Dance, Image, Myth, and Conversion in the Kingdom of Kongo,
      1500–1800   1413
         Cécile Fromont

62   The Indian Conquest of Catholic Art: The Mughals, the Jesuits, and
      Imperial Mural Painting   1438
         Gauvin Alexander Bailey

63   *The Truth-Showing Mirror*: Jesuit Catechism and the Arts in Mughal
      India   1452
         Gauvin Alexander Bailey

64   Africanising Christian Imagery in Southern African Missions   1472
         Elizabeth Rankin

      Index of Places   1489

      Index of Personal Names   1501

Introduction

Dorottya Nagy and Martha Frederiks

Alice came to a fork in the road.
"Cheshire Puss," she began, rather timidly,
(…) "Would you tell me, please, which way I ought to walk from here?"
"That depends a great deal on where you want to get to?" said the Cat.
"I don't much care where—" said Alice.
"Then it doesn't matter which way you walk," said the Cat.
"—so long as I get *somewhere*," Alice added as an explanation.
"Oh, you're sure to do that," said the Cat,
"if you only walk long enough."

> *Alice's Adventures in Wonderland* (Carroll 1865: 89–90)

∵

Some Methodological Reflections

This four-volume anthology *Critical Readings in the History of Christian Mission* has been long in the making. Initially, the request to compile an anthology that would introduce students, fellow researchers, and other interested readers to the academic study of the history of Christian mission seemed straightforward enough. Soon however, like Alice, we were facing forks in the road, each fork prompting the question 'where do you want to get to?' The longer we reflected, the more apparent it became that some fundamental, rather critical choices would have to be made before we could commence the actual process of selecting articles, as each decision had major implications for the type of materials we were to compile. In order to understand—and appreciate—the matrix that eventually became the basis for the current text selection, below a few paragraphs on the forks in the road and the choices we have made.

We began the process by stipulating the notion 'critical readings'. In this anthology 'critical readings' signifies texts that are the product of critical engagement with method, theory, and research data, that intend to enhance critical reflection among the readers. The materials in this anthology are therefore explicitly selected because of their thought-provoking character. These critical writings aim to stimulate discussions and entice the reader to move and think

© KONINKLIJKE BRILL NV, LEIDEN, 2021 | DOI:10.1163/9789004399587_002

beyond his/her academic comfort-zone and interact with theories and methods developed across the width of the academia.

The first fork in the road materialized when we sought to stipulate the second key term of the title: 'the history of Christian mission'. Our understanding of the history of mission as the multidisciplinary and interdisciplinary academic field that engages missionary sources, rather than the prerogative of a single discipline (e.g. mission studies or missiology), decided 'where to get to' at the first fork. We conceive of the history of Christian mission as an academic field of inquiry where numerous disciplines, ranging from social history to linguistics and biology, intersect and interact. This implies that in this anthology the history of mission includes, but is not confined to mission historiography. We have opted for the generic category 'mission' rather than for the plural 'missions' to underscore that as a historical reality mission comprises of more than the sum of activities of missionary societies (Bosch 1997: 391). Featuring contributions from disciplines as wide-ranging as medicine, art history, linguistics, and archaeology, *Critical Readings in the History of Christian Mission* intends to familiarize the reader with this multidisciplinary and interdisciplinary field and its concomitant discussions and theories. Therefore, while this anthology includes some 'classics' from the study of the history of mission, such as "The Colonization of Consciousness" by John and Jean Comaroff (2006: 493–510) or "Eusebius Tries Again: Reconceiving the Study of Christian History" by Andrew Walls (2000), *Critical Readings in the History of Christian Mission* is not a collection of 'classics'. Rather, the volumes primarily seek to introduce and portray the multi- and interdisciplinarity of the field, with a predilection for recent materials that apprise the reader with current discussions, insights, and theories.

The next fork in the road concerned the question of approach. We asked ourselves: what approach would be introductory as well as thought-provoking, and could serve to familiarize the reader with the academic field of the history of mission? While answering this question was relatively simple, it also implied a rather fundamental decision. To quote Fiona Bowie (1993: 3) in the classic *Women and Missions*: "No attempt has been made in this volume to cover all geographical areas, denominations or periods of time. It should also be made clear that our focus is exclusively on Christian mission." This anthology does not intend to present a chronological overview of the history of mission nor opts for a particular linear, longitudinal or spatial approach. Rather, *Critical Readings in the History of Christian Mission* seeks to introduce the reader to methods, approaches, perspectives, and topics relevant to the academic study of the history of Christian mission.

The third major fork in the road emerged, when we reflected on the question of language. Any choice regarding language inevitable implies a methodological choice. After elaborate discussions we decided to select texts in English only. Whether we like it or not, English has become the *lingua franca* of the academic world and the use of English as medium of communication implies accessibility for large groups of readers. Nevertheless, the choice to restrict the selection to texts in English also occasioned some constraints. First, though historically speaking the Spanish-, Portuguese-, and French colonial empires have been of great significance for the history of mission, the number of texts in English reflecting on mission activities in and by these empires, is distinctly limited. As became patent during the process of seeking and selecting articles, there is a distinct correlation between the prevalent language of particular colonial- and mission settings and the language utilized to reflect on them, to the effect that the overwhelming majority of articles in English reflects on mission by the Anglo-Saxon world. Second, while this lop-sidedness may in actual fact be representative of the disproportionate attention for the British Empire experience in the field, the restriction to English publications inevitably further buttresses the already conspicuous Anglophone-Protestant bias in research on the history of Christian mission. Reinforced by matters such as the digital accessibility of British archival materials and the dominance of English as the vernacular of the academic world, we realize that our choice for English may further enhance the preponderance of the British Protestant empire experience in methods and theories regarding the history of mission. Having said this, we have made a concerted effort to move beyond this. We have sought to include publications that reflect on missionary sources in languages other than English, examine the modern 19th and 20th century missionary movement beyond the British Empire, or study the history of mission in the pre-modern period. The paucity of materials addressing the more recent history of mission (e.g. evangelical missions in the former Soviet Union or the contemporary Korean missionary movement) however is striking (Omenyo & Choi 2000; Pelkmans 2007, 2017). We have also endeavoured to make the volumes as polyphonic as possible, incorporating voices from a wide range of disciplines and from different parts of the world; only on rare occasions did we decide to include more than one article by a certain author. The two articles by Gavin Bailey on Jesuit art in Mughal India form a diptych, discussing complementary perspectives on the same topic (Bailey 1998, 1999).

The question how to organize the material presented a fourth fork in the road. In line with the decision that the volumes were to address methodology, approaches, perspectives, and recurring themes in the history of mission, we organized the volumes accordingly. Therefore, the first volume focusses on methodology in the academic study of the history of mission while the second volume discusses approaches to the history of mission; volumes three and four comprise of perspectives (thematic, disciplinary, analytic or theoretical) on recurring topics in the history of mission, such as education, politics, social change, gender issues, and art. Though neatly organized in volumes, the boundaries between methods, approaches, and perspectives are rather fluid.

While neither the choice of approach, the selection of texts nor the organizational structure have been random, we readily acknowledge that other, equally valid, choices could have been made, resulting in a different composition (structure- or content-wise) of the anthology. We are also aware that many issues are left un(der)addressed, such as the relation between missionary organizations and philanthropic and reform movements, mission and slavery, Christian and other missionary movements, the self-representation of the missionary movement, mission and missionaries in literature and movies to name just a few. We have tried to address and remedy this by incorporating an extensive, though no means exhaustive, bibliography in this introduction. Also, while we have attempted to be inclusive in terms of diversity as far as authors, disciplines, and sources are concerned, we are aware that our selection has mainly come from international peer-reviewed books and journals. Relatively few articles were selected from regional or local journals and volumes published in the non-Western world. This was caused partly by accessibility, partly by copyright issues, partly by serendipity, but is in no way intended as a comment on the quality of research published in those media.

The remainder of this chapter serves to present the state of the art in the field of the history of mission, simultaneously introducing and situating the text-selection of the four volumes.

The History of Christian Mission: State of the Art

Sources and Methods
The one thing that all the disciplines working on the history of mission have in common, is that they all use missionary sources. The recognition that missionary sources (like all sources) have their own particularities and peculiarities and require critical usage is hardly new. For all their heterogeneity (e.g. letters, diaries, and journals), missionary materials form a particular genre, written for a particular audience and often with a particular purpose in mind, a genre styled to meet the expectations of its audiences (e.g. in terminology, content, and style). David Arnold and Robert Bickers (1996: 1) have called missionary

materials "a fecund, if often frustrating, source of material to work on". Their significance however far surpasses the mere documentation of the spread of Christianity; the sources yield information on numerous issues, ranging from ornithology, botany, and architecture to language, politics, food, demography, commerce, social change, education, and medicine.

Past research has often tended to spotlight that missionary materials were biased and tainted by racism, chauvinism, and bigotry, and at times has disqualified them because of it. But as Geoffrey Oddie (1996: 204) in his perceptive article "Missionaries as Social Commentators" has noted: "... there is one clear advantage of using them that is not always present in other records, namely, that in the case of missionaries we already know something about their ultimate aims and what their biases are likely to be." He then goes on to demonstrate how missionary sources, because they detail prolonged missionary interaction with ordinary people, constitute "one of the most valuable sources for 'history from below'" (Oddie 1996: 198). When employed critically, they can be utilized to detect voices that are not typically represented in archival resources.

In the last decades scholars from a variety of disciplinary backgrounds have recognized the value of missionary sources. Yet for all their wealth, working with missionary materials remains complex. As Arnold and Bickers (1996) have observed, in addition to the typical missionary biases, documents may reflect the personal quirks and partialities of individuals, materials (even whole collections) may have gone missing or have been destroyed, and researchers who study a topic in a particular region or period, may have to resign themselves to extensive travel, touring the various archival depots.

Studying missionary sources also requires that researchers develop a sensitivity to blind spots in the material. These blind spots could comprise of lack of information about the situatedness of certain materials (e.g. biographical or political backgrounds), of voices that are not represented or have been repressed (women, indigenous workers, children, dissenting voices) as well as of things that are left unsaid (e.g. issues related to sexuality, conflicts, setbacks). These 'gaps' in the material may be as revealing as that which is explicitly recorded and, as postcolonial and gender studies have demonstrated, retrieving them requires particular skills and techniques (Hall 2017; Grimshaw & Sherlock 2007; Maluleke 2000; Peel 1996; Sebastian 2003).

As Anders Ahlbäck's perceptive study of Christian Oldendorp's *Geschichte der Mission der evangelischen Brüder auf den caraibischen Inseln* (1777) demonstrates, missionary periodicals and other published missionary texts form an even more convoluted genre than missionary archival materials (Ahlbäck 2016). Published to solicit spiritual as well as material support, fashioned to inform as well as influence and intended to confirm tropes about missionaries and 'the other', extensive editorial interventions and censorship add additional layers of interpretation to the sources (Barringer 2002, 2004; Jensz & Acke 2013; Miller 2012; Wild-Wood 2010). While, as Terry Barringer has observed in her discussion of missionary periodicals, problematic as sources for understanding developments 'in the field', these texts form a rich resource for "missionary self-understanding and self-representation" as well as for the political climate in a particular period (Barringer 2002: 169; Jensz & Acke 2013: 13).

In recognition of the limitations and complexities of missionary sources, and aware that these limitations and biases imply that the sources can only provide a distinct and therefore partial window into the missionary endeavour, researchers have sought to diversify their sources. On the one hand there has been a trend to supplement the traditional missionary sources such as archives and periodicals, with materials from family archives such as private letters or diaries by missionaries and their relatives (Chu 2007), oral history data (Baker Koons 1985), as well with non-missionary sources 'from the mission field' (Arnold & Bickers 1996). As Wild-Wood (2001, 2008) has shown, triangulation of such sources might yield new, fruitful perspectives.

On the other hand, recent years have also seen a pronounced shift in scholarly attention from written materials to material culture as a source for the history of mission, ranging from photographs, illustrations, cartography, and the magic lantern to art, indigenous artefacts, cloth, and plant specimen (Bailey 1998, 1999, 2013; De Almeida 2003; Fromont 2011, 2014; Jolly 2014; Golvers 2000; Kuo 2016; Simpson 1997; Thompson 2013). The most pronounced example of this 'material turn' has been the growing interest in missionary photography. Spearheaded by Paul Jenkins (1993, 1996; 2001, 2002a, 2002b, 2009), the 21st century has seen a rise in publications on missionary photography (Long 2003; Maxwell 2011; Thompson 2002, 2012). As studies by Jenkins (1996; 2001), Choi (2010), and Reynolds (2010) convincingly demonstrate, missionary photographs are not merely reflections of staged, imperial representations of 'the other', but the product of intricate processes of negotiation and cooperation. Therefore, missionary photographs offer another window into the complexities and relationality of the missionary endeavour and may shed new light on matters described (or omitted) in written sources. In a perceptive article on the role of photography in American evangelical missions, Kathryn Long (2003) for example investigates the role of photographs 'at the home front'. She argues that photographs of missionized as well as missionaries served both promotional and devotional purposes and functioned as "a window through which supporters could view the object of prayer a half a world away" and "sustained a sense of relationship with missionaries, the closest Protestants came to having saints of their own" (Long 2003: 826, 835). A different type of pictorial representation that has received scholarly attention concerns missionary cartography (Kark 1993; Altic 2014; Vasquez 2015; Korte & Onnekink 2020). Pellervo Kokkonen (1993) has for example argued that by inscribing the distribution of mission stations, schools, and churches on the landscape, missionaries were not merely producing 'religious geography', but contributed to the creation and demarcation of what were deemed to be distinct ethnolinguistic groups.

Informed by an anthropological preoccupation with social change, scholars like Margaret Jolly (2014), Latu Latai (2014), Birgit Meyer (1997; 2010), and Jean Mitchell (2013) have followed another line of inquiry. Identifying transformations in indigenous material culture as sites of investigation, their work draws attention to the impact of the twin forces of mission and modernity on issues such as architecture, bodily practices, agriculture, landscaping, and music. In contrast, the work by Gülen Cevik (2011) showcases how missionary encounter with different styles of clothing and furniture influenced trends in fashion and interior design in the home countries.

Both a method to generate data and to interpret them, mission archaeology has also drawn attention to the significance of material culture for the history of mission. Used to engender new data as well as to supplement or validate existent data and theory, mission archaeology is vital when relevant textual materials are absent (Evans, Sørensen & Richter 2014; King & McGranaghan 2018; Martínez D'Alós-Moner 2015). As the research of scholars like Elizabeth Graham (1998), Mark Lycett (2004) and Lee Panich and Tsim Schneider (2015) on early modern America has evidenced, mission archaeology can challenge prevailing narratives about colonisation and mission, uncovering tangible evidence that attests to the creative ways in which local converts "have come to terms with, and possibly eluded and subverted Western domination" (Meyer 1999: xix). And as the publications of Ian Smith and his team (2012, 2014a, 2014b) on 19th century New Zealand have shown, intersecting excavation data with textual materials can be a productive way of mapping the "long conversation" (Comaroff & Comaroff 1991: 11) between missionized and missionaries.

By discussing archaeology, which serves both as a source of and a method for mission history, we have already begun discussing methods in the history of mission. As versatile as the sources, are the methods utilized to investigate the sources. In the paragraphs below we merely spotlight some of the more prevalent methods from the disciplines of history, linguistics, theology-missiology, and the social sciences, used in the study of missionary sources.

Historical methods unquestionably spearhead the research into missionary sources. Mission historiography is perhaps as old as the missionary movement itself, though as an academic discipline it only emerged in the 19th century, typically as a branch of church history. In the 20th century mission history also became part of the subdisciplines of imperial- and world history. Trends in mission historiography have included foci on gender, indigenous agency, contextualisation, mission and colonialism, while current publications tend to focus on the connectivities and interchange between 'metropole' and 'colony' (Becker & Stanley 2013; Becker 2015; Midgley 2000; Price 2008), or remonstrate against tendencies that prolong the dichotomy of Western and non-Western world and subsume the history of Christianity in Africa, Asia, and the Americas under a mission history paradigm, rather than as a part of the diverse history of Christianity worldwide (Cox 2015; Dussel 1981; González 2002).

There is a growing interest in oral history as a method in mission historiography. Oral history has been widely employed to supplement existing data with voices that are typically omitted from the mission archives; in general, the focus has been on silenced voices of people within the Christian fold, such as indigenous workers, women in mission or missionary women and children (Benson 2015; Morrison 2017; Phiri 2000; Verstraelen-Gilhuis 1982). Oral history however could prove a valuable tool in documenting the reception (or rejection) of Christian mission. Oral history methods are also vital for the burgeoning fields of memory and heritage studies. Methods and insights from memory and heritage studies about which things are remembered and how and why they are remembered might yield fertile new ground for the study of mission history (Albert, Bernecker & Rudolff 2013; Erll, Nünning & Young 2008; Sørensen & Carman 2009; Tota & Hagen 2015).

Intersecting historical and linguistic perspectives, missionary linguistics has emerged as an independent academic area of inquiry within the wider field of linguistics. Until the recent past, missionary contributions to linguistics were largely ignored; currently there is, in the words of Marcus Tomalin (2011a: 1), a growing recognition that the "analytical frameworks they [missionaries, the editors] used were often intriguingly heterogeneous, being composed of different approaches derived from a range of distinct grammatical traditions." Tomalin writes:

> While there is a lingering belief that missionary linguists simply adopted some kind of Graeco-Roman grammatical framework, and mindlessly attempted to fit the indigenous languages they encountered into this pre-existing format, this view is largely inaccurate, as many recent studies have demonstrated.

In recognition of the pioneering work of missionaries in linguistics, scholars have begun to analyse how non-native missionaries conceived and described indigenous languages and what these missionary conceptualisations of orthography, lexicology, grammar, and syntax contribute to the field of linguistics (Stolz & Warnke 2015; Zimmermann & Kellermeier-Rehbein 2015; Zwartjes 2011). Missionary linguistics also examines the broader contexts in which language description occurs, studying the dynamics between native speakers and non-native speakers (often missionaries) in language description (Irvine 2008; Samson 2010; Schieffelin 2014) or the standardisation of language brought about by the combined forces of language description and Bible translation (Fulford 2002; Mojola 2001). Also language policy has become a field of inquiry. Clara Mortamet and Céline Amourette (2015: 37) have for example shown how Protestant and Roman Catholic missionary organisations cooperated in adopting and propagating the Latin alphabet for Swahili, in an effort to curb the advance of Arabization and Islamisation in Eastern Africa.

Related to missionary linguistics is the field of translation studies. As Birgit Meyer (1999: xxv) has pointed out: "Translation has to be examined as a 'process of power' (Asad 1986: 148) (…) a creative process, which does not aim for the correct representation of the Other, but which is instead a product of intersubjective and intercultural dialogue (Fabian 1971b)." Derek Peterson's comparison of two contemporary 19th century Kikuyu dictionaries evidences this. Peterson's research reveals that the main differences between the two lexicons concern words about religion and authority. Using a postcolonial analysis Peterson argues that these dissimilarities are not 'mistakes' but rather the outcome of the distinct decisions made in the negotiation processes of each of the dictionaries (Peterson 1999). Marcus Tomalin's appraisal of 19th century Haida New Testament translations discloses comparable findings, possibly indicative of the fact that words pertaining to religion and hierarchy were considered most delicate and therefore most contested (Tomalin 2011b). In a persuasive article on autochthonous medical auxiliaries in Zambia, Walima Kalusa (2007) illustrates how translation could become an instrument of subversion. He argues that by acting as translators for medical personnel and using vernacular categories representing indigenous views on health and healing, medical auxiliaries positioned Western medical healthcare in a continuum with local healing practices rather than as its 'other'; thus, Kalusa maintains, they advertently or inadvertently undermined the project of Christianization through bio-medical healing.

As Jane Samson's work (2010, 2017) displays, translation was rarely the work of individuals but rather a team effort, with translation teams typically consisting of both native and non-native speakers. Samson describes how key decisions were usually preceded by elaborate deliberations, weighing the pros and cons of certain choices. Isabel Hofmeyr's work on Bunyan translations in Africa cogently argues that such hermeneutical negotiations were not restricted to textual translations. Her research evidenced how performances, depictions, partial translations, oral traditions, and other forms of appropriation (wittingly or unwittingly) carry on these hermeneutical processes (Hofmeyr 2001, 2004).

Also theology, and more in particular missiology, has contributed significantly to the study of mission history. In the 19th and early 20th centuries teleological and ecclesiological paradigms of mission history prevailed, but also more recent works such as Lamin Sanneh's *Translating the Message* can be comprehended as teleological projects. Crucial to Sanneh's argumentation is "that all cultures have cast upon them the breath of God's favour, thus cleansing them of all stigma of inferiority and untouchability" (Sanneh 1989: 47) and "that the God whom the missionary came to serve had actually preceded him or her in the field" (Sanneh 1983: 167).

Following the decolonisation and subsequent critical assessment of the missionary movement, the focus in mission history shifted from a mission-centred approach to the reception of Christianity, with special attention for local agency and local manifestations of Christianity (Cox 2015: 28). Theoretically, this move was legitimized by concepts like 'the indigenizing principle' (Walls 2004: 7), 'vernacularization' and 'translation' (Sanneh 1989), and incarnation, inculturation, and contextualisation (Bosch 1991: 430–468). This preoccupation with local expressions of Christianity gave rise to a number of prolegomena questions, such as the relation between church history and mission history (often resulting in the relegation of the term 'mission history'), and the Western normativity in terms of analytical concepts and periodisation and has spurred on a revisionist project that in the words of Dipesh Chakrabarty aims to 'provincialize Europe' in the history of Christianity (Chakrabarty 2000; Dussel 1981, 1992, 1993; González 2002; Hock 2014; Koschorke 2013; Walls 2000). This enterprise, by Paul Kollman (2014) called "the World-Christian turn" in the history of Christianity, acknowledges and at times even lauds Christianity's inherent plurality. World Christianity scholars foreground Christianity's diversity in past and present (Irvin 2008), its multiple centres through time and space (coined 'polycentric structures' by Koschorke & Hermann 2014) and its translocal connectivities.

Recently, some scholars (Cabrita & Maxwell 2017: 21–22) have begun to critique World Christianity scholarship for its fixation on particularity and its disregard for globalizing and integrative forces within the Christian tradition, such as ecumenical organizations, Bible societies, and missionary societies. Others, such as Arun Jones (2014) have pointed out that much 'World Christianity' research continues to work along bipolar lines of thinking, that find their origin in the colonial period, continually producing and reproducing binaries such as 'missionary' versus 'indigenous', 'the West' versus 'the Rest', 'North' versus 'South'. Again others, such as Chandra Mallampalli (2017: 164), have drawn attention to the conceptual entanglement of 'World Christianity' as a field of study with the history of Christianity in Africa and query its usefulness for the academic study of Christianity elsewhere. The impact of these debates surrounding 'World Christianity' scholarship on the study of history of Christian mission and of Christianity more generally is patent; when Stanley Skreslet (2007) reflects on the theological *proprium* in the study of Christian mission, he identifies the concurrent attention for Christian diversity and for local-global dynamics within Christianity as characteristic of a theological-missiological approach to the study of mission history. In view however of these and kindred discussions, Dorottya Nagy (2017) and Nagy & Frederiks (2020) have argued to employ the concept 'World Christianity' solely as the epithet for a particular approach of studying Christianity in past and present.

Postcolonial theologians like Joerg Rieger (2004), Pui-lan Kwok (2005), Rasiah S. Sugirtharajah (2001, 2005), and Musa Dube (2000) have written about the implications of missionary complicity with colonialism for theology and Biblical studies; they maintain that even after the decolonialisation, "colonial intellectual attitudes" still dominate the field of theology (Rieger 2004: 209). Working from the premise that the missionary transmission of Christianity and Christian theology was intertwined with notions of cultural and racial superiority, scholars like Rieger and Kwok have embarked on a project to deconstruct theology and to disentangle it from hegemonic ideas, allowing for the formulation of new, more inclusive theologies; the work by Sugirtharajah and Dube spotlights the imbrication of Bible translations and interpretations in the missionary-cum-colonial project.

Several theologians-missiologists work at the intersection of missiology and the social sciences. As early as 1948 Bengt Sundkler in his *Bantu Prophets* used sociological analysis to examine the political, racial, and religious factors that led Zulu prophets to break with mainline missions and establish independent churches. Paul Kollman's *The Evangelization of Slaves and Catholic Origins in East Africa* (2005) employs sociological and political theories—E. P. Thompson's concept of moral economy and Albert Hirschman's threefold typology of exit, voice, and loyalty—to map African agency in Christian villages of formerly enslaved while Martin Petzke's work (2016, 2018) investigates the sociological and theological presuppositions that undergird the rise of practices of quantification in mission history (e.g. religious statistics) and points to the usefulness of quantitative methods in the study of mission history. Robert Montgomery's *Introduction to the Sociology of Missions* (1999) provides a more generic overview of relevant sociological methods and theory germane to missiologists studying mission history.

Also anthropologists and sociologists have researched missionary sources. The best-known example is John and Jean Comaroff's influential *Of Revelation and Revolution* (2 vols, 1991, 1997); the work analyses the impact of the dual forces of mission and modernity on the South African Tswana (for a discussion of the Comaroffs see below). Anthropological interest in missionary sources has mainly focussed on processes of social change (Jolly 2014; Lankina & Getachew 2012; Meyer 1997, 1999) with the anthropology of Christianity, a recent strand within anthropology that critically engages with anthropology's past entanglement with Christianity (and Protestantism in particular), specifically spotlighting issues of discontinuity, rupture, and deviance in modern mission history (Angrosino 1994; Cannell 2006; Robbins 2014). Also social sciences other than cultural anthropology have engaged mission history. Victoria Burbank's research on health challenges among Aborigines in Australia (2012) is an example of the use of mission archives for medical anthropology, while Richard Schram (2016) discusses semantic and cultural innovations springing from Australian mission work in British New Guinea. Judy Katzenellenbogen, Derek Yach, and Rob Dorrington (1993), working at the intersection of demography and epidemiology, have examined Moravian missionary records to investigate mortality rates and life-expectancy of men and women in the 19th century Western Cape in South Africa.

Approaches and Perspectives

Depending on their interests researchers have chosen different approaches to study missionary sources. Julia Cagé and Valeria Rueda (2017) for example have studied missionary archives to map the correlation between improved colonial infrastructures and the spread of HIV, Paul Smith (2007) and Henry McGhie (2017) to investigate the history of ornithology, William Dunmire (2004) to study patterns of change in horticulture and foodstuffs in New Spain, Gaston Demarée, Astrid Ogilvie, and David Kusman (2019) to investigate historical seismological data, while musicologists like David Dargie (2010) and Anna Celenza and Anthony DelDonna (2014), have utilized missionary sources to detect transformations of musical repertoires. The work of art historian Gauvin Bailey (1998, 1999, 2013) investigates Jesuit utilization of visual art in missionary settings, while musicologist Jutta Toelle (2013) has studied Jesuit missionary use of music. The versatility of missionary sources is such that the list of possible approaches and perspectives is well-nigh endless. We

INTRODUCTION

therefore (again) opt to merely highlight some of more prevalent approaches and perspectives.

Postcolonial scholars and anthropologists have tended to study the sources through a lens of social change and rupture, engendered by the onset of mission and modernity (Cannell 2006; Hunt 1999; Maluleke 2000; Robbins 2004, 2014); most of their work therefore concentrates on the 19th and early 20th centuries. Both postcolonial and anthropological research in the history of mission has been profoundly influenced by Jean and John Comaroff's seminal work *Of Revelation and Revolution* (1991, 1997). The Comaroffs (and scholars working in their tradition) have emphasized the missionary complicity in the colonial project, positing mission and colonialism as twin projects aimed at the colonization (soul, mind, and body) of the subjects of empire.

Missionary schools as well as missionary hospitals as localities where Western cultural values were transmitted, are attributed a pivotal role in this colonization project. There is trail of literature that explores this entanglement of missionary education and medical work with imperial agendas. Modupe Labode (1993: 26) for example writes that missionary education of African women on the 19th century Eastern Cape centred on the creation of Christian homes:

> Simply converting Africans to Christianity was not enough; the missionaries' goal was nothing less than restructuring African society. 'Restructure' suggested physical changes in the household, such as favouring square houses over round huts; these physical changes corresponded to the spiritual changes which took place in the convert.

The education of African girls therefore formed a key strategy in simultaneously Christianizing and civilizing (read 'restructuring') the Cape society. In a similar vein, Chantel Verdeil (2014) has pointed to the profound impact of missionary schools on Ottoman perceptions of time.

Also in medical work, the various agendas were interlocked (Anderson 2017; Kalusa 2007; Gao 2014). Thomas Anderson (2017), discussing British medical work on Madagascar argues that the introduction of the hospital played a central role in missionary strategies. Because missionaries believed traditional medicine to be either superstition or witchcraft and because the hospital was clearly controlled "space of western civilization" (Anderson 2017: 545), missionary clinics and hospitals according to Anderson, could underscore Western superiority and via medical supremacy could debilitate traditional beliefs and thus lay the groundwork for effective evangelization. Or in the words of Walima Kalusa (2007: 61–62):

> As conceptualised by the surgeon and other missionary healers, medical evangelism therefore entailed that African patients would follow a teleological progression from embracing the Christian variety of scientific medicine to abandoning their 'heathen' culture, along with its underlying belief system (...) '[T]he gospel of the syringe' was an integral ingredient of the wider Western 'civilizing mission', which construed all pre-Christian forms of medical knowledge and religion as its 'primitive Other', in dire need of reconstructing in European image.

While an ubiquitous missionary strategy, it often proved to be an ineffective one (Hardiman 2006).

Though hugely influential, the Comaroffs' work has been critiqued for its monolithic conceptualizations of mission and colonialism as well as for the lack of agency accorded to indigenous populations (Dunch 2002; Lankina & Getachew 2012; Meyer 1995; Peel 1995; Peterson 1997, 1999, 2012; Wyss 2012). Based on a study of educational institutions for girls run by the German Kaiserwerth deaconesses in late Ottoman Beirut, Julia Hauser (2016: 475) for example queries "the cultural imperialist thesis" that frames "the civilizing mission" as a unilateral hegemonic project. Her archival work evidences that the deaconesses' educational policy was the product of constant processes of negotiation with their clientele and of adjustments to changing political realities and Roman Catholic competition; a process that according to Hauser (2016: 473) is "starkly at odds with the idea of a unidirectional civilizing mission." Similarly, Kalusa's work on Zambian medical auxiliaries disavows representations of local workers as "mere cogs in the wheels of the 'civilising mission' of their European employers" (Kalusa 2007: 74). Rather, Kalusa's research shows them to be independent actors who functioned as cultural brokers between traditional and western medicine and who by their persistent adherence to indigenous medical cosmologies subverted the project of Christianization through bio-medical healing.

In order to capture these dynamic and reciprocal processes of encounter and interaction, scholars have begun to use the lenses of cultural exchange and transculturation, describing "gradual transformation, mutual appropriation and redefinitions of cultural elements within the colonial encounter" (Schultze 2004: 324). Building on linguistic theory, Mary Louise Pratt (2008: 7–8) has coined the notions 'contact zone' and 'anti-conquest' to describe these encounters. Contact zones, according to Pratt, are "spaces of imperial encounters, the space in which people geographically and historically separated come into contact with each other and establish ongoing relations, usually involving conditions of coercion, radical inequality, and intractable conflict." However, as Cécile Fromont (2011, 2014) has remarked with reference to the early modern world, subsuming all Europe's cross-cultural interactions under the paradigm of colonialism, does not do justice to people in Africa, Asia, and the Americas as "independent influential actors" (Fromont 2014: 9, 15). Therefore Fromont, who studies Christian visual culture in the Kingdom of Kongo in the early modern period, has proposed the notion of "spaces of correlation" (Fromont 2014: 15) as an alternative to Pratt's contact zone.

Despite the critiques on the work of the Comaroffs, there remains a school of researchers that holds on to one-dimensional, rather stereotypical representations of "missionaries as spiritual rapists of the local population, epitomes of intolerance, destroyers of indigenous culture and religion" (Schultze 2004: 324). Most scholars nowadays however agree with the assessment of colonial historian Norman Etherington (1996: 201, 209) "that Christianity was a two-edged sword that could undercut as well as sustain domination" and that "missionaries, who aimed to replace African cultures with European 'civilisation' and who frequently allied themselves with colonial governments, nevertheless transmitted a religion which Africans turned to suit their own purposes: spiritual, economic and political."

Karen Fields' work on British colonial Africa evidences this multifarious relationship between mission and colonialism. She demonstrated for example that attitudes towards chieftaincy were a bone of contestation between missionaries and colonial officers and has argued that missionaries and their indigenous co-workers, in their resistance against African custom, undermined the authority of the chiefs on whom indirect rule depended. Fields (1982: 106) writes: "To the missions custom was a stumbling block, to the regime a prop. Attacking custom, therefore, missionaries attacked indirect rule at its foundation." Fields has been one among many who have pointed to the multi-layered, equivocal relations between mission and colonialism, varying from overt cooperation to outright subversion. Since the 1960s scholars have for example investigated the correlation between mission and the rise of nationalism (Coleman 1965; Moyo 2015; Walshe 1982). James Coleman (1965) and Peter Walshe (1982) identified missionary education as a source of nationalism, while Lamin Sanneh (1989, 1995) has made a case that nationalism was a corollary of the missionary vernacular project. For the Indian subcontinent, scholars like Geoffrey Oddie (1999) and Chandra Mallampalli (2003) have argued that missionary vilification of Hindu practices inadvertently produced Hindu reform movements and Hindu nationalism.

While one line of research has explored the compound relationships between mission and the colonial project (e.g. Blackburn 2000; Hall 2002; Porter 2003, 2004, 2010; Robert 2008; Stanley 1990), another line of inquiry has focussed on heterogeneity in the missionary movement. Part of this research is an attempt to deconstruct the monolithic conceptualization of missionaries, foregrounding the variety in ecclesial and national backgrounds and the differences in attitudes, gender, education, and experience between individual missionaries. As Richard Fox Young (2002: 37) has observed:

> Christian missionaries, far from being cut from the same cloth, ecclesiastical or otherwise, are nowadays regarded as comprising an internally complex, self-differentiated cohort of individuals with little in common except an uncompromising faith in Jesus Christ as the one Lord and a collateral conviction that the gospel's salvific implications are universalistic.

Still, Young hastens to add, this is an insider's perceptive; 'outsiders' who were object of mission were less attuned to these diversities and often conceived missionaries as one homogenous group (Young 2002: 39).

Over the last three decades an important strand within this line of research has sought to remedy past disregard for the contribution of women to the missionary movement. In his seminal essay "God and Nature Intended You for a Missionary's Wife", Valentine Cunningham (1993: 89) evocatively summarized (and critiqued) past conceptualizations of mission and missionaries with the words: "... missionary was a male word"; it denoted "male actors, male actions and male spheres of service." To address this male-biased perspective, Cunningham and others have spotlighted the role of women in mission, such as female missionaries, missionary wives, and the women's support of missionary movement as well as the gendered dimension of the missionary venture (Bowie, Kirkwood & Ardener 1993; Busschers 2015; Choi 2009; Grimshaw 1989; Reeves-Ellington, Sklar & Shemo 2010; Twells 2009; Whiteley 2005).

Research on women and mission began in the 1990s with a surge of publications on women missionaries. While there has been a long, but somewhat under-studied tradition of Catholic female congregations working in missionary settings (Bruno-Jofré 2005; Burke 2001; Chowning 2008; Cowan 2018; Stornig 2015; Thurman 2002), most research has tended to spotlight Protestant women missionaries. Protestant women were not considered missionaries in their own right until the mid-19th century, when spurred on by the slogan 'women's work for women', British and American missions began to send out single female missionaries. It is this group that has drawn most scholarly attention (Beaver 1980; Bowie, Kirkwood & Ardener 1993; Okkenhaug 2002; Robert 1997, 2002; Sasaki 2016). More recent research has focussed on the gendered dimensions of mission, detailing how missionary women (and men) were promoting and imposing Victorian ideals about marriage, domesticity, and propriety (Choi, 2009; Choi & Jolly 2014; Grimshaw & Sherlock 2007; Huber &

Lutkehaus 1999). Elizabeth Prevost (2008: 797) has drawn attention to the irony of the women's work for women project, pointing to the paradox that single women (spinsters) were included in the missionary movement to address "the gendered needs of 'heathen women'", while their lifestyle contradicted the very values they propagated. She writes (2008: 797–798): "[M]issionaries needed to be 'women' for metropolitan purposes of professionalizing women's mission work but not in carrying out that work in the mission field."

Researchers such as Claire Midgley (2000), Anna Johnson (2003), and Patricia Grimshaw and John Sherlock (2007) have drawn attention to the correlation between missionary and imperial projects regarding women on the one hand and the position of women in the metropole on the other. In a thought-provoking article on the practice of *sati*, Claire Midgley (2000) demonstrates how the British campaign against *sati* was simultaneously used to legitimate colonial rule (Spivak's white men saving brown women from brown men) and to enhance political participation of women in the UK. Similarly, Katharina Stornig (2015) shows how the involvement of German nuns of the Servants of the Holy Spirit in obstetric care in New Guinea impacted both Papuan childbirth practices and effectuated shifts in Roman Catholic perceptions of purity and sexuality.

A derivative from approaches centring women and gender, there is a strand of research that focusses on the missionary family as a form of performative mission, embodying the nuclear modern family, and "demonstrating exemplary domestic Christianity to missionary subjects" (Morrison 2017: 431). As part of this approach, research has been conducted into missionary children (Hillel 2011; Manktelow 2016, 2017; Miller 2012; Morrison 2017) as well as in cases of deviance that permeate the clear-cut boundaries between missionary and 'the other' (Manktelow 2012, 2014, 2015, 2017).

Disavowed by apparent missionary complicity in the imperial project and past hagiographic and triumphalist tendencies, missionaries are nowadays rarely a subject matter in their own right, except as perpetrators of vilification and exploitation. While understandable, there are still blind spots in the study of cross-cultural mission, such as how missionaries coped with health and cultural challenges, the omnipresence of death, and new food regimes, how missionaries negotiated expectations from 'back home' when their mission proved uphill work or how missionaries functioned as cultural brokers in the sending countries. Also the relation between mission and science merits further research, as missionary engagement with 'the other' was an important factor in shaping Western intellectual history. Apart from the widely acknowledged missionary contributions to linguistics and ethnography, missionaries functioned as auxiliaries to science by collecting plant specimen for biologists, made ornithological observations, contributed to cartography and medicine and so on (e.g. Bell 2014; Frey Näf 2013; Harries 2012; Kokkonen 1993). But so far little research has been conducted into this aspect of the missionary movement.

More common has been the shift in focus away from Western missionaries to the study of indigenous agency; despite racial, cultural, and religious biases in the sources, the lives and contributions of large numbers of local men and women have been (re)constructed (e.g. Azamede 2010; Brock 2003; Chojnacki 2010; Davis 2018; Grimshaw & May 2010; Tiedeman 1997; Van Valen 2013). Current research, such as Emma Wild-Wood's work on Apolo Kivebulaya makes clear, that many of these local men and women were far more than mere auxiliaries to missionaries; often they were cross-cultural missionaries in their own right, working among neighboring groups (Andrews 2013; Brock 2014; Charles 2010; Chojnacki 2010; Cruickshank 2010; Wild-Wood 2008). There is also a growing body of research on translocal missionaries who did not originate from the centres of empire, so far mainly spotlighting the Black Atlantic missionary work in West Africa, such as 19th century Jamaican Baptist missionaries in Cameroon or 19th century West Indians in the Gold Coast (Kwakye 2018; Killingray 2003; Russell 2000; Wariboko 2004). Possibly with the exception of studies about Bible women (Chang 2006; Kent 1999; Strawn 2012, Yun 2018) and work on indigenous Catholic sisters (Burke 2001; Chu 2016), there is little research on female indigenous agents.

Another trend in the research on indigenous agency seems to move research beyond studies of 19th century missionary sources. Linda Heywood and John Thornton (2007), Edward Andrews (2013), John Charles (2010) for example have focussed on early modern period, with Heywood and Thornton (2007) reconstructing the contribution of Central West Africans to the evangelization of enslaved in the Americas in the 16th and 17th centuries, John Charles (2010) investigating 16th and 17th centuries Andean indigenous agents, and Andrews (2013) studying 18th century native American evangelists, working on the east coast of America.

In recent years also several critical editions of materials written by indigenous agents have been published. Vincent Carretta and Ty Reese (2010) have for example made the letters of Philip Quaque, an 18th century Fante minister who for more than fifty years worked on behalf of Society for the Propagation of the Gospel at Cape Coast Castle (present-day Ghana), accessible for a wider audience, while Peggy Brock (2014) painstakingly transcribed the diaries of the Tsimshian evangelist Arthur Clah. Joanne Brooks' work spotlights the collected writings of the 18th century Mohegan minister Samson Occom (Occom & Brooks 2006), while Ji Li (2015) published a unique set of letters, written by

INTRODUCTION

Chinese Catholic women in 19th century Manchuria to their former missionary, Father Dominique Maurice Pourquié, in France.

In a way, mission history has always been a history of encountering the religious other. Studies that discuss missionary perceptions of and engagement with other religious traditions abound. One strand of current research focusses on the interdependence of theological convictions, political regimes, and missionary representations of the religious other (Botta 2013; Frederiks 2003, 2009; Meyer 1999; Nehring 2003, 2015; Oddie 2006; Porter 2008; Ryad 2015). Sergio Botta (2013) for example demonstrates how in early modern Spain theology rather than phenomenology determined the classifications and representations of newly encountered religious traditions in Latin America. Botta (2013: 12) argues that the classification of indigenous religions in early modern Spain as idolatry served a dual purpose; it theologically positioned the newly discovered religious traditions in relation to Christianity and simultaneously legitimized social control over the conquered cultures. He also demonstrates that by the early 17th century, views gradually began to change and the first notions of polytheism began to be formulated, that formed the foundation for what eventually became a religious studies approach to religion.

Similarly, Geoffrey Oddie's *Imagined Hinduism* (2006) shows how 19th century British missionary conceptualizations of Hinduism were rooted in Enlightenment ideas, Christian understandings of the concept 'religion', and the colonial reality; this resulted in a representation of Hinduism as a unitary, brahman-controlled, ritualistic tradition that embodied 'the other' of British Protestant Evangelicalism. Oddie also contends that by the late 19th century prolonged missionary encounter with Hindus had prompted a more nuanced, mild, and pluriform representation of Hinduism(s). Andrew Porter (2008) points out how the expansion of the British Empire into predominantly Muslim regions occurred at a time of Protestant evangelical millennialism, which ascribed to Islam the role of the antichrist at the end of time, resulting in a resurgence of Protestant missionary work among Muslims. Like Oddie, Porter observes that by the end of the 19th century, due to a changed political climate and experiences on the mission field, more accommodative attitudes towards Islam began to prevail among mainstream missionary societies.

Another strand of research investigates responses to Christian mission. An example of this is a volume edited by Peggy Brock (2005) that investigates the responses of indigenous people (USA, Australia, and New Zealand) to Christian mission. Richard Fox Young (2002) has examined how Hindu elite, who were drawn into the encounter with Christianity and Christian missionaries, demonstrated a surprisingly diverse range of attitudes towards Christian mission, that varied from polemics, to intellectual engagement, appreciation, and conversion. Whereas the 19th century renaissance of Hinduism in response to Christian polemics has received much scholarly attention (e.g. Neufeldt 1993; Śarmā 1988), Andreas Nehring (2003, 2015) has shown that also in 19th century Theravada Buddhism in Burma reforms occurred as a result of encounters with Christian mission. Martha Frederiks (2009) researched the persistent rebuffs of Christian mission by Muslims in 19th and early 20th century Gambia, which eventually led Methodist missionaries to modify their mission strategies, redirecting their efforts to traditional religionists only. Shobana Shankar's study of Muslim responses to Christian mission in Northern Nigeria argues, among other things, that Muslim authorities in Northern Nigeria used the work of medical missionaries to advance their own causes (Shankar 2007, 2014).

Finally

As stated at the beginning of this introduction, *Critical Readings in the History of Christian Mission* presents a selection of texts that intends to introduce students, researchers, and other interested readers to the multi- and interdisciplinary field of mission history by apprising them with current discussions, insights, and theories and by addressing the complexities involved in studying mission history. We designed the volumes in such a way that *Critical Readings in the History of Christian Mission* can serve as basis for course-work and teaching purposes; jointly, the volumes on methods, approaches, and perspectives on topics will give students a comprehensive introduction to the study of mission history.

Throughout the process of compiling this anthology, we ourselves have read and learned a great deal, thereby only increasing our passion for the history of mission. We sincerely hope that the text-selection will be as thought-provoking, stimulating, and inspiring for the readers.

Acknowledgements

This project was initiated some years ago at the invitation of Inge Klompmakers. Since, it has gone through many stages, eventually producing the current text selection. Most of the ideas on how to fashion this anthology were not conceived behind a desk, but rather during long walks through the fields near Ermelo (the Netherlands). However, as Valentina Napolitano (2016: ix) so perceptively writes: "Many voices, people, ideas, and stories, percolate through writings. (…) Ideas are co-created. They emerge in small and big talks, through shared silences, in front of midmorning and late-night coffees. They come through us, more than they are by us." We would therefore like to acknowledge the input of colleagues (cognisant or unaware) in conceiving this anthology.

INTRODUCTION

Inge, Wendy Logeman, Gera van Bedaf, and others of the editorial and production staff at Brill have been patient, encouraging, and helpful throughout the long process of selecting the materials, obtaining permissions, and preparing the materials for this collection. On behalf of Brill, we would also like to thank all the authors and publishers who allowed their work (be it text or image) to be reproduced for this series.

Bibliography

Ahlbäck, Anders (2016). "The Overly Candid Missionary Historian. C. G. H. Oldendorp's Ambivalence over Slavery in the Danish West Indies." In Holger Weiss, ed. *Ports of Globalisation. Places of Creolisation. Nordic Possessions in the Atlantic World*. Leiden: Brill: 191–217.

Albert, Marie-Theres, Roland Bernecker, and Britta Rudolff, eds (2013). *Understanding Heritage. Perspectives in Heritage Studies*. Berlin: De Gruyter.

Altic, Mirela (2014). "Missionary Cartography of the Amazon after the Treaty of Madrid (1750). The Jesuit Contribution to the Demarcation of Imperial Frontiers." *Terrae Incognitae* 46, 2: 69–85.

Anderson, Thomas (2017). "Converting the Hospital. British Missionaries and Medicine in Nineteenth-Century Madagascar." *Itinerario* 41, 3: 539–554.

Andrews, Edward E. (2013). *Native Apostles. Black and Indian Missionaries in the British Atlantic World*. Cambridge: Harvard University Press.

Angrosino, Michael V. (1994). "The Culture Concept and the Mission of the Roman Catholic Church." *American Anthropologist* 96, 4: 824–832.

Arnold, David and Robert A. Bickers (1996). "Introduction." In Robert A. Bickers and Rosemary Seton, eds. *Missionary Encounters. Sources and Issues*. Richmond: Curzon Press: 1–10.

Azamede, Kokou (2010). *Transkulturationen? Ewe-Christen zwischen Deutschland und Westafrika, 1884–1939*. Stuttgart: Franz Steiner.

Bailey, Gauvin A. (1998). "The Indian Conquest of Catholic Art. The Mughals, the Jesuits, and Imperial Mural Painting." *Art Journal* 57, 1: 24–30.

Bailey, Gauvin A. (1999). "The Truth-Showing Mirror. Jesuit Catechism and the Arts in Mughal India." In John W. O'Malley, ed. *Jesuits. Cultures, Sciences, and the Arts, 1540–1773*. Toronto: University of Toronto Press: 380–401.

Bailey, Gauvin A. (2013). *Art on the Jesuit Missions in Asia and Latin America, 1542–1773*. Toronto: University of Toronto Press.

Baker Koons, Jane (1985). "The Midwest China Oral History Collection." *International Bulletin of Missionary Research* 9, 2: 66–68.

Barringer, Terry (2002). "From *Beyond Alpine Snow* and *Homes in the East*." *International Bulletin of Missionary Research* 26, 4: 169–173.

Barringer, Terry (2004). "What Mrs. Jellaby Might Have Read. Missionary Periodicals, a Neglected Sources." *Victorian Periodicals Review* 37, 4: 46–74.

Beaver, R. Pierce (1980). *American Protestant Women in World Mission. History of the First Feminist Movement in North America*. Grand Rapids: W. B. Eerdmans Publishers.

Becker, Judith & Brian Stanley, eds (2013). *Europe as the Other. External Perspectives on European Christianity*. Göttingen: Vandenhoeck & Ruprecht.

Becker, Judith, ed. (2015). *European Missions in Contact Zones. Transformation through Interaction in a (Post-)Colonial World*. Göttingen: Vandenhoeck & Ruprecht.

Bell, Joshua A. (2014). "Bird Specimen. Papua New Guinea." In Karen Jacobs, Chantal Knowles, and Chris Wingfield, eds. *Trophies, Relics and Curios? Missionary Heritage from Africa and the Pacific*. Leiden, Sidestone Press: 57–60.

Benson, John S. (2015). *Missionary Families Find a Sense of Place and Identity. Two Generations on Two Continents*. Lanham: Lexington Books.

Blackburn, Carole (2000). *Harvest of Souls. The Jesuit Missions and Colonialism in North America, 1632–1650*. Montréal: McGill-Queen's University Press.

Bosch, David J. (1991). *Transforming Mission. Paradigm Shifts in Theology of Mission*. Maryknoll: Orbis Books.

Botta, Sergio (2013). "Towards a Missionary Theory of Polytheism. The Franciscans in the Face of Indigenous Religions of New Spain." In Sergio Botta, ed. *Manufacturing Otherness. Missions and Indigenous Cultures in Latin America*. Newcastle upon Tyne: Cambridge Scholars Publishing: 11–35.

Bowie, Fiona (1993). "Introduction. Reclaiming Women's Heritage." In Fiona Bowie, Deborah Kirkwood, and Shirley Ardener, eds. *Women and Missions. Past and Present. Anthropological and Historical Perceptions*. Providence, RI: Berg: 1–22.

Bowie, Fiona, Deborah Kirkwood and Shirley Ardener eds (1993). *Women and Missions. Past and Present. Anthropological and Historical Perceptions*. Providence, RI: Berg.

Brock, Peggy (2003). "Two Indigenous Evangelists. Moses Tjalkabota and Arthur Wellington Clah." *Journal of Religious History* 27, 3: 348–366.

Brock, Peggy (2014). *The Many Voyages of Arthur Wellington Clah*. Vancouver: UBC Press.

Brock, Peggy, ed. (2005). *Indigenous Peoples and Religious Change*. Leiden: Brill.

Bruno-Jofré, Rosa del Carmen (2005). *The Missionary Oblate Sisters. Vision and Mission*. Montreal: McGill-Queen's University Press.

Burbank, Victoria K. (2012). "Life History and Real Life. An Example of Neuro-anthropology in Aboriginal Australia." *Annals of Anthropological Practice* 36, 1: 149–166.

Burke, Joan F. (2001). *These Catholic Sisters Are All Mamas! Towards the Inculturation of the Sisterhood in Africa, an Ethnographic Study*. Leiden: Brill.

Busschers, Iris (2015). "Gendered Remembrance. Women in the Dutch Calvinist Mission and its Historiography, c. 1900–1942." *Trajecta. Religie, Cultuur en Samenleving in de Nederlanden* 24, 2: 285–308.

Cabrita, Joel and David Maxwell (2017). "Introduction. Relocating World Christianity." In Joel Cabrita, David Maxwell and Emma Wild-Wood, eds. *Relocating World Christianity. Interdisciplinary Studies in Universal and Local Expressions of the Christian Faith.* Leiden: Brill: 1–44.

Cagé, Julia and Valeria Rueda (2017). "Sex and the Mission. The Conflicting Effects of Early Christian Investments on the HIV Epidemic in Sub-Saharan Africa." Discussion paper, Center Economic Policy Research London.

Cannell, Fenella, ed. (2006). *The Anthropology of Christianity.* Durham: Duke University Press.

Carretta, Vincent and Ty Reese (2010). *The Life and Letters of Philip Quaque, the First African Anglican Missionary.* Athens: University of Georgia Press.

Carroll, Lewis (1865). *Alice's Adventures in Wonderland.* London: Macmillan & Co.

Celenza, Anna Harwell and Anthony R. DelDonna (2014). *Music as Cultural Mission. Explorations of Jesuit Practices in Italy and North America.* Philadelphia: Saint Joseph's University Press.

Cevik, Gülen (2011). "American Missionaries and the Harem. Cultural Exchanges behind the Scenes." *Journal of American Studies* 45, 3: 463–481.

Chakrabarty, Dipesh (2000). *Provincializing Europe. Postcolonial Thought and Historical Difference.* Princeton: Princeton University Press.

Chang, Sung-Jin (2006). "Korean Bible Women. Their Vital Contribution to Korean Protestantism, 1895–1945." Ph.D. Dissertation, University of Edinburgh.

Charles, John (2010). *Allies at Odds. The Andean Church and Its Indigenous Agents, 1583–1671.* Albuquerque: University of New Mexico Press.

Choi, Hyaeweol (2009). *Gender and Mission Encounters in Korea. New Women, Old Ways.* Berkeley: University of California Press.

Choi, Hyaeweol (2010). "The Visual Embodiment of Women in the Korea Mission Field." *Korean Studies* 34, 1: 90–126.

Choi, Hyaeweol and Margaret Jolly, eds (2014). *Divine Domesticities. Christian Paradoxes in Asia and the Pacific.* Acton: ANU Press.

Chojnacki, Ruth J. (2010). *Indigenous Apostles. Maya Catholic Catechists Working the Word in Highland Chiapas.* Amsterdam: Rodopi.

Chowning, Margaret (2008). "Convents and Nuns. New Approaches to the Study of Female Religious Institutions in Colonial Mexico." *History Compass* 6, 5: 1279–1303.

Chu, Cindy Yik-yi (2007). *The Diaries of the Maryknoll Sisters in Hong Kong, 1921–1966.* Basingstoke: Palgrave Macmillan.

Chu, Cindy Yik-yi (2016). *The Chinese Sisters of the Precious Blood and the Evolution of the Catholic Church.* Singapore: Palgrave Macmillan.

Coleman, James Samuel (1965). *Nigeria. Background to Nationalism.* Berkeley: University of California Press.

Comaroff, Jean and John L. Comaroff (1991). *Of Revelation and Revolution. Christianity, Colonialism, and Consciousness in South Africa*. Volume 1. Chicago: University of Chicago Press.

Comaroff, Jean and John L. Comaroff (1997). *Of Revelation and Revolution. The Dialectics of Modernity on a South African Frontier*. Volume 2. Chicago: University of Chicago Press.

Comaroff, Jean and John L. Comaroff (2006). "The Colonization of Consciousness." In Michael Lambek, ed. *A Reader in the Anthropology of Religion*. New York: Wiley: 493–510.

Cowan, Mairi (2018). "Education, *Francisation*, and Shifting Colonial Priorities at the Ursuline Convent in Seventeenth-Century Québec." *The Canadian Historical Review* 99, 1: 1–29.

Cox, Jeffrey (2015). "Global Christianity in the Contact Zone." In Judith Becker, ed. *European Missions in Contact Zones. Transformation through Interaction in a (Post) Colonial World*. Göttingen: Vanderhoeck & Ruprecht: 27–43.

Cruickshank, Joanna (2010). "Race, History, and the Australian Faith Missions." *Itinerario* 34, 3: 39–52.

Cunningham, Valentine (1993). "God and Nature Intended You for a Missionary's Wife. Mary Hill, Jane Eyre and Other Missionary Women." In Fiona Bowie, Deborah Kirkwood, and Shirley Ardener, eds. *Women and Missions. Past and Present. Anthropological and Historical Perceptions*. Providence, RI: Berg, 85–108.

Dargie, David J. (2010). "Xhosa Zionist Church Music. A Liturgical Expression Beyond the Dreams of the Early Missionaries." *Missionalia* 38, 1: 32–53.

Davis, Joanne Ruth (2018). *Tiyo Sago. A Literary History*. Pretoria: Unisa Press.

De Almeida, André Ferrand (2003). "Samuel Fritz and the Mapping of the Amazon." *Imago Mundi* 55: 113–119.

Demarée, Gaston R., Astrid E. J. Ogilvie, and David Kusman (2019). "Historical Records of Earthquakes for Greenland and Labrador in Moravian Missionary Journals." *Journal of Seismology* 23, 1: 123–133.

Dube, Musa W. (2000). *Postcolonial Feminist Interpretation of the Bible*. St. Louis, MO: Chalice Press.

Dunch, Ryan (2002). "Beyond Cultural Imperialism. Cultural Theory, Christian Missions, and Global Modernity." *History and Theory* 41, 3: 301–325.

Dunmire, William W. (2004). *Gardens of New Spain. How Mediterranean Plants and Foods Changed America*. Austin: University of Texas Press.

Dussel, Enrique (1981). *A History of the Church in Latin America. Colonialism to Liberation (1492–1979)*. Transl. by Alan Neely. Grand Rapids: Eerdmans.

Dussel, Enrique (1992). *Historia Liberationis. 500 Anos de História da Igreja na América Latina*. São Paulo: Ediçoes Paulinas/ Cehila.

Dussel, Enrique (1993). "Eurocentrism and Modernity (Introduction to the Frankfurt Lectures)." *Boundary* 2 20, 3: 65–76.

Erll, Astrid, Ansgar Nünning, and Sara Young (2008). *Cultural Memory Studies. An International and Interdisciplinary Handbook*. Berlin: Walter De Gruyter.

Etherington, Norman (1996). "Recent Trends in the Historiography of Christianity in Southern Africa." *Journal of Southern African Studies* 22, 2: 201–219.

Evans, Christopher, Marie-Louise Stig Sørenson, and Konstantin Richter (2014). "An Early Christian Church in the Tropics. Excavation of the N.ª S.ª da Conceição Velha, Cape Verde." In Toby Green, ed. *Brokers of Change. Atlantic Commerce and Cultures in Precolonial Western Africa*. Oxford: Oxford University Press: 173–192.

Fields, Karen E. (1982). "Christian Missionaries as Anticolonial Militants." *Theory and Society* 11, 1: 95–108.

Frederiks, Martha (2009). "Methodists and Muslims in the Gambia." *Islam and Christian-Muslim Relations* 20, 1: 61–72.

Frederiks, Martha and Dorottya Nagy, eds (2020). *World Christianity. Methodological Considerations*. Leiden: Brill.

Frederiks, Martha T. (2003). *We Have Toiled All Night. Christianity in the Gambia 1465–2000*. Zoetermeer: Boekencentrum.

Frey Näf, Barbara (2013). "Die Pflanzenwelt Südindiens. Johann Jakob Hunzikers Naturselbstdrucke aus dem Jahr 1862." *Bauhinia* 24: 1–14.

Fromont, Cécile (2011). "Dance, Image, Myth, and Conversion in the Kingdom of Kongo, 1500–1800." *African Arts* 44, 4: 52–63.

Fromont, Cécile (2014). *The Art of Conversion. Christian Visual Culture in the Kingdom of Kongo*. Chapel Hill: University of North Carolina Press.

Fulford, Ben (2002). "An Igbo Esperanto. A History of the Union Ibo Bible 1900–1950." *Journal of Religion in Africa* 32, 4: 457–501.

Gao, Xi (2014). "Chinese Perspectives on Medical Missionaries in the 19th Century. The Chinese Medical Missionary Journal." *Journal of Cultural Interaction in East Asia* 5, 3: 97–118.

Golvers, Noël (2000). "Jesuit Cartographers in China. Francesco Brancati, S.J., and the Map (1661?) of Sungchiang Prefecture (Shanghai)." *Imago Mundi* 52: 30–42.

González, Justo L. (2002). *The Changing Shape of Church History*. St. Louis, MO: The Chalice Press.

Graham, Elizabeth (1998). "Mission Archaeology." *Annual Review of Anthropology* 27: 25–62.

Grimshaw, Patricia (1989). *Paths of Duty. American Missionary Wives in Nineteenth-Century Hawaii*. Honolulu: University of Hawaii Press.

Grimshaw, Patricia and Peter Sherlock (2007). "Women and Cultural Exchange." In Norman Etherington, ed. *Missions and Empire*. Oxford: Oxford University Press: 173–193.

Grimshaw, Patricia and Andrew May, eds (2010). *Missionaries, Indigenous Peoples, and Cultural Exchange*. Brighton: Sussex Academic Press.

Hall, Catherine (2002). *Civilising Subjects. Colony and Metropole in the English Imagination, 1830–1867*. Chicago: University of Chicago Press.

Hall, Catherine (2017). "Thinking Reflexively. Opening 'Blind Eyes'." *Past and Present* 234: 254–263.

Hardiman, David (2006). *Healing Bodies, Saving Souls. Medical Missions in Asia and Africa*. Amsterdam: Rodopi.

Harries, Patrick (2012). "Natural Science and *Naturvölker*." In David Maxwell and Patrick Harries, eds. *The Spiritual and the Secular. Missionaries and Knowledge about Africa*. Grand Rapids: Eerdmans: 30–71.

Hauser, Julia (2016). "From Transformation to Negotiation. A Female Mission in a 'City of Schools.'" *Journal of World History* 27, 3: 473–496.

Heywood, Linda and John Thornton (2007). *Central Africans, Atlantic Creoles, and the Foundation of the Americas, 1585–1660*. New York: Cambridge University Press.

Hillel, Margot (2011). "'Give Us All Missionary Eyes and Missionary Hearts'. Triumphalism and Missionising in Late-Victorian Children's Literature." *Mousaion* 29, 3: 179–192.

Hock, Klaus (2014). "Transkulturelle Perspektiven und das Programm einer Polyzentrischen Christentumsgeschichte." In Klaus Koschorke and Adrian Hermann, eds. *Polycentric Structures in the History of World Christianity*. Wiesbaden: Harrassowitz: 399–408.

Hofmeyr, Isabel (2001). "Bunyan in Africa. Text and Transition." *Interventions. International Journal of Postcolonial Studies* 3, 3: 322–335.

Hofmeyr, Isabel (2004). *The Portable Bunyan. A Transnational History of the Pilgrim's Progress*. Princeton: Princeton University Press.

Huber, Mary Taylor, and Nancy Lutkehaus (1999). *Gendered Missions. Women and Men in Missionary Discourse and Practice*. Ann Arbor: University of Michigan Press.

Hunt, Nancy Rose (1999). *A Colonial Lexicon of Birth Ritual, Medicalization, and Mobility in the Congo*. Durham: Duke University Press.

Irvin, Dale T. (2008). "World Christianity. An Introduction." *The Journal of World Christianity* 1, 1: 1–26.

Irvine, Judith T. (2008). "Subjected Words. African Linguistics and the Colonial Encounter." *Language and Communication* 28, 4: 323–343.

Jenkins, Paul (1993). "The Earliest Generation of Missionary Photographers in West Africa and the Portrayal of Indigenous People and Culture." *History in Africa* 20: 89–118.

Jenkins, Paul (1996). "Four Nineteenth Century Pictoral Images from Africa in the Basel Mission Archive and Library Collections." In Robert A. Bickers and Rosemary Seton, eds. *Missionary Encounters. Sources and Issues*. Richmond: Curzon Press: 95–113.

Jenkins, Paul (2001). "On Using Historical Missionary Photographs in Modern Discussions." *Le Fait Missionaire* 10, 1: 71–89.

Jenkins, Paul (2002a). "Everyday Life Encapsulated? Two Photographs concerning Women and the Basel Mission in West Africa, c. 1900." *Journal of African Cultural Studies* 15, 1: 45–60.

Jenkins, Paul (2002b). "Much More Than Illustrations of What We Already Know. Experiences in the Rediscovery of Mission Photography." *International Bulletin of Missionary Research* 26, 4: 157–162.

Jenkins, Paul (2009). "From a Real Body, Which Was There, Proceed Radiations Which Ultimately Touch Me, Who Am Here. An Encounter with a Missionary Portrait of a Precolonial Akan Court Official." *Visual Anthropology* 22, 4: 275–292.

Jensz, Felicity and Hanna Acke, eds (2013). *Mission and Media. The Politics of Missionary Periodicals in the Long Nineteenth Century*, Stuttgart: Franz Steiner Verlag.

Johnston, Anna (2003). *Missionary Writing and Empire, 1800–1860*. Cambridge: Cambridge University Press.

Jolly, Margaret (2014). "A Saturated History of Christianity and Cloth in Oceania." In Hyaeweol Choi and Margaret Jolly, eds. *Divine Domesticities. Christian Paradoxes in Asia and the Pacific*. Acton: ANU Press: 429–454.

Jones, Arun W. (2014). "Scholarly Transgressions. (Re)writing the History of World Christianity." *Theology Today* 71, 2: 221–232.

Kalusa, Walima T. (2007). "Language, Medical Auxiliaries, and the Re-Interpretation of Missionary Medicine in Colonial Mwinilunga, Zambia, 1922–1951." *Journal of Eastern African Studies* 1, 1: 57–78.

Kark, Ruth (1993). "The Contribution of Nineteenth Century Protestant Missionary Societies to Historical Cartography." *Imago Mundi* 45, 1: 112–119.

Katzenellenbogen, Judy, Derek Yach, and Rob E. Dorrington (1993). "Mortality in a Rural South African Mission, 1837–1909. An Historical Cohort Study Using Church Records." *International Journal of Epidemiology* 22, 6: 965–975.

Kent, Eliza F. (1999). "Tamil Bible Women and the Zenana Missions of Colonial South India." *History of Religions* 39, 2: 117–149.

Killingray, David (2003). "The Black Atlantic Missionary Movement and Africa, 1780s–1920s." *Journal of Religion in Africa* 33, 1: 3–31.

King, Rachel and Mark McGranaghan (2018). "The Archaeology and Materiality of Mission in Southern Africa. Introduction." *Journal of Southern African Studies* 44, 4: 629–639.

Kokkonen, Pellervo (1993). "Religious and Colonial Realities. Cartography of the Finnish Mission in Ovamboland, Namibia." *History in Africa* 20: 155–171.

Kollman, Paul V. (2005). *The Evangelization of Slaves and Catholic Origins in Eastern Africa*. Maryknoll: Orbis Books.

Kollman, Paul (2014). "Understanding the World-Christian Turn in the History of Christianity and Theology." *Theology Today* 71, 2: 164–177.

Korte, Hannah de and David Onnekink (2020). "Maps Matter. The 10/40 Window and Missionary Geography." *Exchange* 49, 2: 110–144.

Koschorke, Klaus (2013). *Veränderte Landkarten. Auf dem Weg zu einer Polyzentrischen Geschichte des Weltchristentums. Festschrift für Klaus Koschorke zum 65. Geburtstag.* Cirprian Burlacioiu and Adrian Hermann, eds. Wiesbaden: Harrassowitz Verlag.

Koschorke, Klaus and Adrian Hermann, eds (2014). *Polycentric Structures in the History of World Christianity. Polyzentrische Strukturen in der Geschichte des Weltchristentums.* Wiesbaden: Harrassowitz.

Kuo, Margaret (2016). "China through the Magic Lantern. Passionist Father Theophane Maguire and American Catholic Missionary Images of China in the Early Twentieth Century." *US Catholic Historian* 34, 2: 27–42.

Kwakye, Abraham N. O. (2018). "Returning African Christians in Mission to the Gold Coast." *Studies in World Christianity* 24, 1: 25–45.

Kwok, Pui-lan (2005). *Postcolonial Imagination and Feminist Theology.* Louisville: Westminster John Knox Press.

Labode, Modupe (1993). "From Kraal to Christian Home. Anglican Mission Education and African Christian Girls, 1850–1900." In Fiona Bowie, Deborah Kirkwood, and Shirley Ardener, eds. *Women and Missions. Past and Present. Anthropological and Historical Perceptions.* Providence, RI: Berg, 126–144.

Lankina, Tomila and Lullit Getachew (2012). "Mission or Empire, Word or Sword? The Human Capital Legacy in Postcolonial Democratic Development." *American Journal of Political Science* 56, 2: 465–483.

Latai, Latu (2014). "From Open Fale to Mission Houses. Negotiating the Boundaries of Domesticity in Samoa." In Hyaeweol Choi and Margaret Jolly, eds. *Divine Domesticities. Christian Paradoxes in Asia and the Pacific,* Canberra: Anu Press: 299–324.

Li, Ji (2015). *God's Little Daughters. Catholic Women in Nineteenth-Century Manchuria.* Seattle: University of Washington Press.

Long, Kathryn T. (2003). "Cameras 'Never Lie'. The Role of Photography in Telling the Story of American Evangelical Missions." *Church History* 72, 4: 820–851.

Lycett, Mark T. (2004). "Archaeology under the Bell. The Mission as Situated History in Seventeenth Century New Mexico." *Missionalia* 32, 3: 357–379.

Mallampalli, Chandra (2003). "British Missions and the Rise of Indian Nationalism 1880–1908." In Andrew N. Porter, ed. *The Imperial Horizons of British Protestant Missions, 1880–1914.* Grand Rapids: W. B. Eerdmans Publishers: 151–181.

Mallampalli, Chandra (2017). "The Orientalist Framework of Christian Conversion in India. Three Venues of 'Inducement' from Colonial Times to the Present." In Joel Cabrita, David Maxwell and Emma Wild-Wood, eds. *Relocating World Christianity. Interdisciplinary Studies in Universal and Local Expressions of the Christian Faith.* Leiden: Brill: 162–186.

Maluleke, Tinyiku S. (2000). "The Quest for Muted Black Voices. Some Pertinent Issues in the (South) African Mission Historiography." *Missionalia* 28, 2: 41–61.

Manktelow, Emily J. (2012). "Rev. Simpson's 'Improper Liberties'. Moral Scrutiny and Missionary Children in the South Seas Mission." *Journal of Imperial and Commonwealth History* 40, 2: 159–181.

Manktelow, Emily J. (2014). "The Rise and Demise of Missionary Wives." *Journal of Women's History* 26, 1: 135–159.

Manktelow, Emily J. (2015). "Thinking with Gossip. Deviance, Rumour and Reputation in the South Seas Mission of the London Missionary Society." In Will Jackson and Emily J. Manktelow, eds. *Subverting Empire. Deviance and Disorder in the British Colonial World.* Basingstoke: Palgrave Macmillan: 104–125.

Manktelow, Emily J. (2016). *Missionary Families. Race, Gender and Generation on the Spiritual Frontier.* Oxford: Manchester University Press.

Manktelow, Emily J. (2017). "Making Missionary Children. Religion, Culture and Juvenile Deviance." In Hugh D. Morrison and Mary Clare Martin, eds. *Creating Religious Childhoods in Anglo-World and British Colonial Contexts, 1800–1950.* Abingdon: Routledge: 41–60.

Martínez D'Alós-Moner, Andreu (2015). *Envoys of a Human God. The Jesuit Mission to Christian Ethiopia, 1557–1632.* Boston: Brill.

Maxwell, David (2011). "Photography and the Religious Encounter. Ambiguity and Aesthetics in Missionary Representations of the Luba of South East Belgian Congo." *Comparative Studies in Society and History* 53, 1: 38–74.

McGhie, Henry A. (2017). *Henry Dresser and Victorian Ornithology. Birds, Book and Business.* Manchester: Manchester University Press.

Meyer, Birgit (1997). "Christian Mind and Worldly Matters. Religion and Materiality in Nineteenth-Century Gold Coast." *Journal of Material Culture* 2, 3: 311–337.

Meyer, Birgit (1999). *Translating the Devil. Religion and Modernity among the Ewe in Ghana.* Trenton, NJ: Africa World Press.

Meyer, Birgit (2010). "'There Is a Spirit in That Image.' Mass-Produced Jesus Pictures and Protestant-Pentecostal Animation in Ghana." *Comparative Studies in Society and History* 52, 1: 100–130.

Midgley, Clare (2000). "Female Emancipation in an Imperial Frame. English Women and the Campaign against Sati (Widow-Burning) in India, 1813–30." *Women's History Review* 9, 1: 95–121.

Miller, Karen Li (2012). "The White Child's Burden. Managing the Self and Money in Nineteenth-Century Children's Missionary Periodicals." *American Periodicals. A Journal of History & Criticism* 22, 2: 139–157.

Mitchell, Jean (2013). "Objects of Expert Knowledge. On Time and the Materialities of Conversion to Christianity in the Southern New Hebrides." *Anthropologica* 55, 2: 291–302.

Mojola, Aloo Osotsi (2001). "The Swahili Bible in East Africa from 1844 to 1996. A Brief Survey with Special Reference to Tanzania." In Gerald West and Musa Dube, eds. *The Bible in Africa. Transactions, Trajectories and Trends.* Leiden: Brill: 511–524.

Montgomery, Robert L. (1999). *Introduction to the Sociology of Missions.* Westport, Conn.: Praeger.

Morrison, Hugh (2017). "'It's Really Where Your Parents Were'. Differentiating and Situating Protestant Missionary Children's Lives, c.1900–1940." *Journal of Family History* 42, 4: 419–439.

Mortamet, Clara and Céline Amourette (2015). "Missionary Descriptions in a Colonial Context. The Grammatization of Swahili through the Study of Four Missionary Grammars from 1885 to 1944." In Klaus Zimmermann and Birte Kellermeier-Rehbein, eds. *Colonialism and Missionary Linguistics.* Berlin: De Gruyter: 29–48.

Moyo, Fabulous (2015). *The Bible, the Bullet, and the Ballot. Zimbabwe. The Impact of Christian Protest in Sociopolitical Transformation, ca.1900–ca.2000.* Eugene OR: Pickwick Publications.

Nagy, Dorottya (2017). "World Christianity as a Theological Approach." In Joel Cabrita, David Maxwell and Emma Wild-Wood, eds. *Relocating World Christianity. Interdisciplinary Studies in Universal and Local Expressions of the Christian Faith.* Leiden: Brill: 143–161.

Napolitano, Valentina (2016). *Migrant Hearts and the Atlantic Return. Transnationalism and the Roman Catholic Church.* New York: Fordham University Press.

Nehring, Andreas (2003). *Orientalismus und Mission. Die Repräsentation der Tamilischen Gesellschaft und Religion durch Leipziger Missionare 1840–1940.* Wiesbaden: Harrassowitz.

Nehring, Andreas (2015). "Politics and Meditation. Christian Missions and Theravada Buddhist Reform in Nineteenth Century Burma." In Judith Becker, ed. (2015). *European Missions in Contact Zones. Transformation through Interaction in a (Post-) Colonial World.* Göttingen: Vandenhoeck & Ruprecht, 87–106.

Neufeldt, Ronald (1993). "The Response of the Hindu Renaissance to Christianity." In Harold Coward, ed. *Hindu-Christian Dialogue. Perspectives and Encounters.* Delhi: Motilal Banarsidass: 28–46.

Occom, Samson and Joanna Brooks (2006). *The Collected Writings of Samson Occom, Mohegan. Leadership and Literature in Eighteenth-Century Native America.* Oxford: Oxford University Press.

Oddie, Geoffrey A. (1996). "Missionaries as Social Commentators. The Indian Case." In Robert A. Bickers and Rosemary Seton, eds. *Missionary Encounters. Sources and Issues.* Richmond: Curzon Press: 197–210.

Oddie, Geoffrey A. (1999). *Missionaries, Rebellion and Proto-Nationalism. James Long of Bengal 1814–87.* Richmond, Surrey: Curzon.

Oddie, Geoffrey A. (2006). *Imagined Hinduism. British Protestant Missionary Construc-tions of Hinduism, 1793–1900*. New Delhi: Sage Publications.

Okkenhaug, Inger Marie (2002). *The Quality of Heroic Living, of High Endeavour and Adventure. Anglican Mission, Women, and Education in Palestine, 1888–1948*. Leiden: Brill.

Omenyo, Cephas N. and David Choi (2000). "Korean Missionary Enterprise in West Africa 1979–1999. A Preliminary Study." *Exchange* 29, 3: 213–229.

Panich, Lee M. and Tsim D. Schneider (2015). "Expanding Mission Archaeology. A Landscape Approach to Indigenous Autonomy in Colonial California." *Journal of Anthropological Archaeology* 40: 48–58.

Peel, John D. Y. (1995). "'For Who Hath Despised the Day of Small Things?' Missionary Narratives and Historical Anthropology." *Comparative Studies in Society and History* 37, 3: 581–607.

Peel, John D. Y. (1996). "Problems and Opportunities in an Anthropologist's Use of a Missionary Archive." In Robert A. Bickers and Rosemary Seton, eds. *Missionary Encounters. Sources and Issues*. Richmond: Curzon Press: 70–94.

Pelkmans, Mathijs (2007). "Culture as a Tool and an Obstacle. Missionary Encounters in Post-Communist Kyrgyzstan." *Journal of the Royal Anthropological Institute* 13, 4: 881–889.

Pelkmans, Mathijs (2017). *Fragile Conviction. Changing Ideological Landscapes in Urban Kyrgyzstan*. Ithaca: Cornell University Press.

Peterson, Derek (1997). "Colonizing Language? Missionaries and Gikuyu Dictionaries, 1904 and 1914." *History in Africa* 24: 257–272.

Peterson, Derek (1999). "Translating the Word. Dialogism and Debate in Two Gikuyu Dictionaries." *Journal of Religious History* 23, 1: 31–50.

Peterson, Derek R. (2004). *Creative Writing. Translation, Bookkeeping, and the Work of Imagination in Colonial Kenya*. Portsmouth, NH: Heinemann.

Peterson, Derek R. (2012). *Ethnic Patriotism and the East African Revival. A History of Dissent, c. 1935 to 1972*. Cambridge: Cambridge University Press.

Petzke, Martin (2016). "Taken in by the Numbers Game. The Globalization of a Religious 'Illusio' and 'Doxa' in Nineteenth-Century Evangelical Missions to India." *The Sociological Review* 64 (2 suppl): 124–145.

Petzke, Martin (2018). "The Global 'Bookkeeping' of Souls. Quantification and Nineteenth-Century Evangelical Missions." *Social Science History* 42, 2: 183–211.

Phiri, Isabel Apawo (2000). "African Women in Mission. Two Case Studies from Malawi." *Missionalia. Southern African Journal of Mission Studies* 28, 2: 267–293.

Porter, Andrew (2008). "Evangelicalism, Islam, and Millennial Expectation in the Nineteenth Century." In Dana L. Robert, ed. *Converting Colonialism. Visions and Realities in Mission History, 1706–1914*. Grand Rapids: Eerdmans: 60–85.

Porter, Andrew N. (2004). *Religion Versus Empire? British Protestant Missionaries and Overseas Expansion, 1700–1914*. Manchester: Manchester University Press.

Porter, Andrew N., ed. (2003). *The Imperial Horizons of British Protestant Missions, 1880–1914*. Grand Rapids: Eerdmans.

Pratt, Mary Louise (2008). *Imperial Eyes. Travel Writing and Transculturation*. New York: Routledge (2nd edition).

Prevost, Elizabeth (2008). "Married to the Mission Field. Gender, Christianity, and Professionalization in Britain and Colonial Africa, 1865–1914." *Journal of British Studies* 47, 4: 796–826.

Price, Richard (2008). *Making Empire. Colonial Encounters and the Creation of Imperial Rule in Nineteenth-Century Africa*. Cambridge: Cambridge University Press.

Reeves-Ellington, Barbara, Kathryn Kish Sklar, and Connie Anne Shemo, eds (2010). *Competing Kingdoms. Women, Mission, Nation, and the American Protestant Empire, 1812–1960*. Durham N.C.: Duke University Press.

Reynolds, Chris (2010). "Africa Joins the World. The Missionary Imagination and the Africa Motion Picture Project in Central Africa 1937–1939." *Journal of Social History* 44, 2: 459–479.

Rieger, Joerg (2004). "Theology and Mission between Postcolonialism and Neo-colonialism." *Mission Studies* 21, 2: 201–227.

Robbins, Joel (2004). *Becoming Sinners. Christianity and Moral Torment in a Papua New Guinea Society*. Berkeley: University of California Press.

Robbins, Joel (2014). "The Anthropology of Christianity. Unity, Diversity, New Directions." *Current Anthropology* 55, 10: 157–171.

Robert, Dana L. (1997). *American Women in Mission. A Social History of Their Thought and Practice*. Macon: Mercer University Press.

Robert, Dana L. (2002). *Gospel Bearers, Gender Barriers. Missionary Women in the Twentieth Century*. Maryknoll: Orbis Books.

Robert, Dana L., ed. (2008). *Converting Colonialism. Visions and Realities in Mission History, 1706–1914*. Grand Rapids: Eerdmans.

Russell, Horace O. (2000). *The Missionary Outreach of the West Indian Church. Jamaican Baptist Missions to West Africa in the Nineteenth Century*. New York: Peter Lang.

Ryad, Umar (2015). "Muslim Responses to Missionary Literature in Egypt in the Late Nineteenth and Early Twentieth Centuries." In Douglas Pratt, John Hoover and John A. Chesworth, eds. *The Character of Christian-Muslim Encounter. Essays in Honour of David Thomas*. Leiden: Brill: 288–308.

Samson, Jane (2010). "Translation Teams. Missionaries, Islanders and the Reduction of Language in the Pacific." In Patricia Grimshaw and Andrew May, eds. *Missionaries, Indigenous People and Cultural Exchange*, Brighton: Sussex Academic Press, 96–109.

Samson, Jane (2017). *Race and Redemption. British Missionaries Encounter Pacific Peoples, 1797–1920.* Grand Rapids, Michigan: William B. Eerdmans Publishing Company.

Sanneh, Lamin (1983). "The Horizontal and the Vertical in Mission. An African Perspective." *International Bulletin of Missionary Research* 7, 4: 165–171.

Sanneh, Lamin O. (1989). *Translating the Message. The Missionary Impact on Culture.* Maryknoll: Orbis Books.

Sanneh, Lamin O. (1995). "The Gospel, Language and Culture. The Theological Method in Cultural Analysis." *International Review of Mission* 84, 1: 47–64.

Śarmā, Aravinda (1988). *Neo-Hindu Views of Christianity.* Leiden: Brill.

Sasaki, Motoe (2016). *Redemption and Revolution. American and Chinese New Women in the Early Twentieth Century.* Ithaca: Cornell University Press.

Schieffelin, Bambi B. (2014). "Christianizing Language and the Dis-Placement of Culture in Bosavi, Papua New Guinea." *Current Anthropology* 55, 10: 226–237.

Schram, Ryan (2016). "'Tapwaroro Is True'. Indigenous Voice and the Heteroglossia of Methodist Missionary Translation in British New Guinea." *Journal of Linguistic Anthropology* 26, 3: 259–277.

Schultze, Andrea (2004). "Writing of Past Times. An Interdisciplinary Approach to Mission History." In Frieder Ludwig and Afe Adogame, eds. *European Traditions in the Study of Religion in Africa.* Wiesbaden: Harrassowitz Verlag: 323–328.

Sebastian, Mrinalini (2003). "Reading Archives from a Postcolonial Feminist Perspective. 'Native' Bible Women and the Missionary Ideal." *Journal of Feminist Studies in Religion* 19, 1: 5–25.

Shankar, Shobana (2007). "Medical Missionaries and Modernizing Emirs in Colonial Hausaland. Leprosy Control and Native Authority in the 1930s." *Journal of African History* 48, 1: 45–68.

Shankar, Shobana (2014). *Who Shall Enter Paradise? Christian Origins in Muslim Northern Nigeria, ca. 1890–1975.* Athens, Ohio: Ohio University Press.

Simpson, Donald (1997). "Missions and the Magic Lantern." *International Bulletin of Missionary Research* 21, 1: 13–15.

Skreslet, Stanley (2007). "Thinking Missiologically about the History of Mission." *International Bulletin of Missionary Research* 31, 2: 59–65.

Smith, Ian W. G. (2014a). "Schooling on the Missionary Frontier. The Hohi Mission Station, New Zealand." *International Journal of Historical Archaeology* 18, 4: 612–628.

Smith, Ian W. G., et al. (2012) *Archaeology of the Hohi Mission Station.* Volume I: The 2012 Excavations. Dunedin, New Zealand: Department of Anthropology and Archaeology, University of Otago.

Smith, Ian W. G., et al. (2014b) *Archaeology of the Hohi Mission Station.* Volume II: The 2013 Excavations. Dunedin, New Zealand: Department of Anthropology and Archaeology, University of Otago.

Smith, Paul J. (2007). "On Toucans and Hornbills. Readings in Early Modern Ornithology from Belon to Buffon." In Karl A. E. Enenkel and Paul J. Smith, eds. *Early Modern Zoology. The Construction of Animals in Science, Literature and the Visual Arts.* Leiden: Brill.

Sørensen, Marie Louise Stig and John Carman, eds (2009). *Heritage Studies. Methods and Approaches.* London: Routledge.

Stanley, Brian (1990). *The Bible and the Flag. Protestant Missions and British Imperialism in the Nineteenth and Twentieth Centuries.* Leicester: Apollos.

Stolz, Thomas and Ingo Warnke (2015). "From Missionary Linguistics to Colonial Linguistics." In Klaus Zimmerman and Birte Kellermeier-Rehbein, eds. *Colonialism and Missionary Linguistics.* Berlin: De Gruyter: 3–25.

Stornig, Katherina (2015). "Cultural Perceptions of Purity and Pollution. Childbirth and Midwifery in a New Guinean Catholic Mission, 1896–c.1930." In Judith Becker, ed. *European Missions in Contact Zones. Transformation through Interaction in a (Post) Colonial World.* Göttingen: Vanderhoeck & Ruprecht: 107–123.

Strawn, Lee-Ellen (2012). "Korean Bible Women's Success. Using the Anbang Network and the Religious Authority of the Mudang." *Journal of Korean Religions* 3, 1: 117–149.

Sugirtharajah, Rasiah S. (2001). *The Bible and the Third World. Precolonial, Colonial, and Postcolonial Encounters.* Cambridge: Cambridge University Press.

Sugirtharajah, Rasiah S. (2005). *The Bible and Empire. Postcolonial Explorations.* Cambridge, UK: Cambridge University Press.

Sundkler, Bengt (1948). *Bantu Prophets in South Africa.* London: Lutterworth Press.

Thompson, T. Jack (2002). "Light on the Dark Continent. The Photography of Alice Seely Harris and the Congo Atrocities of the Early Twentieth Century." *International Bulletin of Missionary Research* 26, 4: 146–149.

Thompson, T. Jack (2013). "Lake Malawi, I Presume? David Livingstone, Maps and the 'Discovery' of Lake Nyassa in 1859." *Society of Malawi Journal* 66, 2: 1–15.

Thompson, T. Jack ed. (2012). *Light on Darkness? Missionary Photography of Africa in the Nineteenth and Early Twentieth Centuries.* Grand Rapids: W. B. Eerdmans Publishers.

Thurman, Suzanne R. (2002). "The Medical Mission Strategy of the Maryknoll Sisters." *Missiology. An International Review* 30, 3: 361–373.

Tiedemann, Rolf G. (1997). *Indigenous Agency, Religious Protectorates and Chinese Interests. The Expansion of Christianity in China, 1830–1880.* Cambridge: North Atlantic Missiology Project.

Toelle, Jutta (2013). "'Was michs kostet, die Indianer in unserer Europäischen Music zu instruiren, ist dem lieben Gott allein bekannt'. Kircher und die Jesuitische Mission durch Musik in Paraquaria." In Melanie Wald-Fuhrmann, ed. *Steinbruch oder Wissensgebäude? Zur Rezeption von Athanasius Kirchers "Musurgia Universalis" in Musiktheorie und Kompositionspraxis.* Basel: Schwabe: 93–105.

Tomalin, Marcus (2011a). *"And He Knew Our Language". Missionary Linguistics on the Pacific Northwest Coast.* Amsterdam: John Benjamins Publishing Company.

Tomalin, Marcus (2011b). "Exploring Nineteenth-Century Haida Translations of the New Testament." *Journal of Religious History* 35.1: 43–71.

Tota, Anna Lisa and Trever Hagen, eds (2015). *Routledge International Handbook of Memory Studies.* London: Routledge.

Twells, Alison (2009). *The Civilising Mission and the English Middle Class, 1792–1850. The 'Heathen' at Home and Overseas.* Basingstoke England: Palgrave Macmillan.

Valen, Gary van (2013). *Indigenous Agency in the Amazon. The Mojos in Liberal and Rubber-Boom Bolivia, 1842–1932.* Tucson: University of Arizona Press.

Vasquez, Jean-Michel (2015). "Y a-t-il une Expertise Urbaine dans la Cartographie Missionnaire?" *Chrétiens et Sociétés* 21: 65–77.

Verdeil, Chantal (2014). "Le Temps des Missionnaires. Calendriers et Emplois du Temps dans les Etablissements Scolaires de l'Empire Ottoman à la Fin du XIXᵉ Siècle." *Revue des Mondes Musulmans et de la Méditerranée* 136: 89–108.

Verstraelen-Gilhuis, Gerdien (1982). *From Dutch Mission Church to Reformed Church in Zambia. The Scope for African Leadership and Initiative in the History of a Zambian Mission Church.* Franeker: Wever.

Walls, Andrew F. (2000). "Eusebius Tries Again. Reconceiving the Study of Christian History." In Wilbert R. Shenk, ed. *Enlarging the Story. Perspectives of Writing World Christian History.* Maryknoll NY: Orbis Books: 1–20.

Walls, Andrew F. (2004). *The Missionary Movement in Christian History. Studies in the Transmission of Faith.* London: T&T Clark International.

Walshe, Peter (1982). *The Rise of African Nationalism in South Africa. The African National Congress, 1912–1952.* London: C. Hurst (2nd edition).

Wariboko, Waibinte E. (2004). "I Really Cannot Make Africa My Home. West Indian Missionaries as 'Outsiders' in the Church Missionary Society Civilizing Mission to Southern Nigeria, 1898–1925." *The Journal of African History* 45, 2: 221–236.

Whiteley, Marilyn Färdig (2005). *Canadian Methodist Women, 1766–1925. Marys, Marthas, Mothers in Israel.* Waterloo, Ont.: Canadian Corporation for Studies in Religion.

Wild-Wood, Emma (2001). "An Introduction to an Oral History and Archive Project by the Anglican Church of Congo." *History in Africa* 28: 445–462.

Wild-Wood, Emma (2008). "Saint Apolo from Europe. Or: What's in a Luganda Name?" *Church History* 77, 1: 105–127.

Wild-Wood, Emma (2010). "The Making of an African Missionary Hero in the English Biographies of Apolo Kivebulaya (1923–1936)." *Journal of Religion in Africa* 40, 3: 273–306.

Wild-Wood, Emma (2014). "A Biography of Apolo Kivebulaya." *International Bulletin of Missionary Research* 38, 3: 145–148.

Wyss, Hilary E. (2012). *English Letters and Indian Literacies. Reading, Writing, and New England Missionary Schools, 1750–1830*. Philadelphia: University of Pennsylvania Press.

Young, Richard Fox (2002). "Some Hindu Perspectives on Christian Missionaries in the Indic World of the mid-19th Century." In Judith M. Brown and Robert E. Frykenberg, eds. *Christians, Cultural Interactions and India's Religious Traditions*. Grand Rapids: Eerdmans Publishers: 37–60.

Yun, Zhou (2018). "The Making of Bible Women in Funjian Zenana Mission from the 1880s to the 1950s." In Patricia Chiu, and Wai-Ching Angela Wong, eds. *Christian Women in Chinese Society. The Anglican Story*. Hong Kong: Hong Kong University Press: 59–82.

Zimmermann, Klaus and Birte Kellermeier-Rehbein (2015). *Colonialism and Missionary Linguistics*. Berlin: De Gruyter.

Zwartjes, Otto (2011). *Portuguese Missionary Grammars in Asia, Africa and Brazil, 1550–1800*. Amsterdam: J. Benjamins.

PART 1

Methods

Recent Trends in the Historiography of Christianity in Southern Africa

Norman Etherington

In a survey made a dozen years ago, I remarked on the problems of keeping up with the historiography of Christian missions in Africa.[1] These have not diminished with the passage of time. There is still no specialist journal devoted to the field and major academic presses rarely publish books on the subject. Historians who want to stay in touch must stray far from their usual haunts and cross disciplinary boundaries. Looking narrowly for books, articles and theses with the words 'mission' and 'history' in their titles is a misconceived enterprise which inevitably generates meagre results, even in the present age of computer-assisted keyword searches.[2] To form a proper idea of the work that has been done since the birth of *JSAS* in the early 1970s, it is necessary to cast a wide net across the entire spectrum of religious studies. Publications are widely dispersed across the periodical literature of different disciplines in several different countries. Nowhere, not even in the *Journal of Religion in Africa*, is there the kind of concentrated regular dialogue or the canon of currently approved texts that are available in other lines of research. There are, in current American idiom, several different 'information loops' that rarely intersect. If you want to survey them, you have to work.

Source: Etherington, N., "Recent Trends in the Historiography of Christianity in Southern Africa," *Journal of Southern African Studies* 22.2 (1996): pp. 201–219. Copyright © The Editorial Board of the Journal of Southern African Studies reprinted by permission of Taylor & Francis Ltd, http://www.tandfonline.com on behalf of The Editorial Board of the *Journal of Southern African Studies*.

---

1 N. Etherington, 'Missionaries and the Intellectual History of Africa: A Historical Survey', *Itinerario. Bulletin of the Leiden Centre for the History of European Expansion*, 7 (1983), pp. 116–143.
2 Thus in an interesting article on the sociology of mission stations, Justin Willis is able to write as though the only previous investigations of his topic were made by Oliver, Beidelman, Landeg White and the Comaroffs, thereby missing a large body of relevant literature: The Nature of a Mission Community: the Universities' Mission to Central Africa in Bonde', *Past and Present*, 140 (1993), pp. 127–154.

My principle of selection was to look for items concerned with history at some important level and my starting point was the bibliographies which appear several times a year in the *International Review of Mission*.[3] Building on that base, I next searched the last twelve years of the *Journal of Religion in Africa*. The *South African Historical Journal*'s bibliographies of articles, theses and papers in South African history for the years 1990–1993 compiled by Mary-Lynn Suttie of the University of South Africa Library also proved to be invaluable.[4] The search eventually extended to 65 books, more than 120 articles and a miscellaneous collection of conference papers, anthologies and items from edited books—a fair sample of recent literature but one which for the most part excludes magazines of local history and church affairs directed at non-academic audiences.

Although it is still unusual to find articles on religious history in generalist journals concerned with Africa, in recent years such articles have appeared more often. The table below sets out the results of my survey of periodicals for the years since 1982. After each publication I list the total number of articles concerning southern African religious history (excluding routine reviews) and the median year of publication.

The most striking feature of the table is the figure for the median year of publication. The journals which routinely concern themselves with the history of religion show a median date about mid-way between 1982 and 1994. However, for what Richard Elphick would call the 'mainstream journals', the median is in every case closer to 1994 than 1982.[5] And for several of these, the median is 1990 or later. It may be tentatively suggested on the basis of this survey that after several decades of relative neglect, interest in religion has been growing among secular historians.[6] Further evidence of a trend is the inclusion

---

3 For several decades the diligent compiler has been Andrew Walls.

4 *South African Historical Journal*, 28 (1993), pp. 398–445 and 30 (1994), pp. 222–297. In a broader search of regional literature I also consulted H. C. Price, C. Hewson and D. Blake, *Theses on Africa, 1976–1988 Accepted by Universities of the United Kingdom and Ireland* (London, 1993). For American and Canadian theses, see the very full listings compiled from time to time in the *International Bulletin of Missionary Research*.

5 Elphick commented on the difficulty of getting writing about religion into the mainstream of historical studies in 'Writing about Christianity in History: Some Issues of Theory and Method', paper delivered at the University of the Western Cape at the 1992 Conference, 'People, Power and Culture: The History of Christianity in South Africa, 1792–1992'.

6 Historians have been slow to notice the emerging trend. Michael Twaddle, contemplating the state of African studies in 1986, had nothing what ever to say about religion; 'The State of African Studies', *African Affairs*, 85 (1986), pp. 439–445. John McCracken, as late as last year, contemplating the lost paradise of African history in British Universities, remarked only that several years ago Aberdeen had closed down the distinguished department of Religious

Journal	Total articles	Median year of publication
Journal of Religion in Africa	23	1987
Missionalia	16	1989
International Journal of African Historical Studies	10	1992
Journal of Theology for Southern Africa	7	1984
South African Historical Journal	7	1991
JSAS	7	1990
Journal of African History	7	1988
International Review of Mission	6	1989
International Bulletin of Missionary Research	4	1988
Norske Tidsskrift for Misjon	3	1990
Journal of Imperial and Commonwealth History	2	1992
Journal of Modern African Studies	2	1988
History in Africa	2	1990
Others[a]	8	1991

a   One article each appeared in: *Journal of Religion*; *Journal of Historical Sociology*; *Mission Studies*; *Past and Present*; *Religion in Malawi*; *Theologia Evangelica*; *Svensk Missionstidskrift*; *Bulletin of the John Rylands Library*.

of a chapter on Christianity in a new history of nineteenth century Natal and two forthcoming books, one drawn from papers given at a 1992 conference at the University of the Western Cape, the other a new history of Christianity in South Africa edited by Richard Elphick and Rodney Davenport.[7]

Studies that had been built up by Andrew Walls and Harold Turner; 'African History in British Universities: Past, Present and Future', *African Affairs*, 92 (1993), pp. 239–253. Andrew Porter's inaugural lecture as Professor in King's College, London, began with a familiar lament at the neglect of religion by secular historians in this country; 'Religion and Empire: British Expansion in the Long Nineteenth Century, 1780–1914', *Journal of Imperial and Commonwealth History*, 20 (1993), pp. 370–390. Richard Elphick has complained in very similar terms; see 'South African Christianity and the Historian's Vision', *South African Historical Journal*, 26 (1992), pp. 182–190.

7   Norman Etherington, 'Christianity and African Society in Nineteenth Century Natal', in A. Duminy and B. Guest (eds), *Natal and Zululand from Earliest Times to 1910, A New History* (Pietermaritzburg, 1989). The 1992 papers are included in Robert Ross and Henry Bredekamp (eds), *Missions and Christianity in South African History*, Johannesburg, University of the Witwatersrand Press, 1995. The new history is *Christianity in South African History* (London, 1995).

Distribution of the items in my sample was very uneven. More than half the sample comprises materials focussed on South Africa. Most authors are linked to organised religion in some fashion, either through present or previous employment in churches or missions, or through links to academic departments of religious studies or theology. Males predominate as authors, reflecting their outsize representation among the clergy. African authors are more in evidence than they would have been in a sample of secular historians, because there are many more of them in the church than in university history departments. The aim of most studies is not to gain a better understanding of the past but to provide a better guide to Christian action either in daily life or in the work of evangelisation. Consequently, it is unusual to find articles based on extensive use of primary sources in missiological or theological journals.[8]

Amid all the publications of the last two decades there have been few full-blown histories of individual missions.[9] The most notable of these is John and Jean Comaroff's study of London Missionary Society work among the Tswana.[10] While disclaiming any intention to provide 'an event history' of the mission, the authors take an exemplary approach to their subject, one which gives as much attention to the evangelised as to the evangelisers, and which scrutinises the anthropological background of the European missionaries with the same intensity as the ethnography of the Tswana.[11] Another splendid attempt at a comprehensive mission history is the two-volume study of nineteenth century Norwegian missions in South Africa and Madagascar, produced under the general editorship of Jarle Simensen.[12] The study is consciously materialist and interdisciplinary but does not neglect the theological

---

8   The most important of these journals for Southern Africa is *Missionalia*. For a review of its first 25 years, see J. J. Kritinger, 'The Past 25 years of Missiology in South Africa, A Stock-taking Exercise', *Missionalia*, 22 (1994), pp. 147–162. The same issue contains a listing of 'Missiological Theses Accepted at South African Universities, 1968–1993', compiled by J. J. Kritzinger and P. F. Smit, pp. 163–76.

9   One reviewer of M. L. Pirouet's 1978 book on CMS missions in Uganda called her study an example of 'a nearly extinct genre'.

10   *Of Revelation and Revolution: Christianity, Colonialism and Consciousness in South Africa, Vol. 1* (Chicago, 1991); Vol. 2 is projected for some future time.

11   On a lesser scale, a notable attempt to integrate the story of a mission in its African context is the first part of Landeg White's *Magomero: Portrait of an African Village* (Cambridge, 1988) which retells the story of the first ill-fated effort of the Universities' Mission to Central Africa.

12   Jarle Simensen (ed), *Norwegian Missions in African History, Vol. 1: South Africa 1845–1906; Vol. 2, Madagascar* (Oslo and Oxford, 1986).

aspects of the Norwegian enterprise. Especially noteworthy is its careful delineation of the social origins of the missionaries. An important addendum to the story of Norwegian missions is the published thesis of T. Jorgensen, which argues convincingly that theological discourses were more important than European images of Africa in forming the mindset of nineteenth century evangelists.[13] Until recently, Swiss missions to Southern Africa were barely known to historians. They have emerged from obscurity through the work of Jan van Butselaar and Patrick Harries, who have drawn attention to their sophisticated cultural approach.[14]

It is not unusual for years to pass between the writing of a thesis on mission history and its appearance in book form. A good example is C. J. M. Zvobgo's work on Methodist missions in Zimbabwe which took nearly twenty years to find a publisher, despite its important chapters on church-state relations and conversion.[15] One way of circumventing the time-lag problem is to break a thesis into articles as Brendon Carmody has done with his study of a Jesuit mission in Zambia.[16] Endorsing the conclusions reached by earlier historians, he finds that secular inducements loomed larger than theological teaching in drawing Africans to mission stations.[17]

Others point out that the mission stations were simply one element in the total picture of African religious change, and a small one at that. Richard Gray has argued forcibly that, vital as stations were to the spread of literacy, from the very beginning black evangelists were far more important than white ones

---

13   Torstein Jorgensen, *Contact and Conflict, Norwegian Missionaries, the Zulu Kingdom and the Gospel, 1850–1873* (Oslo, 1990).

14   Jan van Butselaar, *Africains, Missionnaires et Colonialistes. Les Origines de l'Eliglise Presbyterienne du Mozambique (Mission Suisse) 1880–1896* (Leiden, 1984). Although Patrick Harries has not published work directly focussed on missions, he has pillaged the archives of Swiss missions for their information on other subjects. Especially interesting is his work on the thinking of Henri Junod.

15   C. J. M. Zvobgo, *The Wesleyan Methodist Missions in Zimbabwe 1891–1945* (Harare, 1991).

16   Since receiving his PhD from Berkeley Graduate Theological Union in 1986, Carmody has published a critical look at Jesuit tactics in 'Conversion and School at Chikuni, 1905–1939', *Africa*, 58 (1988), pp. 193–209, and a more sympathetic treatment of mission personnel in 'Secular and Sacred at Chikuni: 1905–1940', *Journal of Religion in Africa*, 21 (1991), pp. 130–148.

17   See, for example, N. A. Etherington, *Preachers, Peasants and Politics* (London, 1978), still in print, Boydell and Brewer.

in winning African souls and minds.[18] Despite widespread agreement on this point, only a handful of historical studies have focussed on African agency in religious change and most of these do not stray far from mission station bases.[19] The struggle for freedom from missionary control has been revisited as a factor inhibiting African evangelical initiatives and as a spur to religious schism.[20] On the positive side, Les Switzer has shown how African editors and journalists transformed mission presses into organs of political comment and protest.[21] And, in one of the most riveting accounts ever penned of a single African clergyman, Terence Ranger reveals the power of the international ecumenical movement to counter the local power of white-dominated mission clergy. Going as a delegate to the 1938 world mission conference at Tambaran, Madras, utterly transformed Thompson Samkange's life and work in the Southern Rhodesian Methodist Church.[22] Another notable contribution to the slender literature on African agency has been Deborah Gaitskell's study of the role of women's uniformed prayer organisations in fostering a 'distinctive and fervent female group solidarity which helped to sustain them in times of personal and community upheaval.'[23]

Not all recent work on African agency has been so uncritical. Shula Marks has drawn attention to the role played by African Christians (*kholwa*) in mobilising Zulu ethnic identity around the focal point of the Royal House, an enterprise which is the lineal ancestor of today's controversial Inkatha movement.[24] Picking up on Marks' observation that educated Africans could

---

18   Richard Gray, *Black Christians and White Missionaries* (New Haven and London, 1990), pp. 80–81.

19   See, for example, J. Millard, 'Grass-roots Pioneers of Transvaal Methodism', *Missionalia*, 17 (1989), pp. 188–198.

20   D. M. Balia, '"How Best to Save the Heathen"—Formation of the Unzondelelo Missionary Movement in Natal', *Missionalia*, 18 (1990), pp. 320–329; H. W. Langworthy, 'Charles Domingo, Seventh Day Baptists and Independency', *Journal of Religion in Africa*, 15 (1985), pp. 96–121.

21   L. Switzer, 'Reflections on the Mission Press in South Africa', *Journal of Theology for Southern Africa*, 43 (1983), pp. 4–14.

22   T. O. Ranger, 'Thompson Samkange: Tambaran and Beyond, *Journal of Religion in Africa*, 23 (1993), 318–346.

23   D. Gaitskell, 'Devout Domesticity? A Century of African Women's Christianity in South Africa' in Cheryl Walker (ed), *Women and Gender in South Africa to 1945* (Cape Town, 1990). See also the chapter on the 'Red Blouse Women' in Zvobgo, *Wesleyan Methodist Missions*.

24   See, for example, S. Marks, 'Patriotism, Patriarchy and Purity: Natal and the Politics of Zulu Ethnic Consciousness', in Leroy Vail (ed), *The Creation of Tribalism in Southern Africa* (London and Berkeley, 1989), pp. 215–240, and *The Ambiguities of Dependence*

in some circumstances become 'willing accomplices in their own subjection', John McCracken has portrayed in sometimes gory detail the chequered careers of three Malawian Christian collaborators.[25]

McCracken's caution against a tendency in nationalist writing to treat all African converts, clergy and Ethiopians with undue reverence has yet to make a discernible impact on studies of religious change in the Eastern Cape. This is one of a handful of mission fields on the entire African continent where a rich and concentrated mass of scholarship makes it possible to trace the spread of Christianity through creative African agency over the course of several centuries. Recent studies have demolished the assumption that religious change commenced with the arrival of European missionaries. The century and a half of colonial expansion which preceded the establishment of permanent missionary operations shifted the boundaries of the spiritual universe for Khoisan peoples through the subtle permeation of religious ideas held by settlers and the challenge posed to previous certainties by the experience of dispossession and forced labour. From this forcing house emerged dynamic ideas about cosmology and eschatology which ran ahead of the frontier of settlement and missionary evangelism.[26] Thus, as Janet Hodgson has shown, within a few years of the time when J. T. Van der Kemp's pioneering attempt to plant a mission station among the Xhosa ended in failure and retreat, home grown prophets filled the land with messages which reverberated sympathetically with Christian doctrine.[27] Later, when missions were re-established, it became difficult to draw a hard and fast boundary between purely Xhosa ideas

---

(Baltimore, 1986). Nicholas Cope extends this analysis in 'The Zulu Petit Bourgeoisie and Zulu Nationalism in the 1920s: Origins of Inkatha', *Journal of Southern African Studies*, 16 (1990), pp. 431–451.

25   J. McCracken, '"Marginal Men": the Colonial Experience in Malawi', *Journal of Southern African Studies*, 15 (1989), pp. 537–64.

26   In a ground-breaking analysis, Elizabeth Elbourne has called attention to ways in which, when European evangelists did arrive among the Khoisan, 'mission Christianity was used creatively by many individuals seeking positively to reconstruct a broken world, and ... the meaning and "ownership" of Christian texts were constantly under debate'; see 'Early Khoisan Uses of Mission Christianity', paper delivered to 1992 conference: People, Power and Culture: The History of Christianity in South Africa, 1792–1992, University of the Western Cape, 1992.

27   See, for example, Janet Hodgson, 'Ntsikana—A Precursor of Independency?', *Missionalia*, 12 (1984), pp. 19–33. This is but one of a number of important articles by Hodgson, many of whose key ideas are brought together in *The God of The Xhosa, A Study of the Origins and Development of the Traditional Concepts of the Supreme Being* (Cape Town, 1982).

and Christian ones. In contrast to previous scholarship, which had tended to portray the famous 'Cattle Killing' of 1857 as the final crisis of the old order, Jeff Peires argues that it drew both on Xhosa myths of creation and on an imported Christian idea of resurrection.[28]

In such colonial situations, imported Christianity and 'traditional culture' do not so much constitute separate 'worlds' as poles on a continuum between which individual Africans slid rather than jumped—a cause of continual frustration for nineteenth century European missionaries who drew sharp mental boundaries between believers and pagans. A series of studies has charted the personal dilemmas, misunderstandings, approaches and retreats of individual Xhosa during the long process of Christianisation.[29] Valuable as these are, they concentrate upon the nineteenth century and individuals closely associated with European churchmen.

The decisive struggles for and against religious change in the hinterland are more difficult to chronicle and therefore receive less attention. Paul Landau's study of politics and Christianity in the Ngwato Kingdom of Botswana during the early decades of the twentieth century provides a rare insight into the complicated ways in which the advent of a new religion interacted with social and

---

28 J. Peires, *The Dead Will Arise, Nongqawuse and the Great Xhosa Cattle-Killing Movement of 1856–7* (Johannesburg, Bloomington and London, 1989); 'The Central Beliefs of the Xhosa Cattle-Killing', *Journal of African History*, 28 (1987), pp. 43–63.

29 The missionaries' view of the process is canvassed in W. G. Mills, 'Missionaries, Xhosa Clergy and the Suppression of Traditional Customs' paper delivered to 1992 conference: People, Power and Culture: The History of Christianity in South Africa, 1792–1992, University of the Western Cape, 1992. Hildegarde Fast explores the intersection of cross-cultural understanding in a fascinating study of questions posed to missionaries by the people they aimed to convert: '"In at One Ear and Out at the Other": African Response to the Wesleyan Message in Xhosaland 1825–1835', *Journal of Religion in Africa*, 23 (1993), pp. 147–174. Case studies of individual Africans attempting to reconcile the demands of missionary teaching with their positions of leadership in Xhosa society are presented in: D. Williams, *The Journal and Selected Writings of the Rev. Tiyo Soga* (Cape Town, 1983); W. A. Saayman, 'Tiyo Soga and Nehemiah Tile, Black Pioneers in Mission and Church', *Missionalia*, 17 (1989), pp. 95–102; P. J. Jonas, 'Jan Tshatshu and the Eastern Cape Mission—A Contextual Analysis', *Missionalia*, 18 (1990), pp. 277–292; and Janet Hodgson, *Princess Emma* (Johannesburg, 1987). Hodgson extends her line of thought in 'Soga and Dukwana: The Christian Struggle for Liberation in Mid 19th Century South Africa', *Journal of Religion in Africa*, 16 (1986), pp. 187–208, the central argument of which is that after key individuals had shown that it was possible to be both a Christian and a patriot, the way was paved for large scale conversions, religious independency and nationalist resistance to segregation in the twentieth century.

political institutions beyond the penumbra of mission station influence.[30] He illustrates this by following the career of a single African Christian preacher in the LMS Ngwato Church, which became a state church after Khama III's conversion. After analysing Khama's use of religion to cement central authority, he shows how conflicts with Khama's son, Sekgoma, had more to do with the latter's bid for power than with Christianity per se.

The same tendency to gravitate toward nineteenth century pioneers that can be discerned in studies of African evangelists also afflicts the historical study of missionary thought and biography.[31] After a long period of neglect, attention has begun to be paid to the eighteenth century Moravians in the Western Cape.[32] Early agents of the London Missionary Society continue to exercise a fascination disproportionate to their numbers or evangelical achievements. By looking back to their European origins, recent work has considerably extended our understanding of their broader historical background. Andrew Ross has re-evaluated the ever-controversial John Philip in the context of the Scottish Enlightenment.[33] This, in turn, helps to explain why the free-thinking, hard-living Dutch officer and future missionary Johannes Van der Kemp travelled to Scotland for medical training when he grew tired of soldiering.[34] Counteracting

---

30   P. Landau, 'Preacher, Chief and Prophetess: *Moruti* Seakgano in the Ngwato Kingdom, East-central Botswana', *Journal of Southern African Studies*, 17 (1991), pp. 1–22. For a somewhat similar case of religious entanglement in a political context, see G. Campbell, 'Missionaries' Fanompoana and the Menalamba Revolt in late Nineteenth Century Madagascar', *Journal of Southern African Studies*, 15 (1988), pp. 54–73, which argues that the 1895–99 rising was not so much a revolt against Christianity as struggle to destroy the Merina state, which, following the adoption of Christianity as its religion, used the church as a source of impressed soldiers. Another view of the revolt is taken by Stephen Ellis in *The Rising of the Red Shawls. A Revolt in Madagascar 1895–1899* (Cambridge, 1985).

31   Johannes du Bruyn selectively reviews the development of these studies in 'Missionaries in South African Historical Writing', paper delivered to 1992 conference: People, Power and Culture: The History of Christianity in South Africa, 1792–1992, University of the Western Cape, 1992.

32   H. C. Bredekamp (ed), *The Genadendal Diaries: Diaries of the Herrnhut Missionaries* (Belville, 1992).

33   A. Ross, *John Philip (1775–1851): Missions, Race and Politics in South Africa* (Aberdeen, 1986). In the 1970s Philip acquired new enemies on the left, adding to his legion of settler critics. The new critique emphasised his allegiance to industrial capitalism. For a critical review written from this perspective, see Greg Cuthbertson, 'Van der Kemp and Philip: the Missionary Debate Revisited', *Missionalia*, 17 (1989), pp. 77–94.

34   A biography by the veteran mission educator, I. H. Enklaar, fills in many blanks in the first five decades of this enigmatic missionary's life: *Life and Work of Dr J. Th. Van der Kemp, 1741–1811* (Cape Town and Rotterdam, 1988). See also, Elizabeth Elbourne, 'Concerning Missionaries: the Case of Van der Kemp', *Journal of Southern African Studies*, 17 (1991),

a long-standing tendency to treat the LMS missionaries as agents of European capitalism,[35] Richard Grove reminds us of the millennial thinking of Robert Moffat whose gloomy appraisal of Europe was paralleled by his view of South Africa as a degraded Eden.[36]

Nineteenth century pioneers in Natal and Zululand have also been subjects of ongoing study. While Olav Myklebust's massive book on Norwegian bishop Hans Schreuder is an atavistic example of the hagiographic tradition in missionary biography, it is nonetheless welcome for spotlighting a formidable personality whose involvement with the Zulu monarchy and the government of Natal was previously ignored or underrated.[37] In quite a different vein, the hundredth anniversary of the death of Anglican Bishop J. W. Colenso was commemorated by the publication of Jeff Guy's *The Heretic*, which traces Colenso's progress from mid-Victorian missionary imperialist and scholar to beleaguered defender of Zulu independence.[38] Still awaiting a modern biographer is Colenso's intellectually adventurous colleague, Dr Henry Callaway, whose works on Zulu religion and mythology were highly valued in late-Victorian Britain and whose sympathetic appreciation of African medicine parallels that of his contemporary David Livingstone.[39] While Livingstone continues to occupy a class of his own as a object of study and veneration,

---

pp. 153–164. On Van der Kemp's abandoned mission to the Xhosa, see Janet Hodgson, 'Do We Hear You Nyengana? Dr J. T. Vanderkemp and the First Mission to the Xhosa', *Religion in Southern Africa*, 5 (1984), pp. 3–47.

35   J. and J. Comaroff, 'Through the Looking-Glass: Colonial Encounters of the First Kind', *Journal of Historical Sociology*, 1 (1988), pp. 6–31; and 'Missionaries and Mechanical Clocks: An Essay on Religion and History in South Africa', *Journal of Religion*, 71 (1991), 1–17. Julian Cobbing takes the attack to an unprecedented level in 'The Mfecane as Alibi: Thoughts on Dithakong and Mbolompo', *Journal of African History*, 29 (1988), pp. 487–519, which accuses the LMS mission of covering up their own complicity in the capture and 'sale' of African labour.

36   R. Grove, 'Scottish Missionaries, Evangelical Discourse and the Origins of Conservation Thinking in Southern Africa', *Journal of Southern African Studies*, 15 (1989), pp. 163–187.

37   D. Myklebust, *H. P. S. Schreuder, Kirke og Misjon* (Oslo, 1980). See also 'The Legacy of H. P. S. Schreuder, *International Bulletin of Missionary Research*, 8 (1984), pp. 70–74 and Myklebust's account of his fifty years of research on the bishop, 'Sluttstrek for et Biografisk Engasjement', *Norsk Tidsskrift for Misjon*, 44 (1990), pp. 234–240.

38   J. Guy, *The Heretic, A Study of the Life of John William Colenso 1814–1883* (Braamfontein and Pietermaritzburg, 1983).

39   Callaway and Livingstone are favorably contrasted with later, more arrogant missionary doctors, in N. Etherington, 'Missionary Doctors and African Healers in Mid-Victorian South Africa', *South African Historical Journal*, 19 (1987), pp. 77–92.

the Scots missionaries who followed his footsteps into Central Africa have not fared so well.[40] Appreciation of their successful stand against Cecil Rhodes' bid to swallow Nyasaland is balanced by distaste for their methods of education and discipline.[41]

Fascination with nineteenth century clerical pioneers has not as yet extended to the women who accompanied them. After forty years Wyn Rees' publication of letters from Bishop Colenso's wife Sarah Frances still stands alone in the field.[42] My survey turned up only three recent articles featuring missionary women, one of which is a throwback to Victorian devotional literature about 'good deaths', in this case a wife who succumbed to breast cancer.[43] Dana Robert provides a sample of what can be found by those who go seeking, in a fascinating article on American women recruited from Mount Holyoke College to serve as teachers in Dutch Reformed Church schools.[44] Founded specifically to serve the cause of missions, Mount Holyoke was well-known as 'a "rib factory" where theological students with missionary appointments could count on finding a wife.' Several women from the same school went to Natal as teachers and wives of American Board missionaries. Lack of interest rather than a lack of documents accounts for their neglect by historians.[45]

---

40 The latest biographical study is T. Holmes, *Journey to Livingstone: Exploration of an Imperial Myth* (Edinburgh, 1993). Andrew Walls explores some of the reasons for Livingstone's eminence in 'The Legacy of David Livingstone', *International Bulletin of Missionary Research*, 11 (1987), pp. 125–129.

41 K. R. Ross cites the mission's opposition to Rhodes as a evidence that it was truly engaged in what Lamin Sanneh has called 'cultural translation' of Christianity, in 'Vernacular Translation in Christian Mission: The Case of David Clement Scott and the Blantyre Mission, 1888–1898', *Missionalia*, 21 (1993), pp. 5–18. On the other side of ledger, Peter Hinchliff reviews the way a scandal over corporal punishment and execution of criminals led to an acceptance that colonial rule must displace the Victorian ideal of self-governing missions, in 'The Blantyre Scandal, Scottish Missionaries and Colonialism', *Journal of Theology for Southern Africa*, 46 (1984), pp. 29–36.

42 W. Rees, *Colenso Letters from Natal* (Pietermaritzburg, 1958).

43 J. Millard, 'Anne Hodgson—Missionary and Mystic', *Theologia Evangelica*, 26 (1993), pp. 55–63.

44 D. Robert, 'Mount Holyoke Women and the Dutch Reformed Missionary Movement, 1874–1904', *Missionalia*, 21 (1993), pp. 103–123.

45 As I found when reviewing my own research notes for my paper on gender issues in Natal missions presented to the 1992 conference, People, Power and Culture: The History of Christianity in South Africa, 1792–1992, at the University of the Western Cape. Due to my own oversight, only a sliver of material I collected found its way into *Preachers, Peasants and Politics in Southeast Africa.*

Studies of twentieth century missionaries are very thin on the ground.[46] Joseph Booth remains a figure of continuing fascination because of his influence on African independency in general and John Chilembwe in particular.[47] Other eccentric individuals who carved out careers as white prophets, unsupported by foreign missionary societies, deserve more attention, as Gerald Pillay has shown with his work on John Alexander Rowlands, an Englishman of Quaker background who founded a Pentecostal congregation among Natal Indians.[48] Greg Cuthbertson has helped to fill a gap at the turn of the century with articles about the impact of the Boer war on missionaries and their congregations.[49] Paul Rich, by tracing the impact of imported educational ideas on particular missionaries, has shown how scaled-down expectations and a world-wide vogue for racial segregation afflicted some South African missions.[50] Others have begun to tackle the complex relationship between missionaries and twentieth century anthropology. In many places missionaries were the first ethnographers and linguists. By fixing standard dialects and languages they helped create the 'tribes' who became the subjects of field work by later anthropologists.[51] Missionaries published in anthropological journals

---

46 This is not just true of writing on southern Africa. See T. Christensen and W. R. Hutchinson (eds), *Missionary Ideologies in the Imperialist Era: 1880–1920* (Copenhagen, 1982), which includes some general overviews, regional surveys and chapters specifically on South Africa by N. Bloch-Hoell and N. Etherington.

47 H. W. Langworthy, 'Joseph Booth, Prophet of Radical Change in Central and South Africa, 1891–1915', *Journal of Religion in Africa*, 16 (1986), pp. 22–43. The original account of Chilembwe's Providence Industrial Mission and the 1915 rising by George Shepperson and Thomas Price, *Independent African* now in its fifth edition, has established itself as one of the few enduring classics of African religious history (Edinburgh, 5th edn, 1987).

48 G. Pillay, 'Bethesda Temple among Indian South Africans', *Journal of Religion in Africa*, 21 (1991), pp. 256–279.

49 G. Cuthbertson, 'Missionary Imperialism and Colonial Warfare: London Missionary Society Attitudes to the South African War, 1899–1902', *South African Historical Journal*, 19 (1987), 93–113; '"Cave of Adullam": Missionary Reaction to Ethiopianism at Lovedale, 1898–1902', *Missionalia*, 19 (1991), pp. 57–64. Also on the Boer War, but with an emphasis on Britain, is H. H. Hewison, *Hedge of Wild Almonds: South Africa, The 'Pro-Boers', and the Quaker Conscience* (Portsmouth, NH, 1989).

50 P. Rich, 'The Appeal of Tuskegee: James Henderson, Lovedale, and the Fortunes of South African Liberalism, 1906–1930', *International Journal of African Historical Studies*, 20 (1987), pp. 271–292; 'Bernard Huss and the Experiment in African Cooperatives in South Africa, 1926–1948', *International Journal of African Historical Studies*, 26 (1993), pp. 297–317.

51 Terence Ranger, 'Missionaries, Migrants and the Manyika: the Invention of Ethnicity in Zimbabwe', in Vail (ed.), *Creation of Tribalism*, pp. 118–150. Herbert Chimhundu builds on Ranger's work by providing further examples: 'Early Missionaries and the Ethnolinguistic Factor During the "Invention of Tribalism" in Zimbabwe', *Journal of African History*, 33 (1992), pp. 87–109.

and some were drawn into the developing anthropological profession.[52] In missionary hands anthropology could be turned to a variety of ends. To some it could suggest new approaches to the work of conversion, to others, ways of adapting the gospel to 'African tradition'.[53] In the wrong hands, culture could be a surrogate for race. Brian Du Toit has shown how the nineteenth century idea of self-governing, self-supporting congregations could be married to anthropological concepts of integral cultures; so that, when sons of missionaries in the Dutch Reformed Church became anthropologists and Broederbond members, they were able to suggest missiological and scientific justifications for apartheid.[54]

How is the paucity of studies of twentieth century European missionaries to be explained? One possible explanation is the ebbing of the missionary impulse since its high point at about the turn of the century. Andrew Porter has calculated that the British societies alone had by 1899:

> approximately 10,000 missionaries in the field, thus equalling in numbers some of the middling-sized professions—accountants and architects, for instance.... at that time there were half as many missionaries as there were ordained Anglican clergy, and three times as many as there were Roman Catholic priests. British missionary societies spent annually some £2 million, equivalent to almost two per cent of central government's gross yearly outlay, or as much as the entire annual cost of civil service salaries.[55]

A century later, the corps has shrunk to such an extent that Andrew Walls advises anyone meeting a missionary to assume, in the absence of other information, that the person is an American—and there are not so many of them as there used to be.[56] The study of atrophy and decline is a minority taste in the historical profession.

---

52   P. G. Forster, *T. Cullen Young: Missionary and Anthropologist* (Hull, 1989). See also Patrick Harries' work on Henri Junod discussed above.

53   P. G. Forster, 'Missionaries and Anthropology: the Case of the Scots of Northern Malawi', *Journal of Religion in Africa*, 16 (1986), pp. 101–120.

54   B. M. Du Toit, 'Missionaries, Anthropologists, and the Policies of the Dutch Reformed Church', *Journal of Modern African Studies*, 22 (1984), pp. 617–632.

55   Porter, 'Religion and Empire', p. 372.

56   A. Walls, 'The Old Age of the Missionary Movement', *International Review of Mission*, 76 (1987), pp. 26–32.

Another possible explanation is the unpopularity of missions among influential churchmen, who are quick to damn anything which might associate contemporary Christianity with the imperial past. They seem unaware that secular historians have reached a virtual consensus on the question of Christianity and colonialism. Phrased in different ways by different authors, it is that the missionaries, who aimed to replace African cultures with European 'civilisation' and who frequently allied themselves with colonial governments, nevertheless transmitted a religion which Africans turned to suit their own purposes: spiritual, economic and political. Thus Richard Gray argues that while 'there is much truth in ... [the] critical analysis of the White missionaries' role in colonial Africa' it overlooks 'the complexities of the missionaries' relationships with colonialism.' The 'argument that Christianity in sub-Saharan Africa has been merely part of the ideological superstructure of Western capitalism ignores the fundamental contributions of African Christians and of African cosmologies'.[57]

In a similar vein, Jean Comaroff writes that 'the nonconformist mission in southern Africa helped sow the state of colonialism on which the colonial state was founded' while at the same time providing 'a language for contesting the new modes of domination it had itself helped create'.[58] As Clifton Crais puts it:

> A colonialist institution *par excellence*, the mission station communicated many of the essential ingredients of British rule and the capitalist world economy. Over the course of the nineteenth century evangelical Christianity became a crucible within which a new and syncretic South African culture emerged. This integration of cultural symbols and knowledge could be both hegemonic and potentially revolutionary: religious belief could legitimate the inequalities of the present as well as provide a radical critique and understanding of the alienation which accompanied conquest and dispossession....[59]

This was most likely the reason that 'almost without exception, ... colonial white settler societies were hostile to missionary ambitions and to the consequences of non-European conversions'.[60]

---

57 Gray, *Black Christians and White Missionaries*, pp. 60–61.

58 Jean Comaroff, 'Missionaries and Mechanical Clocks', p. 7.

59 Clifton C. Crais, *White Supremacy and Black Resistance in Pre-Industrial South Africa, the Making of the Colonial Order in the Eastern Cape, 1770–1865* (Cambridge, 1992), p. 104.

60 Porter, 'Religion and Empire', p. 381.

RECENT TRENDS IN THE HISTORIOGRAPHY OF CHRISTIANITY

These days, most hostility to missions comes from within the clergy and departments of religious studies. 'The church in South Africa', writes Charles Villa-Vicencio, 'has since its earliest missionary days shared in the subjugation of the masses.... The mission activity of the English-speaking churches ... destroyed the social structure of African society and ... the church found itself located firmly on the side of ... white supremacy and capitalist exploitation'.[61] Willem Saayman, of the Department of Missiology at the University of South Africa, asks the church, as it contemplates the end of apartheid, to reflect sadly and prayerfully on the unfortunate complicity of Christian missions in colonialism, land alienation and capitalism.[62] Michael Drohan reiterates that in the age of imperialism, Christianity stood for repression of progressive impulses at home and the crushing of cultures abroad.[63] It is important to emphasise that these self-flagellating conclusions do not usually arise from original research. Secondary works by secular historians are mined for negative content, while positive evaluations are ignored.

To understand why the writers who are most closely connected to the study or practice of religion are often the most vitriolic critics of missions, it is necessary to know something of the complex development of contemporary religious thought in Southern Africa and other traditional mission fields. Political dissent within the churches was greatly influenced by the importation of 'Black Theology' from the United States in 1971 through the agency of the University Christian movement.[64] In America, Black Theology was closely associated with the African-American, James H. Cone, who drew together the experience of 'Black Power' politics in the late 1960s and the oppositional

---

61   C. Villa-Vicencio, *Civil Disobedience and Beyond: Law, Resistance and Religion in South Africa* (Cape Town, 1990), p. 131. See also the same author's *Trapped in Apartheid, A Socio-Theological History of the English-Speaking Churches* (Maryknoll, NY and Cape Town, 1988).

62   W. Saayman, 'Christian Mission in South Africa: a Historical Reflection', *International Review of Mission*, 83 (1994), pp. 11–20. See also his *Christian Mission in South Africa: Political and Ecumenical* (Pretoria, 1991) and 'Christian missions in South Africa: Achievements, Failures and the Future', in Martin Prozesky (ed.), *Christianity Amidst Apartheid: Selected Perspectives on the Church in South Africa* (London, 1990), pp. 28–36.

63   M. Drohan, 'Christianity, Culture and the Meaning of Mission', *International Review of Mission*, 75 (1986), pp. 285–303.

64   M. Mothlabi, 'The Historical Origins of Black Theology', in J. Mosala and Buti Thagale (eds), *The Unquestionable Right to be Free; Black Theology from South Africa* (Maryknoll, NY, 1986), p. 44.

theology developed in Nazi Germany by Barth and Bonhoeffer.[65] This combination was hugely attractive to dissenters in South Africa, where the ANC had reluctantly taken up the armed struggle and where the state-sponsored racism of a repressive regime apparently paralleled the German experience of the 1930s so clearly. If one accepts God's direct responsibility for the incarnation of Jesus as an oppressed Jew, then imitation of Christ means identification with His struggle on behalf of all oppressed people everywhere.

A complication for South African churchmen was that Cone's writings strongly suggest that, although not impossible, it is more difficult for a white man to espouse Black Theology than for a camel to pass through the eye of a needle.[66] As a result, the formal Black Theology movement in South Africa—and the journal which bears that title—have remained black in personnel as well as name.[67] On the other hand, as Cone himself discovered, Black Theology reverberates sympathetically with what radical Latin American radical churchmen know as 'Liberation Theology'. Although associated closely with Catholic clergy and linked to Marxism, the intellectual roots of the movement run back to the same German Lutheran sources that Cone drew upon in his initial formulation of black theology.[68] White radical theologians could thus stake out positions broadly in sympathy with Liberation Theology and Black Theology without having to be either Catholic or black.[69]

The common denominator was resistance to apartheid and the churches who had condoned it through complicity or silence. To attack nineteenth and early-twentieth century missions for their active or tacit complicity in

---

65 James Cone's *A Black Theology of Liberation*, first published in 1970, has gone through many editions. Important revisions were made in the 1986 edition, and the most recent includes critical reflections by Cone and a number of other theologians: *A Black Theology of Liberation, Twentieth Anniversary Edition* (Maryknoll, NY, 1990).

66 Ibid., p. 85: 'Jesus is not a human being for all persons; he is a human being for oppressed persons, whose identity is made known in and through their liberation.'

67 Since its foundation in 1970, Basil Moore is the only white theologian to have published in *The Journal of Black Theology in Southern Africa*, founded in 1970. Comparisons and contrasts between the American and South African experience are explored in D. Hopkins, *Black Theology, USA and South Africa: Politics, Culture and Liberation* (Maryknoll, NY, 1989).

68 As Paul Gifford notes in *The Religious Right in Southern Africa* (Harare, 1988), p. 97.

69 Although the linkages have been close, there has not always been perfect harmony between exponents of black theology and white liberationist theologians. For some of the complications, see: David Bosch, 'Currents and Crosscurrents in South African Black Theology', in G. Wilmore and J. Cone (eds), *Black Theology: A Documentary History, 1966–79* (Maryknoll, NY. 1979), pp. 220–337; and John De Gruchy, 'The South African Theological Debate', in C. Villa-Vicencio and J. W. De Gruchy (eds), *Resistance and Hope, South African Essays in Honour of Beyers Naudé* (Cape Town and Grand Rapids, 1985), pp. 85–97.

colonialism was, by implication, to attack present-day clergy who stood aloof from the political struggle.[70] By the same token, courageous missionaries who took a stand against the state and white settlers could be admired as historic exemplars. This helps to explain why the subjects of all the recent biographical studies of individual missionaries have been oppositional figures like John Philip and Bishop Colenso, whose appeal is not limited to academic historians.[71] The Marxist element in Latin American Liberation Theology attuned its South African sympathisers to the importance of the neo-Marxist historical scholarship that flowered in the 1970s and 1980s. The works of such writers as Charles Van Onselen, Colin Bundy, Peter Delius, Phil Bonner, Shula Marks and William Beinart are frequently cited in the writing emerging from strongholds of theological dissent, especially the University of Cape Town Department of Religious Studies.

In the religious history of neighbouring states which shared the experience of settler colonialism, similar tendencies can be noted, although the body of writing is much smaller. The failings of mainstream Christianity have been chronicled.[72] Individual churchmen have been praised for their courage or criticised for collaboration.[73] How far the wheel has turned in the course of this century is dramatically illustrated by Kenneth Ross's article on the Church of Scotland in Malawi which proudly claims that 84 baptised members of the Blantyre Mission joined John Chilembwe's 1915 revolt.[74] At the time of the rising,

---

70 For an exceptionally clear statement of this position, see J. R. Cochrane, *Servants of Power, The Role of English-speaking Churches in South Africa. 1903–1930; Towards a Critical Theology via an Historical Analysis of the Anglican and Methodist Churches* (Johannesburg, 1987).

71 As an example of how easily parallels can be drawn, see D. Whitelaw, 'A Crisis of Credibility; Contemporary Dialogue with Colenso and du Plessis', *Journal of Theology for Southern Africa*, 60 (1987), pp. 12–27.

72 A. Hastings, 'Church and State in Southern Africa', *African Affairs*, 91 (1992), pp. 134–137; J. C. Weiler and J. Linden (eds), *Mainstream Christianity to 1980 in Malawi, Zambia and Zimbabwe* (Gweru, 1984); C. F. Hallencreutz and A. M. Moyo (eds), *Church and State in Zimbabwe* (Gweru, 1988). P. Katjavivi, P. Frostin and K. Kaired (eds), *Church and Liberation in Namibia* (London and Winchester, MA, 1989).

73 In Michael Lapsley's, *Neutrality or Co-option? Anglican Church and State from 1964 until the Independence of Zimbabwe* (Gweru, 1986), Arthur Lewis is the anti-communist villain and Kenneth Skelton is the hero. Skelton has written his own account in *Bishop in Smith's Rhodesia* (Gweru, 1985). In '"On the Side of the Robbed": R. J. B. Moore, Missionary on the Copperbelt, 1933–1941', *Journal of Religion in Africa*, 19 (1989), pp. 44–63, Sean Morrow retails the stormy history of an English Anglican who supported striking African workers.

74 K. Ross, 'Vernacular Translation', p. 18. New light is shed on the consequences of Chilembwe's rising for neighbouring territories in E. Yorke, 'The Spectre of a Second Chilembwe: Government, Missions, and Social Control in Wartime Northern Rhodesia, 1914–18', *Journal of African History*, 31 (1990), pp. 373–391.

missionaries did everything possible to distance themselves from that event and its grisly aftermath.

The advent of black and liberationist theology did not, of course, instigate religious resistance to state-sponsored racism in South Africa. It merely buttressed the intellectual foundations of an ongoing struggle which had involved many prominent representatives of the foreign-based mission churches. As the apartheid state began to slide slowly towards the abyss, an avalanche of Christian literature appeared, chronicling and assessing the role played by the churches at this historic juncture. Peter Walshe provides an invaluable guide to this literature in an article contending that religious resistance did make a crucial difference in speeding the transition to majority rule.[75] Already it is possible to discern the outlines of a Christian narrative of the downfall of apartheid which shadows the explanations devised by lay historians.[76] In the Christian interpretation the drama begins, not with the development of a segregated political economy, but with a theology of separateness nurtured within the bosom of the Dutch Reformed Church. The tragedy of Sharpeville provokes the Cottesloe Statement of the South African Council of Churches in December 1960. While Christian Africans turn to Black Consciousness, white Christian dissidents such as Beyers Naudé are persecuted with banning orders. Following the precedent of the German Lutheran Barmen Declaration of 1934, the oppositional clergy first declare apartheid to be a sin and then, in the Kairos Document of 1985, to be absolute evil.[77] The work of the World Council of Churches eventually brings the imposition of economic sanctions which bring the regime to its feet and change the hearts and minds of crucial Nationalist politicians such as F. W. de Klerk. After the fall of apartheid, the churches are called to play a critical role in the process of reconstruction and restitution.[78]

Alongside the struggle against apartheid, other movements developed within the church—movements whose significance may loom larger now that the last formally racist government in the world has perished. One of these

---

75 'South Africa: Prophetic Christianity and the Liberation Movement', *Journal of Modern African Studies*, 29 (1991), pp. 27–60.

76 The seeds of such an interpretation are present as early as 1985 in Villa-Vicencio and De Gruchy (eds), *Resistance and Hope*.

77 See J. W. De Gruchy and C. Villa-Vicencio, *Apartheid is a Sin* (Grand Rapids, 1983) and The Kairos Theologians, *The Kairos Document, A Theological Comment on the Political Crisis in South Africa* (Bramfontein, 2nd edn, 1986).

78 So, at least, hope J. R. Cochrane and G. O. West, 'War, Remembrance and Reconstruction', *Journal of Theology for Southern Africa*, 84 (1993), pp. 25–40, and C. Villa-Vicencio in *A Theology of Reconstruction: Nation-Building and Human Rights* (Cambridge University Press, 1992).

is the acculturation of Christianity to African modes of life and thought. As a missionary strategy, its roots run deep. Some would trace them all the way to Henry Venn, Secretary of the Church Missionary Society in England from 1841 to 1872 and his contemporary, Rufus Anderson of the American Board of Commissioners for Foreign Missions. Both exhorted their agents to work quickly to establish self-supporting, self-governing, self-propagating churches which should be African rather than English or American in character. The latest study of Venn traces his ideas from early popularity to eventual defeat by the spread of colonial government and the popularity of Livingstone's rival emphasis on European 'civilisation' as an essential accompaniment of Christianisation.[79]

By the 1930s, the idea had revived under the influence of contemporary anthropology, indirect rule and the ecumenical thrust of the international Protestant missionary movement.[80] Not long after the publication of Edwin W. Smith's landmark anthology, *African Ideas of God*, in 1950,[81] the trend toward indigenisation of Christianity became conceptually linked to independence from colonial rule. Throughout the continent scholars and theologians were arguing that knowledge of a High God and many other elements of Christianity had existed in African religious thinking before the arrival of European missionaries.[82] Such arguments brought the very concepts of 'mission' and 'pagan' into question, and ran parallel to nationalists' claims that African states had achieved great things in their precolonial past.[83] In the early 1960s West African clergy were calling for a *'théologie de couleur africaine'*, by which they understood a distinctively African theology which was nonetheless thoroughly Christian.[84]

---

79   P. C. Williams, *The Ideal of the Self-Governing Church: A Study in Victorian Missionary Strategy* (Leiden, 1990).

80   A fascinating account of the transition within a single mission is given by S. S. Ncozana, 'Livingstonia Attitude to Spirit Possession', *Religion in Malawi*, 3 (1991), pp. 43–51.

81   E. W. Smith, *African Ideas of God* (London, 1950). Smith went out of his way to look for acculturating tendency in his biographical study of an American missionary in Natal, *The Life and Times of Daniel Lindley* (New York, 1952). Varieties of indigenisation are discussed in S. Kaplan, 'The Africanization of Missionary Christianity: History and Typology', *Journal of Religion in Africa* 16 (1986), pp. 166–185.

82   Some of this literature is discussed in Etherington, 'Missionaries and the Intellectual History of Africa', pp. 119–123.

83   This led eventually to a call from some African clergy for a moratorium on foreign missions. As E. M. Uka explains in *Missionaries Go Home? A Sociological Interpretation of an African Response to Christian Missions* (Berne, 1989), the broad purpose was not to 'be the end of mission', but to proclaim that 'we shall be the missionaries now.'

84   Gray, *Black Christians and White Missionaries*, p. 72.

African Theology has developed quite apart from Black Theology, and should not under any circumstances be confused with it. During the 1970s, relations between the two movements were strained in South Africa. Adherents of Black Theology complained that the spokesmen of African Theology were politically uninvolved. African Theology treated Black Theology as one more esoteric import from overseas, far removed with African spirituality.[85] Although a truce in the war of words was declared in 1977,[86] differences remained, especially in relation to traditional religion and independent churches.[87] While Black Theology continued to criticise independent churches for their political quietism, African Theology embraced both as part of a broad spectrum of religious truth.

Works produced in Southern Africa have been highly influential in the endless debate about where to draw the line between what is Christian and what is not. As Bengt Sundkler dramatically illustrated by his shift of position from the 1948 to the 1961 edition of his *Bantu Prophets in South Africa*, the line is always on the move—generally away from nineteenth century European conceptions. The issue is fundamental to the historical study of missions. If African prophets such as Isaiah Shembe are counted as Christian, they deserve to be treated as missionaries in their own right whose followers swell the ranks of the faithful. If not, they are at best 'syncretic' and at worst 'heathen'.[88] The contemporary

---

85   See M. Schoffeleers, 'Black and African Theology in Southern Africa: A Controversy Re-examined', *Journal of Religion in Africa* 18 (1988), pp. 99–124, and Takatso Mofokeng, 'Black Theology in South Africa: Achievements, Problems and Prospects', in M. Prozesky (ed), *Christianity Amidst Apartheid: Selected Perspectives on the Church in South Africa* (London, 1990), p. 48.

86   Desmond Tutu, for example, was willing to acknowledge that the African 'was far closer to the Biblical thought patterns than Western man could ever hope to be' (quoted in Schoffeleers, 'Black and African Theology', p. 106).

87   Writing from within an independent church, Sipho Tshelane has complained recently that 'the rise of black theology in South Africa did not extend its praxis to the AICs, although black theologians frequently made positive statements about them': 'The Witness of the African Indigenous Churches in South Africa', *International Review of Mission*, 83 (1994), p. 173.

88   The issue of Shembe's Christianity was revived by the publication of A. Vilikazi, B. Methetwa and M. Mpanza, *Shembe, The Revitalization of African Society* (Johannesburg, 1986). Based on a university thesis submitted by Vilikazi in 1951, it attacks G. C. Oosthuizen for contending that Shembe set himself up in place of Christ—implying at the same time that Oosthuizen was influenced by the 'ethnos' doctrines associated with early apartheid ideology. The issue cannot be decided because Oosthuizen, like Sundkler, has altered his opinions. Although in recent years he has taken a more sympathetic view of Shembe, Oosthuizen still works at drawing fine lines between Christianity and syncretism. See, for example, *The Healer-Prophet in Afro-Christian Churches* (Leiden, 1992). Jack Thompson reviews the controversy in 'Shembe Mismanaged?: A Study of Varying Interpretations of

RECENT TRENDS IN THE HISTORIOGRAPHY OF CHRISTIANITY 59

tendency among those who collect statistics on church membership has been to give most members of independent churches the benefit of the doubt as to their Christianity.[89] A 1990 estimate put the number of independent church members in South Africa at about eight million, distributed among some 4000 denominations.[90]

Nudging the independent churches into closer communion with World Christianity is a modern form of missionary activity that is often overlooked in secular histories. Those most closely involved are generally regarded as scholars rather than missionaries, yet the impulse behind their scholarship ultimately derives from an evangelical purpose.[91] A prime example is M. L. Daneel, son of Dutch Reformed missionaries and author of the multi-volume studies, *Old and New in Southern Shona Independent Churches*.[92] Since 1972 the *Fambidzano* movement, which he helped to found, has worked to promote ecclesiastical unity among the Shona independent churches.[93] Whereas at one time the main aim of missiological scholarship on independency was to prevent 'backsliding' towards traditional religion, nowadays it is more often the promotion of Christian unity through mutual understanding.[94]

---

the *Ibandla amaNazaretha*, *Bulletin of the John Rylands University Library of Manchester*, 70 (1988), pp. 185–196.

89   The lead in the work of quantification has been taken by David Barrett, beginning with *Schism and Renewal in Africa: an Analysis of Six Thousand Contemporary Religious Movements* (Nairobi and London, 1968). For more than a decade his 'Annual Statistical Table on Global Mission' has been published in the *International Bulletin of Missionary Research*. An even wider net has been cast by Harold Turner's 'Study Centre for New Religious Movements in Primal Societies' at Selly Oak Colleges in Birmingham, which keeps a world-wide watch on NERMs (New Religious Movements); see Turner's 'Bibliography on NERMs', *Missiology: An International Journal*, 13 (1985), pp. 103–110.

90   G. C. Oosthuizen, 'Research Unit for the Study of New Religious Movements and Independent Churches (NERMIC)', *Journal of Religion in Africa*, 20 (1990), p. 276. See also, J. K. Coetzee. G. C. Oosthuizen, J. W. De Gruchy, J. H. Hofmeyr and B. C. Lategan, *Religion, Intergroup Relations, and Social Change in South Africa; Report of Human Sciences Research Council, Work Committee on Religion* (Westport, CT, 1988).

91   For a wider survey of this activity, see D. Shank, 'Mission Relations with the Independent Churches in Africa', *Missiology: An International Review*, 13 (1985), pp. 25–44.

92   The latest of these is M. Daneel, *Vol. III, Leadership and Fission Dynamics* (Gweru, 1988).

93   M. Daneel, *Fambidzano, Ecumenical Movement of Zimbabwean Independent Churches* (Gweru, 1989).

94   Sundkler looks back on sixty years of his own work in 'Mina Sextio Ar i Kyrkohistoria', *Svensk Missionstidskrift*, 75 (1987), pp. 73–81. For another example of purposeful missiological scholarship, see H. L. Pretorius, 'Historical Trends in Transkeian Zionism', *Missionalia*, 12 (1984), pp. 7–12 and 'The New Jerusalem: Eschatological Perspectives in African Indigenous Churches', *Missionalia*, 15 (1987), pp. 31–41.

Of course, independent religious movements are not solely studied by churchmen. Their problematic relationship to politics is a perennial topic of interest for secular academics. Colonial governments generally regarded religious innovation with suspicion, reading messages of subversion in the Xhosa 'cattle-killing' of the 1850s, Ethiopianism in early twentieth century Natal, and Watchtower movements in Central Africa. Scholars are tempted to do likewise. The publication of Jeff Peires' *The Dead Shall Arise* in 1989 sparked a renewed controversy over the meaning of the millennial movement in Xhosaland. Peires himself was guarded in his conclusions, pointing out that while colonial oppression was everywhere in Southern Africa, millenarian movements were not. Clifton Crais, mesmerised by potent symbolism, concludes that 'the Cattle-Killing' was 'very much a popular uprising' which 'rejected the colonial order in the symbolic recreation of community'.[95] Timothy Stapleton agrees that it was a movement of resistance but insists that oppressive chiefs were the target.[96] Ethiopianism as political protest and harbinger of nationalism has also remained a popular subject for research.[97]

---

95   C. Crais, *White Supremacy and Black Resistance*, p. 210. In a review of Peires' book, Crais calls for a more post-modern appreciation of the power of signs: 'Peires and the Past', *South African Historical Journal*, 25 (1991), pp. 236–240; other reviews appear in the same number. Another author emphasising the power of symbolism is Jean Comaroff in *Body of Power, Spirit of Resistance* (Chicago, 1985). See also S. Thorpe, 'Religious Response to Stress: The Xhosa Cattle Killing and the Indian Ghost Dance', *Missionalia*, 12 (1984), pp. 129–137, which strangely ignores previous authors such as Lanternari who have likewise drawn a parallel between those movements.

96   T. Stapleton, '"They No Longer Care for their Chiefs": Another Look at the Xhosa Cattle-Killing of 1856–1857', and 'Reluctant Slaughter: Rethinking Maqoma's Role in the Xhosa Cattle-Killing (1853–1857)', *International Journal of African Historical Studies*, 24 (1991), pp. 383–392 and 26 (1993), pp. 345–369. For a related critique, see Jack Lewis, 'Materialism and Idealism in the Historiography of the Xhosa Cattle-Killing Movement 1856–7', *South African Historical Journal*, 25 (1991), pp. 244–268.

97   Les Switzer argues that Ethiopianism led directly to African nationalism in the Ciskei in *Power and Resistance in an African Society, The Ciskei Xhosa and the Making of South Africa* (Madison, 1993), especially pp. 79–192. See also B. Tembe, *Integrationismus und Afrikanismus. Zur Rolle der kirchlichen Unabhängigkeitsbewegung in der Auseinandersetzung um die Landfrage und die Bildung der Afrikaner in Südafrika, 1880–1960* (Frankfurt, 1985). J. M. Chirenje, *Ethiopianism and Afro-Americans in Southern Africa, 1883–1916* (Baton Rouge, 1987), also sees links to politics while tracing fascinating links to African-American figures. South Africa was an exporter as well as an importer of political Ethiopianism as Richard Newman shows in 'Archbishop Daniel William Alexander and the African Orthodox Church', *International Journal of African Historical Studies*, 16 (1983), pp. 615–630 and *Black Power and Black Religion: Essays and Reviews* (West Cornwall, CT, 1987).

RECENT TRENDS IN THE HISTORIOGRAPHY OF CHRISTIANITY 61

The big problem for those who want to read religious innovation as dissent is that for most of this century the independent churches have studiously avoided political action.[98] In a notorious incident of the 1980s a mass rally of South African Zionists cheered a speech by president P. W. Botha. In neighbouring Zimbabwe it has been the spirit mediums of centuries' old cults who have been singled out as key agents of resistance to settler colonialism, not the adherents of independent churches. Since Terence Ranger called attention to their role in the 1896 rebellion against the British South Africa Company, they have been extensively studied. Doubts about their influence expressed in the early seventies were answered by a spate of studies examining their part in the war against the Smith regime.[99] By contrast, the independent churches stood on the sidelines. An important article by Matthew Schoffeleers' reviews conflicting interpretations of Zionist Churches in Southern Africa and puts forward the ingenious explanation that their emphasis on healing individuals runs counter to collective political action.[100]

Whether right or wrong, Schoffeleers performs a service by calling attention to the reasons why Africans join independent churches, which in turn raises the vexed question of 'conversion'. Despite the inherent difficulty of peering into human minds, historians and anthropologists continue to be curious about the process by which one set of religious convictions displaces another. For the last twenty years the speculations of Robin Horton have been the focus of theoretical interest.[101] Beginning with the assumption that, in one form or another, a High God was a universal feature of traditional African religions, Horton argued that the need for a closer relationship to the High God was felt whenever economic and social change widened the boundaries of individual experience beyond the local arena which had been the principal sphere of action for lesser supernatural agencies. Thus, when invading colonialism and capitalism drew

---

98   And some famous cases of political confrontation did not arise from deliberate choice. See R. Edgar, *Because They Chose the Plan of God: The Story of the Bulhoek Massacre* (Johannesburg, 1988).

99   The most important of these is David Lan's *Guns and Rain: Guerrillas and Spirit Mediums in Zimbabwe* (London and Berkeley, 1985). Jean Comaroff quips in 'Missionaries and Mechanical Clocks', p. 7, that 'in the fight for Zimbabwe, it soon became hard to determine who stood in greater awe of the legendary spirit mediums, the whites or the blacks'. In 'Rural Christians and the Zimbabwe Liberation War: a Case Study', M. Bourdillon and P. Dundani argue that it was not just the spirit mediums who had to be cultivated; where Christianity was strong, it also commanded respect: C. F. Hallencreutz and A. M. Moyo (eds), *Church and State in Zimbabwe*, pp. 147–161.

100 M. Schoffeleers, 'Ritual Healing and Political Acquiescence: The Case of the Zionist Churches in Southern Africa', *Africa*, 60 (1991), pp. 1–25.

101 These were first put forward in R. Horton, 'African Conversion', *Africa*, 41 (1971), pp. 85–108.

Africans into vital relationships with distant workplaces and centres of power, they were more inclined to listen to the Christian evangelists. In a later period, those who found the more austere missionary versions of Christianity irrelevant to their instrumental needs for 'explanation—prediction—control' were likely to turn to independent churches, especially those who stressed healing.

Horton's thesis lacks historical specificity and is probably inherently unprovable using the normal processes of investigation and verification. Nonetheless scholars continue trying to prove or disprove it. Misunderstandings abound. Some have assumed that attachment to a mission is the hallmark of conversion and that identifying the motivations which led individuals to reside at missions will tell us about conversion. The most common conclusion is that material incentives were most powerful in drawing people to missions.[102] However, reasons for residence are not the same as reasons for mental transformations and cannot really help to unlock the mysteries of conversion. Another common misconception is that Horton argued that Christian missions were themselves the expanders of macroscopic horizons, in contrast to traditional religions, which could not see beyond their local shrines. Terence Ranger mounts a massive assault on this proposition in a contribution to an important new book on conversion.[103] Deploying the full range of his formidable knowledge of religion in Zimbabwe, Ranger shows how missionaries strove to *narrow* the universe of their converts to the microcosm of the station, while traditional religions spread networks of interaction and spiritual efficacy over vast distances. Energetic and interesting as it is, Ranger's argument does not amount to a knock-down case against Horton. The shattering of microcosms in Central Africa by slavers, traders and invaders was under way long before the arrival of modern missionaries. And, as Horton allowed for the possibility that traditional religions could change to accommodate expanded horizons, it is entirely possible that appropriate transformations predated the arrival of missionaries.[104]

---

102   Among recent examples are: B. Carmody, 'Conversion and School at Chikuni, 1905–39, *Africa*, 58 (1988), pp. 193–209; and J. Simensen, 'Religious Change as Transaction: the Norwegian Mission to Zululand, South Africa 1850–1906', *Journal of Religion in Africa*, 16 (1986), pp. 82–100.

103   'The Local and the Global in Southern African Religious History' in R. W. Hefner (ed), *Conversion to Christianity: Historical and Anthropological Perspectives on a Great Transformation* (Berkeley and Los Angeles, 1993), pp. 65–98. Ranger was responding not only to Horton but to the more recent work of R. Werbner in, for example, ch. 7 of his *Ritual Passage, Sacred Journey* (Washington, DC, 1989), pp. 245–298.

104   How a Central African religion might have transformed itself over centuries is explored in M. Schoffeleers, *Rivers of Blood: the Genesis of a Martyr Cult in Southern Malawi* (Madison, 1992).

All of this leaves the question of conversion unresolved. Richard Gray, among others, is attracted to the proposition that whatever the circumstances of its dissemination, Christianity did contain entirely novel concepts which could attract converts.[105] As we have seen, he contends that the most effective agents for the spread of those ideas were African evangelists, not white missionaries. Although that is generally agreed, historians interested in conversion have continued to direct attention at the mission station, even when researching the careers of black clergy and lay evangelists. I used to believe that when we had studies of mission stations in the era of mass conversions comparable to existing studies of missions in the early eras of pioneering and piecemeal advance, we would have a much better understanding of what conversion was all about. I am now inclined to think that the focus on mission Christianity has been misplaced, that there were never enough mission stations to account for the vast scale of twentieth century conversions and that the most important mental transformations occurred far away from missionary eyes. A seminal contribution to the discussion of those transformations comes from the work of Lamin Sanneh, a West African-born theologian who now occupies the professorial chair of missiology once held by historian Kenneth Scott Latourette.

Sanneh rejects categorically the proposition that Christianity was an essentially European religion foisted upon African societies by missionaries in cahoots with colonialism.[106] At the same time he agrees that there were distinctive cultural characteristics in African societies to which Christianity needed to be assimilated. The process by which that was accomplished he calls 'translation'. Just as signs were found to render the words of German, French or English Bibles into African languages, so, eventually, ways were found to carry the underlying meaning of Christianity into multifarious cultures. Sanneh's approach is rigorously historical. He reminds us of the time when Christianity had to be 'translated' by peoples of the Eastern Mediterranean into concepts that could be understood by Romans. Although the religion flourished in Ethiopia and Nubia long before missionaries carried it to the British Isles, that did not prevent its cross-cultural rendering into the powerful prose of the Book

---

105 Gray, *Black Christians and White Missionaries*, pp. 66–69.

106 He regards the Comaroff's study of Tswana missions, for example, as 'a sophisticated presentation of the classical theory of Christianity as a tool of colonial subjugation, and of Africans as victims'. 'As such', he continues, 'the book represents the European metropolitan viewpoint, the viewpoint of the transmitters over against the recipients of the message', L. Sanneh, *Encountering the West, Christianity and the Global Cultural Process. The African Dimension* (Maryknoll, NY, 1993), p. 91n.

of Common Prayer or the King James Bible.[107] In the modern era, the work of linguistic translation was begun by European missionaries, the work of cultural translation, by African evangelists.

Sanneh's contribution is certainly stimulating and original, but is it capable of being investigated by conventional methods of historical research? How can the lived experience of this ongoing process of translation be conjured up from the dry bones of written records? There are problems even with the translation of individual words, notoriously exemplified in the nineteenth century missionary debates about whether to use Unkulunkulu, Utixo, or some other word for God when preaching to the Zulu.[108] How much more difficult it must be to declare that a whole religious system has been translated? This is more of a worry for secular historians than for Sanneh, who is confident that what is being translated is a transcendent truth. However, it would be a bold scholar who would contend that Buddhism, Islam or Hinduism never successfully crossed cultural borders And what we routinely call European Christianity could not exist unless the religion had emerged virtually intact after crossing many cultural divides. (Some of the first Portuguese missionaries to Southern Africa may well have had only a few generations of experience with Christianity in their own families.)

Then there is the question of verification. A great deal of individual spiritual experience is inevitably lost in missionary accounts of 'conversions', even when the circumstances are recorded in dramatic detail.[109] Leaps of imagination are required from any historian who aspires to describe the process. Although there is little to go on in the archival record, it is worth remembering that processes of commitment, transformation and regeneration can be observed at close quarters any day of the week in contemporary Africa. Anthropologists and theologians have provided a treasure trove of what Clifford Geertz has called 'thick description' of rituals and evangelical methods among independent churches.[110] Combining contemporary analysis with

---

107   For another example of the insights afforded by looking back to the evangelisation of Europe, see H. J. Sindima, *Drums of Redemption, An Introduction to African Christianity* (Westport, CT and London, 1994).

108   Diana Jeater contends in a paper presented to the September 1992, *Journal of Southern African Studies*, 20th Anniversary Conference, York, England, that by adopting a missionary version of their own language, Shona Christians were distanced from the oral vernacular of the common people.

109   As in P. Delius, *The Conversion: Death Cell Conversations of 'Rooizak' and the Missionaries, Lydenburg, 1875* (Johannesburg, 1984).

110   There are too many examples to cite here. In 'Young Puritan Preachers in Post-Independence Malawi', *Africa*, 62 (1992), pp. 159–181, Richard van Dijk identifies weird and perplexing varieties of street-corner preaching. J. P. Kiernan has collected and analysed the hymns

RECENT TRENDS IN THE HISTORIOGRAPHY OF CHRISTIANITY 65

historical research, Schoffeleers has analysed complex to-ing and fro-ing between different kinds of religious belief in southern Malawi, including Pentecostal churches.[111] Pentecostal evangelism provides many excellent examples of contemporary conversion, some under the aegis of white preachers, others under entirely African leadership. Although the recent spread of fundamentalist and Pentecostal churches with right-wing backing from Europe and America dismays many observers, the highly-charged emotional atmosphere in which they operate has lessons for all historians interested in conversion.[112]

If conversion has been born again as a subject of research, other topics remain neglected. It is surprising that contemporary critical theory and post-structuralism have as yet made little impact on the study of religious history in Africa. Textual analysis and heuristics are the bread and butter of theological discussion. Missionary Christianity emanating from different faiths and nations supplies dozens of discourses to deconstruct. With a couple of exceptions, the study of images and representations has likewise been hardly touched.[113] Missionary medicine in the twentieth century is another topic awaiting its historians. Michael Gelfand's survey is little more than a bland chronicle of names, with little discussion of changing medical technologies or public health.[114] Efforts should be made to correct the regional imbalances in literature on religious history. Although other countries lack the personnel

---

used by 22 different Zionist congregations in 'The Canticles of Zion: Song as Word and Action in Zulu Zionist Discourse', *Journal of Religion in Africa*, 20 (1990), pp. 188–204; in another article he decodes the spiritual meaning of Zionist costumes: 'Wear 'n' Tear and Repair: The Colour Coding of Mystical Mending in Zulu Zionist Churches', *Africa*, 61 (1991), pp. 26–39. One way of approaching the subject of conversion is to run the process in reverse, as anthropologist Wim van Binsbergen did when he went through the physical/spiritual process of becoming a 'traditional' diviner/healer, which he describes in 'Becoming a Sangoma: Religious Anthropological Field-work in Francistown, Botswana', *Journal of Religion in Africa*, 21 (1991), pp. 309–344.

111 M. Schoffeleers, *Pentecostalism and Neo-Traditionalism, The Religious Polarization of a Rural District in Southern Malawi* (Amsterdam, 1985).

112 See the work of Paul Gifford: '"Africa Shall be Saved". An Appraisal of Reinhard Bonnke's Pan-African Crusade', *Journal of Religion in Africa*, 17 (1987), pp. 63–92 and *The Religious Right in Southern Africa* (Gweru, 1988), revised and reissued as *The New Crusaders: Christianity and the New Right in Southern Africa* (London, 1991).

113 Exceptions are P. Kokkonen, 'Religious and Colonial Realities: Cartography of the Finnish Mission in Ovamboland, Namibia', *History in Africa*, 20 (1993), pp. 155–171, and G. Prins, 'The Battle for Control of the Camera in Late Nineteenth Century Western Zambia', *African Affairs*, 89 (1990), 97–105.

114 M. Gelfand, *Christian Doctor and Nurse, The History of Medical Missions in South Africa from 1799–1976* (Mariannhill, Natal, 1984). Also disappointing is the guarded treatment of mission doctors and the state, especially in the section on the work of Anthony Barker in Zululand, pp. 305–308.

provided by South Africa's score of university departments of theology, missiology and religious studies, their experience is equally deserving of study. Language barriers have impeded studies of Mozambique and Angola. The German and Scandinavian missions need more work; this is especially true in Namibia, where more than 50% of an overwhelmingly Christian population belong to Lutheran Churches.[115]

Above all, we need more gendered studies. This is not just a matter of writing women into religious history.[116] It requires, as Deborah Gaitskell observes, that we extend our understanding of 'how the spread and appropriation of Christianity has been gender specific'.[117] It also means, as Guy, Schoffeleers and Hinfelaar point out, exploring the way religion could be organised on a gendered basis to protest against ruling elites.[118] Family organisation within new Christian communities is a related matter, as Sheila Meintjes has shown in her work on Edendale, Natal.[119] The recent upswing of interest in the whole field of religious history suggests that we may soon see many others building on these insights.

115 *Church and Liberation in Namibia*, p. xv.

116 Penelope Hetherington's survey of 'Women in South Africa: the Historiography in English', *International Journal of African Historical Studies*, 26 (1993), pp. 241–269, turned up exactly four articles relating in women in connection with religion. Three papers out of 64 presented to the 1991 Durban Conference on Women and Gender in Southern Africa dealt with religion, and only one of these was historical in orientation.

117 D. Gaitskell, 'Devout Domesticity? A Century of African Women's Christianity in South Africa', in C. Walker (ed), *Women and Gender in South Africa to 1945* (Cape Town, 1990).

118 Jeff Guy notices the way in which the emphasis on cattle-killing rather than crop destruction in the Xhosa movement of 1856–57 has obscured the role played by gender differences: see J. Guy, 'A Landmark, not a Breakthrough', *South African Historical Journal*, 25 (1991), pp. 227–232. Other perceptive studies include H. Hinfelaar, 'Women's Revolt: The Lumpa Church of Lenshina Mulenga in the 1950s', *Journal of Religion in Africa*, 21 (1991), pp. 99–129, and Schoffeers, *Pentecostalism and Neo-Traditionalism*, passim.

119 S. Meintjes, 'Family and Gender in the Christian Community at Edendale, Natal, in Colonial Times', in Walker (ed), *Women and Gender in South Africa*.

Writing of Past Times: An Interdisciplinary Approach to Mission History

Andrea Schultze

> Our intentions for the future are grounded in the past and without remembering we cannot see, for how else would we know what we see?
>
> ELIZABETH TONKIN

⁂

To know what we see is far more difficult than appears at first sight. What we see is rooted in past times and most of these lie beyond 'remembering'. Jan Assmann speaks of 'cultural memory'[1] and defines it as the perspective communities or peoples have on the times which lie before those any living human can remember. Assmann explores how a group sees and understands past times and its own history in particular. How is it bound to specific frames of interpretation? How do cultural memories mirror the society from which they originate and reflect their actual discourses (sometimes rather than what happened in the past)? Without going deeper into hermeneutical questions of whether cultural memories are constructions rather than descriptions of the past, the following article aims at summarising some of the most creative approaches to mission history and their interpretations of past times in the last 20 years. It will be focused on mission activities within the colonial context and considers them as part of the colonial society.[2]

Source: Schultze, A., "Writing of Past Times: An Interdisciplinary Approach to Mission History', in F. Ludwig and A. Adogame (eds.), *European Traditions in the Study of Religion in Africa*, Wiesbaden: Harrassowitz Verlag, 2004, pp. 323–328.

---

1 Assmann, 1999.

2 This is not the place to present a complete overview of recent publications, but to highlight some examples instead which have provoked and supported current research on mission activities. Thus far from claiming completeness the article presents a selection only of relevant interdisciplinary contributions.

For a long time mission historiography was undertaken for the most part by mission directors or other high-ranking theologians. Books on mission history were and are regularly published on the occasion of anniversaries of particular mission societies. Their approach was often self-laudatory or at the very least favourably naive or apologetic. Like the mission movement of the 19th century itself, mission historiography was—and to a certain extent still is—a stronghold of Pietist theology.

Mission historiography however changed towards the end of the 20th century. During the era of decolonisation some theologians joined the critical voices who regarded missionaries as henchmen of colonial exploitation and distanced themselves radically from any idea of practising mission—at the same time turning their backs on mission history as well. In the seventies and eighties, the attitudes of theologians to mission and its history ranged widely from naive enthusiasm through apathy to strong condemnation. It was therefore rather *non*-theologians who, once they had somewhat belatedly discovered the hidden wealth of missionary sources and finally overcome their embarrassment sufficiently to use and quote them in their publications, broke the taboo and reclaimed mission historiography as a serious academic discipline. Many, of course, did so in the same Zeitgeist and focused on the intertwined history of mission activities and colonialism.[3]

In fact the first point to be made is that mission historiography as an interdisciplinary academic study has been primarily developed in the last 20 years by non theologians. In the nineties a wealth of new material appeared in the fields of ethnography, social anthropology and history, dealing with mission history and intensively using the archives of (former) mission societies. Among the best-known examples are the publications of Jean and John Comaroff on the Southern Tswana and the activities of the London Missionary Society in South Africa.[4]

1. In the first part of this paper these most recent non-theological approaches to mission history will be evaluated and some of the key theses, insights and terminologies promoted by their scholars shall be referred to. Some of them have not yet been taken up and applied to any great extent by German theologians.

1.1 For some time it was fashionable to make absolutes out of dichotomies. The history of colonialism was described in purely dualistic terms: here the colonisers—there the colonised; here the offenders, there the victims. Mission history was similarly simplified: missionaries as spiritual rapists of the local

---

3 For instance Gründer, 1983.
4 Cf. Comaroff and Comaroff, 1991; 1992; 1997.

WRITING OF PAST TIMES

population, epitomes of intolerance, destroyers of indigenous culture and religion. Unquestionably there is truth in this perspective and it is still legitimate for the descendants of the colonised to demand that European countries admit and apologise for the sufferings of their ancestors.[5] But we also discovered that a dualistic view of history is not the whole truth and that it is not helpful in understanding the complexity of colonial encounters. One of the fundamental changes in our perception of the colonial past was the rediscovery of the fact that the colonial society was not a monolithic bloc but a *"complex collectivity (...) fractured by internal difference"* as Jean and John Comaroff have claimed.[6]

1.2 Taking this into account, Ann Stoler and Frederick Cooper have convincingly pointed to the fact that:

> [c]olonial dichotomies of ruler and ruled, white and black, colonizer and colonized only reflect part of the reality in which people lived.[7]

Instead of drawing attention to the dichotomies, they highlighted the inner contradictions of the colonial system and revealed the *tensions of empire.*[8] Those tensions weakened the colonisers and enabled and allowed resistance from within the system as well as from outside. Cultural encounters cannot be reduced to the confrontation of clearly defined incompatible systems. Instead colonisers and colonised were composed of heterogeneous, often conflicting groups and individuals, who formed changing coalitions according to their often counter-rotating interests and perspectives. Mission societies are likewise being regarded as complex organisations and the focus of research is changing to scrutinise their inner power relations, inherent contradictions and conflicting ambitions.

1.3 In line with the above approach, colonialism is no longer characterised purely as a clash of powers, one culture gaining complete control over the other and destroying and absorbing it. The term 'acculturation' is increasingly disappearing and is giving way to *transculturation*, a term that was coined by the Cuban Fernando Ortiz but which was brought into the recent anglophone discussion by Mary Louise Pratt.[9] Transculturation stresses the fact that cultural encounters started processes in different directions. It describes gradual transformation, mutual appropriation and redefinition of cultural elements

---

5   Lately claimed again by Soyinka, 2001: 55.

6   Comaroff and Comaroff, 1992: 33–34.

7   Stoler and Cooper, 1997: 34.

8   Stoler and Cooper, 1997.

9   Pratt, 1992: 5.

within the colonial encounter.[10] It highlights social and cognitive interactions, in which particular cultural elements are negotiated and translated and new affiliations get constructed.

In theological contexts normally the term '*in*culturation' is common. It seems more suitable than 'acculturation' since it suggests a flexible response to the power of colonisers and missionaries. Yet the implicit suggestion is still to think of colonial or missionary encounters as one way. The local population picks up the new worldview and integrates it into their daily life by adapting and transforming certain elements into their allegedly 'traditional' thinking. In the light or the above, "transculturation" seems to be the most appropriate term. It points to the interdependency of cultures[11] and to the frequently overlooked fact that mission activities also had a strong effect on the sending context, as in Germany for instance.

1.4 Terms like 'transculturation' illustrate that other disciplines have developed a useful vocabulary with which to approach mission history. Another example is the notion of *contact zone*. The term was also introduced by Mary Louise Pratt and is characterised as:

> the space of colonial encounters, the space in which peoples geographically and historically separated tome into contact with each other and establish ongoing relations, usually involving conditions of coercion, radical inequality and intractable conflict.[12]

Pratt talks about 'contact zone' instead of:

> 'colonial frontier',[13] because it draws attention more to aspects of mutual influence than to one sided colonial expansion. She also says: " By using the term 'contact' I aim to foreground the interactive, improvisational dimensions of colonial encounters so easily ignored or suppressed by diffusionist accounts of conquest and domination.[14]

1.5 In naming important contributions to mission historiography the model of the *long conversation*, suggested by Jean and John Comaroff (1991), cannot

---

10   Cf. MS Wirz, 2000: 1.

11   Cf. Said, 1994: 25.

12   Pratt, 1992: 6.

13   The term "frontier zone" was used by Martin Legassick (1969) and his study of the area north of the Cape Colony in the 19th century.

14   Pratt, 1992: 6. Another consistent point of view was taken by Ann Stoler, who claims, "to explore the colonies as more than sites of exploitation but as 'laboratories of modernity'." (Stoler, 1995: 15)

WRITING OF PAST TIMES

be ignored. The metaphor of the *long conversation* describes the encounter between missionaries and 'heathens', mutual influences, misunderstandings, confrontations and long-term processes of cultural, social and religious transformation. It is understood as an *exchange of signs and substance*.[15] Because the long conversation was full of conflicts, yet tied missionary families and their converts closely together (an aspect which is often ignored in mission studies but evident from the archival reports), the Comaroffs also described the missionary encounters of the 19th century as a *mutually constraining embrace*.[16]

1.6 There is another fascinating book I would like to mention. It is Birgit Meyer's *Translating the Devil*.[17] Mirroring an anthropological perspective it aims at illustrating that 'African Christianity is not merely an extension of the missionary impact' but that it is characterised by 'a dialectical interplay of alienation and appropriation.' Meyer shows that there were elements *of choice and transformation*, actively used by the local population when confronted with the new faith, and she unravels:

> the ways in which Africans have elided or even subverted Western domination.[18]

Unfortunately there is no space to address perceptions of mission history already mentioned in greater detail. Many others could be referred to. Summarising this first part one can conclude that colonialism and missionary work—whether in the vanguard or part of the colonial project—imposed very subtle processes of transformation on the protagonists of both sides. Partly because of the steady marginalisation of mission history within mainstream academic theology in the second half of the twentieth century, it has been owing primarily to ethnological, anthropological and historical research that mission historiography has been returned to the level of current academic discourses where its complexity has been rediscovered. These scholars have placed a useful terminology at our disposal, some of which still has to be taken up by their German theological colleagues.

2. Coming to the second part of new approaches to mission history let me now turn to the contributions that might provide helpful insights into mission history. This section focuses to some extent on the German discussions,

---

15   Comaroff and Comaroff, 1991: 11.

16   Comaroff and Comaroff, 1991: 198.

17   According to Meyer (following Fabian, 1971) translation involves a "creative process, which does not aim for the correct representation or the Other, but which instead is a product of intersubjective and intercultural dialogue" (Meyer, 1995: 7).

18   Meyer, 1995: 1.

since it is only possible to make a selection from all the many publications and discourses. Obviously a bridge between all disciplines—theological as well as anthropological, historical and so on—is the topic of the perception of the Other, set out in various approaches by very different people such as Edward Said with his critique of 'Orientalism' (Said, 1978) or Theo Sundermeier with his model of *Konvivenz* (Sundermeier, 1995, 1996)—both being developed from interdisciplinary perspectives but deriving from very different approaches.

2.1 Missiology however, and perhaps, too, religious studies, have for quite some time focused rather on dogmatic issues than on historiography. Mission archives have only recently been rediscovered by professors and Ph.D. students. They were, as has been mentioned, long avoided as a domain for Pietist apologists. There were well-perceived shifts of paradigms in missiology, recently claimed by Konrad Raiser (Raiser, 1989) or David Bosch (Bosch, 1991) for instance, but although they were historically well founded these impulses did not result in a new view of mission history. Other academics, though, such as Werner Ustorf (Ustorf, 1994, 1995). Klaus Koschorke (Koschorke, 1998) and others have stressed the importance of mission history and have used historical methods for its interpretation.

In the following however attention shall be paid to other ways in which theology as an academic discipline enriches mission historiography. Some of the points to be raised are desiderata rather than books which have already been published. On the other hand many of these new contributions are not as new as one might think; rather, they reintroduce earlier debates into the discussion.

2.2 Theology has developed rich instruments for dealing with the Other and more especially with historical documents. *Hermeneutical questions* touch the core of its efforts and are one of the key qualifications of theologians. One may refer to exegetical methods such as redaction, tradition and form criticism, the issue of a 'Sitz im Leben' and so on. Other disciplines are often rather weak at dealing with missionary sources as a methodological and hermeneutical challenge—let alone with our own context and the problem of recontextualisation (Sundermeier, 1995: 88). In addition it is unquestionably an advantage to be acquainted with the Bible and its dogmatic interpretation throughout Christian history for a better understanding of missionary sources and their implicit perspective.

2.3 The second point that has to be mentioned is a recent or, rather, a recently repeated approach which pleads for an *extended perspective* on mission history in terms of *geography, denominations, religions and time*: Christian theology implies a global perspective—mission activities being a historical expression of as well as a reason for it. In the 20th century this global perspective called the ecumenical movement into being or—to put it the other way

WRITING OF PAST TIMES

round—the ecumenical movement fostered the awareness of global relations between denominations and religions and intensified their dialogue. There are three consequences of this commitment: First, mission history today has to be written more decisively as church history of the young churches in the South;[19] secondly it needs to be written from an ecumenical perspective, as Lukas Vischer (Vischer, 1982)—taking up earlier ecumenical attempts—pointed out. Thirdly, we have to take into consideration that other religions also had their mission activities (often in the same geographical location) and that there was a vivid exchange and deep intertwining between those histories. Andreas Feldtkeller therefore pleads for a mission historiography which is embedded in the wider concept of 'missio religionum', the mission of religions—note the plural![20] There is no doubt that mission historiography in a global, ecumenical and inter-religious perspective, elaborated by scholars of theology or religious studies, can make a meaningful contribution to interdisciplinary dialogue and to a deeper understanding of the complexity of mission activities.

2.4 As an aside: Feldtkeller also calls for a mission historiography which extends its perspective in time. Tempted by the narrow period which is well documented in our precious mission archives we tend to focus too much on the 18th and 19th century and so nearly always end up gaining a picture of mission which is closely linked to colonialism. But:

> the period since the founding of most Protestant mission societies does not even cover a tenth of Christian mission history and a much smaller part of the inter-religious connections, in which Christian mission history is embedded.[21]

2.5 Finally, it should be pointed out that it is a privileged experience of European churches today to be closely linked to their partner churches in the South and to the community within the World Council of Churches. Theology in our faculties is therefore linked to a forum where it is questioned by the young Christian churches and constantly has to reconsider its perspective on mission history. More than other disciplines it has a chance to discuss the *shared history* which connects the descendants of missionaries closely to those of early converts. This is indeed a unique opportunity to learn from each other about our collective memories, how to write about past times and how to cope with the challenges of a shared future.

---

19   Gensichen, 1976; Jenkins, 1983; 9.
20   Feldtkeller, 2000, also see: www.missio-religionum.de.
21   Feldtkeller, 2000: 17, my translation.

Bibliography

Assmann, Jan, *Das kulturelle Gedächtnis, Schrift, Erinnerung und politische Identität in frühen Hochkulturen*, München: Beck, 1999.

Bosch, David, *Transforming Mission, Paradigm Shifts in Theology of Mission*, Maryknoll: Orbis, 1991.

Comaroff, Jean and John Comaroff, *Ethnography and the Historical Imagination*. Boulder: Westview Press, 1992.

Comaroff, Jean and John Comaroff, *Of Revelation and Revolution*, 2 vols., Chicago: University of Chicago Press, 1991 and 1997.

Feldtkeller, Andreas, *Sieben Thesen zur Missionsgeschichte*. Berliner Beiträge zur Missionsgeschichte, Berlin: Selignow (1/2000).

Gensichen, Hans-Werner, "Kirchengeschichte im Kontext. Die Historiographie der jungen Kirchen auf neuen Wegen", in: *LR* (26/1976), 301–313.

Gründer, Horst, *Christliche Mission und deutscher Imperialismus: Eine politische Geschichte ihrer Beziehungen während der deutschen Kolonialzeit (1884–1914) unter besonderer Berücksichtigung Afrikas und Chinas*, Paderborn: Schöningh, 1982.

Hastings, Adrian, *A History of African Christianity. 1950–1975*, Cambridge: Cambridge University Press, 1979.

Hastings, Adrian, *The Church in Africa 1450–1950*, Oxford: Clarenton, 1994.

Jenkins, Paul, "Missionsgeschichte. Ein Manifest", *ZMiss* (9/1983), 8–18.

Koschorke, Klaus, *Christen und Gewürze. Konfrontation und Interaktion kolonialer und indigener Christentumsvarianten*, Studien zur außereuropäischen Christentumsgeschichte, vol. 1, Göttingen: Vandenhoek & Ruprecht, 1998.

Küster, Volker, *Konvivenz und Differenz. Studien zu einer verstehenden Missionswissenschaft*, FS für Theo Sundermeier, Erlangen: Verlag für Mission und Ökumene, 1995.

Legassick, Martin, *The Griqua, the Sotho-Tswana, and the Missionaries*, Los Angeles, 1969.

Meyer, Birgit, *Translating the Devil, an African Appropriation of Pietist Protestantism. The Case of the Peki Ewe in Southeastern Ghana, 1847–1992*. Edinburgh: Edinburgh University Press, 1995.

Müller, Karl and Werner Ustorf (ed.), *Einleitung in die Missionsgeschichte. Tradition. Situation und Dynamik des Christentums*, Stuttgart: Kohlhammer. 1995.

Pratt, Mary Louise, *Imperial Eyes. Travel Writing and Transculturation*, London: Routledge, 1992.

Raiser, Konrad, *Ökumene im Übergang, Paradigmenwechsel in der ökumenischen Bewegung?*, Genf, 1989.

Ritschl, Dietrich and Werner Ustorf, *Ökumenische Theologie. Missionswissenschaft*, Stuttgart: Kohlhammer, 1994.

Said, Edward, *Kultur und Imperialismus. Einbildungskraft und Politik im Zeitalter der Macht*, Frankfurt a.M.: Fischer, 1994.

Said, Edward, *Orientalism, Western Conceptions of the Orient*, London: Penguin, 1978.

Soyinka, Wole, *Die Last des Erinnerns. Was Europa Afrika schuldet—und was Afrika sich selbst schuldet*, Düsseldorf: Patmos, 2001.

Stoler, Ann und Frederick Cooper (eds.), *Tensions of Empire. Colonial Cultures in a Bourgeois World*, Berkeley: University of California Press, 1997.

Stoler, Ann, *Race and the Education of Desire*, Durham: Duke University Press, 1995.

Sundermeier, Theo, *Den Fremden verstehen, eine praktische Hermeneutik*, Göttingen: Vandenhoek & Ruprecht, 1996.

Sundermeier, Theo, *Konvivenz und Differenz*, Erlangen: Verlag der Evangelisch-Lutherischen Mission, 1995.

Ustorf, Werner, "Missionsgeschichte als theologisches Problem", *ZMiss* (9/1983), 19–29.

Vischer, Lukas, "Kirchengeschichte in ökumenischer Perspektive, III", *ThZ* (38/1982), 367–472.

Wirz, Albert, Andreas Feldtkeller, Andrea Schultze et al., *Transkulturation—Mission und Moderne*, unpublished manuscript, Berlin, 2000 (quoted as MS Wirz).

'Trained to Tell the Truth': Missionaries, Converts, and Narration

Gareth Griffiths

Missionaries invested an inordinate amount of energy in producing written material. Apart from the obvious priority given to the primary aim of conversion—such as printed Bibles and catechisms in the languages of their intended audiences—missions utilized the whole range of media of their day from print and colour reproduction tracts to screen technology (magic lantern slides). Personal accounts of the newly converted in the form of life stories and autobiographies were particularly widespread. They are among the earliest texts in colonial languages that feature the lives and experiences of colonized peoples. Such accounts were important to the colonized subjects themselves, to the missionaries who wrote them down, and to the Christians readers at whom they were aimed.

As one might expect, the texts were censored through complex systems of patronage and control.[1] What missionaries wrote in their personal diaries, or even in the daybooks of the mission stations, differed significantly in tone and content from accounts submitted to mission headquarters. Mission journals also rewrote such material for their pages, imposing further filters. Shifting from the voice of the native subject to the pen of the mission recorder was only the first step in a long process of control exercised over the record of the lives of their converts. These texts provided the principal lens through which home audiences viewed the imperial world beyond colonial homelands and so decisively shaped the attitudes by which colonized cultures were judged. Despite the profound limitations on personal agency involved in their production, they were also among the earliest means by which the subjects of the imperial venture could communicate some of their own views to those who had invaded their lands and to their fellow colonized people. Eventually, they would even be employed to speak to other colonized people across linguistic and cultural divides. Mission texts, like other texts in the colonial languages, could thus be

---

Source: Griffiths, G., "'Trained to Tell the Truth': Missionaries, Converts and Narration," in N. Etherington, *Missions and Empire*, Oxford: Oxford University Press, 2008, pp. 153–172. Reproduced with permission of the Licensor through PLSclear.

---

1   Anna Johnston, 'Adam's Ribs: Gender, Colonialism, and the Missionaries, 1800–1860', Ph.D. diss. (Queensland, 1999).

both an instrument of oppression and a means of resistance, depending on the circumstances of their production and dissemination.

While societies expended much energy on material for use in the mission field, at least as many of their publications were aimed at encouraging interest and financial contributions from the home audience. By the end of the nineteenth century mission presses rivalled secular publishers and printers in volume of output and had adopted many of the secular presses' genres, forms, and discursive features. This was only to be expected until such time as a significant literate local audience of converted 'natives' existed in the mission field, a phenomenon that came late—usually after the control of evangelistic effort had passed from the hands of Euro-American missionaries into those of local converts. Even then a legacy of mission conventions persisted, partly because institutional control of the publishing remained in overseas or expatriate hands.

Gauri Viswanathan emphasizes that conversion did not necessarily mean a total deculturation, even when it was a massively disruptive event.[2] Since converts frequently continued as an active part of their communities, they retained a significant degree of agency. While acting upon their own society as agents of change, they also brought the values and viewpoints of that society into their dealings with the converting society. The great majority of converts discarded neither their pre-existing culture, nor the totality of their previous identity. Viswanathan emphasizes that new Christians worked for change in two directions. While acting as forces for modernization among their own people, they could simultaneously act as forceful critics of the Euro-American Christian societies—a phenomenon exemplified by such converts as the Revd. Attoh Ahuma and J. E. Casely Hayford in West Africa, and Ham Mukasa in East Africa. The case was quite different when converts had been previously ripped from their cultures, as was the case of the 'recaptives'—people freed from slave ships and caravans through the intervention of British imperial officials. Seldom did they return to their own communities, being consigned instead to artificial communities peopled by other recaptives, who often spoke different languages and practised different customs. For these converts the only convenient vehicles for communicating their stories were the languages and texts controlled by missionaries, texts whose forms were profoundly limiting. However, as these new communities began to succeed in converting people from the established undisrupted African communities, the processes described by Viswanathan in the Indian context slowly come into play.

---

2   Gauri Viswanathan, *Outside the Fold: Conversion, Modernity and Belief* (Princeton, 1998), p. xi.

This chapter employs close analysis of recaptive life stories and personal conversion narratives produced from the 1870s to the 1920s to demonstrate that, even in the most unfavourable circumstances, the voices of the colonized subjects cannot be completely suppressed. The necessity for a narrow focus in such a detailed textual investigation has led this chapter to focus on East and Central African sources dating from about 1870, though the occasional passing reference to texts from West Africa might suggest that in a fuller analysis of such texts a wider range of examples might usefully be compared. The texts reveal how narrative conventions operated to contain the 'native voice' they claimed to express, while, paradoxically, that very act of containment inscribed a record of its presence and even its actual operation in the choices and narrative strategies of the texts themselves. Although the voices of the missionized 'subjects' may seem to have got rather lost in these ventriloquized texts, read against the grain they reveal traces of the silenced voices of the converted colonized subject. Such is the case in West Africa of J. B. Danquah's work, which set out to rehabilitate and reaffirm the value and effectiveness of Akan traditional culture, law, and even religious thought in, for example, *The Akan Doctrine of God: A Fragment of Gold Coast Ethics and Religion.* In East Africa there are comparable cases, such as Jomo Kenyatta's work on the Kikuyu in texts such as *My People of the Gikuyu and The Life of Chief Wangora.* That these figures, both leading nationalists and anti-colonial fighters, felt able to publish in mission series shows how complex were the relations between this generation of African leaders and the missions, and how they felt, even in the 1940s when these texts were published, that mission presses were effective tools for communicating their ideas, if only in indirect and subtle ways. Read in this way, the life stories form an interesting and revealing accompaniment to the self-authored texts discussed by Peggy Brock in Chapter 7 and even the more radical texts by mission-educated nationalists which mission presses produced in the lead-up to decolonization.

These early 'ghosted' accounts of native life and conversion are sometimes openly stated to be the product of the missionary pen, but at the same time purport to give the 'true' account of the life of these subjects, 'as told to' a mission amanuensis. In fact, a dominant concern of these texts is the claim to authenticity. That discloses the troubled awareness the missionary amanuensis had of exercising controlling power over the agency of the colonized convert, a power at odds with the missionaries' stated aim to free these converts. The strenuous assertions of authenticity also reveal uneasiness about the missionary's role in the imperial process. It is clearly problematic to discuss overall how much the mission 'patron' exercised direct control over such texts. In some cases the control was almost total, to the extent that the 'subject' of the text was simply the passive pretext for the authorization of the mission amanuensis's own ideas and attitudes. However, from the earliest period even these ghosted texts allow their subjects' voices to disturb the stereotypical imperial presentation of them and their culture. Of course the missionary discourse of a savage, barbarous, 'dark', and benighted heathenism continued to condition these accounts, but the very presence of this stereotype creates in the gaps and silences of these texts an awareness of its enabling, silenced, and repressed opposite. The question these early conversion accounts pose is what agency, if any, the native subjects of mission texts authored by missionaries on their behalf could achieve within the boundaries of mission literary forms and narrative conventions which still largely represented them. Can the very silences and repressions of these early accounts in which missionary authors speak for the native subject reveal the nature of that control and so reveal through the rents in the veil of a dominant discourse the disturbing presence of the hidden subjects of the tale? And is the repressed desire for control and power of the missionary amanuensis also revealed within the very forms which they create and impose on their subjects, rendering their condition, too, as part of these text's occluded subject?

This is not to claim that the forms of mission narrative examined here were present in all missions. Imperial mission conversion narratives and forms are legion and diverse. The question posed here is simply, how far does the mission text of the high imperial period enable us to assert the existence of a paradigmatic relationship between missionary and native convert lodged within mission narrative form itself? Does it expose the hidden subject of their narrative choices and rhetorical structures, namely the voices of the enunciated colonized native subjects and of their missionary enunciator and the relations between them?

Many narratives published by missionaries in East Africa take the form of 'release' narratives: stories that purport to tell the 'unvarnished tale' of slaves purchased by missionaries, or rescued from slavery by the British Navy and brought to missions where missionary amanuenses write down their life stories. A typical example appeared in *Central Africa*, the journal of the Universities' Mission to Central Africa (UMCA) in 1884, entitled 'The Story of a Nyassa Boy, as Told by Himself'. As with so many similar tales, the actual missionary 'author' claims only to be the 'translator' and/or recorder. 'The following story of a Nyassa boy's life and wanderings, up to the time when he was received by the Mission, was written out by himself in the Swahili language ... There is no reason, from the character and ability of the lad to doubt the story.' Though 'allowance must be made for the fact that he was certainly very young, perhaps ten or twelve years of age at most, when first carried away from his home.

He is now probably eighteen years of age.' Elsewhere the author asserts, 'It is the story of an intelligent boy who has been seven years at the Mission Schools and risen to be a teacher and to promise well for future usefulness.' The final proof for the 'translator' of the truth of the story is the closeness with which it conforms to existing ideological and narrative expectations. In a classic early statement of the conventions of the release form, he offers one final proof of authenticity.

> Lastly, the substance of the story is not only typical of the experiences of hundreds, even thousands, of East African children, but of some intrinsic interest as a picture of the state of society and operations of the slave trade in the Eastern Lake district. The stages may be distinguished as follows: first, the normal state of the Nyasa tribes, war among themselves, and war with their common enemies; next, the sequel of war, the passing of the captives from owner to owner, until they fall into the hands of Arabs forming large caravans for conveyance to the coast; then the long march down to the coast, with all its hardships and terrible cost of human life; lastly, the attempt to ship the slaves to meet foreign demands, their capture by an English man-of-war, and the final consignment of a portion of them to the care of the Universities' Mission.

There could hardly be a clearer statement of the essential features of the 'narrative' mission texts embraced as the 'typical' life of the now freed, once enslaved, convert. It is followed by a renewed assertion of truthfulness on the part of the missionary recorder. 'In translation, care has been taken in no way to make any substantial change in the story, only to render it in simple and readable English.' The assertion is disingenuous. Not only had the 'author' of the original Swahili version been a pupil of the mission for seven years by the time of its composition, but he had become a trusted teacher. In the process of becoming literate in Swahili, and probably having a spoken if not written knowledge of English as well, he would have absorbed the ideological determinants of mission narrative. Thus, while there is truth in the basic facts recorded in the release narrative—experiences common among freed slaves at the mission— the transformation of those experiences into a text was inextricably bound up in the narrative form which focused, shaped, and ordered the raw events that were related. This is a more profound 'translation', which precedes the mere act of transferring narratives from one language to another, or even from a source oral narrator to a missionary-authored written text. By the time this story was published in 1884, the form of the release narrative that shaped it had long been established as the template for all such life narratives.

'TRAINED TO TELL THE TRUTH'

Women were often the authors of mission accounts of African life and experience, partly because many of the journals which printed them had began as children's journals. Thus, in the case of the UMCA they appear mainly in the journal *African Tidings* (originally *Children's Tidings*) rather than in the society's official journal, *Central Africa*. The audience for these stories quickly spread beyond young people as the adult readership broadened to include less educated members of the home congregations who responded to the human appeal of these stories of native life couched in personal rather than official discourse. There was, of course, the appeal of the exotic. The window this kind of account opened for home readers into what they assumed to be the 'true' world of the native, a world recognizably human but tinged with a frisson of horror, gelled with the seemingly perennial taste for the combination of the shocking and the moral, providing them with both a justification for their interest and a sense of satisfaction in their own superiority to the cultures depicted. In this respect the mission journals helped disseminate the wider ideology of imperialism, notwithstanding their unintended effects when read as potential counter-discursive texts. Since the texts examined here emerged from an area later absorbed into the British Empire (Tanganyika–Zanzibar), they are relevant to the wider story this volume seeks to tell. But since this part of Africa attracted attention from several European powers—France, Belgium, Germany, and Britain—and the missionaries came from many nations, the narrative conventions embodied in the texts they produced appear not to be rooted in any particular national culture. They clearly share a broader set of concerns. There was, of course, to some degree a shared culture of mission representation of Africans in this period. However, one must be equally mindful that crucial differences existed in individual missions. In the same way, it is arguable that the similarities these texts display were rooted in the broader structures of imperial control itself, structures common to all the nations engaged in the colonization of Africa, despite their differences in detailed practice.

Thus conversion narratives of an identical kind also occur in the journals of the Catholic society operating in the whole Central and East African region, the Pères de Saint Esprit, or Spiritans, as they came to be more familiarly known, and their accompanying nuns, the Sœurs de Sacré Cœur de Marie, who looked after the rescued girl slaves (it was deemed unseemly for male missionaries to be in charge of females). For similar reasons, by the mid-1880s a substantial force of laywomen were managing the Anglican UMCA reception house at Shangani Point and the girls' training establishment at Mbweni. Unlike women in some other Protestant missions, these High Anglican women were mostly spinsters who remained unmarried and who lived in all-female communities, in effect if not in name an order of Anglican nuns. These unmarried women missionaries, Catholic and Anglican, were often the channels through which the voices of Africans telling their tales were translated. This was especially so in the case of the UMCA, whose missionary laywomen were often from a very highly educated upper-class background, making them perhaps more inclined to engage in this kind of 'literary' work. The UMCA women were frequently independent, intellectual women who resisted the restrictions of a late nineteenth-century marriage. Mission work in East Africa, India, and China offered such women a more independent existence than a late Victorian marriage afforded. While in other Protestant missions marriage to a fellow missionary was sometimes a precondition for acceptance, even then the status and isolated location of these missionary couples afforded women more authority and a broader scope for the exercise of their talents than was usual at home. It was perhaps to be expected that such women would take an interest in the expressions of the voiceless subjects to whom the condition of their gender bound them in coils of sympathy and fellow feeling.

In 1896 the Spiritans' journal printed an example of the classic 'release narrative' which indicates clearly how exactly the Catholic missionaries at Bagamoya reproduced the narrative template employed by their Anglican rivals in the region. The 'Histoire d'Angelina' recounts the story of a woman who comes to beg food in a famine.[3] She is told the mission has only enough food to feed the hungry abandoned children it has taken in and instead is given some advice on how to trade in the local material of the forest to people in the hills for maize and bananas. She returns to tell her story, together with a present of a magnificent woven mat that she has made, clearly a product of the skills she learned as a result of the mission advice. She relates how she was born near Lake Nyasa, and was captured, 'stolen from my parents, like so many others, an Arab from Zanzibar bought me'. The phrase 'like so many others' declares the generic quality of the tale, which the narrator is at no pains to hide, since its stereotypical nature is part of its design and the foundation of the claim it makes on its intended audience of mission supporters at home. After an account of maltreatment rendered in the usual generalized terms, she goes on to tell of her escape and how she learned about the fathers at the mission to which she fled to find the familiar sanctuary. 'Under the protection of the Mission I found happiness. I was instructed in the religion of our Dear Lord Jesus, and baptized.'

---

3 *Annales Apostoliques*, XLII (April 1896), pp. 77–79; my translation.

Another revealing narrative in the standard mould is 'Ambimoya; or, The History of a Young Slave, Told by Himself'.[4] In this case the identity of the amanuensis, R. P. (Reverend Pere Le Roy, later Mgr Le Roy, a significant figure in the Spiritans' African mission), is incorporated into the text. Although the narrative includes few details of the process of the telling, it emphasizes the slowness of the procedure, a feature whose significance will emerge in later discussion of this process of relating and recording the testimonials of the converts. In this case the subject, Patrice Ambimoya, is a Christian child who in earlier times 'has accompanied Mgr. De Courmont on all his travels'. Perhaps the arduous character of one particular journey—'We were still walking, as long as the sun lightened our way, until our legs refused to carry us any further'—and the unusual intimacy inspired the lengthy conversation that ensues, at least in this textual dramatization of the event. 'Gradually a conversation began and Patrice told us his story at length'. This dramatization forcefully claims the authentic voice through the conventions of reported speech: 'I begin', said Patrice. Despite these signifiers of an 'authentic' voice and the unusual amplitude and detail the text affords, it remains confined within the narrative convention of what is by now a classic, well-established form of slave capture and release through Christian conversion.

Patrice, we are told, was born near Ungindo. The grammar and syntax suggest that the stealing and enslavement of children in this inland location were so widespread as to be universal conditions. 'Where I come from they steal children.' The central event of his enslavement, foretold if not almost predestined by the narrative structure, is fulilled: 'The thief seized me. Put me into a sack made from palm leaves and stuffed my mouth with maize paste to smother my cries.' The plethora of similar details serves to reinforce the concrete existence of the source narrator, whose substantive life story the narrative purports to relate. Against such detail is ranged the enveloping narrative patterning into which all such stories are now enfolded, a process of containment, as much, one suspects, for the convert who is their source as for the missionary who is their scribe. That Patrice Ambimoya is an older child and not a recent convert may indicate that he has told this story more than once, indeed, that his life and its memory have been shaped, as in all narratives of the past, by the expectations and conventions of the forms into which they are cast, which in turn were shaped by the audiences for which they are intended. In any case, following more details, including extended dialogues between the narrator and his parents, Patrice is captured and sold. There follows a riveting,

---

4 *Annales Apostoliques*, VI (Apr. 1887), pp. 71–6.

gruesome account of the caravan journey to the coast to Kiloa (Kilwa), along with conversations between Patrice and his various owners. These are far more precisely distinguished than is usual in these narratives; one is 'a great Arab, Abdallah bin Seliman'. These acknowledgements of the different qualities of individual Arab slave owners, differences usually disguised in these texts by a generalized, pejorative characterization and by the use of the generic term 'Arab' or 'Mussulman' in place of individual names, make this a fascinating example of the edges and boundaries of the standardized release narrative genre. This text is also one of the few mission accounts to acknowledge the historical reality that Arabs were not just slavers but also potential rivals in the conversion of their captives: 'An Arab with a white beard appeared, looked me over, asked me some questions, and bought me: "Don't cry," he said, "in ten days we'll leave for Mascate, you'll come with me, you'll be taught the Koran, and God willing you'll be a good Muslim."' For a moment the potential rupture between the viewpoint of the subject of the text and its mission recorder is glimpsed. Of course this textual fissure soon closes. The good master dies and Ambimoya is again sold, but this time he is rescued by the missionaries. However, the presentation of this event once again allows a leakage of unstandardized material into the form of this account of rescue. Ambimoya is terrified since he has been warned while at Kiloa that the white-robed fathers are slavers whose slaves are summoned to service in their 'stone house' by cords, which are attached to them and to the bed of the White Ones (the Spiritans). 'These Whites have houses of stone, and in these houses a type of chair that is like a bed. All their slaves are lodged in adjoining rooms, tied with ropes that are attached to the White's bed. When he wants a slave he pulls on the rope, without disturbing himself, and the slave arrives.'

No wonder Ambimoya is terrified. 'That is why I said to myself "I am lost" upon seeing the Whiteman approach.' This little vignette is clearly designed by the missionary amanuensis to illustrate false ideas about the missions promulgated by the Arab slavers to prevent slaves from seeking the sanctuary of the mission. The preamble is again very revealing. Ambimoya, we are told, has been warned thus by his fellow slaves: 'There are Whites who are wickedness itself, and you should never speak to them concerning yourself, or concerning your village.' The story the missionary amanuensis records is clearly meant to disprove this assertion, showing that Ambimoya can and does speak openly to his new mission friends. But at a deeper and ironic level the warning against revealing anything of oneself or one's society to these intruders may have an unintentional force in a text and form whose ultimate goal is the conversion of the subject and the transformation and 'civilization' of their cultures. At such moments the suppressed, 'disordered' perceptions of the unreconstructed

'TRAINED TO TELL THE TRUTH' 85

narrated subject seem about to erupt into open discourse. Almost, but never quite. In the end even the least well-policed 'authentic' testament must conform to the mission's ideological and narrative patterns. Thus, for all its fascinating detail and moments of textual fracture, the narrative closure is as inevitably fixed by the form as in the most simple example of the genre, ending as early release narrative demands at the moment of baptism ('You have brought me to Bagamoya, you have taught me to work, to read, to wash my soul through baptism, and here I am').

Meanwhile, when the good Arab master dies, the narrator piously notes that it 'is the Good Lord who wished it thus; otherwise where would I be today?' In fact, one might conclude by his own earlier account that had he in fact been taken as a slave to 'Mascate' (Muscat) by this master, been taught to read and converted, his experience might not have been profoundly different from what occurs when he is converted by the white missionary (Le Blanc). The fissures in this version of the release narrative suggest alternative narrative outcomes that lurk within and behind the story that eventually is recorded. Now the further possibilities of reading the text, as counter-discourse for example, may be more easily perceived. The story of Ambimoya reveals how much the mission amanuensis needed to suppress or transform the oral narrative to enable the officially acceptable version of the 'truth' of the convert's experience to be recorded.

Another elaborate example of how such processes operate, entitled 'Panya', appeared in the pamphlet series Stories of Africa, which, although it is undated, was published sometime in the first decade of the twentieth century.[5] This product of the Anglican UMCA mission on Zanzibar recounts the rescue of a 9-year-old girl, Panya, from Arab slavers. The exceptional interest of this tale lies in its foregrounding of the process by which the paradigmatic narratives of the tracts were produced through a controlled transmission of story from 'subject' to 'author'. This example clearly shows how hollow were the claims of the mission amanuensis to be a simple, objective recorder of lives. Panya's tale starts with the customary claim that it is 'as told' by its subject herself to A. F., a female missionary at the Mbweni Training Establishment in 1894–5. Panya had been released from an Arab dhow in April 1893. Her 'conversion' had occurred in the interval between the release and the finding of 'peace' and baptism at Mbweni, a process that is made an explicit subject of the narration.

---

5   A version of the story was first printed in *African Tidings*, XCVI (Feb. 1896), pp. 110–11 and XCVII (Mar. 1897), pp. 120–22. Its reworking in this collection a decade or more later shows how little mission presses cared about the date or provenance of accounts or their relevance to changing circumstances in the field.

Also explicit is the degree to which this transformation and reconstruction is intertwined with the production of the allegedly unmediated 'true' textual narrative of Panya.

The text describes an elaborate training process centred on control of the child's perception and memory. 'I remembered Panya's story,' A. F. observes, 'and I gave her fair warning I should expect it to be ready in a week.' A. F. had taught Panya Swahili but was surprised to find that she had also picked up some knowledge of English. 'I found if I didn't want the Little Pitcher to enjoy all my talks with the other ladies, she must be sent away before we began.' This aside makes plain that A. F. must have translated the Swahili original of Panya's oral narrative into English, a fact that might otherwise have gone unnoticed. Communication then was to be a controlled process, with information flowing from A. F. to Panya only if the missionary chose. Panya, A. F. tells us, had to be 'trained to tell the truth'. That complex process of training is then described, the purpose of which was to determine the 'truth' of Panya's story.

> And now Panya began to tell the truth sometimes. I found she very much disliked having to say afterwards what she ought to have said first, when she had told a lie. At first she only cared a little, but I think each time she cared more, and the last time she lost her temper; in fact, we both did considerably, and she gave me a lot of trouble. But when I came up a long time afterwards, and found her lying with her face pressed down upon the concrete floor, and saw that sympathizing friends were met by silence and kicks, if they came too near, I said to myself, 'Good, we have learnt something at last'. And from that day forward she began to try to speak the truth.

The idea that Panya's anger expressed her frustration at having to modify her story to fit the expectations of her listener and the structure required by mission release narratives does not seem to occur to the amanuensis A. F.

Only after this complex process of control has been narrated is 'Panya's story' told. By this time, of course, the identification of Panya as its controlling agent and A. F. as a mere neutral recorder implicit in the phrase 'as told to' has been exposed as a determining fiction. The story which we now hear is not that story of 'misery' which the 'men and women' of the mission heard from Panya's lips during her illness, but a reorganized, probably bowdlerized, version. What aspect of her story has been altered or suppressed and for what motives? It is possible to speculate that the 'unvarnished tale' described, among other things, a sexual relationship between the child and the slaver. The slavers' sexual abuse of children could not be recorded in the evangelical tracts because of the sensitivity of its intended audience and the negative impact this might have on the mission presentation of Africans as 'innocent victims'. Of course, for late Victorian readers no female victim of sexual abuse could ever be rendered as 'innocent', however traduced and pressured. Whatever adjustments were required of this and other kinds to ensure the 'truth' of Panya's story before it could be released, what this long process of negotiation and control finally produces bears the hallmark of the by now paradigmatic release narrative. Thus A. F.'s struggle with Panya to get her to 'tell the truth' resulted in a narrative that fulfilled all the patterns of the well-established mission narrative of release and conversion. This provides a telling comment on the interchangeability of the concepts of 'training' and 'truth-telling' by which both the subject and the scribe of the text are profoundly overdetermined.

Panya goes on to relate how at 3 years old she went from Uganda to 'live among the Nyamwezi' (how or why is not explained). She is approached by a man who 'carried me away to the houses of his people, and then that deceiver took me away to another house and sold me'. She is sold on until she ends at 'Saadani (an Arab town on the coast, nearly opposite Zanzibar) and we stayed there two months (meaning some little time)'. These internal glosses are interesting both in terms of their stress on the text's intended audience, the 'home' audience, which needs to be 'informed', and, even more significantly, as evidence of the intrusive 'voice' of A. F. even within the narrative we are offered as an accurate 'transcription' of Panya's 'own' tale.

> And we went on from Saadani just the same, only we went in a boat. It was a very large boat, so high that I could not climb up into it by myself. And we stayed in the boat, and we slept in it at night; but the man who had bought me loved me and took care of me in the boat, till one day we landed near a town.

At this juncture an Arab steals her and she is smuggled out of the town on another dhow. After she has been beaten for screaming, Panya's ear is cut off and fed to a dog. Eventually an English gunboat rescues her. The rest of the story concerns her reception and settlement 'in great peace and quietness' at Mbweni. This last phrase suggests none of the complex tensions between Panya and the rescuing missionaries recorded in A. F.'s long preamble. Thus the text reveals the complex, palimpsestic nature of the construction of this text vis-à-vis alternative and more complex 'truths' the tale cannot voice. The tale reveals remarkable open evidence of the process of construction involved in the making of paradigmatic texts of the nineteenth century release narrative, a process that later examples ignore. This may reflect the different practices of the missionary transcribers, but it may also reflect the different instrumental functions of the text with regard to the mission project and the audience it addressed in the different periods of the mission text's production.

The UMCA mission worker Alice Foxley, who worked at the mission on Zanzibar from 1894 until 1911, was almost certainly A. F. because she was the only person at Mbweni in 1894 with those initials. A. F. authored numerous other contributions to mission journals during Foxley's period of residency in Zanzibar, but none appeared after her departure. It may be that the self-revealing discussion of the processes of text production reflected unconsciously an essential sympathy felt by women for the controlled nature of their subjects, though this must remain merely speculative. For whatever reason, it is to a woman missionary, Alice Foxley, that we are indebted for one of the most revealing accounts of the personal life and narrative of an African convert and of the processes by which it was recorded.

Over the course of several decades a shift can be discerned from the texts narrowly focused on the anti-slavery campaigns in the region to the emergence of forms addressing wider concerns. Later texts retailing the experiences of converted natives were designed not only for a home audience but also for a growing body of converted Africans literate in both African languages and English whom the missions wished to provide with appropriate reading matter. These later texts (especially those produced after the First World War) address different concerns, notably those of 'backsliding' by converts under the pressures on these converts of the societies from which conversion has purportedly removed them. That this shift reflected a change in the target audience is confirmed by the fact that the daybooks that have survived at the missions at Bagamoya and at the Anglican Cathedral on Zanzibar regularly record struggles with backsliding converts in entries as early as 1870. Similar accounts appear only rarely in the *published* records until the audience for these publications include literate native converts, perhaps because struggles with backsliding and errant converts held little appeal to a 'home' audience, which needed to hear tales of success to ensure their continued contributions to mission funds. Despite the different emphasis of these later texts and their shift to the concerns of a local target audience, they remain strongly controlled by a process of editing or recording by mission amanuenses. Consequently, they remain equally problematic expressions of the actual concerns of Africans.

The series Little Books for Africa, issued by the Sheldon Press, an imprint of the Society for the Promoting of Christian Knowledge in the late 1920s and early 1930s, typifies the reading materials produced by missionary presses in the period between the wars for congregations of African Christian converts.[6]

---

6 All the titles in the Sheldon series discussed here are lodged in the British Library.

'TRAINED TO TELL THE TRUTH'   89

The series lays frequent claim to African authorship, with titles including the words 'autobiography' or 'as told by himself'. A number of texts are even attributed to specific individuals, thereby implying that they were directly authored by Africans. Despite the increasing claims to be 'authentic' and 'unmediated', the process of transmission and transcription continued to be very problematic, as an investigation of the provenance of the texts being circulated as late as the 1920s and 1930s as 'authentic' life accounts of African converts will reveal.

The Sheldon series includes *Ways I Have Trodden*, subtitled *The Experiences of a Teacher in Tanganyika Told by Himself*.[7] The translation is dated 1932; however, since the text is translated from German, it clearly had a pre-war origin. The collapse of the time frame between the events and the republication is again passed over without comment. This may be because, as with the earlier accounts of pre-Christian and pre-mission Africa recorded in the early release narratives, the point of these stories is to emphasize the unchanging, negative side of African life for those not converted and so saved. Even in the late 1930s they anachronistically conjure up an Africa riven by tribal divisions, warfare, and intertribal enslavement. Moreover, their form retains the features of classic release narratives. A war occurs; the protagonist (male or female) is captured and enslaved, and then sold to slavers. They escape. They are taken into the mission. They are healed in body. They are baptized. These late published stories confirm the view of the African past currently favoured by the mission societies, presenting as they do an essentially anachronistic picture of warfare and enslavement.

Another production of the Sheldon series was *Stories of Old Times: Being the Autobiographies of Two Women of East Africa* (*Narwimba and Chisi-Ndjurisiye-Sichayunga*).[8] Subheadings set out the narrative structures that shape the 'life' of the African subjects: 'Childhood', 'Stolen from Home', 'Slavery', 'Escape', 'Marriage', 'Ill-Treatment', 'Death of my Husband', 'I Marry Again', 'The Sin of Senga', 'Utengule (the Mission Station)', 'Baptism'. This final chapter concludes with the two sentences 'I was baptized on August 1, 1914. I have finished.' The narrative contains its lives within a frame of representation in which the African past—presented as violent, arbitrary, and brutal, especially in its treatment of women—is redeemable only by Christian conversion. The African 'life' is defined in these terms, and the arrival at the state of conversion is literally the 'end of life', that is to say they are not just born again but literally

---

7   *Ways I Have Trodden: The Experiences of a Teacher in Tanganyika Told by Himself*, trans. and abridged by Margaret Bryan from the German of Elise Kootz-Kretschmer (London, 1932).
8   Elise Kootz-Kretschmer, *Stories of Old Times: Being the Autobiographies of Two Women of East Africa* (*Narwimba and Chisi-Ndjurisiye-Sichayunga*), trans. and abridged from German (London, 1932).

disappear from narrative possibility. The convert's life displays no continuity with the past, nor does it connect to a post-conversion present. No indication of how conversion affects the subjects subsequently is aired, nor of how it changes their relations within and towards African society. In the same way the colonized state of recent African history also disappears, overwritten by a determining myth of unchanged and unchangeable heathenism to which only conversion can bring an end. To account for this one might postulate that these pieces dealing with the African 'past' are meant to act as contrasts, and one must ask if they are not preaching (literally) to the converted since by the time they were published or republished in the inter-war years they were dealing with matters decades out of date. Indeed in cases such as *The Story of Dorugu*, set in Nigeria and recorded by the same J. F. Schön who was Samuel Crowther's superior on the 1841 expedition up the Niger–Tshadda, the time lag is obviously much longer.[9] The overriding purpose is to contrast post-conversion African life with the brutish and savage African past from which the present congregations, descendants of these early converts, are now happily released. It is the present Christian congregation that is now the text's determining audience, replacing the 'home' audience for which the earlier release narratives were primarily published. Although the ostensible theme of the text remains conversion, its principal aim is not to encourage new conversions but to confirm the present, already converted audience in its superior status and correctness of belief, and to reinforce its identity as a people saved from darkness.

In some of these later narratives the 'rescue' and conversion theme extends beyond actual enslavement to metaphorical enslavement by ignorance and heathenism. The release is from the demands of their communities and the 'pagan customs' to which they may be tempted to return. In *The Tale of Rachel Dangilo*, also from the Sheldon series, the burden of its narrative concerns post-conversion trials. Although Rachel, the heroine, has her leg saved by the mission doctor after her release from slavery, where she has been tortured, the text stresses that this is not the central miraculous event. The real miracle is her conversion, since even after the operation she remained lame and in pain throughout her life. The main body of the narrative recounts a series of temptations to return to the pre-Christian community structure. Rachel is praised for following the Bible injunction to 'forsake all others and follow me'. Those

---

9   *The Story of Dorugu*, selections from *Magana Hausa* by J. F. Schon (London, 1932). *Magana Hausa* was first published in Hausa in Berlin in 1857, translated into English by Schön himself in 1885, and revised by Charles E. Robinson in 1906. Both these earlier English collections from which *The Story of Dorugu* is taken were published by the SPCK, who therefore had the English-language rights when they abstracted this story from the collection for the Little Books in Africa series in 1932.

she forsakes include even her parents. This allegory of excision from 'pagan' life clearly aims to arm converted people against temptations to regress into 'pagan ways'. The fact that such regression also involves a rejection of traditional and customary practice is, of course, ignored or even seen as beneficial. Since, as Viswanathan and others have pointed out, conversion need not and often does not involve deculturation and may, indeed, act to stimulate a critical attitude to the society and values of the converting culture as much or even more than of the convert's own culture, the politics of these late publications may be seen as part of a powerful attempt to justify the destructive impact of missions and the larger imperial enterprise within which such cultural onslaughts are embedded.

Although this chapter has concentrated on mission texts about conversion, especially the release narrative that served a variety of evangelical purposes in different historical periods, it has argued that the texts provide a paradigm of the kind of control involved in all imperial narratives. Indeed, as a polemic and instrumental form, mission narratives may be especially prone to such control. The release narratives are ranged alongside other related mission genres in these early to mid-twentieth-century mission series, including the 'lives' which claim the status of a full autobiography, since the amanuensis is removed from the narration. An example (this time from West Africa) in the Sheldon series is *The Life of Aaron Kuku of Eweland Born 1860–Died 1929 By Himself.* This 'autobiography' is nevertheless remarkable for the extent to which it replicates the narrative structures of the earlier missionary tales of 'release' through conversion, as witnessed by its subheadings: 'Childhood', 'The Ashanti War 1869–70', 'The Report of the War to the King', 'How I Was Nearly Killed', 'Three Months with Pagan Priests', 'I See my Father', 'Flight', 'The Return to the Ewe Country', 'At Home', 'The Death of my Wife and How I Revenged her Death', 'I See my Mother and Relations Again', 'I Become a Christian', 'My Work as Evangelist', 'How I Teach'. Despite its more sophisticated shape and a time-frame extended again beyond the moment of conversion, the basic account of pre-mission and pre-colonial African life in these later narrative forms continues to stress its disruptive and barbaric nature. This late mission genre of the exemplary life of the famous convert retains the basic evangelical Christian pattern of sin and redemption derived from the earlier narrative form, incorporated now into this overtly historicized 'autobiographical' form. The title claim to first-person authentic authorship disguises this ongoing control, and here, unlike in the earlier examples discussed, the absence of the amanuensis from the text, far from removing the fundamental narrative control implicit in the form, serves only to disguise more successfully the control exercised by the form and by the institution which maintains and produces it, the mission press.

For all their self-consciously 'liberal' surface and overt praise for the individual achievement of exemplary African converts in these late narratives, African traditional societies are still presented in many of these later mission texts as wholly negative. Intertribal warfare is the 'cause' of the enslavement of the Africans either directly, when they are sold as captives, or indirectly, when they are separated from their families as a result of the disruptions caused by warfare. *The Life of Aaron Kuku of Eweland* continues to structure its story along the established narrative spine of the 'release' form, which has become the standardized, seemingly now inescapable, way of framing any mission-generated African life story even in the late colonial period. Before Africans could fully subvert such controlling mission forms and redirect them to new ends, the narrative forms themselves needed to be substantially reworked and their audiences redefined. In particular, the forms of the ethnography, or 'history', and of the 'exemplary life' needed to be released from the narrative spine inherited from the 'release' form of the conversion narrative culminating in baptism and personal salvation. It needed to be directed away from the salvation of the individual subject towards the preservation and development of the social group and culture he or she represents. In addition the audience of mission-educated 'readers' needed to be perceived not simply as converts but as modern Africans, eager to hear their past presented in positive and affirming ways. Thus Jomo Kenyatta's 1942 text *The Life of Chief Wangombe wa Ihora*, which was itself published by a mission press, displays a clear intention to counter the presentation of the past in missionary exemplary lives as 'nasty, brutish and short'. In Kenyatta's text the mission genre of the exemplary life is employed for a much more radical end, divesting itself of concern with conversion as the narrative conclusion or even its principal subject. Now the form is appropriated for the purpose of establishing and celebrating communal African identity as an alternative model for the future of the peoples of Africa. In this thoroughly appropriated form of the mission genre of the exemplary African life narrative Wangombe wa Ihora is presented as a self-sufficient leader whose example provides his people with the strength to resist enemies and also the insight to be able to form alliances with them. The account records how Wangombe negotiates a peace with the Maasai. The wars of Africa in which he is involved are presented not as the brutal tribal encounters featured in earlier mission texts, but as conflicts analogous to European warfare, with causes rooted in similar processes of expansion, economic interest, and cultural pride, able to be resolved by negotiation between peoples. Kenyatta also records how, at the end of his life, Wangombe warns his people to beware the Europeans and to 'learn their clever way of talking for it is by using your wisdom that you may safeguard your country'.[10] The subject of the mission text is now exhorted to resist control by taking over the form rather than allowing the form to take them over. These late texts thus seek to reverse the low of control across the site of the early mission genre and text.

As this account of these earlier texts has also tried to illustrate, even at the height of that textual control, when the native subject of the text had little or no agency through the control of his or her own representation, the very act of the mission amanuenses engaging discursively with the native 'other' created texts which always threatened to escape the control they sought to embody. In the silences and spaces of the classic accounts of the salvation and conversion of the native subject we may now discern personal and cultural engagements which could never be fully contained within the lineaments of the mission text conventions. Speaker and spoken stand revealed in these texts as intimate enemies, bound together in a linked if unequal process of self-definition. The missionary writing down the life of her native convert expressed and revealed the limitations and boundaries of her own subjectivity even in the act of rendering mute the unacceptable truths of that subject's unmediated expression.

Select Bibliography

Danquah, J. B., *The Akan Doctrine of God: A Fragment of Gold Coast Ethics and Religion* (London, 1944).

Griffiths, Gareth and Jamie S. Scott, eds., *Mixed Messages: Materiality, Textuality, Missions* (New York, 2005).

Griffiths, Gareth and John V. Singler, eds., *J. J. Walters's 'Guanya Pau: The Story of an African Princess'* (Toronto, 2004).

Griffiths, Gareth, *African Literatures in English—East and West* (London, 2000).

Hofmeyr, Isabel, *The Portable Bunyan: A Transnational History of 'The Pilgrim's Progress'* (Princeton, 2004).

Huber, Mary Taylor and Nancy C. Lutkehaus, eds., *Gendered Missions: Women and Men in Missionary Discourse and Practice* (Ann Arbor, 1999).

Johnston, Anna, *Missionary Writing and Empire, 1800–1860* (Cambridge, 2003).

Kenyatta, Jomo, *My People of the Kikuyu and The Life of Chief Wangombe wa Ihora* (London, 1942).

---

10   Jomo Kenyatta, *My People of Kikuyu and The Life of Chief Wangombe wa Ihora.* (London, 1942), p. 63.

Stanley, Brian, ed., *Christian Missions and the Enlightenment* (Cambridge, 2001).

Stilz, Gerhardt ed., *Colonies, Missions, Cultures in the English-Speaking World: General and Comparative Studies*, ZAA Studies, XII (Tübingen, 2000).

Viswanathan, Gauri, *Outside the Fold: Conversion, Modernity and Belief* (Princeton, 1998).

The Quest for Muted Black Voices in History: Some Pertinent Issues in (South) African Mission Historiography

Tinyiko Sam Maluleke

It Walks

But to me it is clear
that even the Black man in Africa
must stand on his feet
in matters of worship
like people in other countries
and not
always expect to be carried
by the White man on his back.
He has long
learnt to walk
by leaning on the
White man
but today he must stand
without leaning on anybody
except his God
so that the work of the Gospel should flourish
The child itself
feels it must walk
it
stumbles and falls
takes one step at a time
but the end result is
that it walks

(Pambani Jeremia Mzimba in Chapman & Dangor 1982:31).

Source: Maluleke, T.S., "The Quest for Muted Black Voices in History: Some Pertinent Issues in (South) African Mission Historiography," *Missionalia* 28.1 (2000): pp. 41–61.

How the Theme Came About*

The theme of the conference at which this essay was born was titled "Black Clergy under Apartheid."[1] However, many of the ideas and issues raised in it had been haunting me for a long while. Basic to many of the mission-historiographical concerns I raise is the fact that the recovery of muted voices in history – blacks, women, the poor etc. – is a task more complex than meets the eye. I appreciate the noble motivations and goal of recovering black presence in history. However I do feel that the theoretical underpinnings of many attempts at recovering black presence in history need to be critically examined.

To begin with, the very categories basic to many proposals of historical revisions and projects of historical retrievals are laden with problems of imprecision and ambiguity. In my presentation at the "Black Clergy under Apartheid" conference I questioned the assumptions hidden behind and in the very category "black clergy" as a way of discussing the relationship between black churches and apartheid. I remarked then that not all "black" clergy under apartheid were "black" and that not all "black clergy" would make interesting and constructive discussion in relation to apartheid – therefore the category needed further unpacking. It is therefore not enough to say that we wish to recover black voices, we need to define the category black in ideological as well as ethical terms. The same principle applies to historical quests for the retrieval of muted voices of women (cf Landman 1999); we need to define which are the women whose voices we wish to retrieve[2] and why. Even more basic has been my suspicion that the recovery of black presence in history must entail more than the sheer introduction of a few new black faces to the same old historical narrative. In an earlier work (Maluleke 1995:224), I had noted the following:

> No amount of new faces and forgotten local actors (the so-called unsung heroes) that are imported into mission history, however necessary and welcome that is, will of itself manage to tilt the missiological scales. In fact, the more this is done, the 'nobler' seems the face of Western

---

* The financial assistance of the National Research Foundation (NRF) towards this research is hereby acknowledged. The opinions and conclusions which are expressed in this essay are those of the author and are not necessarily to be attributed to the NRF.

1 The conference – organized by the University of Natal Oral History Project – was held on the 3rd of July 1999 at the same university and I was one of the invited speakers.

2 Incidentally, while Landman (1999) explains very helpfully how (and why) she intends to retrieve and reconstruct the muted voices of women, she tends to operate with a poorly differentiated virtually homogeneous notion of 'South African women' – which is not very helpful.

THE QUEST FOR MUTED BLACK VOICES IN HISTORY 97

Christendom despite all its 'shortcomings.' In any case, such endeavours of 'digging up' forgotten heroes are mortally hampered by the fact that for a large part, the 'primary sources' out of which the 'forgotten stories' must be reconstructed were created by Western Missionaries.

It is therefore in the full realisation of these types of challenges that I, in the poetic epitaph with which I open this essay, invoke the spirit of Pambani Mzimba, the founder of only the second Ethiopian Church in South Africa – The Presbyterian Church of Africa – which he established around 1893. What Mzimba sought in the ecclesiastical sphere – black presence and self-determination – is similar to what we now seek in mission history, namely a black presence which, though impossible to detach completely from the dominant historiography of White Christendom, can nevertheless walk its own walk without a debilitating dependence on the theoretical crutches of established mission historiography. This intention is noble and must be upheld and pursued vigorously, but its ambiguities and complexities must also be faced. This essay affords me the opportunity to develop these concerns further, some of which have been with me for a long time and others that have emerged in dialogue with colleagues over the past few years.

Attempts at retrieving the muted voices of black clergy under Apartheid are merely one illustration of a growing and larger historiographical concern, namely that of giving voice to the voiceless in history. The emergence and sustenance of a black clergy is indeed a potentially fruitful 'test case' in this kind of historical retrieval as the work of the Oral History Project of the University of Natal in recent years has shown. Ironically, Mzimba was "the first ordained Native minister in connection with the Free Church of Scotland in South Africa" (Shepherd 1940:246) – a 'distinction' which he held for twenty years (cf. Introduction in Denis 1995, Atwell 1995, Millard 1995, Burchell 1979).[3] It is therefore most appropriate that the quest for a black clergy presence in history starts off by paying homage to someone like Mzimba. However, while Mzimba might have been the first to be trained in mission Christendom and ordained within it, other black clergy ordained outside of mainline Christendom appeared in the emerging Ethiopian and Zionist Independent Churches.

---

3 I am aware that Tiyo Soga had been ordained nearly twenty years before Pambani Mzimba and that Soga is (Chalmers 1878) therefore, strictly speaking the first Black clergy person to be ordained. However, Soga was both trained and ordained in Scotland rather than on South African soil. Mzimba is still arguably the first known locally trained Black person to be ordained.

Outline of Essay

I want to be up-front about the fact that as a non-historian I am interested in the theology and ideology of a historical quest for a black presence that 'walks' on its own. Indeed, I will even be interrogating the viability of this very ideal. The aim of this essay is to explore the ideological and theoretical issues at stake in projects of historical retrieval of silenced or marginalized voices. As a theologian it is the historiographical issues implied, invoked and provoked by the project on 'Black clergy under Apartheid' that concern me here, rather than the historical details around the skills needed for such a project to ensue. My essay is divided into three parts: In the first part, I make nine theoretical and historiographical suggestions. Secondly, I sample at least two non-theological tools and theories designed to unravel muted and silenced voices in history. Finally, I make a few evaluations and present a few of the challenges lying ahead.

Nine Proposals

Firstly, I am proposing a close *historical* connection between the emergence of Ethiopian Church leaders (and of other African Independent Churches) and the emergence of black clergy within and outside the ranks of the mission churches. No attempt at retrieving the muted voices of black clergy can afford to ignore the emergence of African Independent Churches as the alternative and earliest contexts in which black clergy leadership was exercised and nurtured. It is therefore unfortunate that, except for one paper (Kamphausen 1995, Moripe 1995), almost all the other papers in *The Making of an indigenous Clergy* fail to recognize the connection between Ethiopianism/ Independentism and the emergence of a black clergy. However, historical evidence abounds to indicate direct connection between the emergence of some Ethiopian and other AIC churches and the making of black clergy. In an ironic kind of way, therefore, Sundkler's *Bantu Prophets in South Africa* was one of the first deliberate and ideologically conscious reflections on black, Bantu or 'indigenous clergy in Southern Africa'[4] – even though it has seldom been looked at in this way. Hitherto, black clergy presence in the church had not been the subject of serious theological inquiry beyond the occasional essays triggered off by the fear and alarm over schisms – not that Sundkler's work was free of these fears!

---

4   I am deliberately playing on the title of Denis (1995): *The Making of an Indigenous Clergy.*

Secondly, black clergy are a product of contestation and struggles. Historically, black clergy *emerged* out of three processes: a) as the gradual outcome of a closely managed and monitored process born of (often reluctant) missionary tutelage; b) as actual and mostly defiant initiatives by some black clergy 'to stand on their own feet' in matters of worship; and c) as a massive movement of hundreds of unsung local missionaries – male, female, groups and individuals. All three these processes are hegemonic struggles – contestation for and against control – in which local people had the odds stacked heavily against them. In other words, the very emergence of black clergy is a product and symbol of these struggles. The very need and effort to manage their 'birth' – carefully and 'gradually' – is a sign of contest, calculation and hegemonic battles. Therefore, there has always been something ideological about black clergy, so that to speak of and write about black clergy is to be drawn into an old and ongoing ideological 'battle' – a battle which is old and ongoing at the same time. Old in terms of historical sources but ongoing at a historiographical and ideological level. Even those seemingly innocent black clergy who 'quietly went on with their work' – as it were – have not and cannot escape the ideological taint of which I speak.

Thirdly – and this relates to the foregoing point – if we are to do our job well as historians and commentators on black clergy in Southern Africa, we must do more than unearth new information about Black clergy – necessary though that is. The fact that "indigenous clergy are only mentioned in passing if at all [and that] their views are not reflected in the written documentation" (Denis 1995:9), although they were crucial in mission, is not accidental. These were not 'mistakes' and 'errors' of omission committed under time and space constraints. If we 'do' our black clergy history and black clergy missiology as if all that is needed is to correct omissions, we commit a grave disservice. The absence of black clergy from history books, centenary celebration books and church records has always been ideological and theological – if you like. There were theologies and ideologies of church history that sanctioned and legitimated the 'exclusion' of black clergy. Therefore, my sense is that any attempt to chronicle the black clergy in South Africa must 'do battle' on at least two levels right from the onset, all the time: a) at the level of creativity and innovation in finding or/and constructing sources for histories of indigenous clergy – which is what the Oral History Project of the University of Natal attempts to do[5] – and b) at the level of theology and ideology.

---

5 Something I myself tried to do in my doctoral thesis (Maluleke 1995).

Fourth, there must be some merit in the mere and sheer multiplication of historical narratives on black clergy, so that there is a gradual and deliberate increment of black voices in mission history. It is possible that these individual voices and individual historical accounts may eventually erupt into a powerful choir that will ultimately drown out the powerful hegemonic voice in history. However, I submit that this will not happen automatically through the sheer introduction of new faces into church history. Hegemony and ideology are much more structured and resourceful, and will not be out-manoeuvered by a mere numerical increase. Indeed – as hinted in an earlier quote above – the mere introduction of new black faces into 'official' church histories may achieve the very aim of strengthening and legitimising hegemonic theologies of history – by filling in the 'blank spaces' without subverting the hegemonic frames and the logic that hold the spaces together.

Fifth, for various reasons, the category 'black clergy' must be redefined to mean more than ordained individual black actors. Our interest here is in *the agency of black Christians*, not only in mission but in defining themselves religiously in the face of missionary control, but also in the face of modernity, conquest and dispossession. The ecclesiastical baggage of the term 'clergy' may prove unhelpful – regardless of the adjective we put before it. It is very difficult to move away conceptually from the facile dualism of clergy vs laity – even though such a dualism has proven very difficult to sustain practically in many black churches. As an ecclesiastical guild, the black clergy are a very problematic group – even more problematic than other categories of black Christians. Black clergy were members of an emerging middle class who were "in the frontlines of struggles in a society divided not only by class, but also by race ... [who shared in] the stresses and strains of their class position" (Saayman 1996:59). Worse still, while the term "black cergy" may help us articulate a prophetic word about racism in the church, the term does not even begin to address questions of gender – more precisely the exclusion and devaluing of the role and input of women.

Sixth, since the times of slavery, the designation, definition and naming of black people has been – and appears to continue to be – problematic, much more problematic than the designation 'white', even though the two notions are virtual mirror-image concepts.[6] The reason why the former has always been more problematic is mainly due to the powerlessness that has come to epitomise so much of black existence during the past five centuries at least. In Southern Africa, for example, people of colour have been called 'Natives',

---

6   For a classical discussion on the pathology of *being* black and *naming* black, see Fanon (1986).

'Caffres', 'Africans', 'Bantus', 'Plurals', etc. For roughly comparable reasons the naming of black people in the USA has also been problematic: 'niggers', negros, blacks and more recently African-Americans. The 'restlessness' in the naming and designation of black people is due to the fact that the initiative for their (re)naming has often come from the outside, from powerful *others*. Even when black people have sought to wrest the naming initiative from those who seek to name them from the outside, they have simply increased the intensity and changed the tone of the restlessness rather than eliminated it.

What has all this to do with our historical quest for a black presence that 'walks?' I am suggesting that the category 'black clergy' is necessarily tainted with all the naming and self-definitional problems associated with black peoples. Shall we therefore abandon the designation? No, that is definitely not what I would suggest. My proposal is that the naming 'problems' of black people are, and should be, a legitimate historiographical issue. This is especially the case in such a specific – and I would add ideological – historical quest as the one that seeks to highlight and construct a black presence. In other words, this is as much a historical quest as it is a confrontation with the historical mechanisms, processes and motivations of black self-naming and black 'othering'. I want to suggest – following Black Consciousness – that blackness (or Africanness, for that matter) is a condition – a material, spiritual and cultural condition. It is *more* than skin colour, because there are, strictly speaking no 'black' and 'white' people. Therefore, unlike Denis' definition of 'indigenous clergy' as "any clergy who were born on the African soil" (Denis 1995:10), it would not be enough for someone merely to have a black skin and to be born in Africa for that person to be called black. True, skin blackness would be an important clue and signifier but it is not an ultimate criterion. However blackness must include some ethical and existential set of self-positioning and self-understanding beyond the ontological reality of having a black skin.

Seventh, to advance the foregoing argument from a different angle, not all black people who engaged in mission and ministry would qualify for automatic inclusion in the category 'black clergy'. Not all black missionaries asserted and signified a 'black presence.' In other words, the black agency and presence which we seek to construct is not an arbitrary one, in which all black Christians participate simply by virtue of being Christian, black and clergy. Is it possible that black Christians who were ruthless with their own kind, denigrating their culture and ruthlessly oppressing them, did less for black presence in history – despite their black skins – than the Van der Kemps and John William Colenso's (cf. Guy 1983)? The black presence we seek is not an ideologically neutral one. It is just as possible for a black clergy person to be anti-black and un-African. Not every activity by blacks in mission and ministry attests to black presence in history. Therefore the historical quest for black clergy presence should not amount to a catch-all expedition where every 'black' activity and every apparent black agency is automatically owned. This is a moral, ethical, ideological and theological quest – and 'black presence' must therefore include ethical, ideological and theological dimensions.

Eighth, historiography has to do with the quest to assign meaning to events, whether they be imagined or real. History-writing (especially the history of Christianity) is therefore – whatever else it may be – both an ethical, moral and evaluatory enterprise. Therefore, according to Dussel (1992:12), there should be overt criteria of historical evaluation. He suggests, for example, that if we take the 'bringing of good news' as Jesus'

> specific historical purpose and that of his church, this must also be the absolute and primary criterion of a *Christian* interpretation of the history of the church ... [so that] the meaning of an event, (then), is deduced from the effect (positive or negative) it has on the poor, the oppressed, the ordinary people. The criterion for writing the history of the church is not the triumphalism of the great cathedrals or the splendor of papal coronations of emperors, but the mutual love in the 'breaking of bread' in persecuted, poor, missionary, prophetic Christian communities.

Dussel goes further to unpack the notion of 'the poor' into the categories of those dominated in terms of race, sex and class.

Lastly, recent studies – certainly recent in theology – are suggesting that the manner in which the mutedness, the domination and the resistance of black clergy and black Christians are conceptualized may need to be revisited (De Certeau 1984, Scott 1985, 1990; Harries 1994, Petersen 1995, Comaroff & Comaroff 1992, 1997). The call is for a recognition of the coded 'arts of resistance' (Scott 1990, Petersen 1995) that dominated groups use in order to mitigate, subvert and survive their domination. Consequently it is being suggested that domination, survival, resistance and agency are notions that need to be understood anew if we are ever to grasp what goes on in situations of domination and marginalisation.

Site for the Fiercest Battles

The nine proposals briefly outlined above are, in my opinion, some of the key theoretical issues that need to inform our quests for the retrieval of muted black voices in mission history. How easy our job would have been if it was a clear cut case that black Christians functioned unambiguously, definitively and pro-actively as agents in both Christian mission and modernity! Our quest for a historical presence that 'walks' would then merely be one of documentation, with only the occupational hazard of finding information. But things are more complex than the new proposals (cf. Scott 1990, Petersen 1995) of old suggestions that the dominated were truly, thoroughly and completely dominated.

Neither the whole truth nor the last word has yet been said on these issues – and my efforts in this essay are also not the 'last word' on the subject. As hinted in several places above, the extent, manner and meaning of black presence in both Christian mission is both ambiguous and fiercely contested. For this reason, "the construction of a local 'response' and/or perspective on Christian mission is (therefore) fraught with many difficulties" (Maluleke 1995:23, cf. Maluleke 1993) – both of a practical and interpretative kind. At the practical level there is the lack of written sources, especially those written from an insider's perspective. However, it is at the hermeneutical and theoretical levels that the fiercest contests are being waged and still need to be waged.

Indeed, the very idea that blacks (or indigenous people) acted with creativity and initiative in relation to modernity and Christian mission is a fairly recent one – at least in theology. For a long time, the very possibility was unthinkable. Black people were generally seen by both friend and foe as objects of Christian mission, modernity and history, but seldom as subjects. It is true that individual 'exceptional' and 'model' black 'actors' in mission might have been identified and written about as progenitors – yet even these usually evoked ambiguous if not ambivalent evaluations (cf. Chalmers 1878). And yet this muting of black voices was done and projected not merely because of the badness of the hearts of missionaries and historians. It was the product of complex relations of power and intense struggles for hegemony.

For this reason, attempts at writing blacks (or any other subordinate group) back into history cannot proceed innocently of these complexities. To engage in any attempt at a 'recovery' of black presence in history is to be drawn into the struggles and power relations of the historical actors themselves. To skip over the theoretical issues highlighted above, would be like rushing into a warzone without arms and without ammunition. In South African Black Theology, Mosala (1989) has shown the importance of theoretical astuteness as well as the worrying possibility of 'theoretical bankruptcy' in several theological constructions which purport to be liberative – especially in the construction of those theologies that purport to give voice to the poor and the oppressed.

Recent Notions of Black Agency in History

Central to several proposals in current Black and African Theology is the issue of *agency* (cf. Maluleke 1996a, 1996b, 1997a, 1997b, 1998, 2000): African theologians are no longer satisfied with starting points that portray Africans as passive victims in either the missionary or the colonial process. Many theologians have realized that Apartheid and oppression cannot and do not have the last word on the reality of oppressed and marginalised black peoples. For these kinds of reasons we have seen a search for new theological categories and new conceptualisations of domination and resistance.

Locally and continentally, we have seen an increased unease with 'grand narrative' notions of 'liberation', 'African culture', 'African Theology' etc. among African Christian theologians. Incidentally, and contrary to popular perceptions, this unease predates the more recent suggestions of post-exilic *reconstruction* as a 'replacement' for *liberation* and *inculturation* in African Theology. It must be remembered that Black and African theologies have also functioned as a critique of notions of liberation in both Latin American theologies of liberation and European political theologies. The irruption of feminist and women's theologies on the African continent provided yet another impetus for unease with certain notions of liberation. Therefore, the deconstruction of African theologies predates and supercedes both the ending of the cold war and the ending of Apartheid.

What I find worrying is the lack of awareness, acknowledgement and dialogue between current proposals and previous ones. In fact many current proposals for new approaches in African Theology are not based on clear, incisive, coherent and persuasive deconstructions of such notions as "Africa", "liberation" and the "new world order". Until this is done, I suspect that many of the reconstruction proposals derive more from optimistic excitement about the new world order, packaged in the promises of global capitalism – otherwise known as globalisation. To the extent that I may be correct what is being offered is nothing new – it is old hegemonic grand narratives under new names. The dose of optimism that permeates many current proposals is understandable, and for some even necessary, given Africa's lot in the 20th century. However, much more is needed than the optimistic foregrounding of perceived opportunities for Africa, Africans and African Theology as a result of the alleged momentous socio-political changes ushered in during the last 21 years of the 20th century. For these kinds of reasons I am not yet persuaded by most proposals of reconstruction as a viable paradigm in African theology – and I include in this critique the proposals of Jesse Mugambi (1995) and Kä Mana (2000).[7] Visions and understandings of African agency should derive from more than the end of Apartheid and of the cold war on the one hand or the optimism of a globalizing world. Indeed they need to predate and supercede not only the end of the cold war but its very emergence.

What many current proposals of African agency have in common is that they attempt to re-assert the agency of Black/African actors in history and in this way move away from defeatist victim-portrayals (cf Maluleke 2000). This is done variously, with notions such as translation, reconstruction, reconciliation, post-colonialism and coded resistance playing a key role in these constructions. In this regard, the appropriation of the works of the like of the Comaroffs and Scott (already cited above) – among others – have become popular and important. I think it is important for everyone interested in the recovery of silenced voices to listen to these new emerging approaches. For that reason I shall devote space to a brief discussion of each of them. The value of the excercise is mainly illustrative. The point I am making is that African agency – whether it be couched in the language of historical retrievals of muted voices, or in the enthusiastic quest for an 'African Christian renaissaince' (cf Bediako 1998, Kä Mana 2000, Mugambi 1995) cannot and should not be taken for granted. It needs to be approached and defined in a structured, precise and deliberate manner – otherwise the ambiguities will be missed and the complexities overlooked. The reference to Scott and the Comaroffs below intends to analyse the manner in which they frame agency.

John and Jean Comaroff

Two jointly written volumes, several individual works, as well as some publications in collaboration with others have established the Comaroffs (1986, 1989, 1991, 1997) – anthropologists by training – as key theoreticians on the question of the encounter between Christian missionaries and Africans. They posit a complex notion of agency for the Tswana interlocutors of the 18th and 19th century. Mindful of the deficiencies in earlier anthropological, historical and missiological studies in this area – especially what they see as the over-emphasis on political economy at the expense of ideology, symbolism and culture, the Comaroffs (1991) clearly mean to account for the actions and consciousness of

---

7   I grant that both Mugambi and Kä Mana (2000:26,27) – especially the latter – present powerful and pursuasive suggestions that now is the time for the invention of a new Africa and a new African theology.

both the "agents" of domination (e.g. the missionaries) and the dominated (e.g. the Southern Tswana).

This is a noteworthy point in their methodology. It is a deliberate departure from well-meaning but inadequate studies that merely posit and describe black resistance in homogeneous and simplistic terms on the one hand, and White colonisers and missionaries (in much the same way) on the other. It is this situation which the Comaroffs wish to remedy. What adds value and weight to their work – apart from theoretical erudition – is the empirical basis of the work among the Tswana of Phokeng near Rustenburg:

> We trace out a colonial encounter of the first kind, the moment when two systems of meaning and action – one imperial and expansive, the other local and defensive – begin to engage one another. The process presents itself most accessibly in letters, reports, and published works ... But there is also a discernable Tswana commentary on these events, spoken less in the narrative voice than in the symbolism of gesture, action and reaction and in the expressive manipulation of language. The interplay, of course, was between two parties of incommensurate power; this being reflected in the fact that the evangelists [meaning missionaries, TSM] were acutely aware of their capacity to 'make' history (Comaroffs 1988:6).

This quote captures the basic theory and methodology of the Comaroffs. It is an approach that seeks to reconfigure and even redefine the power terrain between missionaries and local people. In this approach an attempt is made not to dismiss, but to go beyond the written records,[8] by offering a theory for both a 'new reading' of these sources and a gaze towards the local actors. Furthermore, for the Comaroffs, what happened between missionaries and local people was an 'encounter', not straight-forward conquest, cultural invasion or a one-way-traffic evangelistic current from the missionaries to the local people. However, it was also 'a colonial encounter.' The encounter was between two systems of meaning and being – systems that were equally valid as 'plausibility structures' and held equally dearly by both sets of adherents. The Comaroffs argue that a lot more was taking place in the encounter than conquest or the cultural invasion of Christian evangelism. For this reason, they call the encounter a 'long *conversation*' rather than a *conversion* of the one group to the system of the other. As the Comaroffs would be quick to point out, it was

---

8 Although I used written records, it was these kinds of sentiments from the Comaroffs which inspired me to venture into using vernacular novels, plays, poems and history books in my PhD thesis (Maluleke 1995).

not a benevolent fair-play encounter, but a contest for the control of salient signs and symbols. In a passage that reveals both their hypothesis and their conclusions, the Comaroffs argue that the main objective of colonisers – missionaries especially – was to:

> colonize the(ir) consciousness [of local peoples] with the axioms and aesthetics of an alien culture. This culture – the culture of European capitalism, of western modernity – had, and continues to have, enormous historical force – a force at once ideological and economic, semantic and social. In the face of it, some black Africans have succumbed, some have resisted, some have tried to recast its intrusive forms in their own image. Most have done all these things, at one or another time, in the effort to formulate an awareness of, and to gain a measure of mastery over, their changing world. ... no wonder that, in our attempt to understand the Southern Tswana past and present, we kept being drawn back to the colonization of their consciousness and their consciousness of colonization (Comaroffs 1991:21).

Thus should be understood the 'long conversation' between the colonisers and the colonised – a conversation in the process of which "many of the signifiers of the colonizing culture became unfixed ... seized by the Africans and, sometimes refashioned, put to symbolic and practical ends previously unforeseen, certainly unintended ... [inaugurating] a process in which signifiers were set afloat, fought over, and recaptured on both sides of the colonial encounter" (Comaroffs 1991:17). And yet the Comaroffs will not rest their case on signifiers which are constantly and permanently afloat – forever being transformed and interpreted; that would be too postmodernist for them (Petersen 1995:121). They argue that "history everywhere is actively made in a dialectic of order and disorder, consensus and contest," so there emerges even in the face of the 'long conversation' "a new kind of hegemony amidst – and despite – cultural contestation" (Comaroffs 1991:17).

Therefore, the Comaroffs do not give up on hegemony completely; for, although the dominated resist creatively and in various ways, the dominant ideas *do* accumulate and constitute a set of powerful signs that map or classify the world for others. The notions of 'hegemony' and 'ideology' therefore remain crucial theoretical frameworks for the Comaroffs – but they locate these in an analytical répertoire which includes culture, consciousness, power and representation. Rejecting the simplistic notions of cultural imperialism, they nevertheless argue – unlike Scott (1990) – that the colonising project is not a simple dialectic of domination and resistance. The Comaroffs recognize the existence of a realm of the conscious and the unconscious between which there is a liminal space in which people discern acts and symbols but cannot or do not make sense of them with any coherence, so that although they know something is happening to them, they cannot quite put their finger on it.

James Scott

As the title of both his books betray, the work of Scott (1985, 1990) is about domination and the arts of resistance, that is, the 'weapons of the weak.' The Comaroffs and Scott do not appear to be seriously aware of each other's works – although Scott makes two brief illustrative and approving references to the work of Jean Comaroff (1985). Although their works are not synonymous in scope, let alone in orientation and approach, there are points of affinity and comparison – a comparison which unfortunately falls outside the scope of this study.[9] The Comaroffs, on the one hand, are weary of an over-emphasis on political economy at the expense of culture and symbolism that denies black Africans any historical dynamism and runs the danger of painting the actions of all colonisers with the same brush. Scott, on the other hand, is weary of a deterministic understanding of notions such as hegemony and its power over subordinates. Scott casts doubt over the suggestion that subordinates can be thoroughly incorporated into the hegemonic scheme of things through the cultivation and acceptance of a false consciousness. For Scott, there is a different, creative, empirical and more reliable way of understanding the relationship between domination and resistance. A careful study of the arts of resistance among subordinate groups will ensure that "we are not reduced to waiting for open social protest to lift a veil of consent and quiescence. A view of politics focused either on what may be command performances of consent or open rebellion represents a far too narrow concept of political life – especially under conditions of tyranny or near-tyranny in which much of the world lives" (Scott 1990:20).

Similarly, the Comaroffs argue that hegemony is never in total control, but Scott goes further and suggests that even the hold that hegemony seems to have on subordinates is deceptive and unreliable – things are not what they seem to be. Hence Scott distinguishes between public and hidden "transcripts." In public, surbordinates act and speak in the required ways, but there is a

---

9   According to Petersen (1995:100), the Comaroffs, James Scott and Michel de Certeau 'belong together' theoretically: a) they all are concerned with coded resistance, b) 'All of them, but in very different ways, seek to provide means to read beneath the surface on intentionality, self-consciousness, and overt expressions of resistance.' However, Petersen is quick to note that 'they all utilize not only a different conceptual schema for their analyses, but also understand the key notions of consciousness and agency very differently.'

THE QUEST FOR MUTED BLACK VOICES IN HISTORY · 109

"hidden transcript" that happens behind the curtains and behind the backs of the dominant groups. If Scott is correct, then it is the hidden transcripts that our quest for muted voices should focus on. The public arena is unreliable because it provides an "encounter of the public transcript of the dominant with the public transcript of the subordinate" (Scott 1990:13). But, as the subtitle of his book reveals, it is the sphere of "hidden transcripts" – the sphere of infrapolitics – which is the real clue to what takes place in situations of dominance and resistance. To gain new insights into resistance we have to go "behind the official story" (Scott 1990:17) to the hidden transcript where we will observe – as Scott did among peasant Malay rice-farming labourers – that:

> Rather than openly rebel or publicly protest, they adopted the safer course of anonymous attacks on property, poaching, character assassination, and shunning. They prudently avoided, with few exceptions, any irrevocable acts of public defiance (Scott 1990:17).

"Prudent" is a key word here. According to Scott, the dominated "know" the extent or meaning of their domination and are consciously – and prudently – choosing to act in hidden transcript. Therefore, for the surbodinate group, the hidden, transcript is a conscious, calculated and crafty "art" of resistance – "a wide variety of low-profile forms of resistance that dare not speak in their own name." The public transcript is "the *self*-portrait of dominant elites as they would have themselves seen" (Scott 1990:18). Therefore, we must be weary of reading too much into acts of deference expected and "required" of subordinates in highly stratified societies. However, even such acts – whether in word or in gesture – must not be seen "merely as performances extracted by power. The fact is they serve also as a barrier and a veil that the dominant find difficult or impossible to penetrate" (Scott 1990:32).

Domination always implies and provokes resistance of one sort or another. Therefore domination needs resourceful maintenance and constant reinforcement. This, then, is a key function of the public transcript of the dominant elite – to constantly maintain and reinforce domination, through a variety of acts designed to conceal, euphemise and stigmatise the harsher side of power and control, while at the same time seeking to display the power of the dominant through open rituals and ceremonies.

To conclude this section, let me recapitulate. Basically, Scott points to spaces for political life ("sequerated social sites" – Scott 1990:20) which are – in his opinion – seldom recognised in Marxist and even Gramscian political analyses. These spaces lie between the ideas of "command performance of consent" and explicit rebellion – it is the spaces of hidden transcripts.

Unconcluding Thoughts

In the first part of the essay, I have highlighted the kinds of theoretical issues that I believe to be at stake in the quest for black presence and agency in history. These insights are not offered in a dogmatic way, but as possible areas seeking further exploration. It seems as if the notion of agency has become very central to all kinds of revisions of both African mission history and African theology. The emerging discussions around agency are both promising and problematic. The promise of the emerging discussion lies in the fact that several coherent theoretical frameworks are suggested within which historical revision with a bias towards muted voices may be carried out.

Without constructive and well-thought out theories in our hands, many attempts at giving voice to the voiceless in history may fail or – worse still – reinforce the very dominant views we wish to challenge. The notions of infrapolitics, conversation, coded resistance, etc. offer various possibilities for projects of historical retrieval. There is indeed a sense of frustration with starting points that reinforce the victimhood of subordinate and oppressed groups.

However, there are also potential problems and hazards. The overwhelming majority of people advancing theoretical tools with which to understand the survival and "coded resistance" tactics of the poor and marginalised are not themselves members of this class. In other words, it is as if whites were saying that the blacks whom they oppress are not really crushed by their oppression; as if men were discussing the manner in which women subvert and code their resistance against patriarchy; as if the rich were unmasking and praising the survival strategies of the poor, etc.

What function would such discourses serve? What is the ideological function of the rediscovery of the hidden resources of muted voices? Who speaks? Who is silent? Who pays the price? It is one thing when marginalized groups engage in resistance strategies and resistance discourses but quite another when it is done by Whites and by men. Its ultimate function – conscious or unconscious – may be to romanticise life under oppression. But victims of oppression, domination and exclusion know through experience that there is nothing pleasant or romantic about domination or resistance to domination. For outsiders to insist that crushed and brutalized people are not totally crushed is to sustain and perpetuate their brutalization.

Similarly, there is nothing clever or positive about survival – it emanates from pure human instinct. Victimised and poor people do not mistake survival for resistance. A rushed equation of the two might say more about the motives of the dominant than the experience of the dominated. Therefore our historiography cannot buy totally and completely into any of the notions of agency being propagated. Often there is no time or space even for coded resistance. Therefore, contrary to what Scott (1985) suggests, the discourse of coded resistance might in fact be a 'weapon of the strong' rather than a 'weapon of the weak'. For members of the dominant classes to insist that crushed and surviving people are coping and resisting – despite "appearances" – can be just as cruel as crushing and constantly harassing them. Such an insistence benefits the dominant classes more than the dominated. Those who adopt this posture in their attempts to recover muted voices must therefore beware of the pitfalls of an unqualified insistence on the agency of the weak.

Furthermore, not all proposals purporting to highlight African agency actually do that. It is, for example, debatable whether Sanneh's translation emphasis really highlights the agency and initiative of Africans in their encounter with missionary Christianity and colonialism. Apart from attributing almost everything creative done by Africans to the genius and logic of the gospel, the proposal seems more concerned with the activities of missionaries and colonialists than those of Africans.

Equally unhelpful is the insistence and ambition of some: a) to have us all regard the ending of legal Apartheid and of the cold war as the main engine out of which African agency must now be generated, and b) to suggest that there are only two or three umbrella paradigms under which African agency can be explored and asserted, e.g. the paradigms of reconstruction, inculturation, or liberation (understood as a grand narrative). On the contrary, African agency is varied, nuanced and much less romantic than some of the proposals imply. Like the future of African Theology, African agency is no longer what it used to be. Long-held expectations either that the agendas of liberation. and inculturation would embrace, cancel each other out or make way for completely new agendas have not materialized. These agendas refuse to leave us in peace (cf Mveng & Lipawing 1996). If anything, they are complicating, but they are not disappearing. It is not as if reconstruction is or ever will be replacing liberation anymore than is feminism replacing inculturation. Reality is far more explosive and more varied than that. Contrary to previous expectations and predictions, the future is not ONE but MANY. It is therefore in the explosion of variety, nuance and ambiguity and not in the comfort of mono-paradigms that African agency must be sought and constructed. It is my considered opinion that quests for the recovery of black and other marginal presences in past and present history ignore the kinds of issues raised in this essay at their own peril.

List of References Cited

Atwell, David 1995. "The Transculturation of Enlightenment. The Exemplary Case of the Rev Tiyo Soga, African Nationalist". In *The Making of An Indigenous Clergy in Southern Africa*, edited by Philippe Denis. Pietermaritzburg: Cluster, 41–57.

Barret, D. 1968. *Schism and Renewal in Africa: An Analysis of Six Thousand Contemporary Religious Movements*. Nairobi: Oxford University Press.

Bediako, Kwame 1998. "Facing the Challenge: Africa in World Christianity in the 21st Century. A Vision of the African Christian Future". *Journal of African Christian Thought*, 1:1 (June), 52–57.

Burchell, D. E. 1979. *A History of the Lovedale Missionary Institution 1890–1930*. MA dissertation, University of Natal, Pietermaritzburg.

Chalmers, James 1878. *Tiyo Soga. A Page of South African Mission Work*. Edinburgh: Andrew Elliot.

Chapman, Michael & Dangor, Achmat 1982. *Voices From Within. Black Poetry From Southern Africa*. Cape Town: Ad Donker.

Comaroff, Jean 1985. *Body of Power, Spirit of Resistance: The Culture and History of a South African People*. Chicago: University of Chicago Press.

Comaroff, John and Jean 1986. "Christianity and Colonialism in South Africa". *American Ethnologist*, No. 13, 1–20.

Comaroff, John and Jean 1988. "Through the Looking-Glass: Colonial Encounters of the First Kind". *Journal of Historical Sociology*, 1:1 (March), 6–13.

Comaroff, John L. and Jean 1989. "The Colonization of Consciousness in South Africa". *Economy and Society*, No. 12, 267–295.

Comaroff, John and Jean 1991. *Of Revelation and Revolution (Vol.1): Christianity, Colonialism and Consciousness in South Africa*. Chicago: University of Chicago Press.

Comaroff, John and Jean 1997. *Of Revelation and Revolution (Vol.2): The Dialectics of Modernity on a South African Frontier*. Chicago: University of Chicago Press.

Cooper, Frederick 1994. "Conflict and Connection: Rethinking Colonial African History". *American Historical Review*, 99:5 (December), 1516–1545.

De Certeau, Michel 1984. *The Practice of Everyday Life*. Translated by S. Rendall. Berkeley: University of California Press.

De Kock, Leon 1996. *Civilizing Barbarians. Missionary Narrative and African Textual Response in Nineteenth-Century South Africa*. Lovedale: Lovedale Press.

Denis, Philippe (ed.) 1995. *The Making of an Indigenous Clergy in Southern Africa*. Proceedings of the International Conference held at the University of Natal, Pietermaritzburg, 25–27 October 1994. Pietermaritzburg: Cluster.

Draper, Jonathan 1998. "Recovering Oral Tradition from Text in 'Q'". Unpublished Draft Essay.

THE QUEST FOR MUTED BLACK VOICES IN HISTORY 113

Dube, Musa 1996. "Readings of Semoya: Batswana Women's Interpretations of Matt 15:21–28". *Semeia*, No. 73, 111–129.

Dussel, Enrique (ed.) 1992. *The Church in Latin America. 1492–1992*. Maryknoll: Orbis.

Fanon, Frantz 1986. *Black Skin, White Masks*. London: Pluto [First published in 1952].

Guy, Jeff 1983. *The Heretic. A Study of the Life of John William Colenso. 1814–1883*. Braamfontein: Ravan.

Harries, P. 1994. *Work, Culture and Identity. Migrant Laborers in Mozambique and South Africa, c 1860–1910*. Johannesburg: Wits University Press.

Hodgson, Janet 1985. Ntsikana: History and Symbol. Studies in a Process of Change among Xhosa-Speaking People. PhD thesis, University of Cape Town.

Junod, H. P. 1960. *Mufundhisi John Mboweni*. Johannesburg: Swiss Mission in South Africa.

Kamphausen, Erhard 1995. "Unknown Heroes. The Founding Fathers of the Ethiopian Movement in South Africa". In Denis 1995, 83–101.

Khabela, Gideon M. 1996. *Tiyo Soga. The Struggle of the Gods. A Study in Christianity and the African Culture*. Lovedale: Lovedale Press.

Kpobi, David Nii Anum 1993. *Mission in Chains. The Life, Theology and Ministry of the Ex-slave Jacobus E. J. Capitein (1717–1747). With a Translation of his Major Publications*. Zoetermeer: Boekencentrum.

Landman, Christina 1999. *The Piety of South African Women*. Pretoria: CB Powel Bible Centre.

Maluleke, Tinyiko Sam 1993. "Mission, Ethnicity and Homeland – The Case of the EPCSA". *Missionalia*, 21:3 (Nov 1993), 236–252.

Maluleke, Tinyiko S. 1995. "A Morula Tree between Two Fields." The Commentary of Selected Tsonga Writers on Missionary Christianity. DTh thesis, University of South Africa.

Maluleke, Tinyiko Sam 1996a. "Black and African Theologies in the New World Order. A Time to Drink from Our Own Wells". *Journal of Theology for Southern Africa*, No. 96 (November 1996), 3–19.

Maluleke, Tinyiko Sam 1996b. "Recent Developments in the Christian Theologies of Africa. Towards the 21st Century". *Journal of Constructive Theology*, 2.2 (December 1996), 33–60.

Maluleke, Tinyiko Sam 1997a. "In Search of the True Character of African Christian Identity. A Review of the Theology of Kwame Bediako". *Missionalia*, 25:2 (August 1997), 210–219.

Maluleke, Tinyiko Sam 1997b. "Half a Century of Christian Theologies of Africa. Elements of the Emerging Agenda for the 21st Century". *Journal of Theology for Southern Africa*, No. 99 (November 1997), 4–23.

Maluleke, Tinyiko S. 1998. "African Traditional Religions in Christian Mission and Christian Scholarship: Re-Opening a Debate that Never Started". *Religion and Theology*, 5:2, 121–137.

Maluleke, Tinyiko Sam 2000. "Black and African Theology After Apartheid and After the Cold War – An Emerging Paradigm. *Exchange*, 29:3 (July), 193–212.

Mana, Kä 2000. *La nouvelle évangélisation en Afrique*. Yaounde: éditions Clé.

Martin, Marie-Louise 1975. *Kimbangu, an African Prophet and His Church*. Oxford: Oxford University Press.

Millard, Joan A. 1995a. *A Study of the Perceived Causes of Schism in Some Ethiopian-Type Churches in the Cape and the Transvaal, 1884–1925*.

Millard, Joan 1995b. "Educating Indigenous Clergy in Some South African Protestant Churches During the Nineteenth Century". In Denis 1995, 58–68.

Moripe, Simon 1995. "Indigenous Clergy in the Zion Christian Church". In Denis 1995, 102–107.

Mosala, Itumeleng 1989. *Biblical Hermeneutics and Black Theology in South Africa*. Grand Rapids: Eerdmans.

Mosala, Itumeleng 1996. "Race, Class, and Gender as Hermeneutical Factors in the African Independent Churches' Appropriation of the Bible". *Semeia*, No. 73, 43–57.

Mveng Englebert & Lipawing, B.L. 1996. *Theologie, Liberation et Cultures Africaines. Dialogue sur l'anthropologie négro-africaine*. Yaounde: éditions Clé.

Parrat, John 1995. *Reinventing Christianity. African Theology Today*. Grand Rapids: Eerdmans.

Petersen, Robin M. 1995. *Time, Resistance and Reconstruction. A Theology of the Prophetic and the Popular*. Pietermaritzburg: Cluster [Forthcoming].

Saayman, Willem 1996. *A Man with a Shadow. The Life and Times of Professor ZK Matthews*. Pretoria: Unisa Press.

Sanneh, Lamin 1983. *West African Christianity. The Religious Impact*. London: Hurst.

Sanneh, Lamin 1983. "The Horizontal and the Vertical in Mission. An African Perspective". *International Bulletin of Missionary Research*, 7:4 (October), 165–171.

Sanneh, Lamin 1989. *Translating the Message. The Missionary Impact on Culture*. Maryknoll: Orbis.

Sanneh, Lamin 1993. *Encountering the West. Christianity and the Global Cultural Process*. Maryknoll: Orbis.

Sanneh, Lamin 1995. "The Gospel, Language and Culture: The Theological Method in Cultural Analysis". *International Review of Mission*, 84 (No. 332/333) (January/April), 47–64.

Scott, James C. 1985. *Weapons of the Weak: Everyday Forms of Peasant Resistance*. Yale: University Press.

Scott, James C. 1990. *Domination and the Arts of Resistance. Hidden Transcripts*. Yale: University Press.

Shepherd, Robert H. W. 1940. *Lovedale. South Africa. The Story of a Century 1841–1941*. Lovedale: Lovedale Press.

Sundkler, Bengt 1948. *Bantu Prophets in South Africa.* London: Oxford University Press.

Sundkler, Bengt 1976. *Zulu Zion and Some Swazi Zionists.* Oxford: Oxford University Press.

Walls, Andrew F. 1976. "Towards Understanding Africa's Place in Christian History". In *Religion in a Pluralistic Society*, edited by J. S. Pobee. Leiden: E. J. Brill, 180–189.

Walls, Andrew F. 1996. *The Missionary Movement in Christian History. Studies in the Transmission of Faith.* Maryknoll: Orbis.

Sources in Mission Archives

Adam Jones

It is a quarter of a century since Terence Ranger and others drew attention to the need to study African religions—including Christianity and Islam—historically.[1] Although the tendency to describe 'African Traditional Religions' in ahistorical terms and to view Christianity and Islam as 'world religions' rather than African religions remains very much alive today, a number of interesting attempts have been made to approach the subject of religion in Africa diachronically.

Surprisingly few of these studies, however, have been based to any significant degree on mission archives. Missions themselves, of course, have been a major theme in the history of Africa, from Roland Oliver's *The Missionary Factor in East Africa* (1952) onwards. Moreover, there has been a recent upsurge in the publication of articles on the history of African Christianity, both in the *Journal of Religion in Africa* and in collective volumes devoted to particular regions.[2] Yet few authors have done any research in mission archives, and even fewer have taken the trouble to work their way slowly through the hand- or typewritten material there. The main sources used for the history of Christianity and its interactions with other religions in Africa, both in the past and today, have been either books published by missionaries and the periodicals of the missionary societies or material from government archives in Africa and Europe.

Yet strictly speaking, much of this material is not primary at all. By 'primary' I mean, following David Henige's definition, "those pieces of information which stand in the most intimate relationship to an event or process *in the present state of our knowledge*".[3] In this respect historians of religion have of

---

Source: Jones, A., "Sources in Mission Archives," in F. Ludwig and A. Adogame (eds.), *European Traditions in the Study of Religion in Africa*, Wiesbaden: Harrassowitz Verlag, 2004, pp. 39–46.

---

1 Ranger and Weller, 1975; Ranger and Kimambo, 1976 This is not to say that no-one had thought of studying religious history before this time. But awareness of the potential this field offered certainly grew in the early 1970s.

2 E.g., Elphick and Davenport, 1997 for South Africa, or Spear and Kimambo, 1999 for East Africa.

3 Henige, 1987: 54 (italics in the original). It makes sense here to refer to 'primary material' rather than 'primary sources', since a single source may contain primary as well as secondary material.

course not been alone: it is still not unusual to find a dissertation or book on African history based mainly on the printed documents given in Parliamentary Papers or Confidential Print, because it was considered unnecessary—and time-consuming—to examine the original manuscript documents in the Public Record Office upon which these were based. Nevertheless, the archival material of missionary societies has suffered even greater neglect than such governmental material.

One reason for this has been the attitude of some of the missionary societies themselves. I remember visiting a missionary society in Paris in 1977 and being told: "If you intend to write the sort of things that [Jean] Suret-Canale has published, I do not think this is the right place for you." Few mission archivists would be as direct today, and many go out of their way to welcome 'critical but balanced' research. But often one still detects a certain nervousness in the encounter between academia and missions.

Until recently almost all historical research on individual missions was conducted from the inside, often in connection with anniversaries. Some jubilee volumes are better than others, but they are usually characterised by a self-congratulatory approach, in which accounts of the sufferings of the early pioneers and martyrs are counterbalanced by a central narrative of progress, often illustrated by photographs showing church buildings, African Christians in western clothing and so on.

A second reason for neglect has been the diminishing resources of most missionary societies in the course of the second half of the twentieth century, just when African history was 'taking off'. A full-time archivist is a luxury that few societies can afford, and urgent conservation work has in many cases not yet been undertaken because of lack of funding. This is even more true of the written material left by missions in Africa. Insofar as it has not been transferred from Africa to Rome or to a parent institution in Europe, it is generally to be found in mission stations or their successor institutions, but seldom in the form of an institutionalised archive with trained staff.[4]

Given this background of widespread neglect, my paper will deal not so much with what has already been learnt from mission archives as with what might be achieved in the future. I will concentrate mainly on German-language missions.

---

4   See, for example, the information on Moshi (Tanzania) in Jones et al. 2000. Further research on the whereabouts of such material and the conservation problems raised is urgently needed. An interesting project to coordinate archival material in Cameroun has been carried out by Dr. Guy Thomas (now archivist of Mission21, Basel).

Repositories for Mission History?

Two widespread assumptions exist with regard to mission archives:
1) that they are repositories for historical material about 'religion'
2) that this material deals exclusively with 'mission history', conceived in terms of the confrontation between 'Christians' and 'heathen'.

Yet most scholars today would hold that any distinction between 'religion' on the one hand and a non-religious 'secular' sphere on the other is fraught with difficulties. As early as 1926 Carl Meinhof recognised the need to describe African religions—as he put it in the title of one of his books—'in the context of economic life'. More recently Wyatt MacGaffey (1981: 229) has argued that the very notions of 'African religion', 'African art', 'African polities' etc. reflect a preoccupation with the geography of a European city: religion is what one finds in a church, art is kept in the art gallery, politics takes place in the town hall and so on. A less Eurocentric perspective would deal with these topics as overlapping or indeed identical.

As David Arnold and Robert Bickers (1996: 1) have pointed out in their perceptive introduction to a collection of essays on mission archives, the term 'mission history' today signifies something rather different from what it meant to the authors of the multi-volume 'chronicles of ecclesiastical progress' that were still being published two decades ago:[5]

What exactly is 'mission history' and what use is the term? Where do we draw the lines between it and, for example, the history of education in India, or medicine in Africa? Such questions and worries are misleading. Christian endeavour and church history may no longer provide unifying schema for approaching missions, but the bureaucratic competence of the mission societies has supplied a unifying resource: the mission archive.

My own interest in mission archives has little to do with religion, nor with 'mission history' in its original sense. It was first stimulated by brief spells of research in 1976–77 on a precolonial polity in what is now Sierra Leone in the archives of the Church Missionary Society and the Methodist Missionary Society, In the mid-1980s research on the history of women on the Gold Coast (today Ghana) led me to the Basel Mission and the North German Missionary Society, enabling me to publish an article, for instance, on women's ritual in wartime; and a few years later I returned to the Basel Mission's archive to study the background to the publication of books by two missionaries and one African pastor-historian in the late nineteenth century. Other researchers too

---

5   For an even more recent example from my own field of research see Moritzen, 1986.

SOURCES IN MISSION ARCHIVES

have drawn upon the Basel Mission archive in order to discuss non-religious topics: Peter Haenger's book on slavery (2000) is one example.

The best discussion I have read of the kind of material a mission archive can offer a historically minded anthropologist is John Peel's article (1996) on the Church Missionary Society's Yoruba archive. Peel, who recently published an illuminating book dealing with ethnic identity and the relations between traditional religion and society, shows in his article how the incoming correspondence addressed to the Secretary of the Parent Committee contains five main kinds of material:

1) accounts of evangelistic encounters
2) reports of interactions and activities within local Christian communities
3) information on the communities in which the missions operated
4) discussion of regional politics
5) retrospective historical material.

Clearly the accounts of evangelistic encounters and of activities within Christian communities are of crucial importance for the history of religion. This can be seen from the work of another anthropologist, Michelle Gilbert, whose work on material in the Basel Mission's archive shows how in southern Ghana beliefs in the power of ancestors and non-Christian deities "constitute a set of explanations which complement those of Christian doctrine" (rather than competing with it).[6] But it would be unwise to assume that the other three aspects enumerated by Peel are irrelevant to this branch of study. Indeed, his own work has illustrated just how inseparable historiography, local politics and religion are.

One strength of the C. M. S. Yoruba archive which most other mission archives do not share to the same degree is the high proportion of papers sent in by 'native agents': because of the C. M. S. recruitment of 'Liberated Africans' from Sierra Leone, 57 per cent of the authors of papers sent from Yorubaland to London before 1880 were Yoruba,[7] and this makes it possible for Peel to examine changing beliefs and identities in fascinating detail. I know of no mission archive which can compete with this figure, but most mission archives do contain at least a small number of documents written by African Christians. One finds, for instance, letters from Africans to retired missionaries, essays by African schoolchildren about their own culture, or statements by candidates for the ministry concerning why they had become Christians. A few archives have more than this, either in African or in European languages—for instance,

---

6   Gilbert, 1989: 61. The quotation does not refer to the mission archive, but Gilbert's subsequent work has drawn upon the archive's material to elaborate upon this point.

7   Peel, 1996: 77.

historical essays, reports on evangelising journeys, texts of sermons and collections of proverbs or 'legends'.

The nature of what a mission archive can offer depends, of course, on the particular archive concerned—on the philosophy which guided mission work and on the nature of the documentation which was sent back to Europe (itself partly dependent on rules laid down by the mission). It is only gradually becoming clear what strengths and weaknesses individual archives have, Basel, for instance, has a very good collection of photographs (some missionaries were excellent photographers), as well as some remarkable material in African languages.[8] By contrast, the mission archives in Leipzig, Herrnhut and Neuendettelsau contain relatively little linguistic material, and only one or two photographers[9] can compare with those of Basel; but both Leipzig and Herrnhut have an impressive set of diaries, as does the North German Mission.

Given the difficulty of demarcating a separate field of activity which can be labelled 'religion', it would make little sense to identify certain parts of a mission archive as more relevant to the study of religion than others. The further we move away from the old focus upon the 'expansion' of a fixed entity labelled Christianity, the more necessary it has become to look almost everywhere for information on the dialogue or 'long conversation' which, as Arnold and Bickers (1996: 8) point out, took place "not solely between Western and indigenous religious beliefs [...] but also between the missions and their domestic societies". Two different approaches to this dialogue—both of them covering not only religious teaching but also the role of missionaries as transmitters of 'modern'/secular thought and technology—are illustrated by the Comaroffs in their work (1991, 1997) on the Tswana and Meyer in her book on the Ewe (1999).

Much has been written in the past fifteen years about missionary discourse and the ways in which it has influenced academic 'knowledge' about Africans.[10] It has even been argued that the very concept of African 'religion' is a product of missionary attempts to demonstrate the wrongness of analogous practices among non-Christians (Landau, 1999). Missionaries also played a leading role in establishing the genre of the ethnographic monograph, in which individual African societies were described more or less from a synchronic perspective and implicitly in accordance with a questionnaire (cf. Vansina, 1987). However, here too it is striking how little reference has been made in this discussion to

---

8   Some material in Twi and Gã was published in a mission newspaper (cf. Trutenau, 1973); other, unpublished material is currently being studied by several scholars. For an illustration of the kind of historical information that such indigenous sources contain see McCaskie and Wiafe, 1979.

9   E.g., Wilhelm Guth of the Leipzig Mission: see ULPA, Vol. 19.

10   See, for example, De Kock, 1996 and Harries, 1988.

SOURCES IN MISSION ARCHIVES

archival materials. There remains considerable scope for studying how missionaries' assumptions about 'the African' affected what they perceived and wrote, rather than just what they published.

Working in a Mission Archive

Since many researchers arrive in a mission archive with exaggerated expectations and little idea of how to begin, it may be helpful to make a few suggestions.

First, it is wise before visiting an archive to ascertain whether any finding aids are available in print (e.g., the ULPA 'Mission Archives' series) or in the internet. Most visitors to a mission archive hope to spot a few 'juicy' sources, and indeed this will often be possible, especially if there is a good index; but it is equally important to use the finding aid—ideally in combination with a detailed history of the mission concerned—to understand the overall structure of the archive.

To lake a specific example: using the *Guide to the Basel Mission's Ghana Archive (ULPA series. No. 23)*, scholars interested in religion will easily locate manuscripts written by missionaries entitled "Concerning Twi Religion" (D-10.4, 2) or "Religion of the Inhabitants of the Gold Coast" (D-10.4, 3). This is the kind of essay that conventional scholars of African religion write themselves, albeit from a somewhat different perspective; and because of this sense of familiarity, they like to quote such sources. But it is at least as important to do two things more: first, to look at indigenous religious texts, such as such as Fritz Ramseyer's notebook "Some Notes on Fetish and Spirit Worship" (D-20, Sch. 4, 8, which the Guide describes as 'mostly Twi liturgical texts'); secondly, in order to go beyond the theoretical/metaphysical level and examine how religion manifested itself in everyday life, serious historians of religion must be prepared to work their way through the voluminous incoming correspondence (D-1 series), bound in single years. This is where we must look if we are to find the 'confidences, concerns and observations absent from official reports and minutes' and to 'explore the processes by which Europeans met with, and adapted—or otherwise—their preconceptions to fit the realities of a foreign culture and foreign individuals.'[11]

This sounds a daunting task, since hardly any guides to the contents of such volumes exist.[12] Yet there is one well-tried method which can sometimes make

---

11   Arnold and Bickers, 1996: 2, 8.

12   Archival users often complain about the lack of such finding aids; but to prepare them would contradict one of the prime rules of archival science—at least in Germany:

this task easier. This is to start with the material published in the periodicals of the mission concerned—in the case of the Basel Mission, for example, *Der Heidenbote* and the *Jahresberichte*. (In many cases this can be done without travelling to the archive concerned: copies of such periodicals can sometimes be found in public libraries or in the archives of other missionary societies with whom publications were exchanged.[13]) Long extracts from the incoming correspondence may be quoted in such periodicals; but assuming that this correspondence has not been destroyed, the version given in the periodicals is not the closest we can get to what was originally written. Hence, having identified a passage in the periodical which seems particularly informative, it is desirable to turn to the incoming correspondence of the same year and search for the original. Often one will find that the passages used for a publication are crossed through with a vertical line in red or blue pencil. It is worth checking whether these were rendered accurately and to see what was left out. After all, the periodicals selected material partly for propaganda purposes, and modern scholars will have different priorities.

A particularly valuable type of source, much more common in mission archives than in most other archives, is the journal or diary of an individual missionary or a mission station. This can be used to illuminate the thoughts and state of mind of the author, although it must be remembered that most such journals were written not as a private record but with a view to being read by members of the missionary body 'at home'. Indeed, some missions *obliged* their missionaries to keep a diary and send back regular instalments, not just as a means of recording what happened but in order to keep a check on what the missionary himself (or herself) was up to. In certain periods this seems to have applied, for instance, to the Herrnhut Mission (Moravian Church). In addition to this function, of course, diaries provide us with a particular narrative approach to everyday life in Africa, including religion. To some extent their content overlaps with the material found in incoming correspondence, but the emphasis is different. Not surprisingly, quite a few missionary journals were eventually published as books, albeit usually in a heavily edited form which sometimes distorted what the author had actually intended to say.[14]

'Archivists do not read.' An interesting exception is the Basel Mission's guide to its Cameroon Archive. Recently several mission archives have begun to ask users to leave behind brief notes on the contents of the records they consult, for the benefit of future users.

13   For some remarks on German missionary periodicals see Liedtke, 1999.

14   This applies, for example, to the journal of Fritz Ramseyer concerning his captivity in Kumasi (1869–73): see Jones, 1991. The last journals of David Livingstone provide an even more extreme case; see Helly, 1987.

SOURCES IN MISSION ARCHIVES

Of course missionary writings—published or unpublished—are biased and influenced by prejudices, particularly when dealing with religion. This is one reason why many secular historians have preferred to avoid using them. Yet bias is something historians must expect everywhere and must develop skills to deal with. One can even argue that the kind of bias found in missionary writings is less difficult to handle than in certain other sources, since it is 'more clearly acknowledged and belter known.'[15]

Ensuring Accessibility

In Great Britain many missionary societies have handed over their repositories to a university library: thus the Church Missionary Society's archive is now in the University of Birmingham's library, the Methodist Missionary Society's archive is in the School of Oriental and African Studies library in London, and so on. German missions, by contrast, have resisted any suggestion that their archive should be transferred elsewhere, one argument being—as the Director of the Leipzig Mission put it to me—that in order for dialogue between mission and researchers to take place, the archive must remain on the mission's own premises. The one exception in Germany has been the North German Missionary Society, based in Bremen, which a quarter of a century ago handed over its pre-1939 material to the *Staatsarchiv* in Bremen.[16] It is worth noting, however, that the 30-page typewritten list of material drawn up in connection with this transfer remained the only guide to the archive's contents until very recently, when a lecturer at the University of Bremen began to take an interest: hence it would be wrong to assume that a transfer of ownership/residence automatically brings with it an improvement in the kind of archival aids available.

After moving to Leipzig in 1994 it seemed to me that in former East Germany the greatest potential for future research on African history lay not in the records of the German colonial and foreign ministries (at that time in Potsdam but now in Berlin as part of the Bundesarchiv), underused though these were, but in mission archives such as those of the Leipzig Mission, the Moravian Church (Herrnhuter Brüdergemeine) and the Berlin Mission, which had been to a large extent ignored under GDR rule. As a result, together with half a dozen students and ex-students, I have since 1998 been engaged in the preparation of guides to the written, photographic and other material on Africa in these archives. One thing led to another, and work on the Leipzig Mission had to

---

15 Arnold and Bickers, 1996: 4.
16 See Hüttner and Martens, 2001: 1.

be extended to Bavaria: the Leipzig Mission's activity in East Africa had been a sequel to work begun in the 1880s by the Hersbruck Mission, and after the division of Germany following the Second World War the Protestant Church in Bavaria (in Neuendettelsau) largely took over the Leipzig Mission's work. Through collaboration with the University of Bayreuth, we were able to cover these mission archives, and to publish our first guide to a Catholic mission, likewise in Bavaria—that of the Benedictine monks in St. Ottilien. Work on a guide to the Berlin Mission's archive has also begun, although more funding will be necessary if it is to be done thoroughly.[17]

A glimpse of some other work recently done in the field of mission archives may be gained from the website of the International Association for Mission Studies.[18] With regard to Africa the most important entries are:

1) for the C.M.S. records: a statement of intent by the University of Birmingham library, where the records are housed, and a list of microfilm from these records housed at the Billy Graham Center (Wheaton, IL)

2) for the Council for World Mission (formerly London Missionary Society): a detailed list of holdings (including photos, watercolours etc.) housed at the School of Oriental and African Studies (London)

3) Evangelical Mission Archives, kept at the Billy Graham Center[19]

4) records relating to missionary activities at the National Archives Enugu (Nigeria)

5) the Mundus gateway to missionary collections in the United Kingdom.

Conclusion

I have indicated some of the consequences of moving beyond the old view of the mission archive as a place containing material on 'the traditional religion of the X' and on how the light of civilization overcame the darkness of paganism. If we agree that religions in Africa can no longer be described in the form of an ethnographic monograph and that Christianity itself can only be understood in relation to particular historical contexts, the mission archive takes on a new significance as a place where encounter, dialogue and transculturation are documented in everyday life. Mission archives have an important role to play here, and the task has only just begun.

---

17 This project was initiated by the Berliner Gesellschaft für Missionsgeschichte in collaboration with myself and the Theological Faculty of the Humboldt University Berlin.

18 http://www.missionstudies.org/4groups/PADO11/archives.htm.

19 This center has recently made a useful contribution to the discussion of the role of mission archives (notably non-denominational ones): see http://www.wheaton.edu/bge/archives/consult/consult.html.

Bibliography

Arnold, David and Robert A. Bickers, "Introduction", Bickers, Robert A. and Rosemary Seton (eds.), *Missionary Encounters: Sources and Issues*, London: Curzon Press, 1996, 1–10.

Bickers, Robert A. and Rosemary Seton (eds.), *Missionary Encounters: Sources and Issues*. London: Curzon Press, 1996.

Büttner, Manuela and Sandy Martens, *Afrikabestände der Norddeutschen Missionsgesellschaft im Staatsarchiv Bremen*, Leipzig: University of Leipzig Papers on Africa, 2001.

Comaroff, Jean and John, *Of Revelation and Revolution: Christianity, Colonialism, and Consciousness in South Africa*, 2 vols., Chicago: Chicago University Press, 1991, 1997.

De Kock, Leon, *Civilising Barbarians: Missionary Narrative and African Textual Response*, Johannesburg: Witwatersrand University Press, 1996.

Elphick, Richard and Rodney Davenport (eds.), *Christianity in South Africa: A Political, Social and Cultural History*, Oxford: James Currey, 1997.

Gilbert, Michelle, "Sources of Power in Akuropon-Akuapem: Ambiguity in Classification", in: Werner Arens and Ivan Karp (eds.), *Creativity of Power. Cosmology and Action in African Societies*, Washington: Smithsonian Institution Press, 1989, 60–89.

Haenger, Peter, *Slaves and Slave Holders on the Gold Coast: Towards an Understanding of Social Bondage in West Africa*, Ed. J. J. Shaffer and Paul E. Lovejoy. Basel: P. Schlettwein Publishing, 2000 [German original 1997].

Harries, Patrick, "The Roots of Ethnicity: Discourse and the Politics of Language Construction in South-East Africa", *African Affairs* (87/1988), 25–52.

Helly, Dorothy O., *Livingstone's Legacy: Horace Waller and Victorian Mythmaking*, Athens, Ohio: Ohio University Press, 1987.

Henige, David, "The Race is Not Always to the Swift: Thoughts on the Use of Written Sources for the Study of Early African History", in: Beatrix Heintze and Adam Jones (eds.), *European Sources for Sub-Saharan Africa Before 1900: Use and Abuse* (*Paideuma*, Vol. 33, 1987), 53–79.

Jones, Adam, "Four Years in Asante: One Source or Several", *History in Africa* (18/1991), 173–203.

Landau, Paul S., "'Religion' and Christian Conversion in African History: A New Model", *The Journal of Religious History* (23/1999), 8–30.

Langer, Christoph & Steffen Lehmann, *Afrikabestände in evangelisch-lutherischen Missonsarchiven: Leipzig und Moshi*, Leipzig: University of Leipzig Papers on Africa (ULPA), Mission Archives Series No. 9, 2000.

Liedtke, Wolfgang, "Zur Auswertung älterer Missionszeitschriften", in: *Afrikabestände in deutschen Missionsarchiven: Perspektiven ihrer Erschließung*, ed. Adam Jones and Gudrun Miehe, Leipzig: University of Leipzig Papers on Africa, 1999, 17–21.

MacGaffey, Wyatt, "African Ideaology and Belief: A Survey", *African Studies Review* (24/1981), 227–84.

McCaskie, T. C. and J. H. Wiafe, "A Contemporary Account in Twi of the *akompi sa* of 1863: a Document with a Commentary", *Asantesem* (11/1979), 72–8.

Meinhof, Carl, *Die Religionen der Afrikaner in ihrem Zusammenhang mit dem Wirtschaftsleben*, Oslo, 1926.

Meyer, Birgit, *Translating the Devil: Religion and Modernity Among the Ewe in Ghana*, Edinburgh: Edinburgh University Press, 1999.

Moritzen, Niels-Peter, *Werkzeug Gottes in der Welt. Leipziger Mission 1836–1936–1986*, Erlangen: Verlag der Ev.-Luth. Mission, 1986.

Peel, J. D. Y., "Problems and Opportunities in an Anthropologist's Use of a Missionary Archive", *Bickers and Seton*, 1996, 70–94.

Ranger, Terence and I. N. Kimambo (eds.), *The Historical Study of African Religions*, Berkeley: University of California Press, 1976.

Ranger, Terence and John Weller (eds.), *Themes in the Christian History of Central Africa*, Berkeley: University of California Press, 1975.

Seton, Rosemary (ed.), *A Mission for the Future: The Use and Importance of Missionary Archives*. Papers given at a conference organised by the Religious Archives Group in conjunction with the Research Support Libraries' Programme, 16th October 2000 [London 2001].

Seton, Rosemary, "Appendix: Archival Sources in Britain for the Study of Mission History", Bickers, Robert A. and Rosemary Seton (eds.), *Missionary Encounters: Sources and Issues*, London: Curzon Press, 1996, 240–55.

Spear, Thomas and Isaria N. Kimambo (eds.), *East African Expressions of Christianity*, Oxford: James Currey, 1999.

Trutenau, H. M. J., "The 'Christian Messenger' and its Successors: A Description of the First Three Series of a Missionary Periodical with Articles in Ghanaian Languages (Twi and Gã) 1883–1931", *Mitteilungen der Basler Afrika-Bibliographien* (9/1973), 38–53.

ULPA: University of Leipzig Papers on Africa, Mission Archives Series (details under http://www.uni-leipzig.de/~afrika).

Vansina, Jan, "The Ethnographic Account as a Genre in Central Africa", in: Beatrix Heintze and Adam Jones (eds.), *European Sources for Sub-Saharan Africa before 1900: Use and Abuse* (*Paideuma*, Vol. 33), 433–44.

The Midwest China Oral History Collection

Jane Baker Koons

Introduction

The Midwest China Oral History Collection was initiated in 1976 to gather firsthand information from midwestern Americans and others who lived and worked in China before 1952. The oral history collection is a component of the Midwest China Oral History, Archives, and Museum Collection, which is under the auspices of the Midwest China Center in St. Paul, Minnesota. One hundred and twenty narrators have been interviewed for a total of 480 hours of recording. The resulting 11,000 pages of transcript are bound into individual volumes and are available for use.

The China interest generated in the midwest at the end of the nineteenth century and the first five decades of the twentieth century ran high. No region of the United States sent more church workers, health care personnel, educators, agriculturalists, relief workers, and others to China than did the midwest. As P. Richard Bohr writes in the foreword of the guide to the collection: "The narratives in this collection are a living history of Chinese-American interaction during the critical period from the fall of imperial China to the creation of the People's Republic. They tell of Midwestern Americans who went from the world's youngest to the world's oldest nation in search of a new frontier. Inspired by the ideals of humanity, democracy, and individualism, these 'ordinary people' participated in China's modern transformation."

Background research for the Midwest China Oral History Collection, conducted in 1975 and 1976 to determine need and feasibility, revealed large gaps in the existing record. For many of the midwesterners in China there was inadequate documentation of their experiences and perceptions. The turbulence created by the collapse of imperial rule, internecine warfare, the rise of nationalism, the Japanese occupation, the Civil War, and natural disasters resulted in the loss or destruction of both institutional and personal records. The experiences and perceptions of certain individuals—particularly single and married

---

Source: Baker Koons, J., "The Midwest China Oral History Collection," *International Bulletin of Missionary Research* 9.2 (1985): pp. 66–68. Copyright © 1985 by SAGE. Reprinted by Permission of SAGE Publications, Ltd.
The original article holds one illustration which is not included here.

women, who were not always included in the decision-making process—were also inadequately documented. Oral history seemed a natural vehicle for preserving aspects of the lost or unrecorded history of the era.

Collection Background

Once the need for the collection was established, the initial step was to build up a name file of appropriate potential narrators. Guidelines were established to determine which of the more than 300 names on file would be appropriate narrators. During the evaluation process, the following factors were taken into consideration: institutional sponsorship, vocation, gender, geographic location, length of time in China, period when in China, and involvements after leaving. Since one of the objectives of the collection was to represent the diversity of midwestern involvement in China, the narrators selected were not limited to missionaries. Military personnel, diplomats, business persons, and those who went to China independently were also included. However, because of the pervasiveness of religious influence and structures in the midwest, 66 percent of the narrators had been in China under the auspices of an organization with religious affiliations.

The collection also includes the oral histories of a small cluster of Chinese Christians—colleagues of some of the American narrators. An example of these select narratives is the experience of the first Chinese bishop of the Lutheran Church of China as told by his son, who is himself a Lutheran pastor. In working with representatives of sixteen different missions as well as Chinese leaders speaking different dialects, the bishop had his own perceptions of the working relations between Westerners and Chinese.

Selection of the oral history narrators was made with the purpose of developing a multifaceted perspective as well as concentrated clusters of perspectives that permit researchers to compare and corroborate information from a multiplicity of viewpoints.

Certain clusters are geographical. For example, one cluster that provides in-depth perspectives is the narratives of those who were in rural China. These individuals living outside the treaty ports and larger cities and often working outside a compound had opportunities to know rural China intimately. From the narratives of a roving medical team that treated the infectious kala-azar disease, of instructors in the rural literacy programs, of village itinerants and many others, researchers are able to understand more fully how individuals who traveled by foot, horseback, cart, chair, bicycle, and sampan, who wore

THE MIDWEST CHINA ORAL HISTORY COLLECTION   129

queues and padded clothes and slept on straw-filled bags, perceived and grappled with the problems of China's interior.

Other clusters have vocational or institutional foci. An example of such a cluster is the narratives of all six members of a mobile Ambulance Unit of The American Friends Service Committee. Members of Medical Team 19 served in both Nationalist- and communist-held areas. The team members compare and contrast their experiences in the different areas and provide information on Yenan's International Peace Hospital during the civil war.

A third example of a cluster is individuals with common backgrounds, such as children who grew up in China and returned home to work as adults. These narrators, whose first language is usually Chinese and some of whom attended Chinese school, offer a generational perspective on China in the midst of great change.

A fourth example of a cluster illustrates how many of the narratives in the collection intersect. Because Shanghai was one of the few international settlements in the world open to all people regardless of passport or visa, approximately 18,000 to 20,000 European Jewish refugees fled to China between 1937 and 1939 to escape Nazi persecution. Many of the refugees spent the following ten years in China.

Even though China was occupied by the Japanese at the time, both the Chinese and the Westerners responded to the incoming refugees. Americans, including some German-speaking midwesterners, assisted in the processing and settling of the refugees in Shanghai. A small number of the refugees, primarily physicians and other professionals whose skills were critically needed, were integrated into the work of various missions and became associates of narrators in the collection. In rural areas there were grassroots responses from the Chinese. Ladies' Aid societies in the interior, hundreds of miles from Shanghai, sent small contributions to support the refugees. A congregation in Junan, Honan, composed new lyrics to a familiar Chinese melody: "The Jews, the Jews, the chosen people of God, the Jews. Whoever loves them shall be blest; whoever hates them shall be cursed. We shall always remember the Jews." Included in the Midwest China Oral History Collection are the narratives of eight former Jewish refugees who relocated in the midwest after leaving China. In addition, the collection includes the perspectives of midwesterners who either worked with the refugees directly or whose local organizations were involved in their support.

Oral History Methodology

The approach used in conducting the oral history interviews was modified biography. Studies from the Columbia University Oral History Collection suggest that the biographical narrative has the greatest potential usefulness. For this reason, the interviews cover the narrators' family background, including influences in their childhood and youth that may have directed them to China. Extensive coverage of their involvement in China and activities following their return to the United States complete the body of the narratives. Addenda describe cases of restored contacts with Chinese colleagues either through written communications or personal visits to China.

Although certain questions were asked of each narrator to provide a mode of comparison, research was done from primary and secondary sources for every interview, and a specific set of questions was then tailored for each narrator. The interviewers had backgrounds in Sino-American relations and were trained in oral history methodology, following guidelines established by the Oral History Association.

A Particular Value of the Collection

In surveying oral history resources of this nature one value, among many, appears to be the documenting of how individuals responded to their world in various contexts and from differing motives and commitments, ranging from the macro-worlds of international and national structures to the micro-worlds of one individual relating to another. Here are two examples in the Midwest China Oral History Collection of individuals responding in conflicting ways to the China experience.

1. Some individuals on home leave talked to countless church and civic groups about the negative effects of extraterritoriality. A classic midwestern illustration was, "How would you feel if you went up the Mississippi River and found some Russian or British gunboats with guns directed right at city hall, ready to be fired if things went wrong?" Yet these same individuals were carried to the coast on foreign gunboats during the exodus of Westerners in the late 1920s.

2. There were also individuals like Walter Judd, who as a mission doctor in north China treated members of the Eighth Route Army, including communist leaders, and transmitted messages between Yenan and Peking (Beijing). Yet, as a Minnesota congressman, Dr. Judd helped direct American foreign policy, over a period of twenty years, away from the People's Republic to Taiwan.

Use of the Midwest China Oral History Collection

Bound transcripts of the oral history narratives may be used at the Midwest China Center. In addition, volumes may circulate through interlibrary loan or may be purchased at production cost. Copies of the 111-page guide—*Oral History Summaries: A Guide to the Collection*—may be purchased for $5. Information concerning the resources may be directed to the Midwest China Oral History Collection, 2375 Como Avenue, St. Paul, MN 55108. Telephone: (612) 641–3233.

Follow-up Study: The Midwest China Oral History Collection as a Test Case

The development and use of oral history resources is a burgeoning field. Both oral history as a method and the resources generated by that method have become accepted pedagogical vehicles and sources for research, writing, and teaching.

Oral history practitioners and users of oral history resources presume that the impacts of oral history upon the study of history, both content and process, are considerable and are on the whole positive. These presumed impacts, however, remain largely unevaluated and untested. The oral history resources of the Midwest China Oral History Collection were the basis of one of the first empirical studies in the field to test some of the presumed impacts of using these primary resources. The study "Utilization of Oral History Resources in Documented Research Papers: A Study of Impacts" was conducted as part of the collection director's doctoral dissertation at the University of Minnesota. The study investigated the following eight impacts.

1. Because oral history resources are firsthand, primary resources, it is assumed that they humanize and personalize history.
2. The firsthand nature of the oral history resources is assumed to create a sense of authenticity and credibility.
3. Since the oral history resources may provide greater detail than secondary sources, it is assumed that they reflect more accurately the inconsistencies and complexities of the human experience.
4. The use of oral history resources is presumed to counter stereotypes.
5. Oral history is presumed to provide information that can be found nowhere else.
6. Because of the very personal, unedited nature of oral history resources, it is assumed that users are made more aware of the necessity of evaluating the reliability of the source documents.

7. Oral history is presumed to help describe the context in which a specific event or phenomenon occurred.
8. Using oral history resources is presumed to help revitalize the teaching and meaning of history.

A three-tiered procedure was developed to test experimentally in a classroom setting whether or not these impacts occur. The sample for the study included students in modern Chinese history classes in three private liberal arts colleges in Minnesota during the spring of 1983. The sample size was sixty. The students in these three modern Chinese history classes were required to write a documented research paper, with all students receiving the same research topic. Within each class the students were randomly assigned to one of two treatment groups. The study attempted to demonstrate whether or not there were differences in the cognitive and affective reactions of students to the research-paper assignment. Treatment I group utilized a foundation of traditional, secondary bibliographic resources plus an additional bibliography of only oral history resources. Treatment II group utilized the same foundation bibliography plus an additional bibliography of traditional secondary sources.

The structure of the three-tiered experimental procedure was as follows: first, two trained composition raters, using Primary Trait scoring criteria, evaluated the documented research papers; second, one East Asian history instructor and one East Asian teaching assistant, using psychometric scales that purport to measure qualities that are considered important in documented history research papers of college level students, including the presumed impacts of using oral history resources, evaluated each paper on these qualities. In addition, each rater provided qualitative evaluations of each documented research paper. The affective reactions of the students were measured with psychometric scales by means of self-administered questionnaires.

The quantitative analyses and the qualitative evaluations from this sample suggest that there are six impacts in using oral history. The papers that utilized the oral history resources were judged (1) to reflect a greater empathy for individuals and events, and to humanize and personalize history more effectively; (2) to create more effectively the context in which an event or phenomenon occurred; (3) to reflect more accurately the inconsistencies and complexities of the human experience; (4) to provide a greater number of concrete and appropriate details; and (5) to provide more solid, factual information. Finally (6), the students who utilized oral history resources appeared to have a greater interest and enjoyment in the writing assignment.

Although there was no significant difference between the two groups in coherent organization or integration of details, all four raters noted that some students using oral history resources had difficulty handling the multiple perspectives, resulting in inconsistent and contradictory arguments, and problems in proceeding from the concrete to the abstract.

In conclusion, some of the results of this particular design suggest that the use of oral history resources requires a rather sophisticated knowledge of historical methodology. Future studies should include samples of graduate and postgraduate historical researchers to explore further the impacts of using oral history resources.

From *Beyond Alpine Snow* and *Homes of the East*— a Journey Through Missionary Periodicals: The Missionary Periodicals Database Project

Terry Barringer

Historians and anthropologists, Christian and otherwise, who are interested in the meeting of Western and non-Western cultures, the ways each have affected the self-understanding of the other, and the mental images each have held of the other have begun to dig deep into the rich deposits of missionary archives.[1] Rosemary Seton and others have done much to make these sources better known and accessible. The mining of missionary periodicals, however, has barely begun. Several times in the course of the Missionary Periodicals Database Project, we were the first to cut open the pages of a library copy of a missionary magazine.

Missionary periodicals have always had an image problem. Their editorials are full of complaints that even regular church and chapel goers are ill informed and indifferent to foreign missions and regard missionary magazines as uninteresting. They are constantly exhorting their readers to sign up more subscribers. It the missionary magazines had a problem in their own era, it was a long time before scholars took them seriously as source material. Scholars tended to think of them, if they thought of them at all, as covered in a pietistic haze, of interest only to committed missionary antiquarians. Such attitudes are changing. In introducing their important collection *Missionary Encounters: Sources and Issues*, Robert Bickers and Rosemary Seton were able to report that "a broad cross-section of social scientists and humanities scholars are finding the missionary enterprise a fecund, if often frustrating source of material to work on, and use to work through to other issues."[2]

Source: Barringer, T., "From Beyond Alpine Snow and Homes of the East," *International Bulletin of Missionary Research* 26.4 (2002): pp. 169–173. Copyright © 2002 by SAGE. Reprinted by Permission of SAGE Publications, Ltd.

The original article holds one illustration which is not included here.

---

1 *Beyond Alpine Snows* is a missionary periodical published by the Spezia Mission for Italy and the Levant, 1953–73; *Homes of the East* was published for a juvenile readership by the Church of England Zenana Missionary Society, 1904–51. An earlier illustrated version of this article was published as "Why Are Missionary Periodicals [Not] So Boring? The Missionary Periodicals Database Project," *African Research and Documentation*, no. 84 (2000): 33–46.

2 Robert A. Bickers and Rosemary Seton, eds., *Missionary Encounter: Sources and Issues* (Richmond, U.K.: Curzon, 1996), p. 1.

© KONINKLIJKE BRILL NV, LEIDEN, 2021 | DOI:10.1163/9789004399587_009

FROM *BEYOND ALPINE SNOW* AND *HOMES OF THE EAST*   135

The story of missionary periodicals follows that of the modern missionary movement. The Baptist Missionary Society was founded in 1792, followed in quick succession by the (mainly Congregationalist) London Missionary Society in 1795, the (Anglican) Church Missionary Society in 1799, and then many other societies and organizations throughout the nineteenth and twentieth centuries. Beginning with the Annual Reports of LMS in 1795, *Periodical Accounts* by BMS in 1800, and *Proceedings* from CMS in 1800/01, all British mission societies published magazines and periodicals to inform their constituencies and to generate support in prayer, money, and recruits. Some periodicals were generalist, devoted to worldwide mission; others were focused on specific areas. They were denominational, interdenominational, or nondenominational. Some targeted women; others, children; still others, specific social classes or educational levels. Prices ranged from a halfpenny—with bulk discounts for distribution to Sunday school children and the working classes—to expensive annual volumes costing several guineas designed to appeal to the social and spiritual snob. Such was the *Missionary Annual* published in 1833 by the London commercial publishers Seeley and Sons, who advertised their product as a source of "information and pleasure not only to the general reader, but more especially to those who desire to blend piety with their highest gratifications and whose deepest interest is excited by whatever is connected with the advancement of true religion in the world.... The volume, it is hoped, will be generally approved, especially by the friends of Religion, as a beautiful and appropriate present, attractive in its decorations and permanently valuable in the interesting and important nature of its contents."[3]

Study of a run of missionary periodicals shows how ideas and images changed over time, making possible a more nuanced understanding of the much-debated relationship between colonialism and Christianization. Missionary periodicals are valuable sources for the evolution of missionary self-understanding and self-representation. They sometimes make for uncomfortable reading, as there is no shortage of what appears now to be offensive, racist, or patronizing (e.g., *Little Darkie's Budget* or stories of *Wopsy the Guardian Angel* winging round the African jungle rescuing naughty black boys and confronting witch doctors in answer to the prayers of golden-curled Catholic children in England and Ireland).[4] Reading of missionary periodicals must be both sympathetic and critical if it is to be rewarding.

---

3   *Missionary Annual* (London: Seeley and Sons, 1833), Preface.

4   *Little Darkie's Budget* was published for children by the Worldwide Evangelisation Crusade, Heart of Africa Mission, September 1919 to July 1920. Wopsy first appears in the "For the Children" pages of the *White Fathers in Africa*. See "The Adventures of a Guardian Angel: I:

Self-representation is an important theme for missionaries in the field. Even more, committees and editors back home were acutely aware of the need to rally supporters and encourage financial contributions. It was easy to slip from justification by faith to justification by results. Periodicals were used blatantly as public relations tools. Emily Moffat, member of a noted missionary clan in Africa, was delighted when her husband left the London Missionary Society because then it could no longer publish quotes from his letters. "There is so much bosh written and printed," she protested, "so much that is calculated to mislead minds and to give the wrong impressions, that I am disgusted over and over again, while I feel I may do the very same thing myself. The editor's pencil, identifying those passages that are fit for publication, can still be seen on many letters from the field. On one occasion he even writes 'on no account publish this.'"[5]

Gaining Access to Missionary Periodicals

Missionary periodicals are also a rich source of maps, illustrations, and photographs. To tap these riches, however, scholars need to know what exists and where to find it. The Missionary Periodicals Database aims to enable them to do just that. Work on compiling the database began at the end of 1997 under the auspices of the North Atlantic Missiology Project, which promoted scholarly analysis of modern Protestant missions, with Brian Stanley as director. In early 1999 the database project was absorbed within Currents in World Christianity, a three-year international research project on the growth and impact of Christianity in the non-Western world. Funded by a grant from the Pew Charitable Trusts, the project was based in the Centre for Advanced Religious and Theological Studies in the Faculty of Divinity at the University of Cambridge.

Taking Charge," *White Fathers in Africa* n.s. no. 14 (September–October 1940): 100–02. See also "Pip, Pop, and Monica," n.s. no. 40 (October–November 1946): 15–18. Three collections of Wopsy stories by Father Gerald F. Scriven were published in book form between 1943 and 1948.

5 I owe this reference to Mr. Martin Ballard and his unpublished volume "The Christians in Africa." A copy may be consulted in the library of the Henry Martyn Centre, Cambridge, England. See also the discussion of periodicals in Natasha Erlank, "'Civilizing the African': The Scottish Mission to the Xhosa, 1821–64," in *Christian Missions and the Enlightenment*, ed. Brian Stanley (Grand Rapids: Eerdmans, 2001), pp. 141–68.

FROM *BEYOND ALPINE SNOW* AND *HOMES OF THE EAST*   137

The database aims to record all periodicals on foreign missions published in Britain from the 1700s to the 1960s by missionary societies and commercial publishers, giving full bibliographic details, with information on contents and location. Information was gathered by myself and by Rosemary and David Seton from their base at the University of London's School of Oriental and African Studies (SOAS), whose very rich collections of missionary archives notably include those of the London Missionary Society, the Methodist Missionary Society, and the China Inland Mission. The information gathered was mounted on the Web with the aid of technology consultant David Clough, formerly of Yale and now at Durham.

The first surprise in drawing up a list of missionary periodicals was seeing how many there are. We anticipated finding about 200, but the final total came to over 600. A first list was compiled using Rosemary Seton's guides to missionary archives.[6] Library catalogs (especially those of the British Library, Cambridge University Library, and SOAS) were searched under the names of the known missionary societies and for periodicals with titles beginning with "*Mission-....*" Such titles occupy four pages in the *British Union Catalogue of Periodicals*, including for example *Mission to the Kabyles and other Berber Races, Mission Parcel Society Little Papers*, and *Missionary Exhibition Rambler*. Thereafter the list, like Topsy, "just growed." One periodical led to another through advertisements and cross-references. We explored other libraries. Consulting the catalogs was not always enough, for sometimes we had to investigate piles in dark corners. Conversations with friends and colleagues brought other leads as they dredged up memories from childhood Sunday school reading.

Occasional additions and amendments are still being made to the database, but it now has full details for some 500 titles of the 600 title working checklist. The direct address for the database is http://namp.divinity.yale.edu/namp.taf, or it can be accessed via the Web site of the Henry Martyn Centre at Cambridge at www.martynmission.cam.ac.uk.

Searches in the database can be made by region, title, or specific term. To search by region, click on the map on the front page, which brings up a list of periodicals dealing with that part of the world. To do a title search, enter a particular title. Searches by specific term are flexible. For example, it is possible to search by denomination, to look for all periodicals for children, or to call

---

6 Rosemary Seton and Emily Naish, *A Preliminary Guide to the Archives of British Missionary Societies* (London: School of Oriental and African Studies, 1992), and Rosemary Seton, "Archival Sources in Britain for the Study of Mission History: An Outline Guide and Select Bibliography," *International Bulletin of Missionary Research* 18 (April 1994): 66–70.

up a list of all those containing engravings or photographs or advertisements or verse.

The database records the following information for each title: basic bibliographic details, including title and any changes of title, issuing body, place of publication, publisher and printer, dates and numbering system; frequency, whether weekly, monthly, annual, or otherwise (e.g., the *Pentecostal Flames of Fire*, which incorporates *Tidings from Tibet and Other Lands*, carried the statement, "This paper will be issued from time to time as the Lord directs"); price; circulation figures, where these are known; denomination; and region, using the nine areas of Africa, Australasia and the Pacific, East Asia, Europe including Russia, Latin America and Caribbean, Near and Middle East, North America, South Asia, and South-East Asia.

Information is given on specialized work, where appropriate, using categories such as Bible Translation, Jews, Literature, Medical, Welfare and Development, and Women. The database identifies intended readership (e.g., children, women, Sunday school teachers, children's workers), as well as the use of illustrations, distinguishing woodcuts and engravings, black-and-white photographs, color photographs, and portraits.

Illustrations in missionary periodicals are a rich seam. It is my hope that before too long at least one Ph.D. dissertation and one book will be devoted to missionary iconography and use of the camera. Missionaries and missionary magazines were quick to embrace new technologies, and the role of missionary magazines in disseminating visual images of exotic parts of the world can hardly be overestimated. Similarly, there is scope for much work on missionary cartography. Occasionally, the missionary magazines published extremely detailed maps of little-known parts of the world. More often, maps were used to make points about the missionary needs of the world. There is some extremely interesting use of light and shade; among Protestants, mission stations conventionally appear as pinpoints of light in the heathen darkness.[7]

Digging Deeper

Information recorded in the database is quite detailed. The contents of the magazines are logged using the following standard headings: Advertisements, Book Notes and Reviews, Children's Corner, Competitions, Home Supporters'

---

7 For an example of the study of missionary cartography, see Sujit Sivasundaram, "Natural History Spiritualized: Civilizing Islanders, Cultivating Breadfruit, and Collecting Souls," *History of Science* 39, pt. 4 (2001): 417–43.

FROM *BEYOND ALPINE SNOW* AND *HOMES OF THE EAST* 139

Activities, Hymns and Verse, Letters to the Editor, List of Subscribers, Minutes and Proceedings, Missionary Stations and Movements, Obituaries, Prayers and Topics for Prayer, Sermons and Sermon Material, Stories, Suggestions for Further Reading, and Sunday School Teaching Material. A few examples will give the flavor. The heading "Home Supporters' Activities" leads to many examples of busyness at the parish level, such as prayer meetings, sales of work, and sewing parties. On sewing parties, the following is a little gem from the "Ladies" page of *Links of Help* in 1928:

> Not long ago a missionary threw rather a new light on the necessity for neat work in the garments sent abroad. She told me that the natives of the country she represents happen to be excellent needle-women and anything of a slipshod nature received from Christians in Britain conveys an undesirable impression. Not long ago she discovered garments with raw-edged seams in a parcel—little chance for those when handed over to the tender mercies of a washerwoman. Another suggestion was that button-holes should be worked only by experts, as they often have to be done over again before the garments can be laundered. She hesitated about mentioning these little points, as she so deeply values all the lovingkindness shown, but felt sure that all would be glad of any hints that would help to raise their work nearer to the perfection aimed at.[8]

Most missionary societies encouraged their supporters to keep a collection box in their home. The Lakher Mission, working among one of the hill tribes of India, advertised (without further explanation) "missionary boxes in the shape of a telephone." The London Missionary Society favored a replica of its missionary ship the *John Williams* (named for one of its early missionaries and martyrs, who was eaten by South Pacific cannibals). The Regions Beyond Helpers Union used its collection box to give a visual reminder of the comparative statistics of world religions.

Mention of collection boxes leads to an example of hymns and verse as in the following little ditty from the *Mission World*, entitled "An Unhappy Missionary Box":

> Forgotten and forlorn I live
> Upon a dusty shelf.
> And feel so downcast and so sad,
> I hardly know myself:

---

8 *Links of Help with Other Lands* 16, no. 210 (1928): 377.

A missionary box am I
And better days have seen,
For copper, silver—yes and gold
Within my walls have been.

Now I am empty—no not quite,
For something you may hear—
A mournful jingle from my depths
By pennies made, I fear;
I scorn not pennies—no indeed,
Their worth too well I know:
But twopence only in a box
Does make one's spirits low.

The missionaries say, indeed,
That pence to pounds soon grow;
But older people ought to give,
We want our money so.
And thus in emptiness I wait
And dustier grow each day,
While, heedless of my silent plea,
You, round me, work and play.

My words are weak and poor at best,
I know not how to plead,
But look upon the distant fields
To harvest white indeed;
The heathen are in thickest gloom,
Do you need a stronger plea?
Then listen to His voice who said—
"Ye did it unto Me."[9]

---

9   *The Mission World* 3, no. 34 (1896): 568.

FROM *BEYOND ALPINE SNOW* AND *HOMES OF THE EAST* 141

Web-Based Initiatives for Mission Research

Photographs taken in the field between 1850 and World War II represent an important documentary resource for scholars interested in the international missionary movement. In many cases, however, the actual usefulness of these visual archives has been limited by their unorganized state and their dispersion across widely separated mission repositories.

Recognizing the research potential of these photos, the Getty Grant Program is sponsoring the creation of a Web site that initially will feature the collections held by the Day Missions Library at Yale Divinity School, New Haven, Connecticut; the Catholic Foreign Mission Society of America, Maryknoll, New York; the School of Oriental and African Studies, London; the Norwegian Missionary Society, Stavanger, Norway; the Leipzig Mission, Leipzig, Germany; and the Moravian Church, Herrnhut, Germany.

Photographic prints and negatives from these excellent collections will be cataloged in conformity with international archiving standards, then digitized and aggregated into a searchable electronic database, accessible through a Web site hosted by the University of Southern California Library's Archive Research Center. Once launched, this Web-based resource, provisionally called the **Internet Mission Photography Archive**, will evolve and expand as other mission collections are brought online. The goal of the project is to launch this site by December 2004.

Collaborators on this effort will be Jon Miller, Center for Religion and Civic Culture, University of Southern California; Martha Lund Smalley, Day Missions Collection, Yale Divinity School; Rosemary Seton, London University, School of Oriental and African Studies; Paul Jenkins, Basel Mission and Basel University, Switzerland; Nils Kristian Høimyr, Norwegian Mission Society, Stavanger; and Adam Jones, University of Leipzig, African Studies Center.

The **MUNDUS Gateway**, a Web-based guide to more than 400 collections of overseas missionary materials held in archives, libraries, museums, and other institutions in the United Kingdom, provides descriptions for each collection, plus location and access information for each holding institution. There is a facility for free-text searches, as well as searches by personal and corporate names, place-names, and subjects. Maps are provided to assist with regional searches, and there are links to related projects and resources. The MUNDUS Gateway, housed on a University of London computer, can be viewed with a password at www.mundus.ac.uk. Rosemary Seton, Archivist for the School of Oriental and African Studies, London, is the Project Manager. Funding for this project was provided by the Research Support Libraries Programme, Higher

Education Funding Council for England. For more information, visit www.rslp .ac.uk/projects/research/41.htm.

Great poetry or hymnody is rare in missionary magazines, but as a source for the study of popular piety and attitudes, they are a much-neglected source. "Jack Horner Up-to-Date" shows a familiar text reworked in a missionary vein:

> Little Jack Horner,
> Sat in a corner
> Eating a very queer pie:
> He saw in a trice
> It held everything nice
> From the lands where the mission fields lie.
> From Ceylon came the spice,
> And from China the rice,
> And bananas from African highlands;
>
> There wore nutmegs and cloves
> Sent from Borneo's groves.
> And yams from the South Sea Islands.
> There were nuts from Brazil
> All the corners to fill,
> And sugar and sage from Siam;
> And from Turkey a fig
> That was really so big,
> Jack's mouth thought, "It's bigger than I am."
>
> There were pomegranates fair
> Grown in Persia's soft air,
> And tortillas from Mexico found there:
> And there did appear
> Grapes and grain from Korea
> And all the things that abound there.
>
> An Egyptian date
> Did not turn up too late;
> He need not for tea to Japan go;
> Tamarinds were not few;
> There were oranges, too
> And from India, many a mango.

FROM *BEYOND ALPINE SNOW* AND *HOMES OF THE EAST*

"Now," thought little Jack,
"What shall I send back
To these lands for their presents to me?
The Bible, indeed,
Is the gift they most need,
So that shall go over the sea."[10]

Locating Missionary Periodicals

Nothing is more frustrating for scholars than to know that relevant source material exists but not to know where to find it. The database project has therefore placed importance on recording location information. Up to four locations are cited for each title, although often there is only one or two known locations. They are coded to show how comprehensive the holding is at each location, whether complete, nearly complete, moderately complete, or very incomplete.

For missionary periodicals the richest mines arc the British Library; the Oxford and Cambridge University libraries; the School of Oriental and African Studies; the Orchard Learning Resources Centre, Selly Oak, Birmingham; and New College Library, Edinburgh. There are some rich denominational seams such as the Moravian Church Archive and Library and the Library of the Society of Friends, both in London. Full contact details for these libraries are included on the database, as also for libraries such as the Gamble Library of Union Theological College, Belfast, and the Angus Library of Regent's Park College, Oxford. Each of these libraries may be the only known location for a particular title. For some titles no locations have yet been traced, for example, the newsletters of sundry Anglican diocesan associations. Work continues, and the project team would be pleased to hear about any titles and locations that have been missed.

I end not so much with a conclusion as with thoughts about how the study of missionary periodicals can be carried forward. Currents in World Christianity, the parent project, has now come to an end; however, provision has been made for continued maintenance of the Missionary Periodicals Database Web site. If we had unlimited time and funding, it would be good also to record the information in book form. And then it would be good to initiate sister projects recording missionary periodicals published in America, in continental Europe,

---

10   "Jack Horner Up-to-Date," *Young People's Inland Africa* 11, no. 49 (April–May, 1932): 11.

and on the mission fields themselves. I would like to see an anthology/sourcebook/book of readings from missionary periodicals. Finally, all of us involved in this project hope that more and more scholars from a wide variety of disciplines will become aware of the richness of the raw materials to be mined from missionary periodicals.

Missionaries as Social Commentators: The Indian Case

Geoffrey A. Oddie

The purpose of this essay is to discuss missionaries as social commentators with specific reference to British Protestant missionaries in India in the nineteenth century. There is no attempt in what follows to deny that missionary observers shared many assumptions and attitudes in common with other Europeans including aspects of the so-called "orientalist" view of India: the notion that India was essentially different from Europe and generally inferior.[1] The argument of this paper is that, notwithstanding these views and the particular bias inherent in missionary perspectives, missionary comment (if used critically) can provide a valuable and, in some cases, unique insight into social developments in India in the nineteenth century.

The first part of the essay begins with remarks on the extent and variety of comment which was, at least in part, a reflection of the extent to which missionaries succeeded in mixing with various classes in the population. A discussion of the nature and degree of missionary contact with different groups in Indian society is followed by an attempt to identify the main types of social comment; comment which can be categorised according to the missionary's purpose. The question arises as to why the missionaries were drawn into making social comment in the first place and how their aims and objectives affected what they reported and how they wrote. The second part of the paper concentrates on the advantages and problems for the historian of using this type of material with all its limitations of selectivity, bias and unacknowledged assumptions. Here I move from a consideration of more general themes and material to an analysis of individual accounts of particular Hindu socio-religious customs.

Source: Oddie, G. A., "Missionaries as Social Commentators: The Indian Case," in R. A. Bickers and R. Seton (eds.), *Missionary Encounters: Sources and Issues*, Richmond: Taylor and Francis, 1996, pp. 197–210. Reproduced from *Missionary Encounters*, 1st Edition by Robert A. Bickers; Rosemary Seton, published by Routledge. © Curzon Press, 1996. Reproduced by arrangement with Taylor & Francis Books UK.

---

1   For a discussion of the Orientalist view as applied to India see especially Ronald Inden "Orientalist Constructions of India," *Modern Asian Studies*, 20, 3 (1986), pp. 401–46.

One of the first things that strikes the research worker familiar with missionary literature and archival material is the wide range and variety of missionary comment on Indian society throughout the nineteenth century. Almost everywhere they went, the missionaries observed, took notes and commented on the nature of Indian social life and on social conditions and particular problems which claimed their attention from time to time. Indeed it is most unusual not to find somewhere remarks on almost all major issues of social concern raised and discussed in India during this period.

The missionaries were especially interested in the broad question of the relationship between Hinduism and the social system, but apart from that more theoretical consideration, they usually confined their comments to the more down-to-earth problems and issues which arose out of their work and in the context of their particular situation. These issues include many over-lapping matters such as caste and caste conflict, *sati*, early marriage and widowhood, temple prostitution, hook-swinging, the plight of the untouchables, slavery (especially in Travancore), land systems and landlord oppression, the use of coercion in the recruitment and management of labour, racism and oppression by European indigo planters, the sufferings of the peasantry, the partiality of the police and corruption in the courts, the spread of drunkenness, opium cultivation and consumption, famines in south India and elsewhere, epidemics and disease. Apart from comment on these and other specific social issues, some of which were confined to rural areas, the missionary records are also a valuable source of comment on urban life and development. This includes a fairly regular flow of information on intellectual movements and political, religious and social developments among the new Western-educated élites.

But while the coverage and number of topics is impressive, missionary comment was (to state the obvious) always positioned from a particular point of view. The main focus and emphasis in their accounts was, for example, somewhat different from that of government officers concerned with procuring the East India Company's investment or with the problem of reconciling the landed gentry to British rule.

One major and increasingly important focal point in missionary literature was the life and condition of the depressed classes in the rural population: the poor, the marginalised and oppressed, including untouchable communities. As a result of their movement out into the countryside in increasing numbers after 1815, the missionaries became better acquainted with the depressed classes and depressed class problems than most other Europeans. Indeed their letters, journals and reports, and the evidence they gave before various inquiries, constitutes one of the most valuable sources for "history from below".

One of the classical methods of evangelism was through what was known as itineration: going on long tours for days or weeks at a time, camping and preaching in the countryside. Many of the missionaries went on these journeys and their journals provide us with fascinating detailed comment including reports of encounters and conversations with all kinds of people, not the least of whom were the peasants and the poor and oppressed. Mission centres with sub-stations, including schools and chapels, were established in outlying villages in the heart of the countryside and in areas where other Europeans, let alone district officers, were seldom seen. Furthermore, it was the peasantry and poorer class peoples who were among the converts even before the advent of the large scale and more dramatic depressed class movements into Christianity during the last quarter of the nineteenth century.

Secondly, while the missionaries were well acquainted with what was happening at the bottom of the social scale, they were also well aware of some of the developments at the top, more especially the attitude and aspirations of the modern Western-educated élites. Almost all British missionary societies concentrated their energies, at least initially, on trying to capture the hearts and minds of the educated classes. The Protestants were pioneers of education through English and, by the end of the century, they were teaching about 6,000 scholars, or 35 per cent of the total number of college-level students excluding those in professional and technical education.[2] In addition to this some societies like the Cambridge Mission to Delhi and the Oxford Brotherhood in Calcutta devoted much of their attention to work among the same small section in the population: providing hostel accommodation, mounting extra-mural lectures and circulating handbills and newspapers, the most famous of which was the *Epiphany*.

Thirdly, missionary sources also provide a considerable amount of comment on women's issues throughout the century, such as the discussion and debate over *sati*, early marriage, enforced widowhood, female education and other topics. The fact remains, however, that despite agitation aimed at improving the Indian woman's status and condition, males were still the *primary* focus of attention—missionary journals, reports and other papers being much more about men than women.[3] The missionaries preached to audiences which were composed very largely of men and they also worked in an educational system which at least at the college level, was also largely a male affair. It was

2   J. Ritcher, *A History of Missions in India* (translated by Sydney H. Moore) (Edinburgh and London, 1908), p. 320.

3   Ibid., pp. 329–45.

therefore only after the extension of women's work for women—the development of the Zenana visiting system, the further growth of female education and the advent of female missionary itineration—in the last quarter of the nineteenth century, that missionaries in general (male and female) gained a much greater knowledge and understanding of Indian women.[4] In London in 1875 Mrs M. Weitbrecht, wife of a CMS missionary, published a collection of essays entitled *The Women of India and Christian Work in the Zenana*. It included a paper on "Condition of women *as it actually exists* in Bengal and Northwest India", a sad reminder of the state of ignorance prior to 1875. After that period however, female missionaries arrived in India in increasing numbers until they outnumbered male missionaries at the end of the century. Thus while the emphasis in missionary sources is on the depressed classes and the Western-educated élites, it also includes useful material which might be used in research on gender issues.

A major weakness in the range of archival holdings is perhaps in the comparative lack of sympathetic and, in some cases, detailed comment on the life and problems of the more traditional dominant classes in the population. A few individual missionaries were well-acquainted with the life-style and attitude of some of the princes and rajas. There is, for example, substantial missionary material on the Rajas of Tanjore and also valuable evidence of discussions between CMS missionaries and the Raja of Burdwan. But this material really only reminds one of what was exceptional, and of the fact that missionaries in general had comparatively little contact with princes and rajas, or with the traditional (non-Western-educated) landed and commercial classes.

In fact, the Protestants spent most of their time and attention working among people who tended, if anything, to represent a challenge to the power and status of these traditional groups. Furthermore, though the missionaries knew a lot about landlords and landed and tenurial systems this was not out of sympathy for the landlords as a class. It was not for the missionaries to write books like Nirmal Mukherjee's well-known and sympathetic study entitled *Zamindar*, but rather for them to expose the abuses of power and the injustice perpetrated by the landed classes.[5] Indeed, missionaries and landlords were not infrequently in direct conflict, partly because missionaries regarded the latter as an obstacle to the spread of the Christian Gospel and because landlords

---

4 For some of these points on gender and Christian mission I owe a great deal to Helen McCulloch, who recently completed her History IV honours thesis in the Department of History, University of Sydney on "The Female Encounter with Christianity: Protestant Missions in Nineteenth-Century South India".

5 N. Mukherjee, *A Bengal Zamindar: Jaykrishna Mukherjee of Uttarpara and his Times, 1808–1888* (Calcutta, 1975).

MISSIONARIES AS SOCIAL COMMENTATORS 149

felt very directly threatened by the spread of Christianity among their tenants and labourers, mainly because they feared loss of control over them.[6]

In relying on missionary social comment, therefore, the historian is unlikely to obtain a balanced over-view of the different groups in nineteenth-century India, but rather might develop a perspective which emphasises the role of the new élites and which also offers a critique of society from the point of view of the underclasses or dispossessed. Moreover missionary reports probably devote an excessive amount of space to Hindus rather than to Muslims (even when we take into account the higher proportion of Hindus in the population).[7]

If one is to understand missionary social comment, it is not only important to gain some insight into how and where missionaries gained their social information, but also to understand something of their aims in writing. With this latter problem in mind it is helpful to classify missionary comment into three different types according to what appears to have been the author's purpose.

Firstly, there was general comment on social structure, social conditions and the life of the people, told in such a way so as to encourage Christian missions. Secondly, there was similar general information presented not so much with the aim of arousing missionary enthusiasm, but with the aim of providing the general reader with the results of well-researched scholarly investigation; and, thirdly, there was considerable focused and impassioned comment and analysis of particular social problems and issues, material which was presented with very specific goals in mind.

Much of the general comment on Indian society and on the daily life and condition of the people appears in books and pamphlets specifically designed to influence the European public and to encourage greater support for Christian missions. One of the earliest and best known examples of this type of literature was William Ward's *A View of the History, Literature and Mythology of the Hindoos*, first published in 1811, and reproduced with some modification

---

6 On this issue see especially G. A. Oddie, *Hindu and Christian in Southeast India* (London, 1991), pp. 161–62; M. M. Ali, *The Bengali Reaction to Christian Missionary Activities 1833–1857* (Chittagong, 1965), ch. 8; G. A. Oddie, *Social Protest in India: British Protestant Missionaries and Social Reforms 1850–1900* (Delhi, 1979), ch. 4.

7 While a considerable amount of missionary work was conducted among Muslims in the North-West Provinces much less was done elsewhere. According to the Revd F. M. Wherry, one of the speakers at the 1882–3 decennial conference, "though Protestant Missions had been established in India for three quarters of a century, yet there are only two or three foreign Missionaries especially interested in working among the eighteen millions of Bengali Muslims! The case is scarcely better in some other provinces", *Report of the Second Decennial Conference held at Calcutta 1882–83* (Calcutta, 1883), p. 228.

in several further editions.[8] Ward's aim appears to have been to describe Hindu manners and customs in such a way as to demonstrate the enormity of the Hindu system and to show the need to replace it with Protestant Christianity.[9] Other missionaries, while not so condemnatory, were also anxious to encourage an interest in Indian people, and a greater sympathy for them in their "heathen" condition, and to stimulate greater support for Indian missions. Writing in his book *The Land of the Veda*, published in 1854, the Revd Percival declared, for example, that the object of the work was:

> to supply information respecting India, its people and their condition, in such a form and to such an extent as may, it is hoped, contribute to awaken interest where little may have been felt, and to produce among the friends of missions ... a deeper sympathy and greater effort on behalf of Hindus and other Eastern nations, whose intellectual and moral improvement demands from the Church of Christ greater earnestness and self-sacrifice.[10]

W. J. Wilkins, author of *Daily Life and Work in India*, and Henry Rice, author of *Native Life in South India*, were also concerned that their work would awaken sympathy and encourage greater support and activity on behalf of Christian missions.[11]

Secondly, there were other publications, less concerned with Christian missions, where the author's intention appears to have been to make a more scholarly and impartial contribution to knowledge and understanding. Among these more academic works of social observation and comment one might include J. E. Padfield's *The Hindu at Home*, Samuel Mateer's *Native Life in Travancore*, Bishop Caldwell's sketch *The Tinnevelly Shanars* and his *History of Tinnevelly*, and a number of works by James Long.[12] Long, who according to one of his

---

8   *A View of the History, Literature and Mythology of the Hindoos, including a minute Description of their Manners and Customs and Translation from their principal Works in three volumes* (London, 1811).

9   Ibid., introduction to vol. 1, and E. Daniel Potts, *British Baptist Missionaries in India 1793–1837: The History of Serampore and its Missions* (Cambridge, 1967), pp. 92–94.

10 P. Percival, *The Land of the Veda: India Briefly Described in some of its Aspects, Physical, Social, Intellectual and Moral* (London, 1854), p. vi.

11 W. J. Wilkins, *Daily Life and Work in India* (London, 1888); H. Rice, *Native Life in South India: being sketches of the social and religious characteristics of the Hindus* (London, n.d.).

12 J. E. Padfield, *The Hindu at Home, being Sketches of Hindu Daily Life*, 2nd edition (London, 1908); S. Mateer, *Native Life in Travancore* (London, 1883), R. Caldwell, *The Tinnevelly Shanars: A Sketch of their Religion, and their Moral Condition and Characteristics, as a*

colleagues, "delighted in antiquarian and historical researches",[13] was one of the founders of the Bengal Social Science Association which was launched in Calcutta in 1867.[14] As one of its most active members he contributed a number of papers, some of which have recently been republished. These include examinations of Bengali proverbs, the social condition of the Muslims of Bengal, and aspects of social life in Calcutta and Bombay and village communities in India and Russia.[15] Some missionaries also made a contribution to well-known ethnographic and official publications. Gustav Oppert, author of *The Original Inhabitants of Bharatavarsa or India*, and Edgar Thurston, compiler of eight hefty volumes on *Castes and Tribes of Southern India*, as well as *Ethnographic Notes in Southern India*, both made use of missionary social comment and observation. Missionary data was also incorporated into District Gazetteers.[16]

The third main type of missionary comment is observation and argument focused on specific issues and aimed at strengthening movements for social reform. As we have seen, the missionaries campaigned against what were described as Hindu "cruelties"—practices such as the exposure of the sick and dying on the banks of rivers, *sati*, and hook-swinging, customs which the missionaries believed were irrational, barbaric and inhumane. They also advocated some fundamental changes in the socio-economic system, especially in Bengal and Madras. In this respect they had much to say about issues such as caste and untouchability, indigo planting, landlord oppression, and other factors which kept the underclasses in a perpetual state of poverty and dependence on the will of others.

One of the reasons for concern about these problems was a conviction that such conditions, including the unbridled power and attitude of the landed classes, created serious obstacles to the spread of Christianity.[17] It was held that in Bengal, for example, the European indigo planters, "so-called" Christians, set a very bad example in the way they or their agents maltreated their Hindu and Muslim employees. The missionaries were also concerned and frustrated about the way in which Hindu landlords deliberately attempted to prevent tenants

---

    Caste, with special reference to the facilities and hindrances to the progress of Christianity amongst them (Madras, 1840), and *A History of Tinnevelly* (New Delhi, 1982).

13   M. A. Sherring, *The History of Protestant Missions in India* (London, 1875), p. 127.

14   G. A. Oddie, "The Revd James Long and Protestant Missionary Policy in Bengal, 1840–1872," (unpublished Ph.D. thesis, University of London, 1964), pp. 366–72.

15   Ibid., p. 372.

16   G. Oppert, *On the Original Inhabitants of Bharatavarsa or India* (New Delhi, 1986), (first edition 1893); E. Thurston, *Castes and Tribes of Southern India* (Madras, 1909); E. Thurston, *Ethnographic Notes in Southern India* (Madras, 1906). See also *Gazetteer of the Bombay Presidency, Belgaum* (Bombay, 1884).

17   See especially Oddie, *Social Protest in India*, Chs. 4 and 5.

and others from converting to Christianity; and they were also dismayed by the general effect of poverty, which seemed to create a type of religious apathy among the people; the Bengali peasants, for example, being too preoccupied with their immediate needs and suffering in the here-and-now to attend to teachings about their spiritual condition or the life hereafter.

These evangelistic considerations were, however, not infrequently mixed with feelings of indignation, or even outrage, at the level of brutality and injustice inherent in the socio-economic system. Furthermore, linked with a growing recognition of injustices, prevalent especially in rural areas, was a growing consciousness of the powerlessness of the lower classes and a feeling that poor, unorganised and illiterate peoples could do little to help themselves.

Thus the further the missionaries extended their work and the longer they remained, the more they recognised the way in which social and economic conditions seemed to impede the progress of their work; the more they were disturbed by evidence of exploitation and suffering and the more involved they became in social debate and agitation. The end result was a greatly increased degree of social criticism and comment. However, as already implied, it was hardly objective comment In what the missionaries wrote there was no attempt at any kind of dispassionate objectivity. They were passionate one-sided advocates resolutely determined to turn the world upside down.

Issues Related to the Use of Material

Given then that this is the nature of missionary social comment, what are the advantages, or disadvantages of work with this type of material? How difficult is it to use in the reconstruction of Indian social history?

The first point that needs to be stressed with reference to missionary sources as a whole is that there is one clear advantage in using them that is not always present in other records, namely, that in the case of missionaries we already know something about their ultimate aims and what their biases are likely to be. Whereas in some other sources the writers' aims and agenda are not always so clearly apparent, in the case of the missionary material, missionaries seldom tried to hide their objectives or particular point of view.

Furthermore, the material which focused on particular issues such as *sati*, indigo-planting and other topics, though produced in the heat of controversy, is not necessarily misleading or particularly problematic. The missionaries were under considerable pressure to produce the evidence and verify everything they claimed. The very success of their reform crusades depended on their collection of reliable and trustworthy information and on convincing the

MISSIONARIES AS SOCIAL COMMENTATORS   153

sceptics and unbelievers. Moreover, if they were to enlist the support of others they had to do their research and be prepared to defend the findings.

One of the earliest examples of this type of social research, vital if the missionaries were to sway public opinion, were the surveys they undertook in connection with *sati*.[18] In 1803 the Serampore Baptists deputed a number or Indians to travel from place to place within a radius of thirty miles round Calcutta to report on the number of *satis* of which they had heard. In the following years the Baptists and their allies systematically collected a considerable amount of detailed information, material which was published in books and pamphlets and quoted in debates in the House of Commons. This information included the names of the husband and wife, their caste, the age or the widow and the number and age of children left as orphans.[19]

The success of missionary agitation for reforms in the indigo planting and zamindari systems also depended on the extent to which they were able to establish and verify their case. European planters for example, accused the missionaries of ignorance, lies and slander, and the *Hindoo Patriot*, one of the more influential Bengali-controlled papers, declared that: "No body of men have been more bitterly or more grossly or more indecently attacked by the organs of the indigo manufacturing interest in Bengal than the Christian missionaries settled in the country".[20]

Those in the countryside had first to convince their city colleagues, members of the Calcutta Missionary Conference, of the need for reform of the indigo system. Once the missionaries as a body were better informed and more aware of what was involved, leaders of the movement had to be prepared to debate the issues in the public press and eventually to try to convince the government of the need for intervention. When, after the indigo disturbances of 1859, the authorities finally agreed to appoint a Commission of Enquiry the missionaries were once again called to give evidence and substantiate their views. Those who took part in agitation for reform of the zamindari system, for improvement in the position and well-being of pariahs (untouchables) in Madras and for some of the other reforms in Indian society were also well aware of the fact that their case rested, at least in part, on the reliability and persuasiveness of the evidence they produced.

---

18   K. Ingham, *Reformers in India 1793–1833: An Account of the Work of Protestant Missionaries on behalf of Social Reform* (Cambridge, 1956), p. 45.

19   William Johns, *A Collection of Facts and Opinions relating to the Burning of Widows with the dead bodies of their husbands and other destructive customs prevalent in British India* (Birmingham, 1816).

20   Quoted in the *Calcutta Christian Observer*, 30 (February, 1861), p. 83.

In one sense, therefore, missionary records are easier to use than many other sources. The purpose of the missionary's comment—the agenda—is usually fairly clear and, in certain circumstances, the missionaries had every incentive to produce documented and well-founded information. However, this is not to say there are no traps or problems in working on missionary material. On the contrary, these sources present many of the same difficulties and pit-falls which can arise when one is using government or any other records.

Firstly, in some of the published material, including more general comment on Indian society, it is difficult to identify the author's sources of information. Some authors, such as Percival, acknowledge the fact that they incorporated material from other books, and in cases such as these, it is not always easy to distinguish second hand information from comments which were based on experience and observation. Because of the lack of modern forms of documentation the reader must remain uncertain of the basis of information. In some other cases, however, authors were much more conscious of the need to describe their credentials and to verify and check for themselves wherever possible. One such missionary was Henry Rice who in the preface to *Native Life in South India* explained that he had for upwards of eighteen years moved freely among all classes of the people in various parts of the country; that he had taken notes on what he had "seen and heard", and that he had checked on the accuracy of his description of manners and customs with "an educated brahman gentleman". Even if one may doubt whether a "brahman gentleman" was fully qualified to comment on low caste customs, Rice was at least *attempting* to provide the reader with accurate and reliable information.[21]

Secondly, there is the problem of selectivity, the all-too-familiar process whereby commentators ignore material which might have given a more balanced view. For example, there can be no doubt that William Ward witnessed much of what he describes in his *View ... of the Hindoos*. In fact many of the scenes he refers to are recorded in his letters and in a separate diary which is now located in the archives at Serampore. Historians such as K. K. Datta and others who have made use of Ward's book are certainly justified in using parts of his work as evidence, especially where there is corroboration.[22] However, the fact remains that in order to underline the benefits of Christianity, Ward tended to dwell on the darker and more reprehensible aspects of Hinduism and the Hindu social order. This was a technique which some of the more liberal-minded missionaries were inclined to reject. One of these was James Long who commented that:

---

21   Rice, *Native Life in South India*, p. 5.
22   Potts, *British Baptist Missionaries in India*, p. 94.

Many of Mr Ward's remarks respecting the cruelties and immoralities among the Hindus are no more applicable to the body of the people than a description of Billings Gate and the Old Bailey, in London, would be to the inhabitants of the west end of the town.[23]

Thirdly, there are all kinds of personal and cultural factors which one has to take into account when using missionary material. Like most other European writers on India the missionaries were foreigners, on the outside, looking in. Even in their most scholarly work, when dispassionate objectivity was a primary goal, factors in their background, education and European perspective could determine not only what they noticed or looked at, but the way they interpreted or explained what they saw.

One of the best ways of illustrating this point is to take missionary accounts of particular social customs. For example, even a brief analysis of missionary comments on hook-swinging exhibitions will show that the descriptions varied a great deal depending on the background, education and assumptions of the individual observer. Hook-swinging was, for the most part, a form of voluntary or self-imposed bodily penance in which the individual was swung on hooks embedded in the flesh and tendons below the shoulder blades. The aim was usually to fulfil a vow and/or appease the deity on behalf of the rest of the community. The practice, which was widespread in India during the first half of the nineteenth century, was condemned not only by missionaries and other Europeans, but also by an increasing number of Indian reformers.

Missionary descriptions of hook-swinging usually tell us as much about the individual observer as they do about the custom itself. They generally contain some or all of the following components of information. First, information about the observer (who was usually a male): why he went to see the exhibition, how he *felt* and the theological or moral import of what he saw and heard. Second, information about the ritual itself, what the missionary saw and heard and how he interprets or explains the phenomena. Two missionaries who wrote detailed accounts of hook-swinging were James Lynch, a Methodist missionary, and J. E. Sharkey of the CMS. A brief comparison of their descriptions not only helps to pin-point background, cultural and other factors which influenced their accounts, but also highlights limitations which might and should be taken into account by any critical historian looking out for the evidence and attempting to understand hook-swinging rituals at this time.

---

23   J. Long, *Handbook of Bengal Missions, in connection with the Church of England together with an Account of general Educational Efforts in North India* (London, 1848), p. 40.

Lynch visited a hook-swinging exhibition at Royapettah in Madras in August 1820, three years after his arrival in Madras.[24] Not being fluent in Tamil he took a Tamil-speaking friend with him. He described in some detail the temple complex and the appearance of the deity. He noted the extent of animal sacrifice and the fact that hook-swinging was not the only form of self-torture being practised among devotees. He described in detail how the hooks were inserted (an experience which changed his views that the ritual was a fraud) and he also described how the men were swung, what they did while swinging and how they were revered by the crowd. There are, however, limitations in the account. Lynch confessed he did not understand the pedigree of the deity and he made the very serious mistake of thinking the priests were Brahmins, a point which is clearly contradicted by all the other evidence at our disposal. Having recently arrived from Europe, and being familiar with the Brahminical idea of the four *varnas*, he seems to have simply assumed that all priests must be Brahmins, whereas others, more familiar with religion in practice, were aware that many other castes had their own priests and ritual specialists.

J. E. Sharkey described a hook-swinging exhibition at Weyoor in Masulipatam district in February 1848 and again, three years later, in February 1851.[25] He was an Anglo-Indian and, unlike Lynch, fluent in the vernacular and familiar with local custom. He had already had five years of work and experience among the people of Masulipatam district and had witnessed a hook-swinging exhibition in another village and on an earlier occasion prior to his first visit to Weyoor in 1848.[26] In his first account of swinging at Weyoor, Sharkey described the deity and forms of worship and also included comment on why people were attending the festival. His report also included a detailed description of the principal swinger and how the swinging was carried out. Feeling somewhat dissatisfied with this, his first report, and wanting to know more, Sharkey revisited the festival three years later. In the report on his second visit he included a lengthy discussion of the origins and legends connected with the deity, emphasised that the priests were in fact shepherds, and had a great deal more to say about the commercialization of the ritual, and about which particular parties profited most from the practice.

---

24 WMMS, Lynch to Secretary, 25 August 1820. See also N. W. Taggart, "The Irish Factor in World Methodism in the Eighteenth and Nineteenth Centuries" (unpublished Ph.D. thesis, Queen's University, Belfast, 1981), pp. 198–255.

25 CMS Archives, C12/0222/3, Sharkey's Journal for quarter ending March, 1848 and 12/0222/9, Journal, 15 February 1851.

26 CMS C12/0101/5, H. W. Fox, Journal, 26–27 December 1844.

Clearly all reports on hook-swinging have some kind of limitation; and Sharkey himself admitted that observations, as a result of his first visit, were somewhat inadequate and incomplete. Yet it is also apparent that the Sharkey material generally provides the historian with more satisfactory and more extensive data and evidence than the Lynch account. Unlike Lynch, Sharkey was able to take advantage of his fluency in the vernacular to interview the local people. His previous experience, length of time in the country and knowledge of local customs enabled him to explain and interpret much more fully what he encountered at the festival. Furthermore, he asked a broader range of questions and was determined to check the accuracy of his information. While Lynch confessed that he had seen enough, Sharkey confessed no such thing, and revisited the site three years later. This not only enabled him to check his stories and the main events, but also to see the differences between the festival in 1848 and 1851.

If used critically and with common sense much of this type of missionary material is of considerable value to the writer of Indian socio-religious history. The crucial point is for the scholar to ask questions about the observer's credentials. Why was the missionary there in the first place? What was the purpose of the account? What was the observer's past history? What did he or she know of India or social customs? Was the author of the report fluent in the local language? Whom did he or she consult? In other words, who were the informants, and so on?

The author's pre-history has always been an important factor in missionary social comment. It was, for example, an important ingredient which not only affected the way they described and understood hook-swinging, but also the caste system. Coming from what Stuart Piggin has described as a "middling" section of the British population, from a dynamic upwardly mobile class, which placed considerable stress on the importance of individual initiative and talent and on the individual being able to rise through the ranks, they looked for a similar system in India itself. However, instead of finding a system which provided opportunities for the individual they discovered what they claimed was a form of "tyranny" which frustrated individuals, keeping them "locked up" within their social circle. What was not so apparent to missionaries (because it was not something they were looking for) was corporate mobility, a factor which gave the caste system a greater flexibility than many missionary commentators were able to perceive.[27]

---

27   S. Piggin, *Making Evangelical Missionaries, 1789–1858* (Appleyard, Abingdon, Oxford, 1984), ch. 1; Oddie, *Social Protest in India*, pp. 66–67.

Conclusion

Though the purpose of this volume is to highlight issues relating to missionary archives, I have not attempted to distinguish between the archival and other missionary material. While it is true that some missionary records are to be found only in manuscript form in archives, a certain amount of what is in manuscript collections was eventually published, and, added to this, are pamphlets, books and other works which appeared only in a printed form.

I have argued that this material contains a wide range of social comment and that many of the difficulties of working with it are little different from difficulties which arise when one is using government or other specialist data. There too one finds selectivity, a lack of balance, the imprint on the material of particular points of view, cultural bias, presuppositions and so on. What therefore seems to be different about the missionary corpus of social information? It is focused perhaps no more narrowly on particular objectives than, for example, material which was compiled in order to perpetuate empire. Furthermore, missionaries, perhaps unlike some government commentators, were open and frank about what they were trying to achieve. The subject matter and angle of vision is very different from what one sometimes finds in official and government records concerned with the trading and commercial classes or with placating the princes, zamindars and other groups within the established order. Missionary records, by way of contrast, focus primarily on the world of the modern Western-educated élites and especially on the underdog—the underprivileged classes and eventually also on women. Last, but not least, this material also includes much of the available information about the missionaries themselves, their problems and way of life. They were not only observers and commentators on Indian society, but were also (at least temporarily) part of the scene they so often attempted to describe.

Thinking Missiologically about the History of Mission

Stanley H. Skreslet

Is there a missiological approach to the history of mission?[1] Prompting this question is the fact that the history of mission is no longer the special preserve of those who support and participate in missionary activities. Now a growing legion of scholars is being drawn to the study of mission history, among whom we find specialists in politics and economics, Marxists, feminists, historical anthropologists and other kinds of social historians, and Americanists as well as researchers focused on non-Western societies, not to mention religious historians of every stripe who make it their business to study the world's burgeoning collection of faith communities and traditions. All these and more have found in the history of Christian mission a virtually inexhaustible supply of data with which to fuel their various research projects.[2]

Missiologists who study the history of mission share many overlapping concerns with these other scholars, not the least of which is the requirement to practice good historical technique. Some common aims likewise drive much historical work on missions today, and missiologists may find themselves working alongside other scholars who are also seeking to understand the dynamics of cultural and religious change, the emergence and diffusion of modern ideas, the art of apologetics, and the conduct of interfaith dialogue, plus the nature of the church and its place in the world. Mutual interests are thus a part of what needs to be discussed in connection with the question posed above. But this essay also goes on to address the more difficult issue of particularity: do missiological investigations add anything distinctive to these other scholarly efforts?

Source: Skreslet, S. H., "Thinking Missiologically about the History of Mission," *International Bulletin of Missionary Research* 31.2 (April 2007): pp. 59–65. Copyright © 2007 by SAGE. Reprinted by Permission of SAGE Publications, Ltd.

---

1 This essay is based on Stanley H. Skreslet's inaugural lecture as F. S. Royster Professor of Christian Missions, Union Theological Seminary and Presbyterian School of Christian Education, Richmond, Virginia.

2 I wish to thank historian Heather J. Sharkey for her careful reading of an earlier draft of this article.

Common Concerns

With respect to methods, missiologists have no special set of procedures to apply to the problems of history. They must follow the same rules of evidence that pertain to everyone else who studies the history of mission or indeed any other kind of history. If widely recognized scholarly standards of verification in history are ignored, then accuracy suffers, and what purports to be description or analysis slides instead into the category of mere speculation about the past. Therefore missiologists, like other historians, must be concerned about what (if anything) constitutes an objective fact, about how material evidence can be used to buttress or disprove the claims of texts, about the problems of agency and causation in history, plus the need to differentiate between perceptions of an event and the historical event itself.

No scholar has all the evidence that he or she would like for solving the conundrums of mission history. The data are always fragmentary. The memories we have are faulty and sometimes contradictory. The archives are not only incomplete but skewed. On the matter of archives, missiologists working today who specialize in the history of mission are challenged as scholars by the fact that foreign missionaries dominate the accumulated reserve of texts at our disposal. The documents so avidly produced by missionaries and their sending agencies in the past can assume an inordinate degree of authority for us today simply because they often are the only written sources for this history we now possess.[3] This imbalance in the record is a serious methodological problem to be negotiated and overcome, which explains why investigators of every kind (including missiologists) are eager to recover lost voices and to retrieve the contributions of lesser-known actors in the history of mission. Material evidence of indigenous missionary activity, oral history, and other forms of nonliterary self-representation are among the means available to scholars to recover more of what may otherwise be missing from what we know of the history of mission. Filling in the gaps is not the whole story, however. Equally important is the fact that such techniques can enable the living legacies of earlier missionary efforts, the new communities of faith that came into being as a result of Christian mission, to participate more directly in the writing of what is their history too.

---

3 Rachel A. Rakotonirina identifies and addresses some of the problems associated with missionary-stocked archives in her article "Power and Knowledge in Mission Historiography: A Postcolonial Approach to Martyrological Texts on Madagascar, 1837–1937," *Studies in World Christianity* 5, no. 2 (1999): 156–76.

THINKING MISSIOLOGICALLY ABOUT THE HISTORY OF MISSION

Another area where the requirements of competent historical practice are bound to apply equally to missiologists and their counterparts in related fields concerns the way in which the environment of mission is studied. More and more, missiologists are striving to assemble "thick" descriptions of interfaith encounter and Christian witness, rather than simply transcribing stories of heroic missionary action. As Karl Marx famously put it, individuals may make their own history, but they must do so in circumstances not of their own choosing.[4] This point means taking into account large-scale social patterns of which the missionaries themselves may have been only vaguely aware. It means asking about the ways in which factors like geography, economics, organizational theory, and politics not only influenced missionary choices but also perhaps shaped evangelistic outcomes. It means seeking to understand how missionaries could have been unwitting agents of far-reaching but sometimes subtle changes in cultures not their own by reason of birth. Missiologists as a group continue to resist the urge to explain mission exclusively in secular terms (more on this below), but they are more likely than ever before to pay heed to what the eminent Egyptologist Jan Assmann has called the hidden face of history: "History has two faces, one turned toward us, the other averted. The face turned toward us is the sum total of event and remembrance. It is history recalled by those involved in it, as shapers or witnesses, doers or sufferers. The hidden face of history is not what we have forgotten, but what we have never remembered, those products of imperceptible change, extended duration, and infinitesimal progression that go unnoticed by living contemporaries and only reveal themselves to the analytic gaze of the historian."[5]

Distance and Perspective

At first glance, missiologists do seem to face at least one special problem of interpretation when functioning as historians of mission. Many more of them, I suspect, will have previous or current missionary service in their résumés than is true for the rest of the history profession. Is this a disability, a reason to discount the scholarly output offered by missiologists who study the history of mission? I would argue that we have here a slightly different permutation of a persistent scholarly dilemma. Historians have long argued over whether

---

4   Richard J. Evans, *In Defense of History* (New York: Norton, 1999), pp. 160–63, paraphrases Marx's dictum and situates it in a larger discussion about society and the individual.

5   Jan Assmann, *The Mind of Egypt: History and Meaning in the Time of the Pharaohs*, trans. Andrew Jenkins (New York: Metropolitan Books, 2002), p. 3.

participants or more detached observers are better placed to write accounts of the past. Participants have the advantage of direct personal experience, which could be a means to access otherwise poorly documented aspects of the events in question or to gain a "feel" for the time and situation one is attempting to describe. But detachment can serve a purpose too, especially if it enables researchers to avoid telling their stories in ways that inflate their own importance.

The larger question at issue here concerns the different ways scholars more generally relate to their subjects. Missiologists are by no means the only ones obliged to examine their motives for writing history. Biases and partisan concerns threaten to intrude every time historical questions are posed and answered, since no researcher can begin to work without them. In this respect, sound practice in missiology closely resembles the habits of good history. Confessional commitments must be scrutinized, to be sure, but so must all other forms of personal, institutional, or ideological loyalty. Complete objectivity is certainly beyond our grasp, but a measure of transparency regarding intentions and interests can be achieved. Only so may our historical work hope to earn any degree of lasting respect from present and future generations.

A final common expectation that missiologists necessarily share with other students of mission history concerns the written results of their research. As Robert Frykenberg has demonstrated so well, the discipline of history is exceedingly complex.[6] The science of history not only has a distinctive methodology and largely agreed-upon rules with which to evaluate evidence, but it also is practiced as a form of philosophy insofar as it prompts deliberation over questions of language, perception, human experience, and the nature of social change over time. In addition, history is an art. That is to say, it has a creative element, which leaps to the fore as soon as it becomes time to present to the public or to the profession what one has learned about the past.

In this latter respect, we may mention three requirements of good historiography. First, one's written account must be coherent, in the sense that a logical interpretive argument is constructed on the basis of plausible data supported by reputable sources of authority. Second, it should be persuasive, which means putting forward a case that is not just credible but that can move readers to agree with the author's conclusions, even when alternative explanations are given a fair hearing in the presentation. Perhaps the most daunting test of history's contemporary narratives is posed by the question of significance. At the end of the day will anybody care? Probably not, if the product of one's

---

6   Robert E. Frykenberg, *History and Belief: The Foundations of Historical Understanding* (Grand Rapids: Eerdmans, 1996), esp. pp. 253–60.

What Thinking Missiologically Does Not Mean

Before considering what might constitute a missiological perspective on the history of mission, it could be helpful to clarify briefly what I believe is not implied in this way of looking at things. As suggested above, the goal of mission history is not to celebrate missionary heroes. I say this knowing full well that the record is replete with examples of extraordinary dedication and cultural sensitivity, faithfulness, and creativity on the part of Christian missionaries in a variety of very difficult circumstances through the ages. My point is that mission history as a part of the discipline of missiology cannot be fully realized as a form of devotional literature focused on the figure of the missionary. Nor should it be reduced to a kind of cheerleading for "our side" in the global competition of religions.

The reasons for caution here are essentially two. The first, already noted, is that individual missionaries always operate in specific social contexts, and so the circumstances within which they act must be considered in order to appreciate the totality of their effects on others and their surroundings. A too-narrow focus on the person of the missionary may obscure the importance of crucial situational factors. Second, honest missiologists will readily admit that the historical record is full not only of courageous triumphs and self-sacrifice but also of faults, miscalculations, and transgressions—by more than one kind of ethnocentrism and by every manner of unfaithful self-interest. If mission history is made to serve an apologetic purpose, its integrity as a science is undoubtedly put at risk. Put more positively, a mature field of study will reward the investigation of both success and failure, because each of these aspects of missionary experience can shed light on the deepest questions of meaning that mission history inevitably raises. It follows that missiology is not primarily about producing "insider" histories for the purpose of stimulating enthusiasm for contemporary missionary challenges. Nor should practical considerations (e.g., a desire to know "what works" in mission) be allowed to dictate how missiologists approach the history of mission.

Another limitation to be avoided is the misconception that mission history is an unvarying story of missionary initiative followed by indigenous response. Such an assumption—that foreign missionaries acted, but natives could only react—grounded much historical writing on the modern Protestant missionary movement until quite recently, which led to no end of West-centric treatments of mission history. A missiological perspective on the history of mission must be broader. The movements and decisions of expatriate actors are certainly part of what we want to know, especially at the beginning of any new effort to preach Christ where that name is virtually unknown. But no missionary undertaking can be sustained unless indigenous enterprise asserts itself as more than just a reaction to what other, more fully self-aware subjects are doing. As a rule, the earlier a community moves beyond foreign control, the more successful and deeply rooted any new expression of Christian faith is likely to become. Missiologists are accustomed to see in this moment of transition an indispensable act of faith appropriation, on a par with every other attempt to claim the story of God in Jesus as a community's own, reaching all the way back to the first generation of Gentile Christians.

A missiological reading of mission history also must resist the temptation to affect an omniscient point of view with respect to the processes of world evangelization. In other words, missiologists must admit their inability to attain a God's-eye perspective on the history of mission. Methodologically, this constraint means giving up the use of providential frameworks for interpreting the past, which is not always an easy thing to do, especially if one affirms a biblical mandate for Christian mission and believes, as I do, that the church properly responds to the nature of God's Word, which wants to be known, by giving forthright witness to its truth in the world. The danger here lies not in having such convictions but in letting them overrule the demands of sound historiographical practice by subordinating one's account of mission history to a theological point of view. What Andrew Walls has to say about church history applies equally well to missiologists who might hope to write the history of mission: "The church historian cannot present bad history under the plea that it is good theology."[7]

As Paul Kollman has noted in his just-published dissertation on slave evangelization in East Africa, it is also possible to subject the writing of mission history to a *telos* that does not claim a divine origin for itself.[8] His example is the postcolonial nation-state in Africa and how, in particular cases, scholars of African Christianity have cast their stories of mission primarily in terms of whether the foreign missionaries involved either helped or hindered the new

---

7 Andrew F. Walls, "Eusebius Tries Again: The Task of Reconceiving and Re-visioning the Study of Christian History," in *Enlarging the Story: Perspectives on Writing World Christian History*, ed. Wilbert R. Shenk (Maryknoll, N.Y.: Orbis Books, 2002), p. 18.

8 Paul V. Kollman, *The Evangelization of Slaves and Catholic Origins in Eastern Africa* (Maryknoll, N.Y.: Orbis Books, 2005), pp. 9–11.

national entity to come into being. Or the secular end in view could be a conjectured phase of higher development in the history of humankind, such as a post-Christian future for hyperindustrialized societies in the West. In any event, whether religious or secular, it is quite possible for an ideological criterion to undermine the quality of scholarly judgments, especially if ideology is allowed to govern the selection of evidence or in some other way constrict the interpretive freedom of the mission historian. Good missiological technique with respect to mission history will not allow a hoped-for outcome to dominate historical method by guiding the research process to a premature conclusion.

The Missiological Angle on Mission History

What does a missiological approach to the history of mission entail? My argument is that missiologists bring to the study of mission history several important investigative habits or ways of thinking about mission that, when taken together, define a distinctive point of view. I do not propose that missiologists are the only scholars who attend to each of the elements to be discussed. Nevertheless, in the aggregate, I believe we can identify an approach to mission history that grows out of and is intimately related to the field of missiology as it is now conceived and practiced. My essay concludes with a metaphor that suggests how missiologists may be thought to look at the history of mission when it is approached as an integrated whole.

A multivariable approach. We may begin by noting that missiology is, at its heart, relentlessly multivariable. How could this not be the case? Christian mission is a global phenomenon. Given the history of mission over the past two centuries especially, it is now normal for the church to find itself in conversation with the broadest possible array of religious traditions and living cultures. These engagements take place across the full spectrum of human experience, ranging from the cognitive to the material, with the result that the theory and practice of mission are not easily separated. Adding to this complexity is the fact of Christian diversity. Multiple approaches to outreach are to be expected from a worldwide Christian community that has no organizational center or universally shared philosophical framework. In some cases of missionary encounter, competing priorities and disagreements over methods may be traced back to theological differences. In others, the defining issues are more contextual and social.

On the whole, missiologists are not different from other historians when it comes to reckoning with the multifaceted character of Christian mission. The interdisciplinary demands of history weigh equally on all who would hope to study the record of missionary action. As the scholar of comparative religion Eric Sharpe has phrased it, "The ideal missionary historian will be to some extent a social, political, and economic historian; a geographer, ethnologist, and historian of religions; as well as a Christian historian in the more usual sense."[9] A difference arises, however, in the way matters of faith are typically treated by missiologists when compared with their treatment by other scholars of mission history. Simply put, the ethos of missiology encourages its practitioners to take spiritual realities very seriously, even when the researcher does not share the same worldview as those whose history is being studied. Thus, it is not the custom of missiologists to bracket out of their analyses factors of religious conviction. This is the extra variable that often distinguishes the historical work of missiologists from that produced by many secular historians and most social scientists.

A look at two studies of mission will serve to illustrate the point. The first is a pioneering work of historical anthropology produced in the 1990s by a pair of distinguished University of Chicago ethnologists, John and Jean Comaroff. Their massive study of Nonconformist British missions among the Southern Tswana in the nineteenth century, *Of Revelation and Revolution*, interprets these activities within a larger effort to colonize much of southern Africa in the name of Great Britain. The professed aim of the authors is to show how agents of the London Missionary Society and the Wesleyan Methodist Missionary Society functioned as "harbingers of a more invasive European presence" that eventually sought to dominate the Tswana in every possible way.[10] According to the Comaroffs, the missionaries' special preparative role was to shape the collective consciousness of the natives in advance of direct imperial rule, to colonize their minds, as it were, by contriving a new conceptual reality for them that owed as much or more to post-Enlightenment values as it did to the Christian Gospel. In this way, the missionaries became not only "vanguards of imperialism" but also "human vehicles of a hegemonic worldview," whose civilizing axioms "they purveyed ... in everything they said and did."[11]

Of Revelation and Revolution is a formidable scholarly project that successfully presents a deep, thick study of missionary encounter in a particular time and place, which also sheds considerable light on larger issues, like

---

9   Eric J. Sharpe, "Reflections on Missionary Historiography," *International Bulletin of Missionary Research* 13 (1989): 76.

10   Jean Comaroff and John L. Comaroff, *Of Revelation and Revolution*, vol. 2, *The Dialectics of Modernity on a South African Frontier* (Chicago: Univ. of Chicago Press, 1997), p. xvi.

11   Jean Comaroff and John Comaroff, *Of Revelation and Revolution*, vol. 1, *Christianity, Colonialism, and Consciousness in South Africa* (Chicago: Univ. of Chicago Press, 1991), pp. 36, 310.

the relationship of modern missions to European imperialism. Students of nineteenth-century missions ignore this work at their peril. Nevertheless, one can find blind spots in the methodology used. Several anthropologist critics, for example, have taken the Comaroffs to task for reducing the Southern Tswana to inert victims of colonial schemes by effectively denying them any significant capacity to determine their own historical fate as a people.[12] A related concern arises in the way in which the religious behavior of the Tswana is interpreted. The Comaroffs report that the Southern Tswana began to convert en masse to Christianity by the end of the nineteenth century.[13] But what exactly did conversion mean in this context? Why did the Tswana embrace Christianity? Most of the interpretive choices put before the reader are not very generous. They include religious nominality, an awkward imitation of colonial social behavior, an attempt to appropriate by religious means the practical and pecuniary advantages of a foreign civilization, an inadvertent cooptation into the new economic order, a grasping after the white man's power. Unqualified respect is reserved for the notion that these African Christians, through twentieth-century Independency, eventually came to practice "a humanist faith, a faith centered on inspired social action."[14] Perhaps. But when none of the proffered explanations seems to match up with what the principals involved had to say about their own motivations, missiologists will want to ask: are these the only options?

For purposes of comparison, a glance at some recent work by Mrinalini Sebastian on nineteenth-century missions in India may prove instructive.[15] As an Indian feminist scholar of religion and culture, with a particular interest in postcolonial literary criticism and subaltern studies, Sebastian wants to read old missionary texts in new ways, just as the Comaroffs have done. Like them, she wants to understand the corruptive influence of colonialism on European missionary action in the modern era. She does not stop there, however, preferring instead to go on to ask what past evangelistic encounters may have meant to the natives whose stories were captured and represented in missionary narratives. In particular, her article on how to read missionary archives from a

---

12   In their introduction to *Dialectics of Modernity*, pp. 35–53, the Comaroffs offer a spirited rebuttal of their critics.

13   Ibid., p. 107. What follows in the next few sentences is a very compact summary of the argument presented in this second volume of the Comaroffs' project.

14   Ibid., p. 114.

15   Below I highlight Mrinalini Sebastian, "Reading Archives from a Postcolonial Feminist Perspective: 'Native' Bible Women and the Missionary Ideal," *Journal of Feminist Studies in Religion* 19 (2003): 5–25. See also Sebastian, "Mission Without History? Some Ideas for Decolonizing Mission," *International Review of Mission* 93 (2004): 75–96.

postcolonial feminist perspective nicely illustrates the kind of methodology that could support or complement a fully missiological approach to the history of mission.

In her essay, Sebastian focuses on the native Bible women who worked for the Basel Mission in India. She shows how their work was obviously shaped, if not distorted, by Victorian-era missionary ideas about "the Christian home" that only partly rested on Gospel values. A commitment to feminist concerns pushes Sebastian to explore the liberative potential of missionary education for women in India, which connects to her primary topic insofar as these native missionaries, that is, the Bible women, promoted literacy through their activities. She also considers the possibility that the Bible women were among the earliest examples of professional women in India, thereby investing their work with emancipatory significance. Up to this point in her essay, about three-quarters of the way through, I see Sebastian tracking very closely with the approach of the Comaroffs, albeit not at the same level of detail. But then a turn in her investigative strategy comes, which Sebastian describes as follows: "In my engagement with the histories of the Bible women so far, I have tried to present a secularized view of their work. I deliberately have not dwelled too much on either their faith or their attempts to convert other women to Christianity. Yet the primary motive for their becoming Bible women, for their inadvertent transgression [across caste boundaries] was their faith. And the primary purpose of their visits to other women's houses was to communicate the message of the gospel."[16]

A very personal reason lay behind the decision to introduce the factor of faith into Sebastian's scholarly discussion of mission history. As she explains, her own grandmother was a Bible woman in India long before this article was conceived and written, and so she asks: what moved my grandmother and so many other native Christian women to share the story of Jesus with their neighbors in the day-to-day context of Indian village life, sometimes over the course of a lifetime? By raising such a question, Sebastian has chosen to pitch her researcher's tent squarely on missiological ground. Without resorting to a providential framework to explain the workings of history, she has nevertheless allowed the realm of faith to begin to receive a measure of the same consideration so freely given by countless academics to the realm of sight. As historian Mark Noll has observed, this is what missiologists do. They operate somewhere between the "functional atheism of the academy" and the "functional gnosticism of sending churches," which can blind those churches to historical

---

16   Sebastian, "Reading Archives," p. 22.

THINKING MISSIOLOGICALLY ABOUT THE HISTORY OF MISSION

realities.[17] Thus, to think missiologically about the history of mission means, in part, to practice a form of critical empathy with one's subject. A degree of empathy makes it possible to resist the strong modern urge to dismiss—with a Comtean wave of the hand—religious convictions as unimportant.[18] At the same time, a willingness to be critical commits one to a methodology that is suitably rigorous and scientific.

A bias toward the dynamic. Related to the persistently multivariable disposition of missiology is its particular interest in the dynamic character of Christian history. That is to say, there is an inbuilt bias in missiology to concentrate on those points in Christian history where the community acts less like a custodian of tradition or repository of settled answers to familiar questions than as a source of energy for fresh engagements of the Gospel with the world. Missiologists are drawn especially to circumstances of change within Christian history. Efforts to plant the church where it has not previously existed obviously qualify, as would any struggle to understand the Gospel story in new cultural terms. Missiologists also have a special affinity for those parts of the Christian story where conversions into the community, growth, development, and critical self-examination are considered normal aspects of church life rather than the exception.

The effect of these biases on a missiological approach to mission history can be profound. Missiologists have learned, for example, that mission history is not simply a matter of extension and expansion from metropolitan centers to distant peripheries. Thus, they do not expect missionaries to function as mere chutes through which liquid concrete from abroad is poured into forms fashioned out of local materials. Truly missionary encounters in history are intense

---

17 Mark A. Noll, "The Potential of Missiology for the Crises of History," in *History and the Christian Historian*, ed. Ronald A. Wells (Grand Rapids: Eerdmans, 1998), p. 112.

18 On the merits of empathy for the study of religious history more generally, see Richard Elphick, "Writing Religion into History: The Case of South African Christianity," *Studia Historiae Ecclesiasticae* 21 (1995): 1–21. Ogbu Kalu's comment on the importance of respecting faith commitments when trying to write the global history of Christianity is also pertinent here: "It is difficult to tell the story of the church by rejecting its essence." See Kalu, "Clio in a Sacred Garb: Telling the Story of Gospel-People Encounters in Our Time," *Fides et Historia* 35 (2003): 27–39. Auguste Comte (1798–1857) was a French social philosopher who theorized that academic disciplines had to progress through religion and metaphysics before reaching their fulfillment in scientific positivism, at which point knowledge associated with these earlier stages of social development would become irrelevant. Ironically, Comte never completely let go of his own religious sentiments, choosing instead to channel these into a more scientific "religion of humanity" that he thought would one day replace Catholicism.

moments, full of unpredictability but also of promise. Old certainties about what is essential to Christianity may be tested and found wanting in these engagements. New understandings of Gospel truth sometimes emerge out of intercultural and interreligious exchange. In any event, when contemporary missiologists reflect on mission history, they are likely to look for evidence of Christianity as a movement rather than as a set of institutions or a collection of fixed doctrines.

An approach that is both local and global. Next to this interest in the dynamic character of the Christian tradition is a strong tendency within missiology to think about mission history in both local and global terms. The local side of this equation receives attention whenever issues of contextualization are brought into focus. As Werner Ustorf has observed, the Christian faith is by nature "fides semper inculturanda," and nowhere is this quality more apparent than in the history of mission when multiple contemporary contexts are studied side-by-side.[19] The idea of translation is another means by which missiologists explore the local dimensions of Christian outreach. By translation I mean not only the rendering of Scripture into new languages but also the creation of vernacular Christianities that make sense within the context of their particular cultural settings.

The global dimension of missiology is expressed in a variety of ways. One thinks here of the geographic development of Christianity into a truly global religion, and also about the birth of a worldwide ecumenical movement in the heyday of modern Protestant missions. Less often appreciated, perhaps, is the way in which the history of mission itself is stamped with the indelible mark of global interconnectivity. Many eighteenth-century churchgoers in the West, for example, eagerly awaited the latest news of their own missionaries but also began to pray fervently for the spread of the Gospel by others.[20] Acting on the same impulse, the missionary societies founded just before the turn of the nineteenth century sought new ways to share intelligence gained from around the world among themselves and to inform the public of their activities,

---

19   Werner Ustorf, "Mission and Missionary Historiography in Intercultural Perspective: Ten Preliminary Statements," *Exchange* 31 (2002): 210.

20   Intercontinental concerts of prayer on behalf of Christian mission were undertaken as early as the mid-eighteenth century, spearheaded by figures like John Wesley, James Erskine, and Jonathan Edwards. On this development, see Stuart Piggin, "The Expanding Knowledge of God: Jonathan Edwards's Influence on Missionary Thinking and Promotion," in *Jonathan Edwards at Home and Abroad: Historical Memories, Cultural Movements, Global Horizons*, ed. David W. Kling and Douglas A. Sweeney (Columbia: Univ. of South Carolina Press, 2003), pp. 270–74.

hence the creation of the missionary magazine at about the same time.[21] Most intriguingly, we find far-flung modern-era missionaries trying to learn from each other despite the challenges of geography, while also thinking about their work in increasingly global terms. Jennifer Selwyn has provided a wonderful example of this phenomenon in her recent study of early modern Jesuit missions in Naples.[22] As she shows, the Kingdom of Naples became a kind of proving ground within the Jesuit system for would-be missionary candidates to the New World. Coincidentally, theorists in the Society of Jesus considered how certain techniques and ideas learned in one place could be adapted for use elsewhere. In a striking conceptual move, Jesuits assigned to Naples in the sixteenth and seventeenth centuries came to refer to their mission field in southern Italy as "our Indies" or the "Indies down here." This is language that clearly points to a globalized project of evangelization.

Missiology as a scholarly context. Finally, a missiological approach to the history of mission is inevitably affected by and related to everything else that missiologists study. In other words, the rest of what is encompassed by the term "missiology" forms a special scholarly context for studies of mission history undertaken by those who would call themselves missiologists. Missiologists are not unique in this respect. Their situation is parallel, for example, to that which obtains for biblical scholars who study mission in the Scriptures. Should we not expect the exegetes to be influenced by the habits of their guild as they examine the biblical materials pertaining to mission? Likewise for social scientists and other specialists who for one reason or another are drawn to mission-related topics. It would be strange indeed if they went about their work without paying heed to the salient trends and critical research needs that beg for attention in their particular academic patch.

In the case of missiology, the other items on our disciplinary agenda certainly include questions about how Christian mission fits into an increasingly pluralistic world, about the means of outreach most likely to be effective and faithful in our era, about the perennial interface of theology with culture, and about the special vocation of mission service. Missiologists who study the history of mission need not subordinate their investigations to any of these topics, but an awareness of the implications our historical research might have for

---

21   An influential model for this new kind of church periodical was provided by the *Evangelical Magazine*, published in London from 1793. By 1796 the *Missionary Magazine* had made its appearance in Edinburgh. The *Connecticut Evangelical Magazine* and *New York Missionary Magazine*, the first American examples of this genre, followed in 1800.

22   Jennifer D. Selwyn, *A Paradise Inhabited by Devils: The Jesuits' Civilizing Mission in Early Modern Naples* (Aldershot, Eng.: Ashgate, 2004).

these and other questions of pressing concern to students of mission is appropriate. When one puts the study of mission history into such an intellectual context, it then becomes possible for the history of mission to function properly, in my view, as a foundation for other work in missiology.[23]

A Riverine Perspective

To conclude, we may imagine the history of mission as a river, a great flow of ideas, events, personalities, and human encounters taking place over time. Theologically, its headwaters could be identified in the nature of God, the One who sends the Son and the Spirit and in other ways has sought to be known by humankind. Historically, the beginnings of Christian mission might be traced back to the earthly ministry of Jesus or the occasion of Pentecost, with roots in the story of Israel. Where does the river of mission history end? A natural terminus, the particular body of water into which this rushing confluence empties, lies beyond the power of physical sight. Yet, we do have a scene of cosmic consummation described in the Book of Revelation (7:9–12; 22:1–5), with the river of the water of life flowing unceasingly from God's heavenly throne, around which persons from every tribe, tongue, and nation stand praising God and the Lamb.

It is our lot to live downstream, but somewhere before the end of the story. This is the only location now available for those who wish to study the history of Christian mission. But where exactly do we stand to engage this history? Missiologists will not be content to helicopter in every now and again to take a bucketful of water to nourish some parched ground of scholarly labor located far away. Nor can we rely on satellite imaging alone, even though a distant point of view can yield valuable insights.

To adopt a missiological perspective on this history implies a choice to live close by one's subject, taking into account all the elements of approach described earlier. Along the strand one can feel the force of the river, its dynamic aspect, so powerful that it can cut new pathways through rugged and resistant landscape. If a turn is taken at navigating the rapids, direct experience may teach the same lesson, but with greater urgency. A willingness to range far and

---

23   In *Transforming Mission* (Maryknoll, N.Y.: Orbis Books, 1991), David Bosch illustrates how history can operate in this way for missiologists. In this seminal book, Bosch's reading of the history of mission (as a series of partially overlapping paradigms extending back to the New Testament era) clearly influences his exegetical stance, while also shaping his approach to the theology of mission.

wide within the watershed will bring to light the rich complexity of a multivariable and extensive riparian environment. En route one can begin to appreciate how various features of the natural world may have shaped the river's course through time, while also giving thought to the human engineering projects that either succeeded or failed to widen the water's reach. An enduring interest in the local and global dimensions of mission pushes the missiologist further to think about this river as a kind of huge interconnected ecosystem with many different microenvironments. Finally, in our mind's eye, it is impossible to ignore the lush vegetation and diverse wildlife that crowd the riverbank, with each species finding both strength and vitality in the refreshing water. Evidence of life so abundant cannot fail but to remind one of the fundamental significance of this history, not only for the rest of missiology but also for the present and future of the Christian tradition as a whole.

Jesuit Scientific Activity in the Overseas Missions, 1540–1773

Steven J. Harris

Why discuss Jesuit missionaries in the context of national traditions in colonial science? Clearly, the Society of Jesus was not a "nation," not even in the linguistic and cultural sense current at the time of its foundation—though Ignatius, its founder and chief architect, once referred to fully formed Jesuits as members of "an elite race." The Society was not a colonial power, yet it exercised considerable power in the overseas colonies. Nor was it a scientific society, even though its mathematically trained members were upon occasion dispatched with instructions from Rome to procure scientific information. It was, after all, a religious order best known for its colleges and universities in Catholic Europe. It is certain that the Society's overseas missions—and hence its contributions to colonial science—would have been impossible in the absence of state-supported trade and colonial enterprises. Yet the Society's status as an international religious order enabled it to exploit the various modes of colonial practice touched upon in Londa Schiebinger's introduction. Jesuit missionaries were active in the Spanish "territorial colonies" established in the highlands of Central and South America. They were scattered throughout the "trading post empire" of the Portuguese Estado da India as well as the "plantation complexes" in Brazil and the French West Indies. They participated also in the French "settler" and "plural" colonies in Canada.[1] The scientific activity Jesuits undertook in the overseas missions, therefore, displays a complexity and variety commensurate with the complexity and variety of multinational colonial practices upon which it depended.

While several recent works have demonstrated the richness and importance of scientific activity in the Society of Jesus for the early modern period, few have focused on the general character of Jesuit science as practiced beyond the shores of Europe.[2] It would seem that the basic conditions of the Society's

---

Source: Harris, S. T., "Jesuit Scientific Activity in the Overseas Missions, 1540–1773," *Isis* 96.1 (2005): pp. 71–79. Copyright © 2010 by University of Chicago Press.

---

1 Philip D. Curtin, *The World and the West: The European Challenge and the Overseas Response in the Age of Empire* (Cambridge: Cambridge Univ. Press, 2000), pp. 1–7.

2 For references to recent scholarship, see the notes to the editor's introduction and individual essays in Mordechai Feingold, ed., *Jesuit Science and the Republic of Letters* (Cambridge,

colonial science conspire to discourage a synoptic approach. The Society's corporate geography was itself a complex matter. Soon after its foundation in 1540 by Ignatius of Loyola, the Society began both its overseas missions and domestic educational system. At its peak around 1750, the Society operated more than 500 colleges and universities in Europe, a hundred more in overseas colonies (mostly in Spanish America), and roughly 270 mission stations scattered around the globe. The Society, in other words, presided over one of the most extensive and complex institutional networks of the *ancien régime*.[3] A necessary corollary of the geographic dispersion of the Society's institutional network was an extraordinary diversity of cultural and natural environments in which missionaries worked.

That global network, however, operated only as part of a complex web of dependencies involving regional cultural traditions, commercial interests, and state authorities, dependencies that had much to do with the ebb and flow of Jesuit overseas scientific activity. Because it lacked the sort of "vertical control" of, say, the Dutch East India Company—which owned its own ships, hired its own captains, staffed its own factories, and reinvested its own profits—the Society was obliged to negotiate patronage, passage, and protection with a host of other colonial institutions while pursuing its central goal of proselytization. Its success in the overseas missions depended on mastering the intricacies of what sociologists call the "inter-organizational field,"[4] that is,

---

Mass.: MIT Press, 2003). The Society suffered a general suppression in 1773 and was banned throughout the Catholic world. After its restoration in 1814, there were attempts to regain its scientific reputation. The chief centers of scientific research have been astronomical observatories, which, in several cases, have served as nucleation sites for important work in meteorology and seismology. For one of the very few discussions of Jesuit overseas science in the restored Society, see Lewis Pyenson, *Civilizing Mission: Exact Sciences and French Overseas Expansion, 1830–1940* (Baltimore: Johns Hopkins Univ. Press, 1993), pp. 10–15, 157–206 (for China), 207–239 (for Lebanon). For an exhaustive inventory of Jesuit observatories, both in the old and restored Society, see Agustín Udías, *Searching the Heavens and the Earth: The History of Jesuit Observatories* (Dordrecht: Kluwer Academic Publishers, 2003). Because of the limited scholarship on Jesuit colonial science after 1814, I will confine my analysis to the old Society.

3 Steven J. Harris, "Mapping Jesuit Science: The Role of Travel in the Geography of Knowledge," in *The Jesuits: Cultures, Sciences, and the Arts, 1540–1773*, ed. John W. O'Malley, S. J. Gauvin Alexander Bailey, Steven J. Harris, T. Frank Kennedy, S.J. (Toronto: Univ. of Toronto Press, 1999), pp. 216–222.

4 For a useful introduction, see Howard E. Aldrich and Peter V. Marsden, "Environments and Organizations," in *Handbook of Sociology*, ed. Neil J. Smelser (Newbury Park, Calif.: Sage Publications, 1988), pp. 361–392, esp. 383ff. For an analytical overview of recent literature, see Amalya L. Oliver and Mark Ebers, "Networking Network Studies: An Analysis of Conceptual Configurations in the Study of Inter-Organizational Relationships," *Organization Studies*, 1998, *19*:549–583.

the opportunities and constraints arising from the interplay among the major colonial agencies, especially the Spanish Patronato real and the bureaus associated with the Portuguese Carreira da Índia but also military authorities and various indigenous institutions. As Jesuit missionaries insinuated themselves in a field tense with the contending strategic interests of the Portuguese, Spanish, and French crowns as well as foreign rulers and Creoles, they found certain areas of natural knowledge to be useful, either to themselves, to their patrons, or to their foreign hosts—sometimes to all three. Thus the cultural context of Jesuit overseas science was, in fact, profoundly multicultural.

Yet another challenge the historian faces is the multidisciplinary character of the Society's scientific tradition and attendant differences in practices and practitioners. Collectively, Jesuit missionaries made significant contributions to the fields of astronomy, cartography, geography, natural history, ethnography, botany, and *materia medica,* though not consistently in any one missionary theater nor uniformly over any one period. Consider the contrasting patterns of practice in two fields, astronomy and *materia medica.* The China mission is justly famous for the astronomical work Jesuits performed as members of the Imperial Astronomical Bureau in Beijing. Yet with the exception of a brief period in the 1730s under the patronage of the Indian prince Jai Singh and the Venusian transit observations of the 1760s, Jesuit astronomy in the overseas missions was largely a sporadic activity of individual missionaries working with only the most basic instruments and often in near isolation from major observatories. Medical botany, by contrast, was practiced fairly consistently in virtually every missionary theater since it was deemed essential to the health (both financial and physical) of the missions. Astronomy was almost exclusively reserved for "professed" fathers, that is, the elite, university-educated, ordained members who taught, preached, and published. Medical botany was left largely in the hands of lay brothers, or "temporal coadjutors," who neither taught nor preached and only rarely published.

In sum, the complexity of the Society's corporate geography, the diversity of indigenous cultural and natural environments, the Society's dependencies on secular institutions, and the multiple scientific disciplines and practitioners present us with an intricate, but not intractable, set of problems. Or, to turn the matter around, the complexities of Jesuit overseas science offer the historian a number of opportunities to link history of science to institutional history, history of religion, colonial history, and comparative or multicultural history of indigenous peoples. In recent years, scholars from a variety of fields have taken up these questions in a number of case studies. I cannot do justice to all, or even a majority, of their work in the space remaining. I can, however, highlight those works I see as illustrating the most salient features of Jesuit overseas science: namely, the multinational character of the Society's missions and its ability to extract advantage from the interorganizational field; the circulation of natural knowledge selectively appropriated through cross-cultural intimacy; and the multiple uses of published natural histories.

The Society was multinational in a double, or even triple, sense. Because it did not "belong" to any one nation, it drew its talent from every region of Catholic Europe and beyond and sent its talent to every Catholic colony around the globe. Consequently, Jesuit missionaries operated in more lands than the Portuguese, the Spanish, the French, or even the British and the Dutch empires. Moreover, several European cities served the Society as headquarters for overseas missions. While Jesuit superiors strove to make Rome the "central command" for the missions, Lisbon, Madrid/Seville, Paris, and Vienna functioned in turn—sometimes simultaneously—as de facto metropoles. Consider, by way of example, the international and institutional relations involved in Jesuit astronomical work in China. From the time of Matteo Ricci's permanent residency in Beijing in 1601, the mathematical sciences had been an endeavor shared by Italians such as himself as well as Spanish, Portuguese, Polish, Belgian, and German Jesuits.[5] They worked in (or in association with) the Chinese emperor's Imperial Astronomical Bureau in Beijing while under the protection of the Portuguese patronate, headquartered in Lisbon, but taking orders from their superiors in Rome. In the 1680s, the French entered this already-crowded scene. In late December 1684, Jean de la Chaize, Jesuit confessor to Louis XIV, wrote to Charles Noyelles, father general of the Society, in Rome:

> His Majesty being in all respects devoted to the sciences and doing everything possible to acquire knowledge from foreign countries, has ordered

---

5 Jesuit mathematician-missionaries in seventeenth-century China continue to attract considerable scholarly attention. See, e.g., Isaia Iannaccone, *Johann Schreck Terrentius: Le scienze rinascimentali e lo spirito dell'Accademia de Lincei nella Cina dei Ming* (Napoli: Istituto Universitario Orientale, 1998); Franco Demarchi and Riccardo Scartezzini, eds., *Martino Martini: A Humanist and Scientist in Seventeenth-Century China* (Trent: Università degli studi di Trento, 1996); Noël Golvers, *Ferdinand Verbiest, S.J. (1623–1688) and the Chinese Heaven: The Composition of the Astronomical Corpus, Its Diffusion and Reception in the European Republic of Letters* (Louvain: Leuven Univ. Press, 2003); and John W. Witek, S.J., ed., *Ferdinand Verbiest (1623–1688): Jesuit Missionary, Scientist, Engineer, and Diplomat* (Nettetal: Steyler Verlag, 1994).

me to choose ... good missionaries with enough knowledge of mathematics to ... rectify maritime and geographical maps and especially to learn and understand the major arts and sciences of the Chinese ... and thus, while under the pretext of being the observers and mathematicians of the king, [to] instruct the [Chinese] people in the truths of our faith.[6]

By the spring of the following year, a contingent of six Jesuits, all "good missionaries" possessing the desired mathematical expertise, had left the French port of Brest for China.[7] For the next half century, French Jesuits dominated—and altered the character of—the mathematical sciences in the China missions.[8] Most notably, they led the massive cartographic projects commissioned by the Qing emperor Kangxi (r. 1662–1723) to survey his rapidly expanding empire.[9] At the same time, they transmitted an enormous amount of geographic information back to Paris.[10] And so they skillfully fulfilled their twin scientific mandates by interweaving the interests of Versailles, the Forbidden City, the Académie Royale des Sciences, the republic of letters, and their general in Rome. In both the linguistic and Latourian sense, Jesuits were masters of translation.[11]

---

6   Donald F. Lach, trans., *The Preface to Leibniz' Novissima Sinica* (Honolulu: Univ. of Hawaii Press, 1957), p. 22.

7   Florence Hsia, "Jesuits, Jupiter's Satellites, and the Académie Royale des Sciences," in O'Malley et al., *The Jesuits* (cit. n. 3), pp. 241–257. As Hsia notes, the six Jesuit missionaries were trained in observational techniques by Jean-Dominique Cassini (head of the Royal Observatory), given the title *Mathématiciens du Roi*, and (by special dispensation) became members in the Académie Royale des Sciences—an honor otherwise denied members of religious orders.

8   For a discussion of differences between French and earlier representations of geometry in Beijing, see Catherine Jami, "From Clavius to Pardies: The Geometry Transmitted to China by Jesuits, 1607–1723," in *Western Humanistic Culture Presented to China by Jesuit Missionaries (XVII–XVIII Centuries)*, ed. Federico Masini (Rome: Institutum Historicum s.i., 1996), pp. 175–199.

9   Theodore N. Foss, "A Western Interpretation of China: Jesuit Cartography," in *East Meets West: The Jesuits in China, 1582–1773*, ed. Charles E. Ronan and Bonnie Oh (Chicago: Loyola Univ. Press, 1988), pp. 209–251. See also Cheryl A. Semans, "Mapping the Unknown: Jesuit Cartography in China, 1583–1773" (Ph.D. diss., Univ. California, Berkeley, 1987), pp. 173–180.

10   Most famously in Jean-Baptiste Du Halde's four-volume work, *Description géographique, historique, chronologique, politique, et physique de l'empire de la Chine* (Paris, 1735). See also Theodore N. Foss, "A Jesuit Encyclopedia for China" (Ph.D. diss., Univ. Chicago, 1979).

11   Bruno Latour, *Science in Action: How to Follow Scientists and Engineers through Society* (Cambridge, Mass.: Harvard Univ. Press, 1987), pp. 108–121.

It has become something of a cliché in studies of cultural exchange that foreign knowledge and practices are most likely to be accepted if there is some preexisting niche or cultural predisposition to acceptance. The episode of Jesuit mathematical sciences in China was no exception. A number of factors peculiar to late Ming China provided opportunities for certain elements of Western science, as mediated by Jesuit missionaries, to be taken up by Chinese literati.[12] But the cliché also cuts the other way: the sort of natural knowledge that the Society's missionaries were able to appropriate from indigenous cultures depended on Jesuit predispositions and receptive niches. Indeed, selective appropriation of "local knowledges" has emerged as one of the major themes in recent scholarship, especially in the field of medical botany. Sabine Anagnostou, for example, examines "the different ways ... Jesuit missionaries acquired and integrated their knowledge about the New World's materia medica into the Old World's scientific paradigm."[13] Similar questions arise in connection with Ayurvedic medical practices in India,[14] Huron herbal cures in French Canada,[15] and Pima medical lore in the Sonoran Desert of northwest New Spain.[16] Common to all of these case studies are Jesuit openness to "natural cures" and rejection of indigenous ritual/spiritual practices associated with medical treatments. As predisposing factors for the assembly of the Jesuit pharmacopeia, we can point to the missionaries' immediate, pragmatic need for local medical knowledge and their understanding of European "natural

---

12 Nicholas Standaert, "Jesuit Corporate Culture as Shaped by the Chinese," in O'Malley et al., *The Jesuits* (cit. n. 3), pp. 359–360.

13 Sabine Anagnostou, "Jesuits in Spanish America and Their Contribution to the Exploration of the American *Materia Medica*," *Pharmacy in History*, 2005, 47(1) (in press). See also her "Jesuiten in Spanisch-Amerika als Übermittler von heilkundlichem Wissen" (Ph.D. diss., Marburg Univ., 2000) and her "Das Heilmittelversorgungssystem der Jesuiten in den Missionen Spanisch-Amerikas," *Neue Zeitschrift für Missionswissenschaft*, 2001 4:241–259.

14 John M. de Figueiredo, "Ayurvedic Medicine in Goa According to the European Sources in the Sixteenth and Seventeenth Centuries," in *Scientific Aspects of European Expansion*, ed. William K. Storey (Aldershot: Varorium, 1996), pp. 247–257, esp. 228–231.

15 Allan Greer, "The Exchange of Medical Knowledge between Natives and Jesuits in New France," in *El saber de los jesuitas, historias naturales y el Nuevo Mundo*, ed. Luis Millones-Figueroa and Domingo Ledezma (Frankfurt/Madrid: Vervuert-Iberoamericana, 2005), pp. 135–146.

16 Theodore E. Treutlein, "The Jesuit Missionary in the Role of Physician," in *The Jesuit Missions of Northern Mexico*, ed. Charles W. Polzer, Thomas H. Naylor, Thomas E. Sheridan, and Diana Hadley (New York: Garland, 1991), pp. 518–539.

cures" as part of Galenic medical theory. As predisposing restrictive filters, there was their strict conceptual segregation of "natural" from "supernatural" (inherited largely from Thomas Aquinas) and their self-identity as guardians of the Catholic faith and thus of the Christian god as sole proprietor of the supernatural. Especially in the hands of Jesuit missionaries, medical botany was as much a matter of defining and stabilizing "the natural" and monopolizing "the supernatural" as it was of fending off illness.[17]

As to the question of *how* Jesuits were able to gain intimate knowledge from such disparate peoples, we may take our cue from an insightful, but anonymous, preface to a collection of Jesuit travel accounts published in 1714.

> The Missioners being settled Inhabitants of those Countries they write of, speaking the Languages and reading the Books, are able to acquaint us with many Curiosities, which Travellers in passing through can never be Masters of. The Writers of those Letters make the Knowledge of those People they are among their study, and converse with all Sorts from the Highest to the Meanest; they are Men chosen out of Many for that Purpose, and consequently the only Persons that can set us Right in our Notions of those People so remote from us, and so different in all Respects.[18]

Long-term residency, care in learning languages, attention to customs, and the desire to win the trust and confidence of indigenous peoples—these were the distinguishing characteristics of the Society's mission strategy that made its missionaries especially adept at cross-cultural intimacy. Absolutely critical, however, to the circulation of these filtered bodies of natural knowledge was that Jesuits, unlike members of the other major missionary orders, such as the Franciscans and the Dominicans, energetically embraced the task of "setting us Right in our Notions of those Peoples" by publishing literally hundreds of letters, travel accounts, and natural histories on the overseas missions.[19]

---

17   Though not concerned with Jesuit definitions of nature per se, Lorraine Daston's analysis is quite useful: "The Nature of Nature in Early Modern Europe," *Configurations*, 1998, 6:149–172.

18   Anon., *The Travels of Several Learned Missioners of the Society of Jesus* (London: R. Gosling, 1714), unnumbered preface (p. 2).

19   In her study of eighteenth-century medical botany in the West Indies, Londa Schiebinger has uncovered similar patterns in the "bioprospecting" of English, Dutch, and French naturalists—non-Jesuits all—and points to the importance of long-term residency,

JESUIT SCIENTIFIC ACTIVITY IN THE OVERSEAS MISSIONS

Among the various postmodern and postcolonial criticisms of the Enlightenment of the eighteenth century, two are of particular relevance. Despite the modernist perception of the Enlightenment as a fundamentally secular, and secularizing, movement, Lorraine Daston has maintained that "natural theology in all its myriad forms emerges as *the* enlightened science of the eighteenth century."[20] By viewing the Enlightenment from the other side of the Atlantic, Jorge Cañizares-Esguerra has argued that the civil histories of eighteenth-century colonial authors were informed by a "patriotic epistemology" distinct from the predominant epistemology of the northern European Enlightenment.[21] Jesuit missionary-naturalists represent an obvious point of intersection of natural theology, colonial natural histories, and Enlightenment epistemologies. Happily, we now have a collection of essays that explores these themes for the New World.[22] In Eileen Willingham's reading of Juan de Velasco, she finds a "patriotic" voice (as does Cañizares-Esguerra) but one that explicitly incorporates natural as well as civil elements and that privileges the natural knowledge held by "clerical-creoles" such as himself.[23] Kristin Huffine sees a similar pattern in the contemporaneous natural histories of several Paraguayan Jesuits, whose "rhetorical claims ... were now based on statements of fact and first-hand knowledge of the Paraguayan natural world ... [and who now] followed stricter guidelines of disciplinary writing by constructing civil and natural histories in the language of Enlightenment science" in order to refute the derogatory characterization of the natural productions of the

---

selective appropriation among European "information brokers," and circulation of botanical information through publications. See *Plants and Empire: Colonial Bioprospecting in the Atlantic World* (Cambridge, Mass.: Harvard Univ. Press, 2004), pp. 51–57, 73–104.

20 Lorraine Daston, "Afterword: The Ethos of Enlightenment," in *The Sciences in Enlightened Europe*, ed. William Clark, Jan Golinski, and Simon Schaffer (Chicago: Univ. of Chicago Press, 1999), pp. 495–505, 502. However, she immediately acknowledges that "historians of the Enlightenment sciences have yet to fill the historiographic gap between the Boyle lectures and the Bridgewater treatises."

21 Jorge Cañizares-Esguerra, *How to Write the History of the New World: Histories, Epistemologies, and Identities in the Eighteenth-Century Atlantic World* (Stanford: Stanford Univ. Press, 2001), pp. 204–265.

22 See Millones-Figueroa and Ledezma, eds., *El saber de los jesuitas* (cit. n. 15).

23 "Velasco filters indigenous knowledge of Quito's natural world through a lens focused on showcasing his patria's uniqueness and utility, and its Amerindian and criollo inhabitants' intellectual competence." Eileen Willingham, *Locating Utopia: Promise and Patria in Juan de Velasco's* Historia del Reino de Quito, pp. 251–277, 256. Compare Cañizares-Esguerra, *How to Write the History of the New World* (cit. n. 21), pp. 249–253.

New World circulating among northern European naturalists.[24] As Domingo Ledezma emphasizes in his study of the early seventeenth-century Spanish naturalist Juan Eusebio Nieremberg, apologetic natural history served as a literary means of legitimizing the "new kingdoms" of the New World, casting them as figurative—and sometimes even as literal—"new paradises."[25]

The "rare and wonderful" productions of nature in the New World not only animated the imagination of Nieremberg but also inspired Jesuits throughout the seventeenth and eighteenth centuries.[26] In both Willingham's analysis of Velasco and Ewalt's of José Gumilla's *El Orinoco ilustrado* (1741), the rare and marvelous productions of nature in the New World were made to serve God. One of their principal goals was to inspire wonder of God's creation and through wonder to lead the reader to God Himself. Or, in Ewalt's words, "Father Gumilla consciously appropriates wonder and blends natural philosophy and moral philosophy, physics and metaphysics, within a scientific and religious discourse of wonder, where *scientia* as knowledge of nature leads to *Scientia* as knowledge of the Author of nature."[27]

There is one final aspect of the Jesuit scientific tradition I wish to address before concluding. Elizabeth Rhodes is one of the very few scholars to have taken up the question of a distinctive gender system within the Society of Jesus. She has argued that Jesuit religious practice was "characterized by the rhetoric of traditional Masculinity" and that Ignatian spirituality was "distinguished by a particular character of struggle, combat, and activity."[28] Rhodes also notes that Jesuits achieved their greatest influence as professors at

---

24 Kristin Huffine, "Raising Paraguay from Decline: Memory, Ethnography, and Natural History in the Eighteenth-Century Accounts of the Jesuit Fathers," in Millones-Figueroa and Ledezma, *El saber de los jesuitas* (cit. n. 15), p. 282.

25 See Domingo Ledezma "Una legitimación imaginativa del Nuevo Mundo: *La Historia Naturæ, Maxime Peregrinæ* del jesuita Juan Eusebio Nieremberg," in Millones-Figueroa and Ledezma, *El saber de los jesuitas* (cit. n. 15), pp. 53–84, and in his doctoral thesis, "El paraíso en América: Un aporte de los jesuitas en las historias naturales, 1591–1668," (Ph.D. diss., Brown Univ., 2003). Legitimization is also a theme in Margaret R. Ewalt, "Father Gumilla, Crocodile Hunter? The Function of Wonder in *El Orinoco ilustrado*," in Millones-Figueroa and Ledezma, *El saber de los jesuitas* (cit. n. 15), pp. 303–334.

26 Though never a missionary, Athanasius Kircher is the best-studied representative of this tradition. See Paula Findlen, ed., *Athanasius Kircher: The Last Man Who Knew Everything* (New York: Routledge, 2004).

27 Ewalt, "Father Gumilla," in Millones-Figueroa and Ledezma, *El saber de los jesuitas* (cit. n. 15), p. 304.

28 Elizabeth Rhodes, "Join the Jesuits, See the World: Early Modern Women in Spain and the Society of Jesus," *The Jesuits, II: Cultures, Sciences, and the Arts, 1540–1773*, ed.

JESUIT SCIENTIFIC ACTIVITY IN THE OVERSEAS MISSIONS

university, preachers in church, confessors at court, and contributors to the republic of letters; that is, in the public spaces of civic and cultural production—spaces from which all but the most highborn women were categorically debarred. To this inventory of masculine traits and spaces, we may add the work of missionaries in far-off and dangerous lands who engaged in heroic struggles to bring a Christian order to "heathen Nature" as well as to "heathen societies." Through trials of strength and endurance, they gained direct, first-hand knowledge of the natural world. Thus, along with a masculine spirituality, we may also speak of a vigorous, muscular, risk-taking, "masculine science" developing in the overseas missions.

Once we open the door to gender analysis in a single-sex institution such as the Society of Jesus, questions come pouring in. I gather them under four lines of research, though here I can give them only the barest of outlines. First there is the likelihood—indeed, the certainty—that Jesuits availed themselves of female indigenous informants, especially in the field of medical botany. For most societies relying upon a mixture of hunting, gathering, and small-scale agriculture, women tended to be the chief custodians of botanical knowledge. In fact, we know that Joseph-Francois Lafitau's "discovery" of Canadian ginseng in 1716 was merely a matter of asking a Mohawk medicine woman to find the plant for him.[29] Second, there is the virtually untouched question of the gendering of nature in Jesuit natural histories. While the topic has been developed by Londa Schiebinger, among others, for eighteenth-century natural histories generally,[30] the Society's rigid segregation of male from female raises the prospect of distinctive patterns of gendering in Jesuit accounts of the natural order.

Third, the division of labor within the Society, alluded to above with regard to differences in practices, admits the possibility of gender analysis. The influential, public spaces noted by Rhodes were occupied almost exclusively by university-educated, ordained, professed fathers. The duties and spaces of lay brothers, by contrast, were almost exclusively domestic. They were accepted

---

John W. O'Malley, s.j., Gauvin Alexander Bailey, Steven J. Harris, and T. Frank Kennedy, s.j. (Toronto: Univ. of Toronto Press, 2005).

29   The subsequent export of Canadian ginseng to China created the biggest economic boom—and bust—in eighteenth-century French Canada. See William N. Fenton, "Contacts between Iroquois Herbalism and Colonial Medicine," *Annual Report of the Smithsonian Institute*, 1941, pp. 503–526, esp. 518–520.

30   See Londa Schiebinger, "Gender and Natural History," *Cultures of Natural History*, ed. Nicholas Jardine, James A. Secord, and E. C. Spary, (Cambridge and New York: Cambridge Univ. Press, 1996), pp. 163–177, and idem, *Nature's Body* (Boston: Beacon Press, 1993).

into the Society to tend to the "temporalities" of cooking, cleaning, caring for the sick, and generally minding the day-to-day business of Jesuit houses. Temporal coadjutors did what could be defined as the "women's work" of the Society. With regard to the natural and mathematical sciences, very few ever published. Of those who did, the vast majority were employed as apothecaries in the overseas missions.[31] What they published was mostly catalogs of medicinal recipes and handbooks for the healing arts. By the categories of the day, then, theirs could be characterized as deriving from the feminine side of life.

Fourth, one could investigate the relationship between modes of single-gender sociability and epistemic structures along the lines suggested in Mario Biagioli's analysis of the Accademia dei Lincei.[32] Federico Cesi, the founder of the Lincei, consciously modeled his learned academy on the Society of Jesus and composed elaborate rules to govern the behavior, attitudes, and researches of its members. I suspect that an analysis of Jesuit homosocial bonding, either along Biagioli's or different lines of reasoning, could help throw light on the mechanisms of scientific trust, cooperation, and conflict resolution within the Society.

In conclusion, let me return to the matter of the Society's institutional organization. Its tradition in overseas science was neither an accident nor incidental to its *raison d'être.* Rather, it was the outcome of institutional structures, missionary strategies, and proselytizing goals. Unlike any other colonial enterprise of the *ancien regime,* the Society exercised direct control over a unique combination of institutions, namely, its mission stations, its European colleges and universities, and the publication of its members' writings. The Society's heavy investment in education meant that most of its missionaries were themselves well educated and thus well poised to participate in the republic of letters. Mission and publication activities thus became symbiotic; the former provided content for the latter while the latter provided the medium for disseminating remotely gathered natural knowledge to multiple audiences. The interwoven agendas of colleges, missions, and publications gave Jesuits both the "motive and the means" to engage in overseas science, and the missionaries' long-term residency and commitment to cross-cultural intimacy provided

---

31 Sigismund Aperger, Johann Steinhöfer (Esteyneffer), Pedro Montenegro, and Georg Kamel all entered the Society as temporal coadjutors. Collectively, their publications make up the majority of lay-brother publications in the sciences and together number fewer than a score. Professed fathers were the authors of more than 95 percent of the entire Jesuit scientific corpus.

32 Mario Biagioli, "Knowledge, Freedom, and Brotherly Love: Homosociality and the *Accademia dei Lincei," Configurations,* 1995, 3:139–166.

JESUIT SCIENTIFIC ACTIVITY IN THE OVERSEAS MISSIONS

the "opportunity" to engage in the selective appropriation of disparate bodies of indigenous natural knowledge. Yet all of this, Catholic education at home, edifying reports on the wonders of the natural world from abroad, and conversion of nonbelievers throughout the world to the Catholic faith underscores the intricacies of the science-and-religion complex forged by Jesuits of the period. Insofar as there can be a single theme wending its way through the organizational complexities of the Society's mission program, I suppose it would be this: the coherence of the Society's overseas science depended upon Jesuits' ability to retain the traditional meaning of *scientia* as "knowledge of god" and intertwine it with the emerging meaning of *scientia* as "knowledge of nature."

The Global 'Bookkeeping' of Souls: Quantification and Nineteenth-Century Evangelical Missions

Martin Petzke

The last decades have seen the emergence of a sociological and historical literature that, rather than implementing statistics and calculation as a methodological tool, investigates quantification as an object in itself. Its emphasis lies on the reality constructions and "reactive" effects that result when measurements are "fed back" into the social realms to which they refer (Desrosières 1998; Espeland and Sauder 2007; Espeland and Stevens 1998, 2008; Hacking 1982; Patriarca 1994; Porter 1995). Similar constructionist perspectives have been advanced within the accounting sciences, where an extensive literature has employed a broad repertoire of social theory to explore the social implications of accounting (see Burchell et al. 1980; Chapman et al. 2009; Hopwood and Miller 1994). Lately, new work in finance sociology has put forth a related agenda in investigating the role of theoretical models, calculative devices, and computational technologies in constructing and performing the reality of economic markets (Callon 1998, 2007; MacKenzie and Millo 2003).

The previously mentioned literature has dealt with quantification in diverse institutional realms, for instance exploring the relationship of statistics and nation-building; the effects of rankings in the educational sector; and the constitutive role of economic equations in financial markets. Yet, it has remained relatively isolated from scholarship interested in social fields, that is, bounded spheres of action driven by autonomous logics and held together by distinct cognitive frameworks and shared beliefs (e.g., Bourdieu 1996; Fligstein and McAdam 2012; Scott 1994).[1] The mutual neglect of these two literatures is somewhat surprising as many of the previously mentioned studies highlight

---

Source: Petzke, M., "The Global 'Bookkeeping' of Souls: Quantification and Nineteenth-Century Evangelical Mission," *Social Science History* 42 (Summer 2018): pp. 183–211. © Social Science History Association, published by Cambridge University Press.

[1] In this article, I will not discuss the specific differences between the various approaches using the "field" concept but shall stick to this basic definition of a social field as a common denominator.

an important feature of quantification that gains additional relevance from a field-theoretical perspective: Calculative procedures are uniquely capable of constructing particular visibilities and relationships that readily integrate the perspectives of multiple actors. They create numerical entities such as demographics, comparative ranking systems, or prospective stock profits that are likely to foster distinct interests and particular logics of action oriented toward volatile figures and quantities.

In the accounting literature especially, there has been a notable tendency to limit the analysis to the level of a single organization (Vollmer et al. 2009). Where the social beyond the organizational level has come into view, the focus has either fallen on broader institutional environments and pressures, such as on a general proliferation of neoliberal programs and ideas of accountability (e.g., Miller 2008; Power 1997); on a historical genealogy of far-reaching discursive shifts in accounting (e.g., Hoskin and Macve 1986, 1988); or on a "political economy" of accounting, where accounting techniques are implicated in cross-cutting sociopolitical forces and social relations of production (e.g., Bryer 2000a, 2000b; Tinker 1980). To date, only few studies have chosen a *field-level approach* to investigate the effects of accounting practices on dynamics within societal fields or sectors (but see Ezzamel et al. 2012; Oakes et al. 1998). The extent to which calculative technologies shape, transform, or even create fields and field-level processes is still in need of more investigation.

Such questions gain additional urgency in light of an increasing sociological interest in transnational fields (e.g., Go 2008; Go and Krause 2016; Krause 2014). Here, again, the relative ease with which numbers travel across linguistic boundaries and transform the qualitatively and culturally different into a common metric (Espeland and Stevens 1998; Heintz 2010) would suggest a close engagement of the sociology of quantification with the literature on transnationally extending field structures. Yet, extant studies on the relationship of quantification and globalization have either focused on the broader international diffusion and standardization of accounting practices and regulations (e.g., Mennicken 2008; Samsanova 2009), or they have analyzed how accounting technology figures in enacting, appropriating, and rendering practical the global within multinational organizations (Barrett et al. 2005; Cooper and Ezzamel 2013; Cruz et al. 2011). Where social fields have come into view, the focus has mainly been on supranational organizations such as the World Bank, the IMF, or the OECD transforming and homogenizing *local* fields through the promotion of a vocabulary and technology of accounting (Neu et al. 2002, 2006), or the interest has shifted from accounting to the role of the accounting *profession* in the emergence of an increasingly global field of professional business services (Arnold 2005; Suddaby et al. 2007). What is more, a recently emerging literature on global indicators again opts for a view on cross-cutting aspects of power and governance while largely ignoring how such indicators figure in the creation of relatively bounded domains of action with distinct "rules of the game" (e.g., Davis et al. 2012; Hansen and Mühlen-Schulte 2012). With the sole exception of some work in the Luhmannian tradition (Heintz and Werron 2011), the role of quantification in the emergence and perpetuation of transnational fields remains underexplored.

To address these lacunae, this article highlights a case from the religious realm that shows how quantification and accounting can contribute to forging a global field of action and intervention. It investigates how calculative practices were involved in the global outreach of evangelical missions since the nineteenth century. Earlier initiatives by Anglicans and German Pietists notwithstanding, the nineteenth century marks the beginning of an unprecedented Protestant endeavor to bring the gospel to the "heathens" as missions originating from the United States, Great Britain, and continental Europe extended to all continents and into countries and regions previously untouched. This surge eclipsed previous Christian missionary efforts in organizational rationality, geographical scope, and its unambiguous ambition to evangelize the world (see Latourette 1937–45; Neill 1987; Porter 2004; Stanley 1990; Tyrell 2004). The article argues that these missionary motives of world evangelization were decisively fueled by the construct of a "heathen population" in the foreign world fabricated through *practices of quantification.* Religious statistics constructed a visibility of a global distribution of religious adherents that spurred, directed, and perpetuated an interorganizational enterprise geared toward the conversion of the world to Christianity. The discursive production of a "global object" through calculative practices propelled a globally oriented dynamic of evangelization and proselytization.

The contribution of this article is thus threefold. First, it adds to the nascent literature on global fields, where processes of field emergence are still little understood. While recent contributions in this area have stressed the role of cultural beliefs and individual actors with extraordinary "social skills" that purposely fashion (global) fields (Dromi 2016; Fligstein and McAdam 2012), this article, taking up insights from Werner Sombart and finance sociology, instead points to the role of sociotechnical devices and material infrastructures in constructing an object and objective capable of spawning and captivating a field of organizations and individual actors. It underscores the relationship of quantifying technologies and the genesis of particular "meaning systems" (Scott 1994), "institutional logics" (Friedland and Alford 1991), or "stakes"

THE GLOBAL 'BOOKKEEPING' OF SOULS   189

(Bourdieu 1996; Fligstein and MacAdam 2012) that drive the autonomization of transnationally extending supraorganizational realms perpetuated by collective and individual actors who have come to share in a field-specific ontology and worldview.

Second, the study contributes to the literature on accounting, where the debate on accounting and religion has largely been shaped by Laughlin's (1988) seminal paper arguing that the "sacred" cosmos and the "profane" activities of accounting were carefully separated in the Church of England. Since then, many papers have raised doubts about this strict divide by variously revealing how accounting methods can play a constitutive role in religious organizations (Cordery 2006; Irvine 2002, 2005; Jacobs 2005; Jacobs and Walker 2004; Quattrone 2004). This article further adds to this debate by providing an example from the much-neglected macrolevel of social fields. Instead of showing how accounting techniques productively shape spiritual life in individual organizations, it demonstrates how a numerical object constructed through quantification integrates the perspectives and drives the actions of a whole array of religious organizations of various denominations and stripes.

Finally, the article contributes new insights to the history of Protestant missions in the nineteenth century, where such effects of religious quantification have elicited very little attention. It argues that in addition to ideology and structural opportunity, commonly cited as explanatory factors in the literature (Beaver 1968; Latourette 1937–45; Neill 1987; Phillips 1969; Porter 2004; Shenk 2004; Stanley 1990), the constitutive effects of statistics and bookkeeping need to be considered in explaining the rise and logic of nineteenth-century missions and their continuation in the contemporary spread of global evangelicalism.

For data, I use missionary periodicals, sermons by prominent missionaries, and tracts of the late eighteenth and nineteenth centuries. To highlight historical discontinuities, I also look at early treatises on global religion of the seventeenth and eighteenth centuries. As the United States and Great Britain were the two leading missionary "powers" in terms of missionaries sent abroad and funds raised for missions (Warneck 1901: 85–139), I focus on material from these countries.[2] I furthermore limit my analysis of missionary periodicals to the organ of the biggest missionary organization in the United States, the *Missionary Herald* of the interdenominational American Board of Commissioners for Foreign Missions (ABCFM), and to *The Missionary Review* (later: *Missionary Review of the World*), the leading general-interest mission

---

2 I am, however, aware that continental Europe, especially Germany, was also heavily engaged in missionary publishing and that such publications enjoyed a wide readership even in the Anglo-Saxon world.

journal of its time, reaching a circulation of 13,000 by 1900 (Mathews 2006: 116; Robert 2003: 284–94). Annual reports of the ABCFM, the *Missionary Herald*, and the sermons of ABCFM missionaries have been acquired from the ABCFM archives at Houghton Library, Harvard University. Sermons by British missionaries and evidence on British missionary organizations come from secondary sources on British missions. Finally, in pointing out how this particular missionary dynamic has endured until today, I look at online resources for contemporary evangelical missions. I use these data to show how calculative practices are employed in prompting and orienting Protestant missionary endeavors.

I do not discuss Catholicism in this article, for two reasons. First, in contrast to the material on Protestant missions, broadly published in missionary journals and treatises of the time, primary documents on Catholic missions are substantially less accessible. Second, Catholics played a reactive rather than a proactive part in the upsurge of missions at the turn of the century. Indeed, Roman Catholic missions had been at a "low ebb" (Cox 2008: 9) since the political decline of the Roman Catholic imperial powers and the preliminary end of Jesuit missions after the papal dissolution of the order in 1773. To be sure, the fact that Protestants had the initiative in the nineteenth century by no means implies that Catholicism was insignificant. On the contrary, rejuvenated by the Protestant missionary challenge, Catholic orders became a fierce competitor of Protestant organizations, and numerical gains of Catholics were closely monitored in Protestant missionary publications (as was likely true the other way around). However, as this is rather in line with, than contrary to, my argument of numbers and numerical competition fueling an interorganizational field dedicated to evangelization, and as I am more interested in the genesis and perpetuation of this field through technologies of quantification, I consider the focus on Protestantism to be warranted.

The article begins with one of the earliest proponents of a relationship between calculative practices and the emergence of specific institutional orders as it examines Werner Sombart's (1916) classic thesis on the relationship between double-entry bookkeeping, the construction of the category "capital," and the genesis of a capitalist economy. It argues that central elements of Sombart's argument can be generalized to highlight similar developments in fields beyond the economy. Thus, as is shown in the remainder of the article, demographic techniques played a comparable role in the emergence of nineteenth-century missions. Here, they made global categories of religious adherents numerically visible, installing a "bookkeeping rationale" that quite analogously sparked a missionary enterprise dedicated to altering quantitative distributions in favor of Christianity. The article thus identifies a more general mechanism in the

THE GLOBAL 'BOOKKEEPING' OF SOULS   191

quantitative constitution of distinct social fields: in Sombart's case as in the
one presented here, calculative practices merge with particular meaning structures (religious and economic, respectively) to construct a specific *numerical
object* (distributions of religious adherents and "capital," respectively) that in
turn spawns and becomes the center of an *autonomous and recursive institutional order* focused on maintaining or modifying quantitative values of said
object (the missionary movement or capitalism, respectively).[3]

To set the stage for this novel perspective within religion, I first look at early
forms of religious quantification on a global scale, dating back to the early
seventeenth century, in the second section. In the third section, I proceed to
discuss how and why demographic concepts and logics of accounting merged
with a missionary outlook on the religious world in the nineteenth century. In
the fourth section, I focus on the systematic observation of the overall progress of Protestant missions and show how global statistics of religion drove
and oriented missionary efforts. Finally, I flesh out the central analogies of the
emergence of nineteenth-century missions with Sombart's thesis on the birth
of capitalism and highlight the continuities with contemporary evangelical
missionary perspectives.

Sombart's Thesis on Accounting and the Rise of Capitalism

Both Max Weber (1978 [1921], 1981 [1923]) and Werner Sombart (1916) have
pointed to the constitutive role of double-entry bookkeeping in their studies
on the rise of modern capitalism, seeing it as a unique and defining element
of the rational capitalist enterprise. However, it is first and foremost Sombart's
perspective on the relationship of accounting and capitalism that bears subtle
yet fundamental constructionist implications as it points to the "ideational"
consequences of economic bookkeeping for the emergence of a capitalist
economy. According to Sombart, the very practice of bookkeeping essentially *created* the notion of capital as something that could be accumulated—

---

3   While referring to the process delineated in this article as a mechanism, I do not subscribe
    to the methodological individualism that Hedström and Swedberg (1998) tie to the mecha-
    nism concept. The causal chain observed here operates at an institutional level of discourses,
    meanings, and relevance structures as well as at an organizational level, with quantitative
    practices creating discursive objects that influence and orient organizations and organiza-
    tional structures. Consequently, the microfoundations of these processes add little explana-
    tory value. On multiple levels in the analysis of mechanisms see Jepperson and Meyer (2011).

an accumulation in the first place made *visible* through accounting. In Sombart's words:

> The method of double-entry bookkeeping actualizes the complete separation of the funds used in profit making and the funds used for everyday life. Herewith the acquisition principle reaches its full development. *There remains only one single purpose: to increase a measured amount of "value."* To penetrate the mysteries of bookkeeping, one must forget the qualities of goods and services. One must no longer think of ships or shiploads, flour or cotton, but exclusively in terms of quantities, of increasing and diminishing amounts of value. The idea of organic limitation of human needs, expressed in the livelihood principle, is replaced by the principle of *acquisition as an end in itself....* The very concept of capital is derived from this way of looking at things; *one can say that capital, as a category, did not exist before double-entry bookkeeping.*
>
> SOMBART 1953: 38; emphases added

This thesis and the exact nature of the relationship of double-entry bookkeeping and the genesis of capitalism are still lively debated today. As I am more interested in the structure of the argument than in its actual validity for capitalism, I will not discuss this controversy here.[4] Rather, in the context at hand, three interrelated elements of Sombart's proposition are of relevance. I shall call them *construction, catalyzation,* and *rationalization.*

Accounting practices *constructed* a numerical "entity," a specific quantitative distillate first derived from particular calculative procedures. This quantitative construct *catalyzed* a broad and systematic endeavor or "enterprise" geared toward its incrementation (as manifested in individual enterprises); a certain measure thus emerged as the center of attention and action within a largely autonomous sphere—a field fueled by a specific interest or "spirit" inextricably bound to a purely calculative outlook. Finally, accounting methods formed the basis of increasingly *rational procedures* within this field: Where outcomes of previous undertakings could be made visible and compared, future practices could be optimized and selected in terms of desired results.

---

4 For an overview see Chiapello (2007), who offers an analysis of the relationship between double-entry bookkeeping and the emergence of the *theoretical concept* of "capitalism," especially with reference to the work of Marx. Here, one also finds a discussion of the work of Yamey (1949, 1964, 2005), who is among the most adamant of Sombart's critics.

As I will show in the remainder of this article, similar "catalytic" effects of bookkeeping methods as those posited by Sombart can also be discerned in sectors other than the economy. My focus is on the religious realm, where the transposition of demographic "accounting" practices unto religious affairs created novel categories and numerical "objects" that established and set in motion an autonomous social field devoted to modifying quantities of Protestant adherents and "heathens." I thus illustrate how the confluence of demographic perspectives with a missionary discourse led to the construction of "religious populations" and the institution of "bookkeeping" practices in nineteenth-century global missions, dynamizing an endeavor to evangelize the world. To throw the novelty of this perspective on global religions into sharp relief, the following section will first briefly examine early forms of quantifying the worldwide religious landscape before turning to the missionary discourse of the nineteenth century.

Early Quantification of Global Religion

Global accounts of religion date back as early as the seventeenth century. Samuel Purchas's *Purchas, his Pilgrimage, or Relations of the World and the Religions Observed in All Ages and Places Discovered, from the Creation unto the Present*, published in 1613, may be seen as the earliest work of a whole genre of treatises that aimed to comprehensively survey the religions of the globe as it was known then.[5] These treatises adopted a mostly "qualitative" approach to the comparison of religions (classified as Judaism, Christianity, "Mahometanism," and "heathenism"/idolatry) and things religious as they took stock of the customs, the historical past, and the present locations of the various religious traditions.

However, some of these volumes also exhibit a curious way of comparing the world's religions in a quantitative fashion. Thus, in his treatise *Enquiries Touching the Diversity of Languages and Religions Through the Chief Parts of the World*, first published in 1614, Edward Brerewood offers the following account in his chapter "Of the Quantity and Proportion of the Parts of the Earth,

---

5 Masuzawa (2005) has dealt with most of these surveys in her study *The Invention of World Religions*; on the discursive prerequisites of such comparative treatises see Harrison (1990) and Pailin (1984).

Possessed by the Several Sorts of the Above-Mentioned Religions" (Brerewood 1674 [1614]: 144–51):

> It being first supposed ... that the proportions of Europe, Africk, Asia, and America, are as 1—3—4, and 7. And that the professors of the fore-mentioned Religions, possess the several portions and proportions, of each of them, which is before set down: It will be found I say upon these suppositions ... that Christians possess, near about a sixt part of the known inhabited Earth; Mahumetans, a fift part ... and Idolaters, two thirds, or but little less. So that, if we divide the known regions of the world, into 30 equal parts; The Christians part is as five, the Mahumetans as six, and the Idolaters as nineteen, for the poor dispersed and distressed Christians, which are found in Asia and Africk, mingled among Mahumetans, and Idolaters, I receive not into this account, both because they were but thin dispersed ... and because also, many Mahumetans, are found mingled among Christians in Europe, to recompence and countervail a great part of that number. (p. 145)

Brerewood's quantitative snapshot of global religion, relating religions according to the total area of the regions where they are largely professed or encountered, would sporadically reappear unaltered in comparable treatises throughout the next one and a half centuries. An identical account can be found, for instance, in William Turner's *History of All Religions* from 1695. Hannah Adams (1784), a distant relative of President John Quincy Adams and herself renowned for her many encyclopedic surveys of the world's religions, drew a very similar picture still in 1784, though Jews were now included and Greek Orthodox Christians listed separately.

A sensitivity and interest for numerical relations among religions were thus already present before the nineteenth century. Religious quantification could not have elicited much fascination at this early stage, however. Not only was new information widely missing, but also this rather static way of thinking about quantitative relations among religions, that is, in terms of geographic dominance rather than in terms of individual allegiance, did not allow for much observable change. With religious "populations" at best implicitly in the picture, enumerable fluctuations were not to be had. As will be argued in the following, this changed fundamentally as the missionary discourse of the late eighteenth and early nineteenth centuries became wedded to a demographic discourse.

The Introduction of Demographic Perspectives into Missions

The novel religious view on "populations" emerging in the missionary discourse of the nineteenth century is best exemplified by a treatise that is widely considered to be one of the founding documents of nineteenth-century Protestant missions: William Carey's *An Enquiry into the Obligation of Christians to Use Means for the Conversion of the Heathens* of 1792. Carey, a British shoemaker of London who had recently converted to Baptism, showed himself deeply affected by the writings of Captain James Cook, which featured reports on the many heathen tribes encountered during Cook's voyages. Consequently, Carey's tract argues for the undiminished urgency of the Great Commission and calls for the establishment of missionary societies modeled after trading companies.

This treatise is especially noteworthy for its extensive use of statistics and demographic reasoning. Section III of the tract, "Containing a Survey of the Present State of the Globe," provides statistical tables for all continents, with countries listed as rows and their geographical "extent," "number of inhabitants," and "religions" indicated in the columns. Already here, "populations" and "religions" are brought into affinity. The population figures are estimates based on a method that had already been employed by Vauban in 1707: It begins with an approximation of how many people can be sustained by a square mile of land, taking local factors into consideration, and then extrapolates this figure to the total area of the country in question.

It is not the dubious accuracy of this estimate that is of interest here. The importance lies in the discursive shift that is indicated by it. Rather than quantitatively comparing religions by simply putting their geographical extensions into relation as done by Brerewood in 1614 and by Hannah Adams as recently as 1784, the focus is now clearly on *countable individuals*. The shift is purely a matter of semantics, not of new and advanced intelligence, as, obviously, geographical areas are still the basis of this calculation.

In aggregating these estimates, moreover, Carey's tract offers global totals of religious adherence in what may be considered one of the first specifications of a *global religious distribution*; here, the world's *population*, not the geographical world, is dissolved into its various religious segments, putting the discursive innovation markedly into relief:

> The inhabitants of the world according to this calculation, amount to about seven hundred and thirty-one millions; four hundred and twenty millions of whom are still in pagan darkness; an hundred and thirty

millions the followers of Mahomet; an hundred millions catholics; forty-four millions protestants; thirty millions of the greek and armenian churches, and perhaps seven millions of jews.[6]

> CAREY 1792: 62

In arguing his case for global missions, Carey's emphasis lies poignantly on the *quantitative amount* of heathens:

> It must undoubtedly strike every considerate mind, what a *vast proportion* of the sons of Adam there are, who yet remain in the most deplorable state of heathen darkness, without any means of knowing the true God, except what are afforded them by the works of nature; and utterly destitute of the knowledge of the gospel of Christ, or of any means of obtaining it.
>
> CAREY 1792: 62; emphasis added

Similar pleas for global missions had preceded Carey's treatise; they had had, however, comparatively little repercussions and had been largely void of any numerical argument.[7] Indeed, prior to the 1790s, British Protestant missionary endeavors had been, as Stanley (1990: 55) put it, "sporadic and geographically limited," confining themselves mostly to North American settlements. Continental Europe, to be sure, had witnessed an early impulse of global missions in the first half of the eighteenth century when the Danish-Halle Mission and missionaries of the Moravian Church ventured into India, the West Indies, and even Persia and China. However, these momentous initiatives had been unable to sustain a broader influence on Protestantism (Pierard 2011: 294; Warneck 1901: 66–70).

In contrast, Carey's *Enquiry* prefaced an unparalleled surge in missionary efforts from Protestant denominations across the board. Its call for missionary societies was heeded just months later with the formation of the Particular-Baptist Society for Propagating the Gospel among the Heathen (later: Baptist Missionary Society). Before the century ended, the initially ecumenical

---

6   To be sure, instances of quantifying church members can be found at least as early as the sixteenth century as, for example, in the ecclesiastical censuses in England of 1547, 1563, 1603, 1676, and 1688 (Cline Cohen 1999: 36); however, while some of these censuses also surveyed nonconformists, they generally did not dissolve a "population" into religious segments nor were any of them interested in religious adherence on a global scale.

7   See, for instance, the hymns and appeals of Isaac Watts (1674–1748) and Philip Doddridge (1702–52), which already had, according to Stanley (1990: 55), "a distinctly global flavor."

THE GLOBAL 'BOOKKEEPING' OF SOULS   197

London Missionary Society and the Anglican Society for the Missions to Africa and the East (later: Church Missionary Society) had joined the scene. In 1810, North American Protestants followed suit with the foundation of the ABCFM. Similar organizations sprung up in the following years in Germany, Scandinavia, and the Netherlands.

The turn of the century thus saw a striking shift from more locally bounded missionary engagements to endeavors that were truly global in scope, marking an "unprecedented geographical advance of Christian influence" (Stanley 1990: 83). Most importantly, this novel missionary movement was able to persevere over the course of the century and remains vibrantly alive among evangelical factions of Protestantism even today.

As the example of early Pietism shows, it is unlikely to have been the revivalist atmosphere of the century's turn alone that gave this newly roused missionary movement such an unswerving and long-lasting momentum. Rather, as this article argues, the fact that the evangelical fervor of the nineteenth century was channeled into efforts of religious quantification played a decisive role in *durably establishing* a self-perpetuating as well as global dynamic in the realm of Christian missions. For Carey's treatise not only ushered in an era of missions theretofore unequaled in organizational capacity and global expansion. It also set the foundation for the complementary enterprise of *continually monitoring and rigorously quantifying* the world's religious landscape and worldwide missionary progress.

Before elaborating on this aspect, the very coalescence of quantification and missions warrants some attention. What, in the first place, led to the adoption of demographic and quantitative perspectives in the missionary outlook of the late eighteenth and early nineteenth centuries? What, in short, were the prerequisites for this novel way of relating to Christian missions in quantitative *and* global terms as exhibited by treatises such as the one by William Carey?

First, as I discuss in the following, I maintain that the well-documented *soterio-logical and millenarian* features of nineteenth-century Protestant theology, which are generally cited as central factors in the onset of global evangelical missions (Beaver 1968; Latourette 1937–45; Neill 1987; Phillips 1969; Porter 2004; Stanley 1990), bore an elective affinity to practices of accounting and demography and need to be considered also with regard to the quantitative perspectives they helped install. I thus argue that quantification should be viewed as a relevant mediating factor in explaining the emergence and persistence of evangelical missions.

Second, I show that "bookkeeping" perspectives were further consolidated by the missionary societies' practice of *legitimating* missions through detailed reports that accounted for income and donations *as well as* for successful conversions; here, for apparent reasons of parsimony, similar or often even identical notations and tables for both aspects of missions were used, making "gains" in communicants visible and inevitably lending further plausibility to the idea of religious adherents as something to be "accumulated."

3.1   *Theological Prerequisites*

Within nineteenth-century Protestant theology, it was perhaps first and foremost the *soteriological* outlook that leveled the field for the introduction of demographic perspectives. The emergence of modern demography in the seventeenth and eighteenth centuries, with the seminal contributions of John Graunt in England and Johann Peter Suessmilch in Germany, was closely tied to applying bookkeeping techniques to mortality bills and records of "christenings," thus balancing births and deaths of a "population" (Kreager 1988).[8] In light of the soteriological exclusivism of nineteenth-century Protestantism, such deaths, as they were implied in demographic reasoning and the calculation of populations, inevitably gained a special significance when considering the sizable proportion of unevangelized "heathens" among the dead; after all, the dominant doctrine of the time held that those who had not turned to Christ would perish in hell. A sermon by Robert Moffat, missionary of the London Missionary Society in South Africa, delivered to his parish in 1843, makes this quite apparent:

> Who can look to the East Indies now, and to China now, who can look to those interesting portions of the globe, because the most populous, the most dense, without yearning with compassion over the teeming millions that are there moving onward every day like some vast funeral procession; onward and downward, sadly and slowly, but certainly to the regions of woe? "Oh, you are a hard man," some might say; "do you think they will go to hell?" Where do they go? Do they go to heaven? All idolaters, we are told, have their portion in the lake that burneth with fire and brimstone.
>
> cited in STANLEY 1990: 65

As indicated by the mention of India and China, the focus of this particular soteriological perspective inevitably falls on demographic magnitude. Furthermore, such images of "souls" continually "lost" to damnation if not

---

8   On the origin of modern statistics see, for example, Lazarsfeld (1961).

THE GLOBAL 'BOOKKEEPING' OF SOULS

otherwise "won" for salvation resonate with logics of accounting that underlie modern demography in general.

To be sure, an exclusivist stance toward religious salvation is far from unique to this particular period and certainly insufficient as a cause for missions. For the quantity of heathens to even have been of relevance and not just a purely academic question, the idea that the fate of these heathens could be altered by an earthly intervention had to be presupposed. This Arminian notion that man could play an instrumental part in the salvation of others did indeed increasingly supplant orthodox views of predestination in the eighteenth century (McLoughlin 1959; Mead 1942). Not surprisingly, then, the call for global missions often went hand in hand with a piercing critique of those voices that held God alone ultimately responsible for the salvation of the heathens. To illustrate, Lyman Beecher, one of the central advocates of the Arminian "New Haven Theology," preached during his sermon at the annual meeting of the ABCFM in New York City on October 12, 1827:

> The idea that God will convert the heathen in his own good time, and that Christians have nothing to do but to pray and devoutly wait, is found in no canonical book. It is the maxim of covetousness, and sloth, and uncaring infidelity. We have no authority for saying, what some, without due consideration, have said, that God, if he pleased, could doubtless in a moment convert the whole heathen world without the Gospel. It might as well be said, that he can, if he please, burn without fire, or drown without water, or give breath without atmosphere, as that he can instruct intellectual beings without the means of knowledge, and influence moral beings without law and motive, and thus reclaim an alienated world without the knowledge and moral power of the Gospel. It is no derogation from the power of God, that, to produce results, it must be exerted by means adapted to the constitution of things which Himself has established.
>
> BEECHER 1827: 19–20

The quotation exemplifies the reconciliation of profane rationality, "instrumental activism," and the realm of the sacred, which can be seen as a fundamental prerequisite for the "pragmatic" approach of quantifying heathens and converts.

Second, aside from these soteriological features, the specific *millenarian* perspectives of early-nineteenth-century Protestantism were likewise conducive to adopting a quantitative outlook on global missions. Though pre- and postmillenialists disagreed whether the Second Coming of Christ would precede or follow the millennium, both ideological strands converged in the conclusion that missionary endeavors were urgent and critical, either to save as many souls as possible before the imminent day of judgment or to establish the Kingdom of God on Earth and thereby hasten Christ's return. Moreover, successful conversions in themselves were considered a tell-tale sign that these were in fact the end times. Thus, the conversion of the world's population was as much seen as a *task* to take part in as it was considered an *indicator and gauge* of the millennium's imminence; consequently, a numerical accounting of those already won for Christ and those yet to be gained suggested itself somewhat naturally.

Accordingly, petitions and statistical reasoning as they are exhibited in Carey's early treatise would continue to pervade the many missionary publications and sermons of the nineteenth century. The millenarian ambiance, setting the expectation of an imminent dawn of the "Kingdom of God," of which an increasing number of conversions was indicative, as well as the notion of a "soteriological" responsibility for the salvation of the heathens can be said to have borne an elective affinity to calculative practices and demographic perspectives. As we shall see in the following section, a quantitative outlook and practices of religious "bookkeeping" were further enforced by the meticulous reports of Protestant missionary societies.

3.2 *Missionary Reports*

While the theological outlook of late-eighteenth- and nineteenth-century Protestantism invited demographic concepts into a missionary discourse, it was especially the regular reporting of the various missionary societies emerging from the Protestant missionary awakening that consolidated "bookkeeping" practices in the realm of missions.[9] With only a few exceptions, these organizations were voluntary associations that formed outside the official churches and relied heavily on the service of the religious laity. Nonetheless, they were generally run in a highly bureaucratic fashion. A board of missions in the homeland usually supervised and coordinated all missionary activities in the mission fields, which had to be carefully recorded and continually reported (Tyrell 2004).

Nearly every missionary society entertained some publication that made the information from these reports available to the broader public. Such journals

---

9 See Warneck (1901: 85–144) for a list and discussion of the various missionary societies that originated from North America and Europe.

THE GLOBAL 'BOOKKEEPING' OF SOULS   201

interspersed news from the field and other stories relating to mission with detailed financial reports and surveys of the missionary progress. One function of these publications was to pique a general interest for the missionary cause and elicit donations from domestic supporters.

More importantly, however, these journals can be seen as an important means and vehicle of conveying the *legitimacy* of the missionary society to actual and potential donors. The transparency and detail of the financial reports published in these organs can be attributed precisely to this.[10] Carruthers and Espeland (1991) have highlighted the rhetorical functions of economic accounting, which often played the greater part in the early adoption of bookkeeping methods: Beyond its technical advantages, the practice of accounting was from the outset seen as an effective way of conveying to an audience the legitimacy of a business venture. Similar considerations on the part of the missionary "entrepreneurs" can be discerned from the missionary journals. To illustrate, in its organ *The Missionary Herald*, the ABCFM (ABCFM 1882: 342) restated some of its principles as they were elucidated in an 1862 report on the expenditures and finances of the board:

> The Missionary Herald, published monthly, contains an accurate account of all donations received during a previous month, with the name and place of residence of each donor, which corresponds with the sum entered as received upon the cash-book.... This is a very important safeguard, which cannot be had in ordinary business transactions; and this, and other checks adopted by the Board, for the security of its funds, *should give assurance to every donor that his gift will reach the treasury of the Board.* (emphasis added)

Sure enough, the annual reports of the missionary societies did not content themselves with financial statements. Information regarding new communicants as well as general expositions of the further need of missions also played a significant part in the effort to legitimate a missionary enterprise dependent on the benevolence of donors:

> A condensed and succinct view of each missionary station, of the receipts and disbursements of the Treasury, and of various subjects connected with the general cause of missions, is required at the close of each year, to justify, not only the past proceedings, but the future plans of the

---

10   For a similar point on accounting in religious organizations see Irvine (2002).

> Board, *and to satisfy the Christian public, that their labor and sacrifices are not in vain in the Lord.*
>
> ABCFM 1824: 62–63; emphasis added

Hence, annual summaries determining the total number of church members as well as the number of church members added during the year generally appear in the various missionary journals, in *The Missionary Herald* as early as 1829.

The simple contiguity of financial statements and reports on added communicants lent plausibility to thinking about expenditures, income, and converts in very similar terms. In the annual reports of the ABCFM, as elsewhere, expressions such as "net gain," "increase," and "total" were often used to refer to finances and communicants alike.[11] Thus, quantitative perspectives on religious adherents were reinforced through "semantic interferences" with economic bookkeeping practices *sensu stricto*, thereby establishing practices of *religious* "bookkeeping." In essence, the missionary societies' need to assert legitimacy and give some measure of success to convince donors that their charitable investments were worthwhile solidified logics of "accounting" in the missionary outlook on the religious world.

These missionary reports also supplied the necessary data for the construction of an ever-changing distribution of religious adherents that stood at the center of monitoring the overall progress of Protestant missions and of effectively directing and orienting the missionary enterprise. It is to this *global* "bookkeeping" of souls that I now turn.

The Global "Bookkeeping" of Souls

Based on the extensive report system and the many publication organs of the missionary societies, some took it upon themselves to continually pool all the available information to give a *comprehensive overview* of the *worldwide* Protestant missionary enterprise. Many magazines dedicated to such a task were already circulating in New England before Americans even became seriously involved in global missions: *The New York Missionary Magazine* (1800–3), *The Panoplist* (1805–8), and *The Massachusetts Missionary Magazine* (1803–8) are early examples of such publications (the latter two merged in 1808 and were later replaced by *The Missionary Herald*, the organ of the ABCFM).

---

11   See McKinlay and Mutch (2015) for similar transferences of accountability practices between the economic domain and religious (self-)assessments in Scottish Presbyterianism.

THE GLOBAL 'BOOKKEEPING' OF SOULS

Among the most noteworthy and exhaustive of these ventures was *The Missionary Review*, as of 1888 *The Missionary Review of the World*, edited by Royal G. Wilder from 1878 to 1887, by Arthur T. Pierson from 1888 to 1911, and by Delavan L. Pierson from 1911 to 1939. It could already rely on a well-established system of missionary reporting and thus serves well to illustrate *the construction of a continually changing numerical relation between a heathen and a Protestant population* as focal point of nineteenth-century missionary efforts.

During the *Review*'s first decade, an overview of all financial statements and mission reports of every church and missionary society from America as well as Europe would run through all the editions each year to finally conclude in a comprehensive statistical table summarizing, with some reservations, the present state of global Protestant Christendom. As of 1893, two such statistical tables, one summarizing the Protestant missionary efforts originating from the United States and Canada and the other those from Great Britain and continental Europe, would appear in the first two issues of each year. As stated in the tables, the "figures are almost wholly derived directly from the annual reports of the various Societies" (Pierson 1893: 72–73).

These tables are in many ways notable: Each year, the annual progress of a total of more than 100 Protestant missionary societies is surveyed. Moreover, financial statements and notes on the number of communicants and adherents are again brought together *in one table*. Thus, the last three rows of the table in 1884 give "grand totals" of the current year and the preceding year as well as "year's gain" for financial income, administrative costs, *and* communicants of the global Protestant community. Figure 1 shows the second half of the table listing European organizations, with the totals for American organizations brought over.

Such *global* "gains" in communicants "made visible" through accounting practices and tabular devices focalize the missionary endeavor on a global distribution of religious adherents. Moreover, they discursively highlight the *fluidity* and *alterability* of this distribution. They thus serve as the key rhetorical device not only in legitimating but also in *motivating* and *driving* general missionary efforts in the nineteenth century. First, it is the quantified *success* of missions that spurs the missionary undertaking: "Do not these facts present abundant evidence that God is bestowing large and special blessings on efforts to evangelize the heathen?" (Wilder 1884: 464). Second, it is the quantified *need* for missions that serves to stimulate missionary ventures as these figures are balanced against the as of yet unconverted portion of the world's population: "Assume Prof. Christlieb's estimate of 1,650,000 converts from heathenism, as the result of modern missions, to be correct, and yet how small this result compared to the 1,000,000,000 still unevangelized" (Wilder 1881: 34).

EUROPEAN ORGANIZATIONS. Local Preachers.	Home Strength.		Year's growth in comm'ts.		Foreign Missionary Income.		Maximum Salary of		Administration.		Begun For Mis.	Workers from Christendom.				Native Workers.		Native Com'ts	Year's Gain.	
	Ministers.	Com'ts.	Total.	Per cent.	Total.	Per mbr.	Miss'y	Officer	Whole cost.	Cost per c't.		Ord.	Lay	Wo. men.	Oth ers.	Ord.	ers.		In c'm'ts.	Per cent.
51. Gospel Prop. Society,	23,000	13,000,000			$547,862	$ .04	$3,000	$3,000	$ 71,845	11.20	1701	160	61	62	79	1382	28540	1862	6.97
52. Church Miss'y "	"	"			1,126,157	.08	3,000	3,000	120,670	12.00	1799	222	34	15	240	3075	37443	1117	3.07
53. Eng. Baptist	1,882	304,802	28,446	10.29	303,612	.99	1,350	3,000	34,674	12.89	1792	75	20	23	75	477	40247	2050	5.33
54. Gen. " Society.	404	26,153	0	0	43,890	1.64	700	600	3,345	8.67	1816	7		9	22		1175	27	2.35
55. London Miss'y Society.	3,205	360,000	0	0	633,663	1.75	1,170	2,500	50,353	8.64	1795	152		130	383	4920	86422	12660	12.8
56. Wesleyan Meth. " 18,850	2,000	407,085	27	0	846,800	2.08	1,200	2,340	103,962	13.99	1814	270	30	226	270	1789	91276	1927	2.13
57. Prim. " 15,782	1,151	196,480	0	0	13,098	.06	600	942	968	7.98	1843	4		4	2	4	356	0	0.
58. New Connex Meth. So. 1,271	188	33,383	2,578	8.36	27,276	.81	1,250	750	3,360	14.04		5		4	12	43	1161	30	2.65
59. United Free " 3,417	431	84,152	9,256	12.15	70,428	.83	900	900	3,300	10.64	1857	18		8	15	134	7127	344	5.07
60. Bible Christians 1,930	209	33,920	0	0	32,521	.95	400	750	2,414	8.01	1821	59				325	4095	31	0.76
61. Eng. Presbyterians.	273	58,466	1,004	1.74	80,120	1.37	2,250	0	3,740	4.89	1847	18	9	6	15	59	2859	91	3.28
62. Estab. Ch. of Scotland.	1,660	539,292	9,282	1.75	140,112	.26	3,300	750	5,306	3.93	1827	12	11	6	4	98	415	95	29.68
63. Free & Ref. Ch. of Scotland.	1,034	314,027	34,027	12.86	380,180	1.23	1,920	2,000	9,339	2.45	1827	37	35	50	13	425	4443	172	4.02
64. United Presbyterians "	583	178,195	4,638	2.65	182,674	1.02	2,250	2,000	9,766	5.64	1847	55	8	13	20	418	11519	1304	12.76
65. Irish "	632	103,548	723	0.70	54,505	.52	1,780	2,000	2,518	4.62	1840	13	4	8	10	38	370	10	2.77
66. China Inland Mission.	. . . .	. . . .	. . . .		66,168	. . . .	. . . .	800	7,447	12.68	1865	14	42	50	0	102	1100	20	1.85
67. Livingstone "	. . . .	. . . .	. . . .		25,600	. . . .					1878		14	4		4			
68. London Society for Jews.	. . . .	. . . .	. . . .		223,080	. . . .			31,236	16.28	1808	30	28			85			
69. Col. and Cont. Chr. Society.	. . . .	. . . .	. . . .		235,170	. . . .			24,213	11.47	1823	136	44			92			
70. Christian Faith Mission.	. . . .	. . . .	. . . .		11,380	. . . .					1691								
71. So. Am. Miss'y Society.	. . . .	. . . .	. . . .		76,120	. . . .	3,000	3,000	14,217	22.96	1844	14	10	11	0	5	220		
72. Edinburg Medical Society.	. . . .	. . . .	. . . .		44,437	. . . .	1,500	1,500	5,500	14.12	1841	3	5	3		8			
73. British Miss'y Soc'y, Jews.	. . . .	. . . .	. . . .		47,279	. . . .			7,208	15.25	1842	12	9	3		80			
74. Colonial Miss'y Society.	. . . .	. . . .	. . . .		20,091	. . . .			3,083	18.12	1836	. .	. .						
75. Basle Miss'y Society.	. . . .	. . . .	. . . .		254,180	. . . .	1,000	1,000	2,992	7.25	1832	83	34	83	26	286	7268	43	.66
76. St. Chrischona Miss'y Society.	. . . .	. . . .	. . . .		26,021	. . . .			1,856	7.68	1840	4	27	6		10			
77. Rhenish Miss'y Society.	. . . .	. . . .	. . . .		80,000	. . . .					1828	70	6	60	2	180	9150	150	1.66
78. North German Miss'y Soc'y.	. . . .	. . . .	. . . .		24,000	. . . .					1836	10		8		12	250	14	12727
79. Leipzig Miss'y Society.	. . . .	. . . .	. . . .		63,176	. . . .					1819	22	2	10	260	13321	60	0.45
80. Berlin "	. . . .	. . . .	. . . .		88,000	. . . .					1824	57	12	30	2	162	8060	60	0.75
81. Gossner's " "	. . . .	. . . .	. . . .		34,000	. . . .					1836	12	5	10	8	205	12500	1714	15.89
82. Hermannsburg Miss'y Soc'y.	. . . .	. . . .	. . . .		70,500	. . . .					1853	40	55	55	22	188	3920	120	3.15
83. French Evang. " "	1,500	630,000	. . . .		64,616	. . . .	1,000	1,000	4,000	6.59	1832	25	6	26	2	130	6820		
84. Netherland Ref. " "	1,612	425,000	. . . .		40,800	. . . .					1797	11	8	6	2	35	12650	630	5.41
85. " " Ms'y Union.	. . . .	. . . .	. . . .		12,000	. . . .					1858	8		8		1	150		
86. Utrecht Miss'y Society.	. . . .	. . . .	. . . .		18,000	. . . .					1859	10		8		12	110		
87. Java Comité.	. . . .	. . . .	. . . .		7,500	. . . .					1855	6	3		1	13	350		
88. Mennonites Miss'y Society.	. . . .	. . . .	. . . .		6,500	. . . .						3		4		12	100		
89. Ermelo Miss'y Society.	. . . .	. . . .	. . . .		8,000	. . . .					1856	6		4		14	50		
90. Christian Ref. Ch. Ms'y Soc.	. . . .	. . . .	. . . .		7,000	. . . .					1860	3		4		5	40		
91. Dutch "	. . . .	. . . .	. . . .		7,500	. . . .					1860	3		2		5	150		
92. Norwegian " "	. . . .	. . . .	. . . .		51,500	. . . .					1842	38	4	16	6	220	2000	320	19.04
93. Lunds " "	. . . .	. . . .	. . . .		7,000	. . . .					1845	7	2	4	0	14	80	30	60.00
94. Stockholm Stads Miss'y Soc.	. . . .	. . . .	. . . .		4,000	. . . .					1853	2		2			300		
95. Finnish Miss'y Society.	. . . .	. . . .	. . . .		20,150	. . . .					1859	5	3	7		6	8	2	33.33
96. Ansgarius Union,	. . . .	. . . .	. . . .		3,500	. . . .					1865	1		1					
97. Free Ch. Canton de Vaud.	. . . .	. . . .	. . . .		10,815	. . . .					1859	5	3	5		6	100	40	66.66
98. Danish Ev. Miss'y Society.	. . . .	. . . .	. . . .		7,800	. . . .					1826	8	2	5		30	120	25	0.32
99. Jerusalem " "	. . . .	. . . .	. . . .		5,095	. . . .					1852	4	2	3		3	210	33	18.04
100. Universities' Mission.	. . . .	. . . .	. . . .		65,170	. . . .					1859	19	11	10	1	32	250	30	13.63
European Totals, ... 41,250	32,854	16,694,443	89,991		6,203,237	. .			527,317			1,780	549	1030	1241	15420	396715		
American Totals, ... 36,758	76,640	10,484,289	179,897		3,420,613	. .			233,595			975	129	1112	1102	10936	248079		
Grand Totals in 1882–3 . 78,008	116,494	27,178,732	269,888	0.44	9,623,850	. .			760,912			2,755	678	2102	2343	26356	644794		4.22
Grand Totals in 1881–2 . 78,009	118,264	27,057,012	155,914	1.31	8,967,500	. .			723,451			2,729	608	2013	2210	22719	618657		7.64
Year's gain, ...	1	2,270	121,720	113,974	$656,350	. .			37,461			26	70	149	133	3637	26137		

FIGURE 1   Table quantifying foreign missions in 1882–83 (European organizations, and American and European totals) by Wilder (1884: 460–61)

Accordingly, the "bookkeeping" of communicants and adherents is flanked by diligent calculations regarding the conditions for an evangelization or conversion of the world "in twenty years," thus "before the year 1900" (Pierson 1881: 437), or "in this generation" (Pierson 1892: 143). Hence, Arthur T. Pierson (1881: 438) writes in *The Missionary Review*: "Think of it! We may take *one in ten* of the Protestant church members and with them bring the whole population of the world to the knowledge of the Gospel, by simply securing this result: that each of that elect number shall in some way bring the gospel into contact with three souls each year for twenty years" (emphasis in the original).

Of course, the uneven terms regarding natural demographic increases are seldom overlooked in this matter: "During the century since Carey went to India, Dr. Murray Mitchell computes that *at least* 200,000,000 have been added to the pagan population of the globe; and that for every 10,000,000 added to nominal Christendom, fully 15,000,000 have been added to heathen-dom" (Pierson 1889: 69; emphasis in the original).

However, the continual review of missions had to go beyond statistical ag-gregations to effectively orient the missionary cause. After all, the main objec-tive of *The Missionary Review*, aside from rallying support for the missionary enterprise, was to furnish missionaries with the proper knowledge needed to conduct foreign missions efficiently and rationally and to counter the "lam-entable lack of information, even among Christians, as to the real state of the heathen" (Wilder 1878: 7).

Consequently, efforts such as the one put forth by *The Missionary Review* consisted not only in making the amount of heathens visible and numerically relating them to Christian adherents and communicants in regular intervals. They also included extensive discussions and comparisons of the conditions and proceedings in the various local mission fields. The *Review* thus featured several articles on specific countries and continents. Moreover, under editor-in-chief A. T. Pierson, a section "The Monthly Concert of Missions," later called "Field of Monthly Survey," was introduced with the explicit intention "during the twelve-month to turn the whole wheel round and bring successively to view every part of the world-wide circle of missionary labor" (Pierson 1889: 67). Here, the January issue usually featured "Facts and Figures about the World-Wide Field" (Pierson 1891: 72), while the following issues of each year explored particular countries on all of the continents.

These articles address anything of relevance to missionary work: that is, the properties and degree of difficulty of local languages; the customs of the local people; general facts on the geography and demography of the land; or the basic tenets and practices of local religions, especially as the latter gained more and more contour in Western discourse on "other" religions. Furthermore, statistical data on the missionary progress are given, usually offering trends regarding conversions as well as figures on the missionary societies and mis-sionaries active in the country.

As these paragraphs and articles on the various countries broke the numbers down and put them into context, they were no less compelling than the gen-eral surveys and tracts. They painted the grim yet urging picture characteristic of Carey's early treatise as they highlighted the *sizable populations* untouched by the gospel or clinging to "false" religions: "But of whatever races the popu-lation [of Guatemala] is made up, here are 1,200,000 fellow men, without, so far as we know, a single Protestant preacher of the Gospel to tell them of Jesus and the resurrection" (Wilder 1882: 260). Furthermore, missionary progress was rarely stated matter-of-factly but more often reported in an encouraging, if not at times triumphalistic, manner: "But best of all, the church members, in five years, from 1883 to 1888, grew more than five-fold, from 5,000 to 25,514 [in Japan]! Buddhist priests are in danger of being driven to work to avoid starvation" (Pierson 1889: 702). Finally, reviews of the general conditions of the land and the people usually played into the theme of "Divine Providence" regarding the *kairos* of current missions: "Never was such opportunity [in Japan] presented to the Church of Christ; and woe be to us if we come not up to God's help in this juncture" (ibid.: 703).

While the actual direction of missionary endeavors was still often opportunistic in character, such demographic reasoning did weigh in heavily in the allocation of evangelistic efforts and resources. Indeed, as Phillips (1969: 57–58) has pointed out, the perceived "numerical strength of Oriental Paganism" was a decisive factor in directing the service of American missionaries to foreign fields in the first place—after all, the American continent was not without "heathens" in alleged need of the gospel. Hence, in a sermon delivered in 1812 in Philadelphia prior to his departure to India, ABCFM missionary Gordon Hall argued:

> While on the most liberal calculation, there are but a very few millions to the *west* of us, there are in the *east* more than *five hundred millions*, who are perishing for lack of vision. How immense the difference here? And ought not the principal exertions to be directed towards the principal mass of souls?
>
> HALL 1815: 16; emphasis in the original

Likewise, as the events that unfolded in connection with the Opium Wars in the decades between 1830 and 1860 opened China for missions, the sense of a pressing need to seize this opportunity was fueled first and foremost by numerical considerations. Thus, in 1858, the year when further treaties that guaranteed noninterference with Christian missionaries were signed in Tientsin, an annual report in *The Missionary Herald* read:

> There are reasons which give great force and urgency to the call for more laborers in China; reasons which exist in no other part of heathendom, in the same manner and degree. In no other empire is there such a multitude of human beings; no where else are there so many precious souls to be lost forever, or to be saved by the ministration of the Gospel.
>
> ABCFM 1858: 206–7

THE GLOBAL 'BOOKKEEPING' OF SOULS 207

The missionary activism of James Hudson Taylor in Great Britain was to have an especially profound effect in the context of China's opening. Taylor famously couched the criticality of missions to China in drastic numerical terms and a language of potential "gains" and "losses." His treatise, "China: Its Spiritual Need and Claims," published in 1865, poignantly asserted: "Every day 33,000, every month 1,000,000 subjects of the Chinese Emperor pass into eternity, without ever having heard the gospel.... Oh! Let us shew our interest in these sin-sick, perishing souls, by making strenuous efforts to bring them to the Great Physician" (Taylor 1865: 37). The tract, "reprinted twice within the year" and running "through eight editions before 1900" (Austin 2007: 80), made ample use of lively analogies and illustrations to contrast the unthinkable dimensions of the Chinese empire with those of, say, Scotland or England, and is considered to have had a similar impact on missions as did Carey's Enquiry in 1792 (Austin 2007: 80; Latourette 1944: 328). In 1865, the same year he first published his treatise, Taylor founded the China Inland Mission, a nondenominational organization dedicated to the rapid evangelization of China. With its vivid slogan "a million a month," referring to Chinese souls continually lost to damnation, it was able to acquire funds not just from Britons but also from international sources, especially from the United States, Canada, and Australia, and grew to be one of the most important missionary ventures in China (Latourette 1937–1945, vol. 6: 326–31). To be sure, other societies also benefited from the newly aroused enthusiasm for ministering to the unevangelized Chinese multitudes. As Stanley (1990: 79) notes for Great Britain:

> Missionary giving reached an exceptionally high level in 1858, and remained well above average until 1861. Buoyant giving was matched by rising recruitment. The [London Missionary Society] noted in April 1858 that "an unusually large number of suitable men had within the last weeks offered themselves for Missionary Service." The [Church Missionary Society] received seventy-eight applications from British candidates in 1858, more than in any other year between 1850 and 1875.

Accordingly, by 1890 China had overtaken the Near East, Latin America, and Africa as missionary targets and ranked only behind India among the principal fields of British as well as American missions in terms of deployed missionaries (Field 1974: 34–36). Thus, as one would expect in a domain where the quantification of heathens and conversions plays a constitutive role, once all diplomatic obstacles were removed the two most densely populated countries constituted the two principal missionary fields of Great Britain and the United

States, the key players in the Protestant missionary endeavor. Overall, while in 1858 there were but 81 Protestant missionaries in all of China, the number had risen to 1,296 missionaries by 1889 and to 3,445 missionaries by 1905 (Latourette 1929: 405–406; McGillivray 1907: 674). The numerical rhetoric of the tracts, sermons, and articles cited in the preceding text thus closely matched the observable rationale of the missionary enterprise.

Missionary publications of the nineteenth century, feeding off the annual reports of the missionary societies in foreign fields, thus constructed an ever-changing quantitative relation among blocs of religious adherents and established a primary focus on demographic magnitude. As I shall elaborate further in the following section, the consequences of these quantitative perspectives in the religious realm are in essence analogous to those attributed to double-entry bookkeeping in the economic realm by Werner Sombart.

The "Sombartian Dynamic" in Evangelical Missions

The analogy of this article's argument to Sombart's claim about the relationship of double-entry bookkeeping and the genesis of a capitalist sphere can now be restated in more detail. As illustrated in the preceding text, for Sombart accounting gave birth to a capitalist economy first and foremost through the creation of a novel category. In separating funds, it essentially constructed a visibility of "capital" as the "amount of wealth … used in making profits" (Sombart 1953: 38), which consequently led to the installation of an economic field unreservedly committed to its rational accumulation. I used the terms *construction*, *catalyzation*, and *rationalization* to highlight these general components of Sombart's argument.

An analogous relationship between calculative operations, on the one side, and the emergence of a self-perpetuating domain of action, on the other, can be observed in the case of nineteenth-century missions. As demographic concepts and with them a logic of "accounting" merged with missionary perspectives, they, too, *created* a visibility of global quantities of religious adherents. Carey's missionary treatise that helped spark nineteenth-century missions first brought attention to the vast amount of "heathens" among the world's population. Subsequent missionary tracts continued to point to exorbitant numerical figures representing the proportion of non-Christians or "heathens" on the globe.

As we have seen, this fostered very specific relevance structures for a social field of global missions. To a substantial degree, though not solely, missionary success was assessed in terms of numerical gains in communicants or adherents. Missionary societies documented yearly growth in converts in their annual reports, and journals such as *The Missionary Review of the World* continually surveyed the progress of Protestant missions as a whole. Numbers (of heathens) attested to the need for missions, numbers (of heathens) geographically oriented missions, and numbers (of converts) legitimated the continuance of missions. A global distribution of religious adherents—a numerical object that was not "in the world" before a demographic perspective and quantitative practices entered a missionary discourse—thus *catalyzed* and *perpetuated* a worldwide missionary operation as it became its focal point. Finally, an element of *rational* allocation and direction of missions came to the fore as missionary articles helped identify regions with comparatively dense populations of heathens.

Consequently, what Anthony Hopwood (1987: 225) has stated regarding the introduction of accounting systems into an organizational context also holds true for this particular social field: "[A] socially constructed visibility created an enterprise organisationally dependent on the resultant knowledge." In essence, the missionary movement of the nineteenth century created its own object of interest. It is precisely this fascination for "heathens" as a *numerical category in flux* that gives this missionary enterprise its self-perpetuating features.

While mainstream Protestantism has largely shed the focus on world evangelization after World War I, emphasizing the humanitarian aspects of missions over the element of conversion, evangelical Christianity today is still a stronghold of the quantitative perspective on global missions.[12] Indeed, the element of *a rational orientation and direction* of missions has become even more profound since the nineteenth century—a rationalization that is still part and parcel to the *numerical* outlook of the many vociferous proponents of global missions to non-Christians within evangelicalism today.[13]

---

12   On the liberal paradigm shift in mainstream Protestant missions after World War I see Hutchison (1987); for an evangelical perspective on this development see Glasser and McGavran (1983).

13   Indeed, one may argue that the rationalization of evangelical missions since the nineteenth century resonates as much with an encompassing "occidental rationalism" as it is a specific instantiation of such rationality within an autonomous sphere of missions. On the universality and "sphere-of-life" specificity of rationality and rationalization in the work of Max Weber see Kalberg (1980). On shared "plausibility structures" between evangelical revivalism, political republicanism, and a penetrating market economy in nineteenth-century America see Thomas (1989). For a neoinstitutionalist perspective on Pentecostal organizations exhibiting "isomorphism" with secular organizations in using legitimately "rational" technologies and techniques in the implementation of their albeit nonsecular goal of spreading the gospel, see Lechner and Boli (2005: 173–90).

Thus, in this continuing project of quantifying missions, the notion of "unreached people groups" is now occupying the position formerly held by the term *heathens* in missionary discourse. Following the assumption that culture and language play a decisive role in missions, this perspective dissolves the world into several thousand "people groups" according to linguistic, ethnic, and sociocultural variables, while quantitatively assessing the extent to which they already have been brought into contact with the gospel. Interactive global maps (using Google Maps as a platform) and regularly updated status reports on each "people group" are available online on websites such as The Joshua Project, an organization formally affiliated with the US Center for World Mission, or Operation World, an online resource of a reference book project by British evangelical Patrick Johnstone.[14] A plethora of statistical indicators regarding Christian outreach is also supplied by the World Christian Database of the Center for the Study of Global Christianity in Massachusetts.[15] It continues the work of late missiologist David B. Barrett and others, whose *World Christian Encyclopedia* provided such telling country measurements as "evangelistic offers per capita per year," "costs per baptism" in US dollars, and "responsiveness" of each people group to efforts of conversion (Barrett, Johnson et al. 2001; Barrett, Kurian et al. 2001).

The extent to which such statistical exercises continue to potentially orient and direct missions is perhaps best exemplified by the concept "10/40-window," which is directly related to the idea of "unevangelized" non-Christians. It refers to the region between 10 degrees and 40 degrees north latitude allegedly harboring "an estimated 3.02 billion individuals [living] in approximately 5,579 unreached people groups" (Joshua Project, n.d.). There is an explicit call to prioritize this region in evangelical missions, which includes Northern Africa, the Middle East, India, and China. The term *10/40-window* has gained wide currency within evangelical discourse and is referenced on most evangelical mission websites. It attests to the extent to which quantification is still a driving factor of global evangelical outreach.

Conclusions

Extending sociological perspectives on quantification and the emergence of global fields, this article adds new insights into the workings of

---

14   See www.joshuaproject.net and www.operationworld.org (accessed January 3, 2017).
15   See www.worldchristiandatabase.org (accessed January 3, 2017).

nineteenth-century evangelical missions as it identifies a broader macrostructural mechanism at play in the perpetuation of a global missionary endeavor. Generalizing Sombart's thesis regarding the relationship of double-entry bookkeeping and the genesis of a capitalist sphere, the study argues that quantification bears specific potentials to merge with particular meaning structures and consequently form distinct numerical objects that move to the center of an autonomous and self-propelling sphere of action and attention. Insofar as such objects transcend regional boundaries, the mechanism described here points to a dynamic of globalization as it highlights the emergence of a *global* field dedicated to altering or conserving specific global "quantities."

Thus, in the case at hand, the confluence of millenarian ideologies and demographic perspectives constructed a visibility of a worldwide distribution of religious adherents and yearly gains in Protestant communicants that spurred, legitimated, sustained, and oriented a global enterprise of Protestant missions. This has been demonstrated in four significant ways. First, as one would expect if quantification indeed played a decisive role in the early mobilization of the missionary endeavor, numerical arguments figured prominently and centrally in pleas for missions, beginning with Carey's tract giving concrete figures of the vast amounts of heathens in the world, and continuing in articles, tracts, and sermons pointing out the work to be done in quantitative terms designed to shock and impress.

Second, as one would expect if demographics were indeed momentous in directing missions to foreign lands, numerical comparisons were a central motif in urging missionaries not to content themselves with bearing witness in their homeland but to travel to more populous locations.

Third, as one would expect if demographic considerations were indeed consequential, the most resources were allocated to the most populous regions. Despite the many other motives and opportunity structures undoubtedly in play, India and China moved to the forefront of missionary efforts once all diplomatic barriers were cleared, and constituted the largest missionary fields of Great Britain and the United States.

Finally, as one would expect if quantification was indeed integral to the sustenance of foreign missions, numerical arguments were routinely employed in exhortations to continue or invigorate the missionary effort. Quantifications of successful conversions, often to the point of triumphalism, demonstrated the legitimacy of the missionary enterprise, while quantifications of heathens continued to serve as a reminder of the unresolved task. Both approaches were reconciled in numerical calculations considering the possibility of evangelizing the world "in this generation," validating the feasibility of the missionary endeavor as such.

What is borne out of quantification, then, is a novel "quantity," a "heathen population," giving rise to a field geared toward manipulating *worldwide quantitative* relations among religions—a field that still has a strong hold on a large array of evangelical organizations dedicated to world evangelization and conversion today. Numerical figures become the center of attention and the focal point of action of a whole legion of missionary societies as does the category of capital within an economy of capitalist enterprises in Sombart's account of the emergence of capitalism.

The study thus illuminates the potentials of calculative technologies in catalyzing global fields with distinct logics, a topic underexplored both in the literature on fields and the sociology of quantification. The numerical construct of a global "heathen population" was able to focalize the ideological currents of nineteenth-century Protestantism and channel them into a sustained effort of global outreach. Quantitative reasoning pointing to the large number of "uncivilized heathens" catered also to another popular motive of nineteenth-century Protestant missions. Much of the nineteenth-century missionary enterprise identified with a broader "civilizing mission," an ambition to transform a culture regarded as inferior by imposing upon them Western standards and notions of progress, enlightenment, and instrumental rationality (see Fischer-Tiné and Mann 2004). Consequently, missionary journals also featured anecdotal articles on the "cruel rites" of the heathen as well as on natives' lives "sublimely" transformed by conversion.

Even though the common project of a "civilizing mission" was often grounds for partnership and cooperation between missions and colonial powers, especially in the sphere of education (Copland 2006), this in no way undermines the principal autonomy of the social field of global missions. Indeed, there is now an increasingly consensual view in the literature that there was no fundamental collaborative tie between missions and empire, and that both rather constituted two independent realms with autonomous goals and rationales (see Porter 2004; Stanley 1990). In this regard, nineteenth-century missions were in many ways different from the Catholic conquista missions of previous centuries (Tyrell 2004: 56–76). As opposed to the latter, the Protestant missionary effort of the nineteenth century was not a state-sponsored operation and, as seen, even relied mostly on voluntary associations outside of traditional church structures. What is more, colonial officials often dreaded missionary efforts for their politically disruptive effects among the indigenous subjects and imposed many restrictions on Christian missions while showing little interest in curtailing "heathen practices," much to the chagrin of the missionaries. Thus, forced conversions, short-circuiting the realms of colonial power and religious meaning, a common fixture of previous missionary centuries, had no place in nineteenth-century missions. The autonomy of the missionary enterprise is finally evidenced by the numerical construct of global heathendom and the calculation of worldwide religious distributions: These are objects devoid of political meaning and incongruous with political demarcations. As seen in the preceding text, colonial openings were evaluated in light of structural opportunities and *demographic* considerations, not nationalist sentiment. As a result, colonial territories with "heathen" populations attracted missionary organizations from various sending countries, not just the metropole.

In highlighting the emergence of a field of missionary organizations, commonly oriented to a quantitatively fashioned object of global religious affiliations, the study furthermore adds to extant work on accounting and religion. Instead of focusing on individual organizations using accounting techniques in their spiritual affairs, this article shows how a discourse fed by tracts and general-interest journals pooling all available data constructed an object of interest for a broad field of Protestant missionary organizations of various denominations. Indeed, the orientation to a common objective of world evangelization did not always suppress the particularistic perspectives of each missionary society. Much collaboration notwithstanding, the common fascination with global figures of unevangelized heathens also gave rise to much competition among the various denominations (ibid.: 119–20), an interorganizational dynamic likewise resting on the shared ontology constructed by an infrastructure of calculative technologies.

This "Sombartian dynamic" described here should be generalizable to other institutional orders as well. In the political sphere, the Foucauldian example of a biopolitical maintenance of a "social body," to no small extent constructed through modern demography, is a case in point (see Foucault 1980; Hacking 1982). Furthermore, university rankings as analyzed by Espeland and Sauder (2007) can be seen as another instance in the realm of education: Here again, numerical indicators institute novel categories (of quality) and thus give rise to actions directly aimed at their manipulation as these figures move to the center of attention of the universities subjected to such measurements. Though the focus of the authors is on the specific mechanisms that underlie the "reactivity" of public measures of performance, their findings also point to the emergence of a new social "space" with autonomous "rules of the game" as universities begin to actively compete for ranks; they can thus be recast in these generalized Sombartian terms.

More importantly, however, it is the globalizing potentials of this mechanism that merit further comparative analyses. For instance, in the mid-twentieth century the macroeconomic abstractions of national income accounting and the cross-country comparisons made possible by them similarly produced a globally oriented sphere of foreign development and social engineering aimed at attenuating the huge international discrepancies that became numerically "visible" for the first time (Speich 2011). Comparative research could further highlight similarities and differences in the way quantification creates (or alters) autonomous social fields centered on newly instituted "quantities" of particular relevance and how it contributes to global orientations of such orders. The questions arising from such research perspectives would need to relate not only to the specific effects of quantitative measures but also to the historical contingencies that lead to the invention of particular quantitative "entities" as well as to the meaning structures that render them relevant.

References

ABCFM (1824) "Fourteenth annual report." The Missionary Herald 20 (2): 62–63.

ABCFM (1858) "Shanghai mission: Annual report." The Missionary Herald 54 (7): 205–7.

ABCFM (1882) "Expenditures and finances of the board." The Missionary Herald 78 (9): 336–41.

Adams, H. (1784) An Alphabetical Compendium of the Various Sects Which Have Appeared in the World from the Beginning of the Christian Era to the Present Day. Boston: Edes.

Arnold, P. J. (2005) "Disciplining domestic regulation: The World Trade Organization and the market for professional services." Accounting, Organizations and Society 30 (4): 299–330.

Austin, A. (2007) China's Millions: The China Inland Mission and Late Qing Society, 1832–1905. Grand Rapids, MI: Eerdmans.

Barrett, D. B., G. T. Kurian, and T. M. Johnson (2001) World Christian Encyclopedia, 2nd ed. Oxford: Oxford University Press.

Barrett, D. B., T. M. Johnson, C. R Guidry, and P. F. Crossing (2001) World Christian Trends, AD 30–AD 2200: Interpreting the Annual Christian Megacensus. Pasadena, CA: William Carey Library.

Barrett, M., D. J. Cooper, and K. Jamal (2005) "Globalization and the coordinating of work in multinational audits." Accounting, Organizations and Society 30 (1): 1–24.

Beaver, R. P. (1968) "Missionary motivation through three centuries," in J. C. Brauer (ed.) Reinterpretation in American Church History. Chicago: University of Chicago Press. 113–51.

Beecher, L. (1827) "Sermon at the annual meeting of the American Board of Commissioners for Foreign Missions in New York City on October 12, 1827." ABCFM Archives, 1810–1961 (ABC 84.2), Houghton Library, Harvard University, Cambridge, MA.

THE GLOBAL 'BOOKKEEPING' OF SOULS 215

Bourdieu, P. (1996) The Rules of Art: Genesis and Structure of the Literary Field. Stanford, CA: Stanford University Press.

Brerewood, E. (1674) [1614] Enquiries Touching the Diversity of Languages and Religions through the Chief Parts of the World. London: Printed for S. M., J. M., and H. H. and are to be sold by Walter Kettilby.

Bryer, R. A. (2000a) "The history of accounting and the transition to capitalism in England. Part one: Theory." Accounting, Organizations and Society 25 (2): 131–62.

Bryer, R. A. (2000b) "The history of accounting and the transition to capitalism in England. Part two: Evidence." Accounting, Organizations and Society 25 (4–5): 327–81.

Burchell, S., C. Clubb, A. Hopwood, J. Hughes, and J. Nahapiet (1980) "The roles of accounting in organizations and society." Accounting, Organizations and Society 5 (1): 5–27.

Callon, M. (1998) "Introduction: The embeddedness of economic markets in economics," in M. Callon (ed.) The Laws of the Markets. London: Blackwell: 1–57.

Callon, M. (2007) "What does it mean to say economics is performative?," in D. MacKenzie, F. Muniesa, and L. Sui (eds.) Do Economists Make Markets? On the Performativity of Economics. Princeton, NJ: Princeton University Press: 311–57.

Carey, W. (1792) An Enquiry into the Obligations of Christians to Use Means in the Conversion of the Heathens. Leicester, UK: Ann Ireland.

Carruthers, B. G., and W. N. Espeland (1991) "Accounting for rationality: Double-entry bookkeeping and the rhetoric of economic rationality." American Journal of Sociology 97 (1): 31–69.

Chapman, C. S., D. J. Cooper, and P. Miller, eds. (2009) Accounting, Organizations, and Institutions. New York: Oxford University Press.

Chiapello, E. (2007) "Accounting and the birth of the notion of capitalism." Critical Perspectives on Accounting 18 (3): 263–96.

Cline Cohen, P. (1999) A Calculating People: The Spread of Numeracy in Early America. London: Routledge.

Cooper, D. J., and M. Ezzamel (2013) "Globalization discourses and performance measurement systems in a multinational firm." Accounting, Organizations and Society 38 (4): 288–313.

Copland, I. (2006) "Christianity as an arm of empire: The ambiguous case of India under the Company, c. 1813–1858." The Historical Journal 49 (4): 1025–54.

Cordery, C. (2006) "Hallowed treasures: Sacred, secular and the Wesleyan Methodists in New Zealand, 1819–1840." Accounting History 11 (2): 199–220.

Cox, J. (2008) The British Missionary Enterprise since 1700. New York: Routledge.

Cruz, I., R. W. Scapens, and M. Major (2011) "The localisation of a global management control system." Accounting, Organizations and Society 36 (7): 412–27.

Davis, K., A. Fisher, B. Kingsbury, and S. E. Merry, eds. (2012) Governance by Indicators: Global Power through Classification and Ranking. Oxford: Oxford University Press.

Desrosières, A. (1998) The Politics of Large Numbers: A History of Statistical Reasoning. Cambridge, MA: Harvard University Press.

Dromi, S. (2016) "Soldiers of the cross: Calvinism, humanitarianism and the genesis of social fields." Sociological Theory 34 (3): 196–219.

Espeland, W. N., and M. Sauder (2007) "Rankings and reactivity: How public measures recreate social worlds." American Journal of Sociology 113 (1): 1–40.

Espeland, W. N., and M. L. Stevens (1998) "Commensuration as a social process." Annual Review of Sociology 24: 313–43.

Espeland, W. N., and M. L. Stevens (2008) "A sociology of quantification." European Journal of Sociology 49 (3): 401–36.

Ezzamel, M., K. Robson, and P. Stapleton (2012) "The logics of budgeting: Theorization and practice variation in the educational field." Accounting, Organizations and Society 37 (5): 281–303.

Field, J. A. Jr. (1974) "Near East notes and Far East queries," in J. K. Fairbank (ed.) The Missionary Enterprise in China and America. Cambridge, MA: Harvard University Press: 23–55.

Fischer-Tiné, H., and M. Mann, eds. (2004) Colonialism as Civilizing Mission: Cultural Ideology in British India. London: Wimbledon.

Fligstein, N., and D. McAdam (2012) A Theory of Fields. Oxford: Oxford University Press.

Foucault, M. (1980) The History of Sexuality. Vol. 1, An Introduction. New York: Random House.

Friedland, R., and R. R. Alford (1991) "Bringing society back in: Symbols, practices, and institutional contradictions," in W. W. Powell and P. J. DiMaggio (eds.) The New Institutionalism in Organizational Analysis. Chicago: University of Chicago Press: 232–63.

Glasser, A. F., and D. A. McGavran (1983) Contemporary Theologies of Mission. Grand Rapids, MI: Baker Book House.

Go, J. (2008): "Global fields and imperial forms: Field theory and the British and American Empires." Sociological Theory 26 (3): 201–29.

Go, J., and M. Krause, eds. (2016) Fielding Transnationalism: Sociological Review Monograph 64 (2). Chichester, UK: Wiley-Blackwell.

Hacking, I. (1982) "Biopower and the avalanche of printed numbers." Humanities in Society 5 (3–4): 279–95.

Hall, G. (1815) The Duty of the American Churches in Respect to Foreign Missions, 2nd ed. Andover, MA: Flagg and Gould.

Hansen, H. K., and A. Mühlen-Schulte, eds. (2012) The Power of Numbers in Global Governance. Special Issue of Journal of International Relations and Development 15: 466–557.

Harrison, P. (1990) "Religion" and the Religions in the English Enlightenment. Cambridge, UK: Cambridge University Press.

Hedström, P., and R. Swedberg (1998) "Social mechanisms: An introductory essay," in P. Hedström and R. Swedberg (eds.) Social Mechanisms. Cambridge: Cambridge University Press: 1–31.

Heintz, B. (2010) "Numerische Differenz: Überlegungen zu einer Soziologie des (quantitativen) Vergleichs." Zeitschrift für Soziologie 39 (3): 162–81.

Heintz, B., and T. Werron (2011) "Wie ist Globalisierung möglich? Zur Entstehung globaler Vergleichshorizonte am Beispiel von Wissenschaft und Sport." Kölner Zeitschrift für Soziologie und Sozialpsychologie 63 (3): 359–94.

Hopwood, A. G. (1987) "The archaeology of accounting systems." Accounting, Organizations and Society 12 (3): 207–34.

Hopwood, A. G., and P. Miller, eds. (1994) Accounting as Social and Institutional Practice. Cambridge: Cambridge University Press.

Hoskin, K., and R. Macve (1986) "Accounting and the examination: A genealogy of disciplinary power." Accounting, Organizations and Society 11 (2): 105–36.

Hoskin, K., and R. Macve (1988) "The genesis of accountability: The West Point connections." Accounting, Organizations and Society 13 (1): 37–73.

Hutchison, W. R. (1987) Errand to the World: American Protestant Thought and Foreign Missions. Chicago: University of Chicago Press.

Irvine, H. (2002) "The legitimizing power of financial statements in The Salvation Army in England, 1865–1892." The Accounting Historians Journal 29 (1): 1–36.

Irvine, H. (2005) "Balancing money and mission in a local church budget." Accounting, Auditing and Accountability Journal 18 (2): 211–37.

Jacobs, K. (2005) "The sacred and the secular: Examining the role of accounting in the religious context." Accounting, Auditing and Accountability Journal 18 (2): 189–210.

Jacobs, K., and S. P. Walker (2004) "Accounting and accountability in the Iona community." Accounting, Auditing and Accountability Journal 17 (3): 361–81.

Jepperson, R., and J. W. Meyer (2011) "Multiple levels of analysis and the limitations of methodological individualisms." Sociological Theory 29 (1): 54–73.

Joshua Project (n.d.) "What is the 10/40-window?," joshuaproject.net/resources/articles/10_40_window (accessed January 3, 2017).

Kalberg, S. (1980) "Max Weber's types of rationality: Cornerstones for the analysis of rationalization processes in history." American Journal of Sociology 85 (5): 1145–79.

Krause, M. (2014) The Good Project: Humanitarian NGOs and the Fragmentation of Reason. Chicago: University of Chicago Press.

Kreager, P. (1988) "New light on Graunt." Population Studies 42 (1): 129–40.

Latourette, K. S. (1929) A History of Christian Missions in China. New York: Macmillan.

Latourette, K. S. (1937–45) A History of the Expansion of Christianity. 7 vols. New York: Harper.

Laughlin, R. C. (1988) "Accounting in its social context: An analysis of the accounting systems of the Church of England." Accounting, Auditing and Accountability Journal 1 (2): 19–42.

Lazarsfeld, P. F. (1961) "Notes on the history of quantification in sociology: Trends, sources and problems." Isis 52 (2): 277–333.

Lechner, F. J., and J. Boli (2005) World Culture: Origins and Consequences. Malden, MA: Blackwell.

MacGillivray, D. (1907) A Century of Protestant Missions in China. Shanghai: American Tract Society.

MacKenzie, D., and Y. Millo (2003) "Constructing a market, performing theory: The historical sociology of a financial derivatives exchange." American Journal of Sociology 109 (1): 107–45.

Masuzawa, T. (2005) The Invention of World Religions. Chicago: University of Chicago Press.

Mathews, M. B. S. (2006) Rethinking Zion: How the Print Media Placed Fundamentalism in the South. Knoxville: University of Tennessee Press.

McKinlay, A., and A. Mutch (2015) "'Accountable creatures': Scottish Presbyterianism, accountability and managerial capitalism." Business History 57 (2): 241–56.

McLoughlin, W. G. Jr. (1959) Modern Revivalism: Charles Grandison Finney to Billy Graham. New York: Ronald Press Company.

Mead, S. E. (1942) Nathaniel William Taylor: A Connecticut Liberal. Chicago: University of Chicago Press.

Mennicken, A. (2008) "Connecting worlds: The translation of international auditing standards into post-Soviet audit practice." Accounting, Organizations and Society 33 (4–5): 384–414.

Miller, P. (2008) "Calculating economic life." Journal of Cultural Economy 1 (1): 51–64.

Neill, S. (1987) A History of Christian Missions. Harmondsworth, UK: Penguin Books.

Neu, D., E. Ocampo Gomez, C. Graham, and M. Heincke (2006) "'Informing' technologies and the World Bank." Accounting, Organizations and Society 31 (7): 635–62.

Neu, D., E. Ocampo Gomez, O. G. Ponce de León, and M. F. Zepeda (2002) "'Facilitating' globalizations processes: Financial technologies and the World Bank." Accounting Forum 26 (3): 271–90.

Oakes, L. S., B. Townley, and D. H. Cooper (1998) "Business planning as pedagogy: Language and control in a changing institutional field." Administrative Science Quarterly 43 (2): 257–92.

Pailin, D. A. (1984) Attitudes to Other Religions: Comparative Religion in Seventeenth- and Eighteenth-Century Britain. Manchester, UK: Manchester University Press.

Patriarca, S. (1994) "Statistical nation building and the consolidation of regions in Italy." Social Science History 18 (3): 359–76.

Phillips, C. J. (1969) Protestant America and the Pagan World: The First Half Century of the American Board of Commissioners for Foreign Missions, 1810–1860. Cambridge, MA: Harvard University Press.

Pierard, R. V. (2011) "German Pietism as a major factor in the beginnings of modern Protestant missions," in C. T. Collins Winn, C. Gehrz, G. W. Carlson, and E. Holst (eds.) The Pietist Impulse in Christianity. Eugene, OR: Pickwick: 285–95.

Pierson, A. T. (1881) "Can this world be evangelized in twenty years?," The Missionary Review 4 (6): 437–41.

Pierson, A. T. (1889) "The monthly concert of missions." The Missionary Review of the World 2/12: 67–71, 144–50, 223–26, 305–9, 380–84, 465–70, 539–45, 625–30, 700–5, 781–87, 865–70, 935–42.

Pierson, A. T. (1891) "The monthly concert of missions." The Missionary Review of the World 4/14: 72–74, 144–52, 228–31, 308–11, 391–95, 544–48, 624–28, 707–11, 786–90, 866–70, 943–48.

Pierson, A. T. (1892) "Editorial notes on current topics." The Missionary Review of the World 5/15(2): 141–44.

Pierson, A. T. (1893) "General missionary intelligence." The Missionary Review of the World 6/16(1): 64–80.

Porter, A. (2004) Religion versus Empire? British Protestant Missionaries and Overseas Expansion, 1700–1914. Manchester, UK: Manchester University Press.

Porter, T. M. (1995) Trust in Numbers: The Pursuit of Objectivity in Science and Public Life. Princeton, NJ: Princeton University Press.

Power, M. (1997) The Audit Society: Ritual of Verification. Oxford: Oxford University Press.

Purchas, S. (1626) [1613] Purchas, His Pilgrimage, or Relations of the World and the Religions Observed in All Ages and Places Discovered, from the Creation unto the Present. London: Printed by William Stansby for Henrie Fetherstone.

Quattrone, P. (2004) "Accounting for God: Accounting and accountability practices in the Society of Jesus (Italy, XVI–XVII centuries)." Accounting, Organizations and Society 29 (7): 647–83.

Robert, D. L. (2003) Occupy Until I Come: A. T. Pierson and the Evangelization of the World. Grand Rapids, MI: Eerdmans.

Samsonova, A. (2009) "Local sites of globalisation: A look at the development of a legislative framework for auditing in Russia." Critical Perspectives on Accounting 20 (4): 528–52.

Scott, W. R. (1994) "Conceptualizing organizational fields: Linking organizations and societal systems," in H.-U. Derlien (ed.) Systemrationalität und Partialinteresse. Festschrift für Renate Mayntz. Baden-Baden, Germany: Nomos: 203–21.

Shenk, W. R., ed. (2004) North American Foreign Missions, 1810–1914. Theology, Theory, and Policy. Grand Rapids, MI: Eerdmans.

Sombart, W. (1916) Der moderne Kapitalismus. Vol. 2, Das europäische Wirtschaftsleben im Zeitalter des Frühkapitalismus. Munich: Duncker und Humblot.

Sombart, W. (1953) "Medieval and modern commercial enterprise," trans. excerpt from Sombart (1916), in F. C. Lane and J. C. Riemersma (eds.) Enterprise and Secular Change: Readings in Economic History. Homewood, IL: Irwin: 25–40.

Speich, D. (2011) "The use of global abstractions: National income accounting in the period of imperial decline." Journal of Global History 6 (1): 7–28.

Stanley, B. (1990) The Bible and the Flag: Protestant Missions and British Imperialism in the Nineteenth and Twentieth Centuries. Leicester, UK: Apollos.

Suddaby, R., D. J. Cooper, and R. Greenwood (2007) "Transnational regulation of professional services: Governance dynamics of field level organizational change." Accounting, Organizations and Society 32 (4–5): 333–62.

Taylor, J. H. (1865) China: Its Spiritual Need and Claims; with Brief Notice of Missionary Effort, Past and Present. London: Nisbet.

Thomas, G. M. (1989) Revivalism and Cultural Change: Christianity, Nation Building, and the Market in the Nineteenth-Century United States. Chicago: University of Chicago Press.

Tinker, A. M. (1980) "Towards a political economy of accounting: An empirical illustration of the Cambridge controversies." Accounting, Organizations and Society 5 (1): 147–60.

Turner, W. (1695) The History of All Religions in the World from the Creation Down to the Present Time. London: Printed for John Dunton.

Tyrell, H. (2004) "Weltgesellschaft, Weltmission und religiöse Organisationen—Einleitung," in A. Bogner, B. Holtwick and H. Tyrell (eds.) Weltmission und religiöse Organisationen. Protestantische Missionsgesellschaften im 19. und 20. Jahrhundert. Würzburg, Germany: Ergon: 14–134.

Vauban, S. L. de (1707) Projet d'une dixme royale (n.p.).

Vollmer, H., A. Mennicken, and A. Preda (2009) "Tracking the numbers: Across accounting and finance, organizations and markets." Accounting, Organizations and Society 34 (5): 619–37.

Warneck, G. (1901) Outline of a History of Protestant Missions from the Reformation to the Present Time. New York: Revell.

Weber, M. (1978) [1921] Economy and Society, trans. G. Roth and C. Wittich. Berkeley: University of California Press.

Weber, M. (1981) [1923] General Economic History, trans. F. Knight. New Brunswick, NJ: Transaction.

Wilder, R. G. (1878) "To our readers." The Missionary Review 1 (1): 3–12.

Wilder, R. G. (1881) "Editorial comment on 'Mountain Musings, from India.'" The Missionary Review 4 (1): 33–34.

Wilder, R. G. (1882) "Guatemala as a mission field." The Missionary Review 5 (4): 258–61.

Wilder, R. G. (1884) "Foreign missions in 1882–1883." The Missionary Review 7: 27–52, 114–33, 206–20, 288–302, 357–79, 447–64.

Yamey, B. S. (1949) "Scientific bookkeeping and the rise of capitalism." The Economic History Review 1 (2–3): 99–113.

Yamey, B. S. (1964) "Accounting and the rise of capitalism: Further notes on a theme by Sombart." Journal of Accounting Research 2 (2): 117–36.

Yamey, B. S. (2005) "The historical significance of double-entry bookkeeping: Some non-Sombartian claims." Accounting, Business, and Financial History 15 (1): 77–88.

The Visual Embodiment of Women in the Korea Mission Field

Hyaeweol Choi

In his preface to the catalogue of a pioneering exhibition of photography from the Korea mission field, Donald Clark argues that missionary photography offers a unique window on the Korean experience with the modern, and perhaps more importantly, the dynamic transcultural interactions between Koreans and Western missionaries.[1] To put it differently, missionary photography can serve as a critical device for excavating the complex realities missionaries and Korean converts experienced within the specific historical context of the Korean mission that began in the late nineteenth century. Despite its analytical importance for gaining a fuller understanding of Korean modern history as well as the history of Protestant Christianity in Korea, missionary photography has drawn relatively little attention from the scholarly community.[2] This article is a modest attempt to fill the gap by exploring the complementary role that photographic images fill in interpreting the Korea mission field when they are construed in relation to textual representations. It is also an endeavor to probe the ways in which photographs—either in natural or staged

---

Source: Choi, H., "The Visual Embodiment of Women in the Korea Mission Field," *Korean Studies* 34.1 (2010): pp. 90–126. Republished with permission of University of Hawaii Press, Permission conveyed through Copyright Clearance Center, Inc.

The original article holds an illustration, (fig. 9), which is not included here. The location of this illustration is marked with an * in the text.

---

1   Donald N. Clark, ed., *Missionary Photography in Korea: Encountering the West through Christianity* (New York: The Korea Society, 2009), 6.

2   Some recent studies incorporate missionary photography into their analysis. See Clark, *Missionary Photography in Korea*. Sung Deuk Oak compiles a large number of missionary photographs to introduce the history of the Great Revival movement in Korea, which culminated in 1907. See *Hanbando tae puhŭng: sajin ŭro ponŭn han'guk kyohoe, 1900–1910* [The Great Revival in Korea: A pictorial history of Korean Protestant Christianity] (Seoul: Hongsŏngsa, 2009). In addition, there have been growing efforts to digitalize missionary photographs and make them available for the public to view on the Internet. Examples include the University of Southern California's The Reverend Corwin & Nellie Taylor Collection (http://www.usc .edu/libraries/archives/arc/libraries/eastasian/korea/resources/kda-taylor.html) and the American Theological Library Association's Cooperative Digital Resources Initiative (http:// www.atla.com/cdri/cdri.html).

settings—were taken, circulated, and appropriated for the purposes of missionary goals.[3]

From the viewpoint of missionaries, photography was an indispensable tool for recording, categorizing, and publicizing "the other" as it captured the presumed essence of the local people, the unique, unusual objects and exotic natural setting, as well as the triumphs and tribulations of the mission field. According to Helen Gardner and Jude Philp, from the 1850s "missionaries around the world had turned the new science of photography to the service of the mission."[4] By the time the first group of American Protestant missionaries arrived in Korea in 1884, the modern form of photography had already gained popularity in the United States,[5] and especially from the 1890s, missionary photographs began to provide a much more vivid portrait of Koreans and Korean customs in the pages of mission journals.[6] Many images from the photographs, ranging from candid shots of scantily clad, dirty, vacant-looking locals in the streets to the staged group portraits of recent converts in front of the Western-style churches, schools, and hospitals newly built by the missionaries, present a visual manifestation of the imagined gulf between the West and the Other, the urgency to civilize the people of non-Christian countries by spreading the gospel, and the triumphant spirit of missionaries in Christianizing the world.

---

3 Two mission archives are the major source of missionary photography for this article. One is the General Commission on Archives and History (GCAH), The United Methodist Church, Drew University, Madison, New Jersey. GCAH holds more than two thousand photographs with the originals well-preserved, and photocopies of the originals are available for viewing. The other is the Presbyterian Historical Society (PHS), Philadelphia. The photographs at the PHS are arranged in folders indexed either by the individual missionary or by relevant subject matter. I chose these two archives because the Methodist and Presbyterian denominations constituted the majority of the Protestant Christian missions in Korea. In addition, missionary journals (Methodist and Presbyterian), online digital photos (Cooperative Digital Resources Initiative), and secondary book sources are also used.

4 Helen Gardner and Jude Philp, "Photography and Christian Mission: George Brown's Images of the New Britain Mission 1875–80," *The Journal of Pacific History*, 41, no. 2 (September 2006): 176.

5 A photo of "Pioneer Protestant Missionaries," Seoul, 1887, William Elliot Griffis Collection, Rutgers University. Cited from Clark, *Missionary Photography in Korea*, 68–69.

6 When Mary F. Scranton, the first woman missionary in Korea, began to report her work from Korea, she included a picture of Ewha Hakdang (Ewha Girls' School). In this way missionaries accompanied photos of the institutions or people they worked for. Mary Scranton, "I Hoa Haktan, Seoul, Korea," *Heathen Woman's Friend*, 20, no. 7 (January 1889): 173–74. Aside from sending photos to the mission journals, individual missionaries amassed large collections of photographs in their own albums, some of which were sent to their family members, church organizations, or mission archives after retirement.

The early Korean Christian converts remained illiterate for the most part and thus could not leave much in the way of literature to convey their own experiences. The visual images of the people, objects, and surroundings projected through the camera can provide an alternative means to give voice to people who were not equipped to express their thoughts and experiences in writing.[7] To be sure, the converts were largely the subjects of missionary photography, and missionaries framed the images, determining how the Koreans would be presented, similar to the way they were represented in a particular way in the missionary discourse. However, the simple fact of their being in front of the camera and choosing certain poses (or being asked to pose in a certain way) in a specific time and place can offer a myriad of insights into the "referent" (i.e., the subject of the photograph).[8] In their analysis of the visual culture of American religions, David Morgan and Sally Promey stress that the analysis of images helps us understand the "nonverbal articulation" of place, status, power, alliance, affection, class, race, and gender.[9] It is in this "nonverbal articulation" of the material, institutional, discursive, and human conditions that visual images uniquely contribute to our understanding of the complex and dynamic interactions between the missionaries and the missionized.

The article specifically examines the visual embodiment of women in the Korea mission field. There are two reasons for this focus. One is that the history of Christian women in modern historiography still remains scant and underexplored despite the significant role that women had in expanding church membership.[10] The other is related to the expediency of gender as an analytical

7   One of the rare literary pieces to vividly convey the voices of early Christian women can be found in a book titled *Victorious Lives of Early Christians in Korea: The First Book of Biographies and Autobiographies of Early Christians in the Protestant Church in Korea* (Seoul: The Christian Literature Society, 1927). The book was edited by Mattie Noble, a Methodist missionary stationed in P'yŏngyang, and was written in Korean. Its Korean title is *Sŭgni ŭi saenghwal*.

8   Roland Barthes, *Camera Lucida: Reflections on Photography*, trans. Richard Howard (New York: Hill and Wang, 1981), 9–10.

9   David Morgan and Sally Promey, ed., *Visual Culture of American Religions* (Berkeley: University of California Press, 2000), 16.

10   Some recent studies shed light on the rich history of Christian women in Korea. See Gari Ledyard, "Kollumba Kang Wansuk, an Early Catholic Activist and Martyr," in *Christianity in Korea*, ed. Robert Buswell Jr. and Timothy Lee (Honolulu: University of Hawai'i Press, 2006), 38–71; Donald Clark, "Mothers, Daughters, Biblewomen, and Sisters: An Account of 'Women's Work' in the Korea Mission Field," in Christianity in Korea, 167–92; Kelly Chong, *Deliverance and Submission: Evangelical Women and the Negotiation of Patriarchy in South Korea* (Cambridge: Harvard University Press, 2008); Hyaeweol Choi, *Gender and*

category for a fuller understanding of the Korean experience of the "modern," in which Protestant Christianity played a significant role. As is well known, the "woman question" took center stage in the discourse and practice of modernity after Korea began its open-door policy in 1876, and Protestant Christianity was pivotal in fashioning modern womanhood. American women missionaries, in particular, have been heralded as the pioneers who ushered in the example of modern gender roles. The fact that the majority of "educated" new women in Korea at the turn of the twentieth century had been exposed, directly or indirectly, to Christian mission schools and churches suggests the extensive influence Christianity had in shaping modern Korean womanhood.[11] Adopting postcolonial and feminist perspectives, I have discussed elsewhere the power of missionary discourse and the politics of gender and race that shaped a certain kind of new and modern womanhood within the particular historical circumstances of early modern Korea.[12] Building on these earlier analyses, this article centers on the visual to complement our understanding of the gender dynamics in the Korean mission field within the context of Korea's pursuit of modern nationhood.

In attempting to read visual representations in missionary photography, I have found it useful to adopt Kathleen Canning's thesis on the body as a historical method in the analysis of the transcultural encounters between

---

Mission Encounters in Korea: New Women, Old Ways (Berkeley: University of California Press, 2009).

11   Yi Paeyong in cooperation with Son Sŭnghŭi, Mun Sukchae, and Cho Kyŏngwŏn, "Han'guk kidokkyo yŏsŏng kyoyuk ŭi sŏngkwa wa chŏnmang—Ewha yŏja taehakkyo rŭl chungsim ŭro" [Accomplishment and prospect of Korean Christian education for women— With focus on Ewha Womans University], *Ewha sahak yŏn'gu*, 27 (2000): 9–36; Kang Sŏnmi, "Chosŏn p'agyŏnyŏ sŏn'gyosa wa (kidok) yŏsŏng ŭi yŏsŏngjuŭi ŭisik hyŏngsŏng" [Women missionaries sent to Korea and the formation of feminist consciousness among Christian women] (Ph.D. diss., Ewha Womans University, 2003); Insook Kwon, "'The New Women's Movement' in 1920s Korea: Rethinking the Relationship between Imperialism and Women," *Gender and History*, 10, no. 3 (November 1998): 381–405; Clark, "Mothers, Daughters, Biblewomen, and Sisters."

12   In my work, I underscore the complexity in the nature of "new" and "modern" gender ideology, which has been presumed to have been shaped by American women missionaries, through an examination of what constituted "the modern" in missionary discourse and institutional engagements. See Choi, *Gender and Mission Encounters in Korea*; Hyaeweol Choi, "'Wise Mother, Good Wife': A Trans-cultural Discursive Construct in Modern Korea," *Journal of Korean Studies*, 14, no. 1 (2009): 1–34.

Korean women and American missionaries.[13] The body—physical, social, and cultural—has been understood as a signifier of nation, state, class, and other social categories. Within the hierarchical power relations that were in place at the height of imperialism and foreign missionary enterprise in the late nineteenth and early twentieth centuries, the body served as an effective marker to measure the level of civilization a society had achieved in the Westerners' point of view. However, the construction of the "modern" body in the mission field was never a forced process imposed by the missionaries but rather was a product of inter-cultural negotiation. The embodied images, gestures, and practices in photography are, therefore, an important repository for understanding this dynamic process and context.

The first section of the article traces the earliest pictorial and photographic images in major missionary journals for women to illustrate the multiple representations and realities that characterized the relationship between American missionaries and Korean women, with particular attention to both the tensions and complementarities that existed between the textual and visual representations of Korean women. It also analyzes a gradual shift in visual representations of Korean women from nameless, exotic creatures not yet converted to Christianity to transformed individuals, often baptized and taking Western names, who are actively pursuing the "truth." The second part focuses on one of the most noteworthy visual spectacles captured in missionary photographs—the public display of bare breasts by local women. This section discusses how such photographs, some of which were staged, were consumed as a manifestation of paganism but simultaneously became the site of cultural negotiations over what might be considered proper bodily presentation in public space. The portrayal of Bible women is the focus of the last section. Korean Bible women were indispensable for the success of the evangelical endeavors of the mission. Against the background of the interdependent relationship between American missionary women and Korean Bible women, the last section closely reads the visual messages of the photographs in terms of the impact of the encounters between American and Korean women in the midst of the patriarchal organization of the church and Korean family. In its analysis of these aspects of missionary photography, the article argues that visual images are a useful focus for analysis in order to re-articulate missionary desire and bring out the hidden voices of Korean women.

---

13   Kathleen Canning, "The Body as Method? Reflections on the Place of the Body in Gender History," *Gender and History*, 11, no. 3 (November 1999): 499–513.

Visual Images of the "Heathen" Women from Afar

The Heathen Woman's Friend (1869–1895), published by the Woman's Foreign Missionary Society of the Methodist Episcopal Church, was one of the most influential women's mission journals.[14] In that journal, the first article on Korea was printed in the January issue of 1885, immediately after the first group of American Protestant missionaries had arrived in Korea in 1884. The article, "A Call from Corea," was written by Rijutei and bears the dateline "Tokio, August 8, 1884." Rijutei (also known as Yi Sujŏng) was a newly converted Korean man residing in Japan. He went to Japan in 1882 as part of a special envoy team from the Korean government. From that time, he developed intellectual and religious ties with both American missionaries and the Japanese Christian elite.[15] The crux of his "call" was to urge Americans to send women missionaries to Korea in order to educate Korean women because he believed that "to elevate and reform people, to educate children, to lead their husbands to virtue, are woman's mission [*sic*]." He depicted Korean customs that "are quite unlike either the Chinese or Japanese, *the power of the sex being about equal*" (emphasis added). He further elaborated by saying: "If wives are ever so bad, they cannot be divorced; so if an unhappy match is made, it must extend through life. On the other hand, though the husband be ever so ill-mannered, if he have a good wife he will become a better man. For though he be ever so bad, and dislike his wife's good character, he cannot divorce her, and she must ever exert a correcting influence on his life." Given this power of the Korean woman as a moral arbiter, Rijutei strongly advocated women's education as part of Korea's enlightenment project, and he felt that American missionary women would provide invaluable support in the initial stages.

Along with his plea, Rijutei noted that he wanted to mail to the journal "a photograph of a common Corean woman ... as it may give you a general idea of the appearance and dress of the women in my country."[16] This photograph, which was actually a hand-painted portrait likely based on a photograph, appeared the following year (1886) in the same journal in an article called "A Woman of Korea," written by Mrs. E. W. Rice (fig. 1). It was the first picture of a Korean woman ever published in *Heathen Woman's Friend*. The article noted:

---

14   *The Heathen Woman's Friend* continued under the new title, *Woman's Missionary Friend* (1896–1940). The new title came about after it was decided that the word "heathen" was derogatory.

15   Yi Kwangnin, *Kaehwap'a wa kaehwa sasang yŏn'gu* [Study of the Enlightenment group and its thought] (Seoul: Ilchogak, 1989), 43–62.

16   "A Call from Corea," *Heathen Woman's Friend*, 16, no. 7 (January 1885): 158–59.

FIGURE 1
A Korean woman
FROM *HEATHEN WOMAN'S FRIEND*,
17, NO. 8 (1886): 182

"Of the name and personal history of the woman of the picture, we know nothing. She is simply a Korean woman, whose picture has come to us by way of Japan. She may stand as a representative of her race, and her life history may be easily guessed."[17] Judging from her hair style, the picture is a portrait of a married woman, wearing traditional Korean dress and sitting on the floor. Although the flowers of the plant boxes that flank her soften the background somewhat, her stern face, upright posture, and piercing eyes looking straight back at the viewer convey that role of woman as the moral guide for men and children that was described by Rijutei.

In the two-page essay that accompanies this picture, Mrs. E. W. Rice, who did not serve in the Korea mission field but very likely did work at the journal *Heathen Woman's Friend*, presents a sketch of Korean womanhood, including

---

17   "A Woman of Korea," *Heathen Woman's Friend*, 17, no. 8 (February 1886): 182.

the practice of physical "seclusion" after age seven if the girl belonged to the upper class, the arranged marriage, and her subordination to her husband and his family. She acknowledges "a certain sort of outward respect" shown to women in Korea, noting that a Korean woman "is addressed in terms of honor. The man steps aside to let her pass him on the street, and holds a fan before his face lest he should catch a glimpse of hers.... For a man to speak to her would be a gross insult to her, and worse still, a dire breach of manners for him." She continues, "in spite of all this formal politeness to woman, the Korean believes her destitute of moral existence, a being without a soul, unworthy of a name, a creature without rights or responsibilities, only a convenient adjunct to some man—his daughter, his wife, his mother! Ages of mental and moral degradation have, perhaps, taught the woman herself to believe what her lord believes, almost to be what she thinks herself." Rice concludes, "Verily, women should thank God for birth in a Christian land!"[18]

One can readily see certain contradictions when the Korean (Rijutei's) and the American (Rice's) discourses are juxtaposed. Rijutei's description of the active role of the Korean woman as the example of moral virtue is undermined by that of Rice, in which the Korean woman is ultimately relegated to the status of "only a convenient adjunct to some man" without her own soul or morality. While each writer presented a positive view of the role that Christianity could have in the future of Korea, they clearly had different agendas to put forward: Rijutei's pursuit of modern Korea with the help of Christianity and Western education as opposed to Rice's interest in promoting the foreign mission to save non-Christian women from misery and "moral degradation." The different subjectivities of the authors with different mandates render contradictory representations of the status of Korean women. It is noteworthy that Rijutei's contribution to *Heathen Woman's Friend* was a very rare occurrence of a foreign voice in the journal. For the most part, mission journals were almost exclusively an outlet for American missionaries or workers in mission organizations at home. As is demonstrated by Rice's piece, writers at home sometimes penned articles for the mission journal with no firsthand knowledge of the place they were writing about, using information they had gathered from available publications and reports. However, once field-based missionaries began to accumulate direct experience with the local cultures, the missionaries themselves were the vast majority of the authors of journal articles.

Missionary reports from the field were accompanied by pictures and photographs, which helped readers visualize the local people and scenes. A case in

---

18   "A Woman of Korea," 182–83.

FIGURE 2
A Korean mother-in-law and her daughter-in-law
FROM *HEATHEN WOMAN'S FRIEND*, 20, NO. 2 (1888): 47–48

point is an article titled "Korean Girls" (1888) in *Heathen Woman's Friend*, reported by Mrs. Ella Appenzeller, one of the first Methodist missionaries (1885–1902). Appenzeller offers ethnographic details of the lives led by the local girls and women, sharing her observations about children in Korea as "bright and pretty."[19] She makes particular note of "a girl of perhaps twelve or thirteen, whom I saw with her mother" and reports of learning that "she was not a girl at all, but the wife of the son of the woman" (fig. 2). Appenzeller asks the readers to imagine: "How would you like to leave papa and mamma, and the sweet little baby brothers and sisters, and go to live with some one you had never seen nor heard of, and never go out any more, only in a close-covered box, or in the evening with your mother-in-law? You would not like it at all; neither should I." She deplores the lot of Korean girls, who are destined to comply with the custom of early marriage and domestic seclusion. At the same time, she suggests, a light of hope shines as Mrs. Mary Scranton, a pioneering Methodist missionary, had just opened the "first Korean Sunday-school," where girls aged

---

19   Mrs. Ella Appenzeller, "Korean Girls," *Heathen Woman's Friend*, 20, no. 2 (August 1888): 47–48.

THE VISUAL EMBODIMENT OF WOMEN IN THE KOREA MISSION FIELD   231

six to fifteen could learn lessons from the Bible. Appenzeller specifically profiles some girls as well as adult women in attendance at the Sunday school, including "Patty," a girl who "was found sick unto death by the roadside."[20] The discourse has progressed from the nameless "heathen" Korean woman of Rice's essay to the newly converted individual who is specifically referred to using her baptismal Anglo names and can be seen as an example of successful evangelism in Korea.

George Gilmore, another early Methodist missionary in Korea (1886–1889), offers a fascinating portrait of Korean women in his essay, "Social Phases in Korea" (1890) in *Heathen Woman's Friend*.[21] He includes two images—one is a picture of women ironing clothes, and the other is a picture of a woman making rice cake, or *ttŏk*—in order to provide "a glimpse of women at their household occupations."[22] In the essay, he views the seclusion of Korean women to be "the most noticeable difference between social life in America and Korea." He notes that this gendered quarantine is so strictly observed that "a male visitor is met by the master of the house at the entrance, and is entertained in what corresponds to our hall or ante-room, or in the guest-chamber, neither of which permits a view of the rooms where live the mother and daughters." However, he emphasizes, despite the secluded life of women, "it must not be supposed that the position of woman there is a low one ... she is treated with respect by the husband. She is spoken to in honorific terms, and her judgment is sought when matters of importance are to be considered." In an earlier report, Gilmore had pointed out: "The position of woman in Korea is much misunderstood. It has been supposed that they are not held in respect, and are considered the meaner part of the population. This is doubtless a mistake.... It is an open secret that Her Majesty has more than a little to say in the conduct of the affairs of the kingdom. Undoubtedly the women of Korea generally are a power in the land."[23] He echoes Rijutei's assertion about the moral power of women in the context of Korean culture; however, given the relative isolation

---

20 In the beginning of the mission, it was difficult to recruit Korean girls and women to church or mission schools, largely because of the "inside outside rule" (*naeoebŏp*) that prevented older girls and young women from being seen in public and also due to the widespread, unflattering rumors about Westerners. As a result, the early converts and students at mission schools tended to be orphans or come from impoverished families. See Choi, *Gender and Mission Encounters in Korea*, 90–91.

21 Geo. W. Gilmore, "Social Phrases in Korea," *Heathen Woman's Friend*, 22, no. 1 (July 1890): 3–5.

22 Gilmore, "Social Phrases in Korea."

23 Geo. W. Gilmore, "Two Interrogations Answered about Korea," *Woman's Work for Woman and Our Mission Field*, 4, no. 9 (1889): 237–38. "Her Majesty" refers to Empress Myŏngsŏng also known as Queen Min.

that Korean social practices imposed on women, Gilmore regards the matter of greatest urgency facing the mission to be recruiting "more women [missionaries] to work among women."

Based on his direct contact with local Korean men and women, Gilmore reports a rather surprising reality in which "[Korean] women, after becoming acquainted with us and our ways, have shown no reluctance to meeting gentlemen, and are fond of paying visits to the wives of such foreigners as they know, often manifesting not the slightest embarrassment at being seen even for the first time by strange gentlemen." One example in point is the wife of his Korean language teacher. After working with Gilmore for three months, the teacher wanted to bring his wife to Gilmore's home so that she could see how foreigners lived. Gilmore describes her behavior during her first visit to his house: "looking at everything with great enjoyment. She sat at lunch with us, and soon was cracking jokes with great gusto." More importantly, Gilmore offers an important clue about mission photography in the same essay. He notes that before they left, "she sat with her husband for her picture, which I [Gilmore] took, and a copy of which is now in my album." The photograph of the couple that Gilmore took is not included in his essay.[24] However, his description of the situation provides a glimpse into how Korean subjects were captured by missionaries' cameras. As Helen Gardner and Jude Philp argue in their article on photography and the Christian mission, the relationship between the missionary photographer and the photographic subject is not a simple one-way connection. Rather photography was used to "establish and maintain relations with local people." More importantly, the agency of the photographic subjects is clear.[25] As Gilmore notes, because the Korean teacher had acquired some level of familiarity with foreigners, he was willing to introduce his wife to them and even to pose for a photograph. Without that familiarity, "he [the Korean teacher] would have been shocked and perhaps would not have come near the house again" if Gilmore had asked him to bring his wife for a visit.

As implied in Gilmore's essay, Koreans were curious about "foreign" lifestyles and the material objects from overseas that could be found in missionary homes, including photographs.[26] The introduction to photographs and

---

24   While the exact explanation is unknown, part of the reason why Gilmore did not include the photo of the couple might be related to the high expense or technological limitations involved in publishing photographs in the journal at that time. However, situations greatly changed from the 1890s when a large number of modern photographs began to appear in mission journals.

25   Gardner and Philp, "Photography and Christian Mission," 175.

26   Sadie Welbon, "Foreign Woman's Evangelistic Work in City and Country," *Korea Mission Field*, 6, no. 10 (1910): 259–61.

THE VISUAL EMBODIMENT OF WOMEN IN THE KOREA MISSION FIELD   233

FIGURE 3   A woman Christian convert in a missionary's room
            THE REVEREND CORWIN & NELLIE TAYLOR COLLECTION, UNIVERSITY
            OF SOUTHERN CALIFORNIA, LOS ANGELES, CALIFORNIA

hand-drawn pictures for most ordinary Koreans came when they first came into contact with missionaries. Susan Doty, an early Presbyterian missionary (1890–1931), describes a typical visit by some Korean women to the missionary residence as follows: "Large numbers of them [Korean women] come to my house as women at home go to the museum. They marvel over the organ, the music-box, sewing machine, foreign chairs, pictures, mirrors and beds…. Before they go, I always show them pictures illustrating the life of our Lord, and often give them books and invite them to Sabbath services."[27] Given the language barrier in the encounters between Koreans and American missionaries, pictures would have been useful as a medium for communication. Furthermore, as Doty seems to imply, the pictorial images would serve to pique interest so that people might be motivated to learn more about Christianity. Figure 3 shows a Korean woman convert, a nurse-in-training, sitting in a room filled with Western objects, including an organ, a table, a chair, a lamp, books, and picture frames. A photograph of a male figure hangs prominently in the upper right, and just underneath are three smaller photos of children. In the hallway

---

27   "Korea," *Woman's Work for Woman and Our Mission Field*, 4, no. 12 (1889): 329.

on the left side one can see another set of photos. This converted Korean woman, wearing typical Korean dress in white, is seated on Western-style furniture in the midst of all these decidedly Western artifacts. Given the rarity of the opportunity to have one's picture taken at that time, the act of being posed in front of a camera and then seeing a photograph of herself might have given her a feeling of privilege or status. In this way, pictures and photos were among the exotica that attracted Koreans and became another important evangelical tool for missionaries, serving as a medium for introducing and distributing the gospel and for establishing and maintaining relationships with the local people.[28] Soon after the working relationship was established, many photographs of newly converted Christians and Bible women were introduced in the mission journals along with the stories of their conversions to demonstrate the success of the evangelical effort to bring secluded Korean women out to Christian churches.

The first modern photograph related to Korean women appears in 1892 in *Woman's Work for Woman*, a prominent women's missionary journal of the Presbyterian Church. In her essay, "The Women Who Labor with me in the Gospel," Harriet G. Gale, an early Presbyterian missionary (1885–1908), offers a brief summary of the life paths of the Korean Christian women she worked with, and a group photo is included (fig. 4).[29] Gale's perceptive portrayal of each individual woman in the photograph, ranging from a "light-hearted and almost careless, always smiling" woman to a woman who "fears nothing and will talk about the Bible and read it anywhere," helps readers get a glimpse into the background of these women and what personality or inclinations motivated them to seek the new religion despite the difficulty that publicly embracing Christianity could bring at the time.[30] Gale's "best and brightest of all is dear old Holmonie [*halmŏni*, grandmother]," who is the second from the left in the front row of the photo. Gale describes her first encounter with Holmonie, noting that "unlike most Koreans, she looked straight into my face and not at my

---

28   W. J. Hall, "Pioneer Missionary Work in the Interior of Korea," Gospel in All Lands (July, 1894): 331–32; Rosetta Sherwood Hall, "Kwang Hya Nyo Won or Woman's dispensary of extended grace," Annual Meeting of the Woman's Conference of the Methodist Episcopal Church in Korea (Seoul, May 13–19, 1899), 14–18; Mary Hillman, "Evangelistic Work and Day School, West Korea District," Annual Meeting of the Woman's Conference of the Methodist Episcopal Church in Korea (Pyeng Yang, May 6–21, 1902), 20–21.

29   Harriet G. Gale, "The Women who Labor with me in the Gospel," *Woman's Work for Woman*, 7, no. 8 (August 1892): 215–17.

30   Chŏn Samdŏk, "Nae saenghwal ŭi yangnyŏk" [History of my life], in *Victorious Lives of Early Christians in Korea*, 12.

FIGURE 4   A group of Korean Christian women
FROM *WOMAN'S WORK FOR WOMAN*, 7, NO. 8 (1892):
215–17

dress, as if to see if I myself were really so different from all the people she had ever known…. She came, day after day, caring nothing about the strange [foreign] things she saw, but eagerly devouring chapter after chapter of the Gospel." In a significant way, this photo succinctly captures the wide range of age groups that were drawn to the new religion. The grandmother Gale introduces here is not an exceptional case. As amply demonstrated in later photos, many elderly women actively worked as Bible women.

The growth in the number of new converts was naturally a favorite topic of mission journals, and photographs of those women, both individually and in groups, were frequently showcased (fig. 5). The sheer number of attendants at Bible classes was a point of pride for missionaries. As Mattie Noble, a prominent Presbyterian missionary stationed in P'yŏngyang (1892–1934), proudly notes in her description of her "Bible Institute," many local women enthusiastically responded to the opportunity to learn about the new religion and participate in a variety of activities offered by the missionaries. Noble noted that "two

FIGURE 5 Bible class
THE REVEREND CORWIN & NELLIE TAYLOR COLLECTION,
UNIVERSITY OF SOUTHERN CALIFORNIA, LOS ANGELES,
CALIFORNIA

hundred and fifteen earnest women and girls" attended a 1906 Bible Institute, and among them "one hundred and eight women walked in from the country, a half to four days' traveling."[31]

In addition to the growing number of converts, the success of the evangelical effort was highlighted through the stories of former shamans who had played a significant role as spiritual leaders in old Korea but then converted to Christianity. A case in point is an essay by Blanche Webb Lee (1892–1912), "Christianity's Message to Woman" (1897), with a photo of a Korean female shaman (fig. 6).[32] Lee introduces the shaman who "has been a servant of Satan" for more than fifty years and "by her lies and wickedness won much money and did much evil." The caption of the photo reads: "This one by posing before the camera with all her appliances for divination about her plainly exhibits the money-making character of her calling. At Christmas service (1896) in Pyeng Yang, 400 to 500 people were present and heard short talks from three

---

31   Mattie Wilcox Noble, "A Bible Institute in Korea," *Woman's Missionary Friend*, 38, no. 11 (November 1906): 399–400.
32   Blanche Webb Lee, "Christianity's Message to Woman," *Woman's Work for Woman*, 12, no. 5 (1897): 119–20.

FIGURE 6   A Korean female shaman
FROM *WOMAN'S WORK FOR WOMAN*, 12, NO. 5 (1897): 120

converts: I.—A Former blind sorceress. II.—A devil exorcist. III.—A grave-site diviner." One former shaman pledged, "I consecrate myself and all I have to God's service. I mean to go back and teach the women of Whang Hai Province about Jesus." This type of photograph and story sent a powerful message to the readers at home that shamanistic practices, emblematic of the ultimate form of "paganism" in the eyes of missionaries and Westerners, would be defeated by Christianity, a triumph of missionary labor and evidence in their minds of the superiority of their religion.[33]

The mission journals were produced largely for the consumption of the audience at home.[34] Missionary discourse accompanied by photographs and pictures provided an effective medium for demonstrating what missionaries in the field had accomplished and thus served as a crucial medium for fundraising activities at home that would help secure financial resources that could

---

33   L. A. Miller, "The Conversion of a Sorceress," *Korea Mission Field*, 2 (February 1906): 65.
34   A quotation cited in *Korea Mission Field* in 1908 reads, "The crux of the missionary question, as far as it relates to Korea, is not here on the field but is at home, on the threshold of the church in America. No obstacle appears ahead of us to prevent the saving of hundreds of thousands of Koreans. It is only a question of whether the church at home will make good the opportunity which has been given her of God—to bestow upon one nation, during this generation, the priceless boon of becoming Christian in its national and individual life." *Korea Mission Field*, 4 (March 1908): 1.

be channeled into the mission field so that missionaries could continue to carry out their goal of "saving" the pagan. Bishop David Moore succinctly dramatizes the effective use of the mission journal as a conduit for fund-raising. He writes: "Alas, for the woman of Korea! Until the Gospel crowns her, she is nothing and nameless. Christ's love in her heart, the missionary's hand in holy baptism upon her head, and she goes forth as 'Salome,' 'Martha' or 'Mary,' a new and glorified creation. And it requires but thirty-six dollars, gold, to support a Bible-woman for a year! My American sisters, is this the 'open door' you are seeking?"[35] The formerly nameless "heathen" woman bears her newly acquired Western baptismal name in a photograph that clearly individuates her as a tangible, visible, and transformed being. In this vein, photographs added a more vivid and presumably "realistic" portrayal of the local people and culture with the marked sense of pride on the part of missionaries for their success.

The Body as a Marker of "the Other"

In foreign mission fields throughout the world, the body and the state of dress (or undress) of the local people served as one of the most tantalizing points for understanding the stark differences between the Eurocentric notion of civilization and the primitiveness and savagery of "the Other." Especially the *lack* of clothing on the "natives" was a constant source of disgust and fascination among Western colonialists, travelers, and missionaries.[36] It is important to note that while local women's bodies and their lack of clothing were often framed by the particular worldview and gender practices that Westerners embraced, they also shed light on the ways in which the body—physical, cultural, and societal—was a site of "intervention or inscriptive surface" on which bodily norms and values are newly inscribed or refuted through the transcultural encounters.[37] Tony Ballantyne and Antoinette Burton propose that "the body-as-contact-zone is a powerful analytical term ... precisely because it allows us to navigate the dynamic relationship between representation and 'reality' and to see the work of mediation that embodied subjects perform between the

---

35   Bishop David H. Moore, "Slavery in Korea," *Woman's Missionary Friend*, 35, no. 9 (September 1903): 319.

36   Philippa Levine argues that "Any investigation of unclothedness in a British context must, however, begin with Christianity, which has had much to say on the topic of the unclothed body. Missionaries working in colonial sites looked upon colonial undress as a profound spiritual hazard. The three 'c's of Christianity, civilization, and clothing were surely as important in the missionary ethos." Philippa Levine, "States of Undress: Nakedness and the Colonial Imagination," *Victorian Studies*, 50, no. 2 (2008): 191.

37   Canning, "The Body as Method?," 500–506.

FIGURE 7   A Korean family in the street
GENERAL COMMISSION ON ARCHIVES AND HISTORY, UNITED
METHODIST CHURCH, DREW UNIVERSITY, MADISON, NEW JERSEY

domestic and the foreign, the quotidian and the cyclical, the dynamic and the static."[38]

Some of the most remarkable photographs that illustrate "the body-as-contact-zone" theme were those photographs that showed Korean women with their breasts exposed. The design and fashion of women's clothing in Korea at the turn of the twentieth century was typically an extremely short jacket, which reached down to just under the armpit, and a long skirt that wrapped around the breasts. Given the style, it was very easy to see the gap between the jacket and skirt if a woman lifted her arms to steady something she was carrying on her head. Figure 7 provides an illustration in point. It is a snapshot taken in the street. A family—husband, wife, and children—are on a trip. In

---

[38]   Tony Ballantyne and Antoinette Burton, "Postscripts: Bodies, Genders, Empires: Reimaging World Histories," in *Bodies in Contact*, ed. Tony Ballantyne and Antoinette Burton (Durham, N.C.: Duke University Press, 2005), 407. The notion of "contact zone" Ballantyne and Burton use is drawn from Mary Louise Pratt's definition of contact zone as "the space of colonial encounters, the space in which peoples geographically and historically separated come into contact with each other and establish ongoing relations, usually involving conditions of coercion, radical inequality, and intractable conflict." Mary Louise Pratt, *Imperial Eyes: Travel Writing and Transculturation* (London: Routledge, 1992), 6.

this photo, the woman is carrying a basket on her head and steadying it with her right hand, which has resulted in her jacket being lifted so that her breasts are exposed. From the viewpoint of the American missionaries, who held the Victorian, Protestant, white-middle-class norms and sensibilities of their time, the "private" body should be properly covered in public, and what they saw in the street was beyond the bounds of acceptable bodily presentation.[39] Annie Baird, a prolific Presbyterian missionary (1891–1916), vividly describes a scene where an American woman from Kentucky was so upset at the sight of the exposed breasts of a Korean woman in the street that she tried to pull the Korean woman's top jacket and skirt to cover the breasts but to no avail.[40]

What is significant in fig. 7 is that while the "exposed" body signified a pagan condition from the Western point of view, the "exposure" itself does not seem to even register in the minds of the subjects of the photograph. The woman's facial expression and, more importantly, her husband's smiling at the camera, make it amply clear that they are not embarrassed or even aware that the display of her breasts could be seen as improper. Here one can see the dynamics involved in the interpretation of dress and the body in the contact zone. In this case, the unwittingly revealed "private" body of the subject was captured by the "public" eyes of the missionary photographer that were trained to read the body and dress in a particular way.[41] In many candid photographs of this type taken in the street[42] and even in some of the *posed* photographs of local women,[43] the photographer's aim was to capture an embodiment of "paganism" in the women's "indecent" displays of their bodies and portray them as objects

---

39 Ryu Taeyŏng, *Ch'ogi miguk son'gyosa yon'gu: 1884–1910* [Early American missionaries in Korea: 1884–1910] (Seoul: Han'guk kidokkyo yoksa yŏn'guso, 2001). In this book Ryu provides detailed stories about the middle-class background of American missionaries who came to Korea.

40 Annie Baird, *Inside Views of Mission Life* (Philadelphia: Westminster Press, 1913), 18–19.

41 Dress scholar Carole Turbin notes that "(b)ecause dress is not a simple cultural expression of society or individuals but a form of visual and tactile communication linked to the body, self, and communication, it is paradoxical and double-edged, both public and private, individual and social." Carole Turbin, "Refashioning the Concept of Public/Private: Lessons from Dress Studies," *Journal of Women's History*, 15, no. 1 (2003): 45.

42 Chŏng Sŏnghŭi, *Chosŏn ŭi sŏngp'ungsok* [Sexual culture in the Chosŏn dynasty] (Seoul: Karam kihoek, 1998), 244; Cho Hŭijin, *Sŏnbi wa p'iŏsing* [Literary scholar and piercing] (Seoul: TongAsia, 2003), 71–86.

43 Blanche Stevens' folder at Yenching Library, Harvard University. In this folder, a number of photos are included, donated by Jim Carlson in Virginia. One of the photos is a picture of lower-class women—three young adult women and one old woman whose breasts were exposed. They were standing in a row, looking straight into the camera. They look as if they were asked to pose in that way.

THE VISUAL EMBODIMENT OF WOMEN IN THE KOREA MISSION FIELD   241

to be civilized, while the Korean subjects often cast a seemingly blank stare at the never-before-seen exotic device in the hands of the foreigner.

It is noteworthy that these types of sensational photographs from Korea were not printed in mission journals. This is not to say that such photographs were unusual in the Korea mission field. Many photographs of women in states of partial undress in Korea are preserved in mission archives in the folders of individual missionaries. One might also argue that such photographs might have prompted a sense of urgency in the readers of mission journals at home about the need to "rescue heathen women" from a "profound spiritual hazard" and civilize them with an appropriate sense of modesty and thereby prompt greater support.[44] Indeed, these journals did reproduce images of naked or half-naked "pagan" women from missions in other parts of the world to show the success the mission had had in converting "wild" or "cannibal" natives.[45] However, the mission journals did not include such photographs of Korean women. One clue as to why such photographs did not appear in mission jour- nals might be that the missionaries came to be aware of the class distinctions among women of Korea in terms of their dress code and thus avoided oversim- plifying the world of women in Korea. More seasoned and perceptive mission- aries and travelers understood dress to be a marker of social classes in Korea. In his book, *Chosŏn, the Land of Morning Calm*, published in 1885, Percival Lowell describes women's clothing in Korea and notes that the unexpected exposure of breasts might be found only among women of the commoner class when they carry water in a pot on their head.[46] Huldah Haenig, a Methodist mission- ary (1910–1915), illustrates the common scene of the women in Korea on the streets, noting that "[m]any of the grown and married women ... shield them- selves from the public gaze by the green coat thrown over head and shoul- ders.... Not all women, however, are able to guard their modesty so. Babies astride their backs, heavy burdens on their heads, and all too scanty clothing, are everywhere seen to be a common lot of the women."[47] Indeed, missionar- ies often saw "proper" Korean women, especially young unmarried ones, cover

---

44   Levine, "States of Undress," 191.

45   Joseph H. Reading, "Fangwe Cannibals," *Woman's Work for Woman and Our Mission Field*, 4, no. 6 (June 1889): 149; "The Indians of Brazil," *Woman's Work for Woman and Our Mission Field*, 4, no. 11 (November 1889): 294.

46   Percival Lowell, *Chosŏn, the Land of the Morning Calm* [Nae kiŏk sok ŭi Chosŏn, Chosŏn saramdŭl], trans. Cho Kyŏngch'ŏl (Seoul: Yedam, 2001), 259. See also J. Devika, *En-Gendering Individuals: The Language of Re-forming in Twentieth Century Keralam* (New Delhi: Orient Longman Private Limited, 2007), 253–91.

47   Huldah A. Haenig, "From West Gate to East Gate," *Woman's Missionary Friend*, 43, no. 1 (January 1911): 9–11.

FIGURE 8
A Korean woman ready for church
FROM *WOMAN'S WORK FOR WOMAN*, 38,
NO. 3 (1906): 83

their bodies with long-sleeved clothing in the public space to "shield themselves from the public gaze" (fig. 8).[48] In addition, women of the upper class, who did not have to engage in physical labor such as carrying baggage or water, were always represented in their fine clothing posed with great dignity.

Awareness of class distinctions became a crucial component in developing the mission's strategies for approaching women of different social classes and envisioning what constituted ideal or proper bodily presentation in the public space within the Korean cultural context. As Philippa Levine aptly points out, "What constitutes a state of unclothedness is fluid and unstable—a historical problem, a problem of spatiality and of temporality."[49] In her analysis of the secularization of the breast in Western art, Margaret Miles argues that the "exposed breast" of the Virgin Mary holding the infant Jesus was a powerful religious icon; however, it was eventually transformed from "a religious symbol" to an erotic and medical sign over the course of the early modern period

---

48   Minerva L. Guthapfel, "How They Come Into the Kingdom," *Woman's Missionary Friend*, 38, no. 3 (March 1906): 81–84.
49   Levine, "States of Undress," 190.

THE VISUAL EMBODIMENT OF WOMEN IN THE KOREA MISSION FIELD 243

in Western Europe.[50] Numerous paintings depict mother and child in Western art, and the Madonna has been a central figure. For example, in Joos van Cleve's *Virgin and Child* (1525), the Virgin's breast figures prominently in the portrait, with the child closing its eyes and touching his mother's breast in profound comfort.[51] The bodily function of a mother nursing and comforting a child is aesthetically and culturally constructed as beautiful, even sacred. However, the distinction between the body of a *mother* nourishing her child and the body of an eroticized or *pagan woman* is crucial here. The bare breast is readily justified when it serves a maternal or religious end, while it can invite social condemnation if it is interpreted as a mark of promiscuity or pagan practice.

In this vein, one of the most fascinating interpretations of Korean women's presentations of their bodies, especially the exposure of the breasts, is that of Annie Baird, a veteran missionary woman of the Presbyterian church. She offers her own cultural interpretation that the exposure of women's breasts should not be understood solely from a Western viewpoint. Rather, she argues, it should be understood in relation to the status and role of Korean women within the particular cultural context of Korea. That is, being a mother is the ultimate role and duty of Korean women. It provides them with power and authority. Fulfilling one's motherly duties, including nursing, is so important that women's clothing is designed to make this maternal function easy and efficient.[52] Baird makes the point that, because this duty is understood to be first and foremost for a woman in Korean culture, it removes any sexual connotation from the image of the mother's body. In other words, by emphasizing these maternal functions, she succeeds in de-sexualizing the body of woman and in turn presenting woman as the site of nurturing and care for the future of the society. While ordinary Korean women's bare breasts in the street stirred Western missionaries' sensibility in the beginning, nursing a child in public must have been understood by missionaries as a standard practice in Korean society. In a 1917 portrait of a Bible class in Taigu (Taegu), a woman in the lower left front row (in the rectangle) is nursing her child with her breast slightly exposed*. What the picture suggests is that breastfeeding in public was something that was done commonly without any self-consciousness or embarrassment. This natural and matter-of-fact pose of the breastfeeding woman in front of a camera also manifests missionaries' compliance to such local practice.

---

50   Margaret Miles, *A Complex Delight: The Secularization of the Breast 1350–1759* (Berkeley: University of California Press, 2008).

51   Marita Sturken and Lisa Cartwright, *Practices of Looking: An Introduction to Visual Culture* (Oxford: Oxford University Press, 2001), 37.

52   Baird, *Inside Views of Mission Life*, 18–19.

In a significant way, this staged picture is a classic example that demonstrates the success of evangelical work, showing undeniable "progress" from "heathen" to Christian civilization. The sheer size of the class is an obvious reflection of this. Moreover, the picture illustrates the shifting horizon of society from the old to the new by centering on the larger, more imposing Western-style building—a church—as a symbol of Western modernity and locating the old, traditional Korean house off to the side. While women of old Korea largely remained illiterate, many of the girls and women in this Bible class are holding the Bible, signifying their literacy. The top jacket that many of the women are wearing is significantly longer than was the style in earlier times, suggesting some form of dress reform.[53] In addition, a few women (circled in the picture), who are likely to be leaders of the Bible class, are wearing a "modern" hairstyle, which became popular in the 1920s. In this way, many of the images contained in this picture suggest ongoing changes in the notion of proper space and bodily presentation of women in Korea. Yet, the simultaneous existence of a church member who was openly breastfeeding in front of the camera succinctly shows the extent to which the missionary efforts in "civilizing missions" were inscribed but at the same time negotiated in the face of the local cultural particularities regarding what are the acceptable limits of bodily presentations in public.

The Bible Women and Women Missionaries

The majority of photographic representations about the "progress" in the mission field focused on Bible women. The importance of Bible women in the mission field cannot be overemphasized. Lulu Frey, a teacher at Ewha Girls' School (1893–1920), declared that "the Bible Woman seemed to be regarded as the most important factor in the work among the Korean women of Korea. Since they know what Korean women are and what they experience in their lives,

---

53   Some leading Korean intellectuals made critical comments on the traditional dress style and wanted to reform it to make it more practical and hygienic. Kim Wŏnju, for example, proposed a dress reform to correct the reality in which unmarried women tended to compress their breasts too much by wrapping their skirts around them tightly, and other women especially in the countryside carelessly allowed their breasts to be exposed although not intentionally. She made a point that such scenes were embarrassing, particularly for foreigners. See her article, "Puin ŭibok kaeryang e taehan ŭigyŏn" [Thoughts on the women's dress reform], *Tonga ilbo* 10 through 14 September 1921. Cited from Kim Iryŏp, *Chaet pit chŏksam e sarang ŭl mutko* [Burying love under the ash-colored jacket], ed. Kim Sangbae (Seoul: Sol moe, 1982), 221–26.

FIGURE 9   A Bible training class in P'yŏngyang
NORMAN THORPE COLLECTION

the bible woman can approach other Korean women more effectively with great sympathy."[54] In addition to their easy and direct contact with Korean women, the Bible woman was "a good model for the rest of women because the bible woman is able to read the Bible (all except a very few had learned to read)."[55] Becoming literate was one of the requirements to be appointed as a Bible woman.[56] Given the exceedingly low literacy rate at the time, the prospect of learning how to read served as an attractive factor in recruiting future Christians. As Nellie Pierce Miller, a Methodist missionary (1897–1937), noted, some of her new students at her Bible school attended the school "simply because they want to study."[57] Figure 9 gives us a glimpse of students attending Bible classes and what was taught in Bible classes. The open books and the content on the blackboard demonstrate that Bible classes provided instruction in numeracy and literacy, which were not a small attraction for Korean women. Indeed, the rather happy faces of two Korean women in the front row subtly but powerfully convey the meaning of attending Bible classes. Becoming a Bible woman was more than simply becoming a devoted Christian. It was an opportunity to learn and earn income. Missionaries preferred to train widows as Bible women because those women did not have as many family obligations

54 Lulu Frey, "The Bible Woman," *Korea Mission Field*, 3, no. 2 (1907): 42.
55 Frey, "The Bible Woman," 42.
56 Kate Cooper, "The Bible Woman," *The Korea Magazine* (January 1917): 6–10.
57 *Woman's Missionary Friend*, 37, no. 8 (August 1905): 291.

as others and could devote themselves to the evangelical work full-time.[58] In addition, widows had particularly low status in Korea, and thus the chance to become a Bible woman must have been a welcome opportunity to have a distinct identity other than as widow and, perhaps more importantly, to gain some level of financial independence as they were paid for their work. These full-time Bible women provided crucial assistance to missionary women in the proliferation of evangelical work, especially in small villages away from the city centers. While the evangelical task was the priority in the work of the Bible women, they also engaged in the reform of old habits and customs. For instance, some gave up side businesses selling wine because they were told that Christians should not engage in such activity.[59] A Bible woman named Abigail, who had at one time been a concubine, left her man after she converted to Christianity.[60] As noted earlier, the stories of converted shamans (*mudang*) also provided particularly powerful examples for showing the "superiority" of Christianity, given the centuries of influence shamanism had in Korea.[61]

Many missionaries—both women and men—expressed gratitude for the exceptional contribution of Bible women to the evangelical work. Nellie Pierce Miller talked about her experience in training Bible women as something that gave her "exceeding joy and satisfaction."[62] In her description of her Bible woman, Martha Pak, N. M. S. Hall MacRae, an Australian Presbyterian missionary (1915–1940), says she considers Pak to be "truly my dear friend and fellow worker as if her skin had been white and her language my native tongue ... I think of her earnestness, her charming personality, and untiring zeal in the Master's service."[63]

There is no doubt that the relationship between missionaries and Bible women began as teacher-student and was thus a hierarchical one with the American missionary in the dominant position and the Korean woman in the subordinate role. That hierarchy is enacted in fig. 10, in which a missionary teacher sits on a chair while her Korean students sit on the ground, and the image of the missionary as a guide/teacher to Korean women is heightened by the attentive gazes of the Korean students. At the same time, one can also see the congenial and collaborative relationship between the missionaries and Korean women played out in images like fig. 11. In this photo, Gertrude Snavely,

---

58   Cooper, "The Bible Woman," 7.

59   Mrs. A. F. Robb, "Our Bible Woman, Dorcas," *Korea Mission Field*, 3, no. 1 (January 1907): 6.

60   Lillian Nicholas, "The Story of a Bible Woman," *Korea Mission Field*, 8, no. 7 (July 1912): 207.

61   Miller, "The Conversion of a Sorceress," 65.

62   Third Annual Meeting of the Woman's Conference of the Methodist Episcopal Church in Korea (1901, Seoul. May 9–14), 13.

63   "Biblewomen," *The Korea Review*, 6, no. 4 (1906): 141.

THE VISUAL EMBODIMENT OF WOMEN IN THE KOREA MISSION FIELD   247

FIGURE 10   Chemulpo Bible Institute group
THE REVEREND CORWIN & NELLIE TAYLOR COLLECTION,
UNIVERSITY OF SOUTHERN CALIFORNIA, LOS ANGELES,
CALIFORNIA

a Methodist missionary (1906–1940), sits in the center and Blanche Bair (1913–1938)[64] at one end of a semicircle. Snavely was the senior missionary and Bair the junior in training. The fact that Bair is part of the "student" group in the composition of this photo and that everyone can see each other suggests a different dimension in the missionary-Korean relationship—a more interactive, mutual, open, and less hierarchical relationship. To be sure, Snavely still sets herself apart by wearing a modern-style hat while all the other women have bare heads, and by taking a position at the center she is presented as the leader of the group. Yet, there is no distance between the missionaries and the Korean women. Indeed, the physical closeness (their knees seem to be touching) suggests a dynamic more like that of a peer group than a hierarchical teacher-student group. The Korean woman to the immediate right of Snavely casts a

---

64   In the description of the photo in the Methodist archive, the other missionary is identified as "Miss Bailer." However, no missionary named Bailer was ever sent to the Korea mission field. It is very likely that there is an error in the record and the person in the photograph is actually Blanche Bair, who was working in Haeju, where Gertrude Snavely was working prior to Bair's arrival in 1913.

FIGURE 11   Gertrude Snavely and her Bible class
GENERAL COMMISSION ON ARCHIVES AND HISTORY, UNITED
METHODIST CHURCH, DREW UNIVERSITY, MADISON, NEW JERSEY

gentle, downward gaze at the Bible Snavely is holding. Her subtle smile can be interpreted as a quiet manifestation of the satisfying and comfortable relationship between them.

A more direct and intimate contact between missionaries and Korean Bible women is illustrated in fig. 12, in which Louise McCully (the first person on the left in the second row), the first woman missionary sent to Korea by the Woman's Missionary Society of the Canadian Presbyterian Church (1900–1934), is holding hands with Ch'oe Maria (the second from the left in the front row), a Korean Bible woman. McCully was originally sent to China, but at the outbreak of the Boxer Rebellion in 1900, she found refuge in Wŏnsan, Korea. Upon arriving in Korea in 1901, McCully "quickly proved herself to be an indefatigable evangelistic worker and champion of women's place within the church."[65] The relationship she had with Ch'oe Maria through Bible classes and evangelical activities for women lasted more than three decades. Ch'oe was one of the most active Bible women in the region of Hamhŭng. It is claimed that she was the first Korean woman converted to Christianity in Hamhŭng. She began to teach Korean and Chinese characters to children when there was

---

65   A. Hamish Ion, *The Cross and the Rising Sun* (Waterloo: Wilfrid Laurier University Press, 1990), 31.

FIGURE 12   An example of intimate contact between missionaries and Korean Bible women is seen in the clasped hands of Louise McCully, at left in second row, and Ch'oe Maria
From Helen F. MacRae, *A Tiger on Dragon Mountain: The Life of Rev. Duncan M. MacRae, D.D.* (CHARLOTTETOWN, PRINCE EDWARD ISLAND: A. J. HASLAM, 1993), 150

no school in the region. This initial instruction offered by Ch'oe ultimately led to the establishment of Yŏngsaeng Girls' School.[66]

The photographs of Korean Bible women and American women missionaries complement our understanding of their shared lot and aspirations not only for their religious faith but also for their careers and independent lives. For Korean women, it was in mission schools and Sunday schools that they received literacy training for the first time. It was also mission organizations that began to offer job opportunities for Korean women as Bible women, school teachers, and nurses. Career opportunities such as these were rare for women at the time. In this way, conversion to Christianity opened up unprecedented opportunities for Korean girls and women in pursuing higher education and professional careers. Similarly, the foreign mission enterprise provided relatively well-educated women in the West with an unprecedented opportunity to fulfill their religious and professional ambitions within the "woman's work

---

66   Han'guk kidokkyo yŏksa yŏn'guso yŏsŏngsa yŏn'guhoe, *Han'guk kyohoe chŏndo puin charyojip* [A sourcebook on Bible women in the Korean Christian church] (Seoul: Han'guk kidokkyo yŏksa yon'guso, 1999), 332–33.

for woman" by working as missionaries overseas.[67] Despite the exceptional opportunities both Korean women and women missionaries had in the mission field, as many research studies have demonstrated, both missionary women and Korean Bible women were significantly constrained by a patriarchal church structure that institutionalized gender inequality, which is evidenced in the lack of women in leadership positions, a wide salary gap between men and women workers, and the overall subordinate status of women.[68] The fact that women have long been overlooked or sidelined in the historiography manifests the vastly unequal treatment of women in church history in Korea and the West.[69] These photographs offer a glimpse of their interdependent and shared lives as women who still had to confront the patriarchal organization of church and family and constantly engage in negotiations between the old and the new and between indigenous and foreign ideas and practices.

Conclusion

Photography is often understood as a "scientific" and "trustworthy" reflection of the objects and people captured by the modern instrument, the camera.

---

67 Jane Hunter, *The Gospel of Gentility: American Women Missionaries in Turn-of-the-Century China* (New Haven: Yale University Press, 1984); Patricia R. Hill, *The World Their Household: The American Woman's Foreign Mission Movement and Cultural Transformation, 1870–1920* (Ann Arbor: University of Michigan Press, 1985); Leslie A. Flemming, ed., *Women's Work for Women: Missionaries and Social Change in Asia* (Boulder, Colo.: Westview Press, 1989); and Dana Robert, *American Women in Mission: A Social History of Their Thought and Practice* (Macon, Ga.: Mercer University Press, 1996).

68 Choi, *Gender and Mission Encounters in Korea*, 29–30.

69 A noteworthy effort in recording systematically the history of Korean Christian women was initiated by Han'guk kidokkyo yŏkyŏn'guso yŏsŏngsa yŏn'guhoe. This research group compiled and published biographical notes of Korean Bible women who served in various locations until 1945. See *Han'guk kyohoe chŏndo puin charyojip*. See also Yang Migang, "Ch'amyŏ wa paeje ŭi kwanchŏm esŏ pon chŏndo puin e kwanhan yŏn'gu: 1910-yŏn-1930-yŏndae rŭl chungsim uro" [A study of Bible women in terms of participation and exclusion: From the 1910s to the 1930s], *Han'guk kidokkyo wa yŏksa*, 6 (1997): 139–79; Yang Migang, "Ch'ogi chŏndo puin ŭi sinang kwa hwaltong" [The faith and activities of early Bible women], *Han'guk kidokkyo wa yŏksa*, 2 (1992): 91–109; Yang Hyŏnhye, "Han'guk kaesin'gyo ŭi sŏng ch'abyŏl kujo wa yŏsŏng undong" [The structure of sex discrimination in Korean Protestant Christianity and the women's movement], in *Han'guk yŏsŏng kwa kyohoeron*, ed. Ewha yŏja taehakkyo yŏsŏng sinhak yon'guso (Seoul: Taehan kidokkyosŏhoe, 1998), 200–48. For the lack of attention to women missionaries in the West, Jane Hunter's *The Gospel of Gentility* was the seminal work that stimulated the topic further. See also Sandra Taylor, "Abby M. Colby: The Christian Response to a Sexist Society," *New England Quarterly*, 52, no. 1 (March 1979): 68–79. In this article, Taylor examines the life of Abby M. Colby, a missionary in Japan who spoke up for women's rights.

However, those images captured by the camera are also an expression of a "dynamic field of aesthetic and social relations and contestations."[70] What I have intended in this article is to explore the politics of missionary photography concerning the "objective" and "subjective" projection of images from the Korea mission field—the interplay between "truth-telling" and the "missionary desire" to convey success stories. When tracing the early pictorial images *in relation to* missionary writings, one can readily detect the prevailing worldview in mission photographs that portrays Western and Christian civilization as superior to non-Western societies. However, those photographs also reveal fluid and dynamic interactions between the missionaries and the missionized. Understanding local cultural particularities was both challenging and beneficial to missionaries in approaching and converting local people. The awareness of class distinctions and gender practices in Korea, especially among veteran missionaries, helped them gain better rapport with the locals. The photographs published in mission journals or donated to mission archives reflect these dynamic interactions.

Given the sheer paucity of Korean women's voices in the writing that survives to today, missionary photography also offers a rare glimpse of this group whose lives and history have largely been overlooked in the history of Korean Christianity. To be sure, Korean women converts were not the photographers who could shape, frame, or emphasize certain aspects of their photographic subjects; however, being posed for the camera is not a completely passive activity. Reflecting on his own experience, Roland Barthes argues that "once I feel myself observed by the lens, everything changes: I constitute myself in the process of 'posing,' I instantaneously make another body for myself, I transform myself in advance into an image."[71] In other words, the imminent situation of being captured by the camera can create a moment to "constitute" oneself. In this vein, regardless of the intention of the photographer, the Korean women more readily come to the viewers. Accompanied by particular material culture, they reveal both expected and sometimes unexpected gestures and expressions. It is these unexpected, surprising details of the images that shed light on the depth and complexity of the interactions between Korean women and American women missionaries in the contact zone.

The visual embodiment of Korean women in missionary publications changed over time from a nameless, generic figure to a named (often baptized), contextualized individual and from someone who needed to be rescued from

---

70   Karina Eileraas, "Reframing the Colonial Gaze: Photography, Ownership, and Feminist Resistance," *MLN*, 118 (2003): 807–40 (from 810). See also Sturken and Cartwright, *Practices of Looking*, 16.

71   Barthes, *Camera Lucida*, 10.

FIGURE 13   A postcard from Korea (1903)
From Kwŏn Hyŏkhŭi, *Chosŏn esŏ on sajin yŏpsŏ* [Postcards from Korea] (SEOUL: MINŬMSA, 2005), 87

heathenism to an indispensable co-worker in spreading the gospel. Missionary photography encapsulates the dynamic changes in the Korea mission field, recording not only the simplistic (sometimes mistaken) first impressions but also the highly sophisticated knowledge of Korea that came as missionaries gained more nuanced insights into the intricate cultural and social network in Korea. It often sheds light on the multidirectional interactions between missionaries and Korean women, who found both difficulties in negotiating a different mode of thinking and behavior and opportunities for their own pursuit of evangelical goals or a new sphere of life.

Missionary photography is an expedient analytical tool that adds to our understanding of the dynamic field of the Korea mission because certain visual representations of people or societies overlap with the myriad of material and institutional cultures as well as overt and covert human desires.[72] It tends to open up new areas of research that can fruitfully link the study of Korean Christianity and American missionaries in Korea with a broader cultural and social history of modern Korea. For example, although it is beyond the scope of this article and thus not dealt with here, future research studies may explore

---

72   When W. H. T. Mitchell coined the phrase, the "pictorial turn," he emphasized that it is "not a return to naïve mimesis, copy or correspondence theories of representation" but a "rediscovery of the picture as a complex interplay between visuality, apparatus, institutions, discourse, bodies, and figurality." W. H. T. Mitchell, *Picture theory* (Chicago: University of Chicago Press, 1994), 16.

FIGURE 14
Ewa, the protagonist of W. Arthur Noble's novel *Ewa: A Tale of Korea* (New York: Eaton & Mains, 1906), frontispiece

the intersections of missionary photography and Korean commercial photographic industries. Just as missionaries amassed photos of Korean people, nature, and artifacts for their audience at home, so did Koreans represent Korean customs and people for the viewers overseas. Missionaries borrowed or appropriated some of the commercially successful postcards in their depiction of Korean women. To mention a couple of examples, fig. 8 was originally a postcard produced in 1903 and sent to Paris. The photo was meant to show a typical Korean woman with *changot*, a body-covering cloth that women used as a sign of proper woman when they were in public space. The same photo, however, was titled, "Ready for Church," when it was published in a mission journal in 1906 (fig. 13). Another example is found in a book titled *Ewa: A Tale of Korea*, authored by W. Arthur Noble.[73] The author includes what is supposed to be a photo of the female protagonist of the novel (fig. 14). However, the image is actually one of the most widely circulated *kisaeng* (woman entertainer) postcards (fig. 15), and Ewa is not a *kisaeng* in the story.[74] Modern photographs

73 W. Arthur Noble, *Ewa: A Tale of Korea* (New York: Eaton & Mains, 1906).
74 Yi Kyŏngmin, *Kisaeng ŭn ŏttŏk'e mandŭrŏ chyŏnnŭn'ga: kŭndae kisaeng ŭi t'ansaeng kwa p'yosang konggan* [How was kisaeng created: The birth of modern kisaeng and the representational space] (Seoul: Sajin Ak'aibŭ Yŏnguso, 2005), 46–47. For an analysis of the novel, Ewa, see Hyaeweol Choi, "(En)Gendering a New Nation in Missionary Discourse: An Analysis of W. Arthur Noble's *Ewa*," *Korea Journal*, 46, no. 1 (2006): 139–69.

FIGURE 15
Widely circulated postcard image of a Korean woman entertainer (*kisaeng*)
From Yi Kyŏngmin, *Kisaeng ŭn ŏttŏk'e mandŭro chyŏnnŭn'ga: kŭndae kisaeng ŭi t'ansaeng kwa p'yosang konggan* [How was the kisaeng created: The birth of the modern kisaeng and the representational space] (SEOUL: SAJIN AK'AIBU YŎN'GUSO), 46–47

produced for commercial purposes were deployed by Koreans and then appropriated by missionaries.

This article is intended as an exploratory attempt to emphasize the role of missionary photography as a rich reservoir in enhancing our understanding of Christian mission history by deploying both discursive and visual materials and interpreting the tensions between the two as well as complementary roles. Photographic images can serve as a powerful supplement, or perhaps an alternative, to missionary discourse as they reveal what is visible, obvious, and intended but also hidden, ambiguous, and unintended.

Notes

I would like to express my sincere appreciation to two reviewers for their insightful comments that helped me clarify and strengthen my argument. The present article is based on a paper I presented at the Association for Asian Studies in 2009. I would like to thank Donald Clark for inviting me to join the panel to explore the topic of missionary photography. Timothy Lee, as the discussant of the panel, provided me with astute comments that enabled me to rethink some of the major issues. Lastly, I greatly benefited from a highly stimulating discussion with Nancy Abelmann and graduate students at the University of Illinois during a visit to their campus.

On Using Historical Missionary Photographs in Modern Discussion

Paul Jenkins

Missionaries' history as creators and users of photographs is not the least of the surprises with which our surprising ancestors can electrify us. As late as the 1980s the existence of mission photography as a major source for historical studies was more or less unknown, even to experts in mission history. But now we know that even before the industrial production of ready-to-use film, when photography was truly an craft involving many uncertain manipulations of chemicals by hand, some missionaries were using cameras thousands of kilometres and many weeks' transport from the industrial base which made photography possible, and developing their negatives in primitive dark-rooms under thatched roofs. At the moment the first person I know of who took photographs in a mission context was William Ellis, an LMS representative in Madagascar in 1852. By the 1860s all the signs I have seen are that the then functioning missionary societies had members of staff who were taking photographs—this certainly applies, in the German-speaking world, to the Barmen, Basel, and Bremen Missions. The result is that large numbers of photographs still exist from the half century before the First World War, if one sets out to look for them, and if one not only looks for photographic prints but also for the engravings based on photographs published in mission periodicals. In Basel it turned out that of the 50,000 images we hold in the archive for the period 1860–1945, something in the region of 14,000 date back to before 1914. And one must look for holdings of mission photography outside mission head-quarters, too. The energetic organisers of an exhibition of missionary photographs at the Landeskirchliches Archiv in Ludwigsburg located a surprising number of albums of missionary photographs from this period still in private hands in south-western Germany.[1] Judging by the photographs displayed in Nos surprenants ancêtres the Swiss Mission in South Africa and Mozambique

---

Source: Jenkins, P., "On Using Historical Missionary Photographs in Modern Discussion," *Le Fait Missionnaire* 10.1 (2001): pp. 71–89.

---

1   See the exhibition catalogue Der ferne Nächste, Bilder der Mission, Mission der Bilder, 1860–1920, 233 p.

© KONINKLIJKE BRILL NV, LEIDEN, 2021 | DOI:10.1163/9789004399587_015

followed this trend too. It applied itself early in its history to the use of photography in communications.

But is it really surprising that missionaries took photographs? And are their photographs in themselves surprising? It is, of course, possible to create a mental framework which minimises the impact of the rediscovery of missionary photography on our actual attitude to the history of missions in their overseas environments. Sceptical voices from the secular world have been heard arguing that Missions have a major concern with cash-flow in the regions which support them. They go on to argue that photographs were primarily taken to support missionary fund-raising activities at home. Implicit in this argument is the assertion that a missionary society has a clear editorial policy aimed at maximising support (and not primarily at communicating knowledge or experience "from abroad"), and that it is in a position to communicate this policy to its overseas workers who then take the appropriate photographs (and do not waste financial resources or personal energy taking other kinds of photograph).

People with experience of missionary societies may, in their turn, be sceptical about their ever having had such a stream-lined, clear-sighted organisation. And I maintain that there are enough indications available to make us pay careful attention to the possibility of other major missionary motivations when taking photographs. There were missionaries who found non-western cultures fascinating and whose photography reflects, perhaps, a greater freedom to pursue this interest than did their verbal reports to the guardians of orthodoxy at home. And there were missionaries whose quality of close relationships with their non-christian neighbours also, as the German-American anthropologist Christraud Geary has remarked, resulted in photographs of a rare intimacy—and, one might add, anthropological accuracy—despite the racial and cultural barriers erected by the colonial world.[2]

Truly incorporating photographs in discourse about the past—truly, in other words, exploring the surprises they can offer us—requires us, however, to amplify and retool both the way we look at photographs and the way we construct that discourse. And at the moment the Mission House in Basel is one of the places where one can sense how true that statement is. Thanks to a number of Basel and international foundations we have been able to carry through a careful pilot project with 28,000 photographs designed to enhance radically

---

2 Geary, Christaud, Images from Bamum: German Colonial Photography at the Court of King Njoya, Washington, 1988, 151 p.

ON USING HISTORICAL MISSIONARY PHOTOGRAPHS 257

standards of conservation and access.[3] From the point of view of this essay the important part of the project is that devoted to access, i.e. the development of a database to enable us to find photographs, and the experiences we have had while making increasingly close and detailed examination of individual photographs or groups of photographs. The central point is the importance which must be attached to defining the moment when a photograph was taken, i.e. answering the questions when it was taken, where, by whom, and of what or whom. These questions are not necessarily going to be answerable in respect of any specific photograph. But even in the worst case they sharpen our sense of ignorance. And as time has gone by in Basel we have experienced with many photographs how our analyses can become progressively deeper and more cogent by paying attention to these basic questions, and setting up thereby a dialectic relating a photograph to what, in its broadest sense, can be called its documentation.[4] The results show a mission and indigenous church history which gains new dimensions by incorporating visual sources in its discourses. But clearly, beyond that, lies the possibility of recapturing dimensions in the history of environing societies and cultures which our sources so far have not been able to display.

The two examples offered in this short essay illustrate these two aspects of the use of photographs in historical analysis. They also demonstrate the use of photographs in different levels of analysis, the first being a more simply academic analysis, the second linked to work in adult education (German: Bildung).

• • •

The first photograph looks too simple to be much of a surprise when incorporated in historical discourse. It shows an African family wearing predominantly European clothes—a much photographed theme in colonial photography. Its caption refers to it as a portrait of the family of the Ghanaian Basel Mission

---

3　We have published an illustrated final report on this project: Frey-Näf, Barbara & Jenkins, Paul, Arresting Entropy Enabling New Synthesis—Conservation, Access and the Photographic Record of the Basel Mission 1850–1945. Final Report of a Project 1990–1998, Basel, 1999, 36 p.

4　In work on our collection "documentation" includes the original caption given to the image, any old annotations on its mount, and information from any historical registers we may hold on a specific group of photographs. "Documentation" also refers, however, to information generated by modern cataloguers, including conclusions they may reach (not least through comparing and networking photographs with more and less adequate original documentation) as to when and where a photograph was taken, and who or what it depicts.

pastor Simeon Koranteng, who was active over the years c. 1870 to c. 1910. The actual German expression used to describe Simeon Koranteng in the original Mission caption is Negerpastor, with its clear implication, in the pre-1914 German colonial framework, of second-grade people and second-grade professionals with a European title, but nevertheless needing the tutelage of nicht-neger—white—superiors. The picture's caption, in other words, incorporates this group into the world of hierarchical, colonial mission, but also into a world easily accessible to the picture's viewers in Europe. The profession of pastor, the implied status of pastor's wife, and the existence of a pastor's family were all phenomena known to every village protestant who might have seen this photograph. Having been told who these people are, someone looking at this photograph in Europe sensed no need of further information about them. Instead the use of the adjective neger makes them not only an example of a familiar category, but creates a—for the European—comfortable feeling that superiority is on his side and dependence on the other. Nothing in the image itself demands immediately that we look for other approaches. A reading very sensitive to signs that a non-western culture has influenced the picture may raise some questions, as we shall see. But the carefully suited pastor and the European-style clothing of the children—worn in spite of an equatorial climate—seem to confirm this picture of a family living in a wholly mission-dominated and Europeanised context.

We can only answer the question as to when this photograph was taken approximately—probably in the early years of the 20th century. The question where leads us to the certainty that it was taken in one of the towns of the traditional southern Ghanaian state of Akwapim, and probably in the state capital, Akropong, the site of the oldest Basel Mission inland station in Ghana (started 1835, restarted 1842). The question by whom can be answered with considerable certainty—by a Basel Mission doctor named Rudolf Fisch. But it is the answer to the question of whom which radically changes the orientation of our analysis. The answer is based not on mission sources, but on correlative information on this family especially from non-mission sources—although it has to be added that this information can also be found in the Basel Mission archive, but has been largely laid to rest and "forgotten" by the Basel Mission, and also by most of the Ghanaian parties involved in the situation we now describe.[5]

---

5   The essay which brought Akua Oye/Amelia Koranteng to the focus of attention again was Gilbert, Michelle, "The Cimmerian Darkness of Intrigue. Queen Mothers, Christianity and Truth in Akuapem History", Journal of Religion in Africa, 1993, pp. 2–43.

FIGURE 1 The Black Pastor [German: *Negerpastor*] Koranteng and his family
PHOTOGRAPHER: RUDOLPH FRISCH, PROBABLY IN AKROPONG, C. 1900. BASEL MISSION ARCHIVE, REF. NO D-3.11.018

The pastor's wife depicted in this photograph turns out to have had two roles in life, and not one—and correspondingly two names, not merely one. She was, on the one side, Amelia Koranteng, pastor's wife. But she was also, in the years around 1900, the Queen Mother of Akwapim—the female head of the royal family, and in some important ways female head of the kingdom. She was the Ohemaa Akua Oye.

My theme is not least the importance of the basic documentation about where, when, etc., when analysing a photograph and incorporating it as source in historical discourse. This image offers us food for thought. Firstly, it very quickly becomes clear that this new information changes the way we perceive the photograph. A point which some people notice spontaneously is that it is the matriarch who sits at the centre of the group, and not the patriarch. And the children group themselves around her, almost to the exclusion of him. This becomes much more than merely a matter of chance when we know that Mrs Koranteng held high political office when this picture was taken, and that in this matrilineal setting the children (surely grandchildren, or nieces and nephews reckoned matrilineally) gained their inherited status from her, and not from him. Secondly, however, although this single photograph may seem to weigh little against the massed message of Ghanaian oral tradition and the Basel Mission's own self-image in relation to traditional culture, it can well serve as the grain of sand in the oyster which produces a large pearl of unusual, but very persuasive colour. In other words knowing the status of the pastor's wife and having seen that one can read the photograph "from her angle" gives the image a weight which should lead to changes in the current of established historical discourse about the Basel Mission and its successor church in Ghana.

One may start with the photographer. Rudolf Fisch was a missionary doctor who believed that western medicine must have the authority to determine how people responded to illness and infection. He was a puritan and crusading missionary—one of the many missionaries who, in spite of a preparedness to learn the Twi language, nevertheless acted as if traditional culture in southern Ghana would and should die away.[6] He will almost certainly have been someone who believed that the Koranteng family should ideally be seen exclusively in the context of Simeon Koranteng's position in the Church and the Basel Mission's rules for family life. But in spite of this his portrait of the family has Mrs Koranteng—Akua Oye—at the centre. Something—presumably the power of Mrs Koranteng's character and the way the Korantengs handled their double status—brought Rudolf Fisch to take a photograph at variance with his fundamental beliefs and perceptions. This speaks to me of the categorical need in the Basel Mission Church in Ghana at the beginning of the last century to respect and be in dialogue with other—indigenous—systems of organisation and status. Nothing in the Mission's self-portraiture in its literature from the colonial period prepares me for this. This photograph by itself has the impact of raising serious questions about the accuracy of the general traditional picture of the Basel Mission in Ghana before World War One—i.e. as having pursued an uncompromising course in building up christian communities with no reference to existing cultural forms.

The photograph also, of course, has—complementarily to its significance for Basel Mission history—importance as a source for the church history of the kingdom of Akwapim. Outsiders interested in African church history (especially outsiders interested in women's history....) will find their surprise with this photograph not least in the way Akua Oye/Amelia Koranteng was, as it

---

6   There is an excellent broad-focussed biography of Rudolf Fisch: Fischer, Friedrich Hermann, Der Missionsarzt Rudolf Fisch und die Anfänge medizinischer Arbeit der Basler Mission an der Goldküste (Ghana), Herzogenrath, 1991, 585 p.

were, filed and forgotten decades ago. The reasons for this rapidly become apparent. In the years around 1900 Akua Oye was at the centre of bitter controversy in the kingdom. And the church has never come to terms with the existence of large numbers of traditional office holders who are sincere christians but placed under church discipline because of their participation in traditional rites of ancestor veneration. Investigations of recent Akwapim history working with oral tradition in the 1970s and 1980s seemed to be being told that Akua Oye was not a rightful Queen Mother. Indeed, after performing strongly in a constitutional crisis in the kingdom in the early 20th century, in which she played a key role in destooling a reigning chief and enstooling one of her own sons, Akua Oye later seems to have lost her position as Queen Mother as the pendulum of general support swung away from her sons to other branches of the royal family. At that stage a ruling which she had been able to obtain when she was elected Queen Mother—that she could delegate a non-christian relative to participate in rites in which she as a christian could not carry out without coming under church discipline—became a fatal source of weakness in traditional politics. Her opponents could claim that her delegate, and not Akua Oye herself, was the "real" Queen Mother. In this context the existence of this photograph, the information additional to the old mission documentation which I have considered here, and the portrait we seem to be seeing of a strong personality with determination and inner power, all point to the need to unroll the history of Akua Oye again. At a simple level it would be interesting to know what the "facts" about her really were. And does she, indeed, appear anonymously in other photographs? At a more complicated level it is clear that Akwapim does have an indigenous church history. And knowing about Akua Oye is a very quick step to seeing that this history is complex and in no sense simply a history of institutions and office-holders which can be understood purely and exclusively in western ecclesiastical terms.

• • •

If the analysis of the last photograph was an example of the way answering fundamental questions about the moment the photograph was taken transforms our reading of its contents and significance, the next group of photographs have, perhaps, more diffuse lessons to teach. I describe and analyse here not least the use which I have made of them in adult education. As we shall see they prompt one to raise a quite acute question as to the traditionality of a certain "traditional" object in Ghanaian life. I comment on them here in order to show something of the potential these sources have in promoting a tight dialectic between a discourse/discussion which can develop quite original ideas,

FIGURE 2   Fritz Ramseyer speaking to the Chief of Obomeng, Ghana, and his people. Between 1888 and 1896.
PHOTOGRAPHER: F. RAMSEYER (WITH DELAYED-ACTION SHUTTER). BASEL MISSION ARCHIVE. REF. NO QD-30.043-0042

the photographs themselves, and an increasingly accurate understanding of local indigenous history.

First of all, at a general level the when-, where-, by whom- and of whom- questions relating to the group of three old photographs which I present can be answered quite concretely. They were all taken in or near the small Ghanaian town of Obomeng, up on the Kwahu scarp, between 1888 and 1895. The first photograph shows a missionary, Fritz Ramseyer, addressing a chief whose name we know—Abankwa—and his court. The second shows a close-up of the chief and the people immediately around him on that same occasion. The third picture portrays his servants, grouped by the photographer to show off their symbols of office, or rather the objects which each of them is responsible for keeping and using, and which demonstrate the majesty, power and wealth of the chief. The photographs are regarded as having been taken by Ramseyer himself. Certainly the photos were taken with his equipment, and he will have either taken the first one by delayed-action shutter or by having someone, presumably on his staff, to activate the shutter.

Adult education groups in Basel invariably start their analysis with the figure of the missionary, when presented with pictures like these. The missionary, with his right-hand index finger raised in warning, is a figure many modern viewers heartily detest and they see in him a symbol for old-fashioned

ON USING HISTORICAL MISSIONARY PHOTOGRAPHS

mission's quite illegitimate attempt to impose its world-view on other people and, even confronted with this picture, see mission as, in some indeterminate way, destroying traditional culture. My strategy as tutor is to raise the possibility that the missionary is not having everything his own way in this photograph. We can start with etiquette. The missionary stands to speak, the chief is sitting.

This corresponds with traditional etiquette in an Akan chief's court. Furthermore the missionary will probably take a seat after he has finished speaking (on his box in the left foreground). At this very elementary level the missionary is not dominating and structuring the situation. He is bowing to traditional etiquette, and in what we see as traditional etiquette in the Ghana of the second half of the twentieth century he does not have the last word either. A "linguist" of the court will stand and summarise his words and communicate them to the chief and people. The same, or a similar, official will later formulate a response and communicate it to the missionary after some discussion. It may well include questions and objections related to the intellectual content of the sermon, if the missionary has been preaching. The event may have had other major concerns, of course, like the missionary's search for land to build a church, or the chief's desire to have a school and a teacher in his town. But whatever the themes which were handled there will have been, in effect, a dialogue between the two sides, and no missionary monologue. At issue here is an important point: fundamentally such assemblies are to be seen as one major root of the indigenous church developing from sustained indigenous interest. It is most important not unthinkingly to perpetuate a picture of missionary dominance which the missionaries of that time liked to propagate.

Trying to reinforce this picture of an active indigenous involvement in the scene being played out here is not necessarily easy, however. One problem is Abankwa's top hat, which is frequently seen as a sign that he no longer lives his culture in a pure form, but has been corrupted by contact with Europe into accepting aspects of the late nineteenth century version of European consumer culture. The reply to that is fairly simple—that this particular African culture—Akan culture—has grown up in trading contact with Europe since the 15th century, and in some ways is a response to the presence of European trading posts on the coast. European objects have been absorbed into indigenous status systems. The hat should be seen as having been co-opted into indigenous culture rather than as a symbol of Abankwa's alienation.

But it is important to help viewers of such photographs to develop their own inner discussion about the non-western aspects of what is on show—the massed men (no, or hardly any, women) and the many objects on display—state swords, tobacco pipes, golden discs on the chests of certain specific office holders, drums, weapons, stools, etc.

FIGURE 3
The Chief of Obomeng in close-up (on the same occasion as Photograph 2)
BASEL MISSION ARCHIVE, REF. NO QD-30.043-0041

From this point of view the group portrait of the chief's servants with their symbols of power and majesty is a great gift. It enables people to see and understand for themselves what I mean when I say that a chiefdom like that of Obomeng is partly a system for concentrating the surplus above pure subsistence achieved by the population and turning it into instruments of chiefly policy. The photograph is impressive in demonstrating how many different objects, clearly beautiful in themselves and the products of non-European craftsmanship a chief like Abankwa could gather around him. Indeed, the display is all the more impressive when one knows that in the chiefly hierarchy in Kwahu the Obomenghene is in the third rank—he is neither the local King nor a so-called "wing chief", but traditionally subordinate to his neighbour, the chief of Obo, head of one of the "wings" of the Kwahu army. I suspect that this photograph is evidence of inter-chiefly competition in display, and that the Obomenghene was making a bid, with this display, to enhanced status. But people looking at these photographs and are usually prepared ultimately

FIGURE 4   The Chief of Obomeng's servants, with the symbols of majesty and chiefly rule. Details as Photograph 2
BASEL MISSION ARCHIVE, REF. NO QD-30.043-0043

to develop their own understanding of the way a chief's court like this really represents the peak of indigenous civilisation and culture in this part of Africa.

The argument, trying to use photographs like this to recall the active roles of indigenous people in discussions with missionary, moves now to a different plane. If a chief's court is the peak of indigenous civilisation in terms of material objects, it is also the peak of indigenous civilisation in terms of invisible values like rhetoric, eloquence, and knowledge of the indigenous history and religion/philosophy specific to this region. I argue, with photographs like this before me, that African societies value(d) gifted people. One gift warmly acknowledged in Ghana is the gift of eloquence, of being able to speak well and wittily, and having the power to persuade people, of being able to use knowledge of the cultural resources—history, proverbs—needed to convince people. In an Akan chief's court the office of "linguist" (Twi: okyeame) is tailor-made for someone with these gifts. He speaks for the chief, and he interprets for chief and court the messages being brought in by outsiders. I was brought to this view of photographs 2–4 by the results of a group discussion about this matter during a History Workshop in Stuttgart in the mid-1990s. The group who analysed the photograph included a couple of Ghanaians. It decided to present its results in improvised theatre. The Ghanaians were careful to make sure that those naive and inexperienced Europeans had walk-on parts only—they were made members of the body-guard. The one who owned a hat was made the non-speaking chief for the day, etc. One Ghanaian played the missionary, and another the okyeame. The two created a wonderful chapter of misunderstanding as the missionary preached his complicated message, clearly puzzled by the okyeame's attempts to clarify it by questions ... At any rate for them it was axiomatic that an okyeame will have been present on his occasion and will have taken a central role in proceedings.

At this point I have to admit how slow-moving and imponderable my brain is when working with photographs. The idea of the okyeame and his skills as being a peak of invisible values in Akan culture pleased me, and I have used it frequently in talking about photographs like those preproduced here from Obomeng. It was not until I visited Ghana in the summer of 1999 that I realised that this interpretation has to face a major problem: where, indeed, is the okyeame on these photographs of Abankwa and his court around the year 1900? It is not difficult to see why the question came up when I visited Ghana. I was present at a Durbar in Kwahu—in the mission house compound in Abetifi. The King of Kwahu and many chiefs were present.[7] Large numbers of linguists were also present, escorting their chiefs, and holding their staffs of office (see picture 5). None of the Kwahu photographs taken by Ramseyer, and they include a number of other shots of chiefs' courts, includes anything like the modern linguist's staffs carved of wood and covered with gold leaf. Almost certainly my analysis of the importance of a linguist in the discussion between Ramseyer and Abankwa, and the other Kwahu chiefs, is correct. But the linguist is probably the man squatting on Abankwa's right, holding a staff at the bottom which Abankwa himself is grasping at the top. Both his posture and his staff are, in my experience, unknown in a modern chief's court. Photographs in this case can not only provide a stimulating basis for a historical discussion in general terms. They can document changes in matters which, in indigenous oral discourse, are regarded as "traditional" and "unchanging". They can, in this sense, help to recapture the African past for discussions of historical dynamics.

The question may very well be posed in general terms: what is, or will be, the contribution of historical mission photographs to historical discussion in general? And what does a photograph offer us as a historical source, which a detailed word description of the same object or situation could not communicate? But it is almost impossible to answer these questions at this level of generalisation—there are so many historical discourses, so infinitely many

---

7   August 1999.

FIGURE 5
A massed array of linguists and their carved staffs on the Mission station, Abefiti, August 1999. They are seated to the right of the King, whose umbrella would have been visible at the top of this photograph if it had been taken as general view.
PHOTOGRAPHER:
ROSMARIE TSCHUDIN

themes which historians may come to deal with that the only appropriate answer here is "go and see for yourself".

Adam Jones, Professor of African History in the University of Leipzig, pressed me on this sort of issue recently, and the points I made on that occasion do perhaps, nevertheless bear repeating.[8] The photograph under discussion showed a group of Ghanaian woman teachers of the Basel Mission c. 1890, wearing what we nowadays regard as "traditional clothing". It was immediately clear with that example that very detailed word descriptions might have been possible of the women, their clothing, their jewellery, and the posture with which they model their clothes. But in practice such verbal descriptions scarcely exist in

---

8 Adam Jones deserves to be better known among missiologists than he is. For many years his work as a general historian on our search for sources for West African history has kept a careful eye on documents originating with missions and indigenous churches. In recent years he has directed a project financed by the Volkswagenstiftung to improve indexing and organisation of the Africa holdings in the mission house archive in Leipzig, and in the central Moravian archive in Herrnhut.

the Basel Mission archive, probably not least because the missionaries had no command of the specialist professional vocabulary which such descriptions usually demand. Thus we can say with confidence that historical photographs are sources of major importance as soon as something needs to be discussed where the visible exterior plays a major part in its general importance, or in its incorporation in historical discourse.

It is also clear with the Basel experience that photography documents matters which are often marginal to the main thrust of our traditional sources, or regarded as unimportant by them—and that this documentation exists at a level which facilitates deep analysis. I am thinking here of an example like the documentation of the use of wooden shingles for roofing in southern Ghana after the missionaries had introduced this roofing technique. This whole episode in Ghanaian architectural history is very inadequately documented in written sources, but roofs and ceilings are typically shown on the upper edges of photographs—features of a scene which appear by accident, or almost by accident. Or again: one of the most pressing needs at the moment in African History and in African Church History can be answered in the same sort of way—the need for sources about women. Of our c. 5,000 photographs from Ghana naturally far more than 50% show portraits of, or scenes involving, women. Investigating when and where you see them (and when and where you do not, as in these group portraits of chiefs' courts from Kwahu), what they are doing, how they are grouped, what they are wearing, etc., offers a major possibility of extending the sources available on women's history in and around mission stations.

A last point: as historian and archivist my strong tendency is to see photographs and their documentation as documents which can be incorporated in historical discourse. Even this is not uncomplicated: learning how to incorporate quite new kinds of material in forms of discourse still dominated by the analysis of word-sources is, as I have tried to show in this essay, an interesting but demanding activity.

Beyond this rather academic discussion, however, we also have to do with the whole question of the role of photographs in the modern world—as objects which many people use to confirm their identities and reflect their longings, and as objects which journalists and advertisers use to guide and manipulate public opinion. In other words, work with many of our photographs involves struggling against the first-world reading of such images which is widespread and reliable enough for advertisers to plan it into the reactions they can expect their images to have. In this sense adequate work with these photographs involves going through a kind of "school for seeing", or experiencing a transformation in the way we look at them. So work with historical photographs is not (only!) a pleasant niche for the nostalgic. Properly handled holdings of historical mission photographs can clarify intercultural communications, especially in terms of opening up new lines of analysis and experience. As I have tried to show in this essay, the style of photographic analysis developing around the collection of old mission photographs in Basel is closely meshed with the attempt to engage with the degree of otherness in non-European cultures whose order of magnitude is consistently underestimated here.

The Anthropology of Christianity:
Unity, Diversity, New Directions
An Introduction to Supplement 10

Joel Robbins

Sometimes one would like the chance to begin an article twice. This is one of those times. It is one of those times because I would like to begin by saying that the anthropology of Christianity is 15 years old, and then I would like to go on to make a point about what it means for an area of academic study to be that age. But I know from long experience that I cannot begin quite this way, because as soon as I say the anthropology of Christianity is about 15 years old, I have to pause to defend this claim against those who argue that it is much older—if not as old as the discipline of anthropology itself, then at least as old as the first ethnographic writings focused on Christian groups. And once I pause to make that point and address it in the detail it deserves, I have lost any momentum my argument about what it means to be a 15-year-old area of study might have had. So what I would like to do at this point is announce that in the section that immediately follows I will make an argument about why it is reasonable to claim the anthropology of Christianity is roughly 15 years old. And then I would like to be allowed to begin this opening section again with the assertion that it is.

The anthropology of Christianity is roughly 15 years old. In academic years (to be understood here on something like the model of "dog years"), this turns out to be middle-aged. The image of middle age fits the contemporary anthropology of Christianity in several senses. It has gone from being an upstart to being respectable (at least in many quarters); it is less interested in picking fights with more established anthropological programs than it once was; and it is possessed of a rapidly maturing second generation, the members of which have never been part of a discipline of anthropology that did not pay a good deal of attention to Christianity. But one sense in which the image of middle

---

Source: Robbins, J., "The Anthropology of Christianity: Unity, Diversity, New Directions. An Introduction to Supplement 10," *Current Anthropology* 55.10 (2014): pp. 157–171. Copyright © 2014 by University of Chicago Press.

age is perhaps slightly inappropriate when applied to a 15-year-old academic trend such as the anthropology of Christianity is that many anthropological movements never make it much past this age. Often enough, by the time a given anthropological enthusiasm reaches 15 years of age, it is well on its way out of the center of disciplinary attention. Middle age, then, is at once a satisfying and worrisome time for any would-be intellectual movement, at least in an academic field as mobile as sociocultural anthropology.

This issue, like the conference from which it sprang, has been designed both to take advantage of the middle-aged situation in which the anthropology of Christianity finds itself and to consider some of the dangers that come with reaching this point. At the most general level, the issue's goals are twofold. On the one hand, it aims to assess what the anthropology of Christianity has accomplished in terms of producing new ethnographic materials and new theoretical arguments and to ask what novel developments in these areas might be on the horizon as a second generation of scholars, some junior and some more senior but moving in from other anthropological areas, begins to produce significant work. On the other hand, in a more reflexive mood, it aims to assess whether the anthropology of Christianity as a "movement" or "trend" or "subfield" or however it might best be described ought to continue to develop in the way it has—as something that for at least some of those who have contributed to it has been a self-conscious collective project—or whether the time has perhaps arrived for it to become something more diffuse, as arguably happens to most successful middle-aged anthropological developments once scholars who once framed much of their work in trend-relevant terms begin to take as background knowledge much of what they have learned from being part of a growing movement and go on to pursue new questions.

From the start, then, this issue has been conceived both as a forum for the presentation of the empirical and theoretical results of some current anthropological research on Christianity and as an opportunity to reflect on the anthropology of Christianity as a phenomenon within anthropology. As the issue has turned out, the articles it collects are for the most part explicitly engaged in the first of these goals: presenting new developments in the anthropological study of Christianity. A few of the authors were tasked by the original conference plan with taking up now established themes in the anthropology of Christianity, such as those involving materiality, cultural change, and the nature of religious experience. Others were asked to engage with a host of emergent concerns, including schism and the nature of Christian social organization, gender, space, and how anthropologists might study religious (and nonreligious) practices at the boundaries of Christianity. In taking up both kinds of topics, contributors have understandably focused on making new arguments and presenting new research materials, and with few exceptions the reflexive side of the design of the conference has been set aside.

Yet even as the articles in this issue are mostly focused on the presentation of new ethnographic and historical materials and new theoretical arguments concerning Christianity, the conference discussions themselves were, as planned, also rich in reflexive discussions concerning the nature of the anthropology of Christianity as a project, its past, and its potential future viability. In this introduction, I will take up issues belonging to these reflexive kinds of discussions, drawing on themes that emerged at the conference and those that have been raised in the broader anthropological literature on the anthropology of Christianity. I will also consider several of the most important theoretical and empirical developments charted in these articles, arguing on the basis of these developments that the anthropology of Christianity is perhaps set to transform itself in important ways that might justify it hanging around for at least one more turn around the very fast track of live anthropological concerns. First, though, by way of introducing the anthropology of Christianity and situating it in relation to other developments both within and outside of anthropology, I want to return to the question of how old this trend might reasonably be said to be.

Where Did the Anthropology of Christianity Come from, and How Old Is It?

Having already made much of the age of the anthropology of Christianity and having noted that this is controversial topic, it makes sense to begin my discussion of critical questions bearing on the history, status, and possible future of this area of research by taking up the question of how old it really is. On the face of things, the case for suggesting that the anthropology of Christianity is more or less a child of the new millennium is not hard to make. The appearance in 2003 and 2006 of two edited collections entitled *The Anthropology of Christianity*, one edited by myself (Robbins 2003*a*) and the other by Fenella Cannell (2006*a*), and the publication also in 2006 of a volume edited by Matthew Engelke and Matt Tomlinson entitled *The Limits of Meaning: Case Studies in the Anthropology of Christianity*, might be taken as marking something of a watershed (and, indeed, these works have often been treated together in something like these terms in subsequent discussions, such as Barker 2008; Hann 2007; Jenkins 2012; McDougall 2009*b*). The editors of all three volumes claim that, at the time they were writing, the anthropology of Christianity was something new and that anthropologists had in the past largely ignored the study of Christianity, at least relative to the attention they had paid to other religious traditions, including other world religions. Furthermore, by the time these volumes appeared, many of those scholars who would become important figures in the early years of the anthropology of Christianity had already begun working in this area, and quite a few of them were numbered among the volumes' contributors. And, finally, few will dispute that by around 2010 anthropological work on Christianity had begun to appear in such quantity that it came to occupy a position of prominence in the discipline of a kind it never had before. The appearance of these volumes in rapid succession, then, along with exponential growth in the number of publications focused on Christianity that began around the time that they appeared, all contribute to the plausibility of the claim that the anthropology of Christianity arose as a new development in the early years of this century (for a review of some of the literature from this early period, see Bialecki et al. 2008).

Yet in spite of how easy it is to make a case that something new was afoot about 15 years ago, in casual conversation, and certainly in the peer review process, those who assert that the anthropology of Christianity is a recent arrival are familiar with the retort that in fact there is nothing new about it. Anthropologists, the argument goes, have been producing work on Christians for a very long time. From anthropological work on African Independent Churches that has been growing apace since the 1960s (Fernandez 1978) to studies of European communities in which Christianity is the dominant religion, there are many ethnographic works focused on Christian populations that appeared well before the alleged rise of the anthropology of Christianity. Moreover, Edith and Victor Turner had published high-profile work on Christian pilgrimage by 1978 (see Coleman 2014), several edited volumes focused on ethnographic studies of Christianity had been published near the end of the 1980s (Barker 1990; James and Johnson 1988; Saunders 1988), Jean and John Comaroff had published the first volume of their highly influential study of missionization among the South African Tswana in 1991, and Robert Hefner had published an important edited book focused on the study of conversion to Christianity in 1993. In light of observations of this kind, Chris Hann (2007:394) has given published voice to the widespread concern that long before what some consider a new "anthropology of Christianity" began to emerge, there already existed a "far from inconsequential corpus" devoted to this topic (see also Chua 2012; Comaroff 2010).

How, then, to settle the question of origins? In some respects, where one comes down on the question of whether the anthropology of Christianity appeared as something new in the early 2000s is going to be a matter of interpretation. Some people are allergic to finding breaks in history or are at least very cautious about doing so, and the historical record is generally complex enough to sustain at least some kind of argument that there is never anything new under the sun (a fact that should teach us something important about the nature of processes of even rapid social and cultural change). I remember one very prominent senior anthropologist telling me in the mid-1990s that the whole notion of globalization was nothing new. After all, he pointed out, anthropologists had been studying diffusion and acculturation for a long time. For someone of this cast of mind, it is unlikely that counterarguments that something new has in fact emerged will carry much weight. And more than this, given how important the theme of discontinuity and change has been in the anthropology of Christianity (see below), it is possible that those who are involved in studying at least some forms of the Christian tradition are predisposed to find themselves on the side of those who tend to see new things emerging whenever they can. If this is true, perhaps even in matters of their own historical experience they cannot be counted as reliable witnesses when they claim to have lived through a more or less sharp intellectual break with what came before.

Yet even taking into account the difficulty of settling on appropriate grounds for deciding whether the anthropology of Christianity is really something new, it remains the case that several interesting and important questions arise if one argues that it is, and perhaps in intellectually pragmatic terms this makes its novelty worth positing. I would like to examine two of these questions here. The first question takes up the issue of the sense in which the anthropology of Christianity might be said to be new. If there have long existed at least some ethnographic studies of Christian populations, what is new about the work on Christianity that began to be published around the turn of the millennium, beyond the simple fact that it is appearing in much greater quantity than it was before? At least one important answer to this question is that the authors of this work were consistently self-conscious in several respects about what they were doing (Jenkins 2012: 462). They were, for example, self-conscious that they were trying to get scholars working on Christianity to talk across boundaries of theoretical emphasis and regional ethnographic focus (see, e.g., Robbins

2003c). They were self-conscious about trying to use the vantage point provided by ethnographic work on Christians to push anthropological theory in new directions (e.g., Tomlinson and Engelke 2006). And they were self-conscious in exploring the ways anthropology as a discipline has been profoundly shaped by the Christian tradition (Cannell 2005, 2006b). Further, all of them were self-conscious about trying to explain why, at least as they saw it, anthropologists had relatively neglected Christianity in the past. To borrow terms I had used in my own first piece on the anthropology of Christianity, from the start, the current wave of the anthropology of Christianity has not been a matter of something that has happened simply "in itself"; it has also happened "for itself" as a deliberate effort to move the study of Christianity closer to the center of anthropological concern while at the same time constantly interrogating what this move might mean for the development of anthropology as a field (Robbins 2003c). Or, as Debra McDougall (2009b:168) has more recently put it, anthropologists have responded to Cannell's (2006b:1) crucial early question of "What difference does Christianity make?" by "considering not only what difference it makes to believers but also what difference it makes to anthropology."

The second question we can ask if we assume that there is something new about the recent anthropology of Christianity—something that I have argued at least minimally consists in the self-conscious quality with which it approaches itself as a kind of anthropology—is why it happened when it did. Why did anthropologists begin to pay much more attention to Christianity around the year 2000, and why did they feel that the fact that they were doing so was of some significance to anthropology? In an early piece that represents a remarkable feat of writing intellectual history as it happens, Bronwen Douglas (2001) reviewed the uptick of work on Christianity in Melanesia that was then just beginning to become apparent against the background of a history of how anthropologists of the region had treated Christianity in the past. In the course of her discussion, she posed in very useful terms a regionally phrased version of a question I want to explore in more general terms here: was the study of Christianity in Melanesia suddenly beginning to accelerate because Melanesia was changing (e.g., because Christianity is becoming more important there) or because anthropology was changing (e.g., by beginning to redefine what counts as a legitimate object of study)? The answer she offered, and supported with exemplary thoroughness, is that both things were happening at once.

In a very sophisticated recent article that I have already cited for its assertion that what is new about the recent anthropology of Christianity is its self-conscious quality, Timothy Jenkins (2012) makes a point akin to Douglas's own when he argues that this self-consciousness was borne of changes at once in the world and in anthropology. On Jenkins's account, what allowed for the advent of this self-consciousness about the place of Christianity within anthropology during the late twentieth century was the changing position of religion more generally in the world, including in the Western societies from which most of the new anthropologists of Christianity came, or in which they received their academic training. As Jenkins (2012:472) puts it, during this time period "the trajectories of secularization and modernization [came to] appear less convincing, or, at least, less simple to apprehend." These changes allowed religion to reoccupy social space (outside the academy, of course, but also within it) that it had ceded during the height of secularist modernism, ringing changes both in the ways in which anthropologists encounter religion in the field, where its public presence and broad relevance to many domains of social life in many places are now difficult to ignore, and in the intellectual settings in which anthropological ideas find their final development (see also Bandak and Jørgensen 2012:452–453). The story of the public return of religion around the world that Jenkins alludes to here is by this point extremely well known, being told to great effect in José Casanova's now foundational book from 1994 and in literally thousands of other books and articles across the social sciences and humanities since that time. Jenkins's (2012:463) grounding of his historical account in a careful discussion of Susan Harding's (2000) *The Book of Jerry Falwell: Fundamentalist Language and Politics*, a work that, he suggests, shows that "the categories of the investigating community may have been altered as part of the processes she is investigating," demonstrates quite convincingly that both kinds of changes stirred the pot in which the contemporary anthropology of Christianity would eventually come to a boil.

Seen in the terms Jenkins lays out, the rise of the anthropology of Christianity 15 or so years ago needs to be counted as one of a number of academic responses to the changing role of religion in the world. I will mention just a few of the kinds of academic responses I have in mind here, sticking primarily to ones that have had some influence on the anthropology of Christianity itself. But even an abbreviated list of this kind ought to provide an indication of why it might make sense in intellectual historical terms to focus on the novelty of the kind of anthropology of Christianity that arose during the period in question.

Along with the development of a strong interest in the public role of religion that I have already mentioned, one has to count as a child of the period of change that preceded and then overlapped with development of the anthropology of Christianity the vigorous debate that has followed attempts to deconstruct the category of religion itself, which is best known among anthropologists through Talal Asad's (1993) groundbreaking contribution, though the literature in this area is by now voluminous and spans many social science and humanities disciplines. When combined with the related and very wide-ranging debate about the nature of secularism that has flourished over the past decade (e.g., Asad 2003; Taylor 2007), these developments attest quite directly to a growing scholarly worry that our older understandings of the religious field no longer get much traction on the worlds we are trying to explore. Similarly, one should also note the turn within continental philosophy and critical theory toward a reengagement with religion (best known through the work of Agamben, Badiou, and Zizek), the growing prominence within more mainstream political philosophy of a call to recognize the importance of religion in people's lives (familiar from the more recent work of Habermas, Rawls, and Taylor), and the emerging concern with political theology more generally, which, as Gil Anidjar (2009:374) notes, has been "quickly and deftly universalized" so as to be a phenomenon one can presumably find and study everywhere (de Vries and Sullivan 2006; Tomlinson and McDougall 2013). And along with all of this recent ferment in corners of the humanities and social sciences that had not in the second half of the twentieth century been known for a preoccupation with issues of religion, it is also noteworthy that within religious studies, history of religions, and theology, the same period that birthed these developments also saw the rise of a new discourse of "world Christianity" that has quickly begun to lend its imprimatur to institutes, academic positions, and textbooks (J. Cabrita, personal communication; see also Stanley 2011). The meaning of the label "world Christianity" is still a work in progress, but minimally it responds to the recognition that demographically speaking, at least, and in growing ways culturally speaking as well, Christianity is no longer best described as a "Western" religion (or, as insiders to this discourse often put, a religion of the "global North"; Philip Jenkins 2002 has been a foundational and much debated text for setting these terms for the discussion of world Christianity). As Kwame Bediako (2011:244) puts it, these changes render it "undeniable that what has occurred is a reconfiguration of the cultural manifestation of the Christian faith in the world, a phenomenon that one may also describe as a shift in the center of gravity of Christianity."

One could expand the list I have offered here of signs that the place of religion both in the world and in various intellectual discourses has been in a state of rapid and creative change over the past two decades or so. But I hope to have said enough to carry the main point I want to make: if we take the anthropology of Christianity as it is currently constituted as something new that has arisen over the past 15 years, then it makes sense to see it as one current in a much larger stream of contemporary work that attempts to explore the possibilities that come from rethinking academic approaches to the study of religion. The disciplinary self-consciousness of the anthropology of Christianity has rendered it a particularly anthropological contribution to this churning set of debates, and recognizing its novelty within the discipline itself is important for the way it will eventually allow us to determine what it shares with these other temporally overlapping intellectual developments and what its unique contributions to wider debates might turn out to be.

In the confines of this introduction, I cannot do justice to the issue I have just raised about the specifically anthropological contributions the anthropology of Christianity is making to wider debates about religion, and it might be too early in historical terms to address it very fully in any case.[1] It is worth mentioning, however, that as a fieldwork discipline, sociocultural anthropology might be taken, at least when it is at its best, to be a scholarly endeavor that is unusually quick to register changes in the worlds that scholars study and not just in the intellectual frameworks by means of which they study them (I realize that this distinction between the worlds we study and the terms in which we study them is not an easy one to make in scholarly practice, but the openness to the world of fieldwork-based anthropology is point worth clinging to nonetheless—as Borneman and Hammoudi [2009] compellingly argue). In the spirit of this point, I want to draw attention to one further change in the world that Jenkins (2012) does not highlight and that scholars involved in the intellectual trends I have just enumerated, with the notable exception of those who write about world Christianity, tend to ignore. This is the fact that one of the great historical developments in the Christian tradition itself has occurred in the years immediately preceding the rise of the anthropology of Christianity and the other trends to which I have just referred.

The development to which I refer is the explosive growth of Pentecostal and charismatic Christianity around the world and particularly in Asia, Africa, Latin America, and the Pacific. This growth began in the 1980s, and this form of Christianity now numbers roughly 580 million adherents around the globe

---

1   I should note, however, that Robbins and Engelke (2010) have begun to explore these kinds of issues, suggesting ways the anthropology of Christianity might develop points of dialogue with those interested in the notion of world Christianity and with those interested in the new continental philosophical engagement with religion. This article is the introduction to a journal issue devoted to contributions to this kind of dialogue from scholars from a range of interested disciplines (Engelke and Robbins 2010).

(Pew Research Religion and Public Life Project 2011).[2] It is sufficiently different from other forms of Christianity that many scholars are inclined to treat it as a distinct stream within the broader Christian tradition, joining Orthodoxy, Catholicism, and Protestantism as a fourth "major" strand of the faith (Jacobson 2011:49). Considered in such terms, Pentecostal and charismatic Christianity are distinguished from other forms of Christianity by the stress they place on the assertion that the power of the Holy Spirit is available to all believers, allowing them to heal, prophesy, preach with authority, and exercise other gifts. Churches in this tradition foster a religious life in which prayer and other forms of ritual occur in all manner of contexts and in which religious concerns permeate both public life and private life. They foster, that is to say, a kind of religiosity that at once looks like the kind of total social phenomenon anthropologists of religion have long been used to studying and that it is impossible for field-workers to ignore.

The rapid growth of Pentecostal and charismatic Christianity since the 1980s has meant that just as the place of religion in the world in general was changing in the ways Jenkins points out and just as scholars in a wide range of disciplines were beginning to register this fact, anthropologists in the field were encountering a new kind of Christian religiosity that made insistent claims on their attention. It is thus not surprising that much, though by no means all, of the early work in the anthropology of Christianity focused on churches of this kind. Indeed, almost from the outset of the development of work in this field, scholars of other kinds of Christianity worried that the anthropology of Christianity would end up becoming the anthropology of Pentecostalism (Howell 2003; see also Coleman 2014; Engelke 2014; Marshall 2014). Subsequent developments in the field and the contents of this issue itself put paid to this worry, but the fact that it was at the beginning a legitimate one points to the extent to which the growth of Pentecostal and charismatic Christianity was another worldly change that helped create the soil in which the anthropology of Christianity took root.

I will leave off at this point considering the kinds of issues one can address if one takes the anthropology of Christianity to be something new that began to develop about 15 years ago. Understood in this way, the anthropology of

---

2   Pentecostalism had been rapidly spreading around the globe since its origin in the early 1900s, while the charismatic movement (which arose when non-Pentecostal churches begin to allow their members to engage in Pentecostal-style spiritual practices) dates to the 1960s. After the rise of the charismatic movement, the Pentecostal-charismatic tradition began to grow exponentially in the 1980s (for a brief history of Pentecostal-charismatic Christianity oriented to anthropological readers, see Robbins 2004; for a longer but very accessible account, see Synan 1997; on its rapid growth in recent decades, see Jacobsen 2011:60).

Christianity takes its place alongside a wide range of other very broad developments in the academic study of religion during this time period, developments that have themselves been responses to a number of changes in religion and its place in the world. Even as I hope by means of this discussion to have offered some support for the claim that the anthropology of Christianity is something new and to have specified some of the senses in which such a claim can be reasonably made (one of which is decidedly not the sense that would suggest that no serious ethnographic work on Christianity had been done before the advent of the anthropology of Christianity), I have also endeavored to sketch in some of the context in which some scholars have made a recent push for an anthropology of Christianity.[3] This work of specification and contextualization should be worthwhile regardless of where one comes down on the question of whether this recent push is or is not unprecedented in the history of anthropology. The articles in this issue for the most part set aside this question of origins and instead focus on a range of new arguments and findings produced by anthropological research on Christianity. In the sections that follow, I consider the contributions of these articles and set them in relation to the more general development of this field.

Beyond Culture: Christian Institutions and the Study of Church, Denomination, and Schism

One persistent criticism of the anthropology of Christianity is that it has been largely idealist in orientation (Hann 2007: 402, 407; McDougall 2009a), perhaps even spearheading a return to an emphasis on culture within anthropology, particularly in the United States (Comaroff 2010:529). One could launch a serious theoretical discussion around this kind of complaint by asking precisely what aspects of human life are and are not cultural, for these critics generally at least imply that political-economic factors are outside of culture in some sense and that anthropologists of Christianity have ignored them for this reason. One wonders whether most anthropologists of Christianity would parse the human world into cultural and noncultural bits in this way (of course, their failure to do so might be taken as a symptom of their culturalism, but such a

---

3   As one anonymous reviewer of this article astutely noted, this periodization also opens up the question of how to think about what may have been distinctive of anthropological work on Christianity carried out before the development of the anthropology of Christianity and about the ways this work might have cohered as a body of literature in spite of its relative lack of self-conscious emphasis on producing such coherence. This strikes me as a very worthy task, though it's not one I have been able to carry out here.

failure would not be the same thing as wholly ignoring what others take to be the noncultural bits). Moreover, it often seems as if these critics do not look with much care at the monographic literature the anthropology of Christianity has generated, for much of what they claim to find missing in the various programmatic writings they consult often is at least to some extent present in longer ethnographic accounts (as McDougall [2009a], for example, evenhandedly shows in her critical reading of my own work).

Yet even if charges of culturalism and idealism are too broadly framed to be fully convincing, they are not without any merit at all. One of Hann's (2007:407) most telling points in this regard is his claim that anthropologists of Christianity tend to use an idealist definition of Christianity as something like a culture to tie together disparate ethnographic cases in a single bundle. That is to say, anthropologists of Christianity proceed as if they know what Christianity is apart from the various instances of it they study, but they are able to do this, and hence to render diverse cases comparable, only by assuming an idealist definition of Christianity focused on Christian cosmological conceptions and values more than on Christian institutions. In doing so, it is probably fair to say that anthropologists of Christianity have given less attention than they might have to the ways in which Christian social institutions such as churches, denominations, and practices of schism might be also taken to provide grounds for comparability across cases. This is an oversight a number of the contributions to this issue go a long way toward correcting.

John Barker (2014) tackles the issue of institutional invisibility most directly in his contribution. Taking on board the suggestion that to this point the "tendency has been to explore the nexus between global and local Christianity in broadly cultural terms," he goes on to suggest that it is rather "in the domain of church structures and practices that locally diverse Christians engage a relatively unitary Christianity." Barker substantiates this claim by looking at the long-term stability of the Anglican church as an institution among the Uiaku of Papua New Guinea. Even as he explores the various ways in which the church has been open to localization in Uiaku, he also shows that it has remained "obviously Anglican" in institutional form and emphasis. In this regard, he suggests, the Uiaku case is not unusual, for "one of the defining characteristics of the two thousand year expansion of Christianity across the globe is the planting of enduring institutional structures operating at local, regional and international levels." As easily as we can identify various groups of Christians by their shared cosmological concerns or values, Barker is telling us, we can also recognize them by the kinds of institutions they inhabit. In light of Barker's argument, one might suggest that anthropologists have not reckoned as fully as they might with the long-standing ecclesiological classification of types of church polity into only three kinds: episcopal, Presbyterian, and congregational. The very brevity of this list, even as it can be subject to all kinds of qualifying complications, is a hint that Barker is on a fruitful track in suggesting that looking at church structures is a promising way of reckoning with Christian diversity without losing momentum toward the development of the anthropology of Christianity as a comparative project (see Bialecki 2012 on issues of definition and comparison more generally in the anthropology of Christianity).

Chris Hann (2014), in his article in this issue, also stresses the importance of looking at differences between church institutions, which for him is one part of a project of reorienting the anthropology of Christianity by means of attending to "macromaterialities" that he claims play a leading role in shaping religious life. In line with this assertion, he works throughout his article to show that Protestant, Catholic, and Orthodox churches are not representatives of different civilizations or in possession of distinct ontologies but are rather differentiated by their patterns "for institutionalizing religion in the contemporary world" and their different political-economic situations across history. A key case for Hann's argument that it is institutions and not ontologies that distinguish these churches is his careful analysis of the diffusion of the symbol of the Sacred Heart of Jesus and Mary to some churches but not others over the past 300 years. Like Barker's piece, Hann's contribution demonstrates the value of attending to church structures (as well as to wider political-economic variables) in the comparative study of Christianity.

The rest of the articles in this section follow Barker's and Hann's lead by attending both to church organizations and to the institutionalized means of transforming or leaving them—the characteristically Christian form of bringing about social change by means of schism. Courtney Handman (2014), looking at the history of Lutheran missionization and later schisms from the mission church and from its first successor church among the Guhu Samane of Papua New Guinea, explores how schism is rooted in "critique" of existing churches and their practices, a kind of critique that is generated on the basis of "the ethical demands of Christianity." Such critique of existing church groups and practices is not an end in itself, however, for it leads first to "separation" from the rejected group and then "unification" either in a new church or with a reformed version of the one formerly left behind. As such, schism stands as a key Christian process of "group formation"—a social practice Handman pits against the better-studied tendency of some forms of Christianity to work toward producing the individual as their primary institutional accomplishment (especially, in Handman's argument, the individual understood as a sincere

THE ANTHROPOLOGY OF CHRISTIANITY 283

speaking subject; Keane 2007; Robbins 2001*a*). Jon Bialecki (2014), in his contribution, traces this same kind of process of critical group dissolution and reformation, understanding it as rooted in Christian tendencies to endorse ideals that can never be fully realized, hence leaving room at all times for internal critique (Niebuhr 1957 [1929] is a key reference for both Handman and Bialecki in this regard). In a move similar to the one Barker makes of offering the enduring qualities of church institutions as something that can help to define Christianity as an anthropological object across otherwise diverse cases, Bialecki suggests that one task for the anthropology of Christianity in the future is to explore how schism-generating attempts to realize Christian ideals within earthly church institutions can be seen as "a continuing [Christian] problem, one that endures and which must always be grappled with anew as circumstances change" (emphasis removed). The study of Christian critique and schism as social processes is thus a promising new area for the development of the anthropology of Christianity beyond its cultural turn.

As Handman notes, one might think of schism as a fundamentally Protestant social form, and both her own and Bialecki's articles are focused on Protestant or Protestant-looking charismatic cases. But it is worth noting that perhaps the first work in dialogue with the anthropology of Christianity to take up the study of schism was Douglas Rogers's (2009) study of Russian Old Believers, a group that long ago broke with Russian Orthodoxy and that is also the focus of Caroline Humphrey's (2014) exploration of schismatic social processes in her contribution to this issue.[4] In conversation with older work in the anthropology of Christianity on rupture and discontinuity, Humphrey looks at the specificity of Old Believer notions of schism as a kind of change, wrapped up as they are in collective efforts to preserve tradition and to protect the church from a corrupting outside world in thrall to the antichrist. Humphrey considers the respects in which Old Believer practices of schism might further provide a viable model of revolution, thereby connecting the study of this kind of Christian social processes with that of other forms of fostering social change and new kinds of group formation not by making very broad general statements about the influence of Christianity on modern political forms but by tracing the interaction of various models of change in situations in which they have historically developed in relationship to one another. As one reviewer of this introduction notes, the points Humphrey and other contributors to this section make indicate ways in which the anthropology of Christianity might

4 In Bandak's (2014) article, he also notes that Orthodox and Catholic churches as well as Protestant ones are subject to schismatic change.

contribute even more than it already has to the general study of social movements (see also Shah 2014).

The move all of the authors in this section make toward studying specifically Christian institutions and social processes is a genuinely new development in the anthropology of Christianity (though it is in some respects foreshadowed by Bielo's [2009] important study of the Bible study group as an important evangelical social institution). It is likely that this move will not be enough to satisfy those critics of the anthropology of Christianity who lament what they see as its culturalist tendencies, for in most cases (though perhaps not fully in Hann's) it stops short of privileging political and economic forces, understood as in no significant way shaped by religion, as the sole or only really important historical influences on the ways in which Christianity has developed and on the ways Christian people live their lives. But even if the anthropology of Christianity turns out to be no better suited than any other anthropological trend to date of serving as an arena for settling the conflicts between cultural and materialist understandings that beset the discipline, the turn represented here toward attending to Christian social institutions as a crucial area of study will undoubtedly enrich the anthropology of Christianity as it moves forward.

Christianity, Space, and Place

Almost from the outset, anthropologists of Christianity attended to the various ways in which Christian groups figure time, both eschatologically and in the before and after rhythms of conversion (e.g., Robbins 2001*b*; Schieffelin 2002). By comparison, there has been less work explicitly focused on issues of space. The articles in this section fill this gap. In doing so, they also carry forward some of the institutional and political concerns of the articles discussed above, indicating that perhaps the shift to focusing on such issues is becoming something of a general one.

Bambi Schieffelin's (2014) article looks at how Christian Bosavi of Papua New Guinea have learned to deploy new linguistic resources in ways that remake traditional notions of place. Concerned with mapping new centers and peripheries within the Bosavi world and with sorting those converts who dwell in the center from those who remain on the periphery, Bosavi Christians pepper their speech with forms that index a new sociospatial reality, one profoundly disconnected from the densely relational traditional Bosavi landscape. In effect, Schieffelin shows us the microlinguistic machinery that renders socially effective the kind of critique to which Handman and Bialecki drew our attention. As Schieffelin herself puts it, the new ways of speaking she charts

THE ANTHROPOLOGY OF CHRISTIANITY 285

attest to the ways "critical embodied practices ... can lead the charge toward discontinuity" by enacting a schismatic break from traditional sociality.

Andreas Bandak (2014) and Jianbo Huang (2014) each look at urban situations in many respects far removed from the rural world of the Bosavi. Although anthropologists of Christianity have long worked in both rural and urban settings, little has been done to consider systematically the differences and similarities that mark the way Christianity is lived across this sociospatial divide. In this respect, it is intriguing that one does find some similarities in the place-making practices of the Bosavi and those discussed by Bandak and Huang. Bandak concentrates on the ways minority Catholic and Orthodox Christians in Damascus inhabit urban space. Drawing on Deleuze's notion of the refrain, he examines how insistent, oft-repeated ways of appearing in space, through such means as song, visual display, and religious architecture, render the city a setting for competing religious territorializations. He also attends to the varying identities and spatial spans Damascene Christians work to territorialize as they sometimes foreground their place as members of the Syrian nation while at others stressing their Christian minority status. In relation to the new maps Bosavi Christians work to install, Schieffelin notes that by speaking in terms of them "enough times, Christians hoped to produce a new social reality." The insistent quality of their efforts echoes the repetitive quality of the Damascene Christians' refrains. In both places, Christians work diligently to claim their earthly space.

The conjunction of Schieffelin and Bandak's arguments about the repetitive, interactive nature of earthly place making provides a good opportunity to pause to take up an issue that is relevant to many of the articles in this collection, as well as to the anthropology of Christianity more generally. There has been some concern among critics of the anthropology of Christianity that many of the topics that it deals with are not specific to Christian populations. Hann (2014), who has made such arguments before, reprises them in his contribution to this volume. This is quite obviously true in relation to these two articles about space. Bandak (2014), who is drawing on a Deleuzian model of refrains that is itself phrased in universal terms, states explicitly that "my argument is not that refrains are Christian per se." Furthermore, he documents Islamic as well as Christian practices of refrain making in his article. Schieffelin (2014), for her part, builds her article around a very subtle argument about the role of general language socialization and linguistic practices in bringing about cultural change. Like other contributions to this issue, neither of these authors is making an argument only about Christianity. But it is also the case that both Bandak and Schieffelin are attending carefully to the way the general processes they are examining are lived out by Christians and the ways these processes are inflected by the Christian concerns of those that are undertaking them. Surely, this is enough to render their contributions important to the study of Christianity, as well as to the general anthropology of space and of language. One would not want to set the search for Christian uniqueness as the only or even the primary goal of every contribution to the anthropology of Christianity.

Yet having made this point, it bears noting that in Huang's (2014) article in this section we also find a hint of a very characteristically if not uniquely Christian reason why space making might be a key concern for members of many Christian churches. Huang's focus is on Chinese churches that cater primarily to recent urban migrants from the countryside. By means of the phrase "rural churches in the city," he quite elegantly captures the complexity of the sociospatial location of these churches. Both in their membership, which is predominantly made up of migrants, and in their style of Christian worship, which Huang characterizes as more emotionally than intellectually oriented, these churches remain "rural" even as they help their members adapt to life in urban settings. But one of the things the churches offer their members in this latter regard is a second map of meaningful space that competes with the urban/rural one that so clearly shapes their experience. This is a map of earth and heaven, in which life on earth is transitory and lacks ultimate importance compared to that in heaven. Bosavi Christians work with this kind of map as well. It is an ordering of space that throws into relief the relative and ultimately fragile nature of the earthly spatial order, even as it makes inhabiting space appropriately on earth a key salvational goal. By contrast, the heaven/earth mapping does not appear to figure very importantly for the Damascene Christians Bandak discusses, or at least not in the account he offers here. Preoccupied as they are with their earthly minority status and perhaps also influenced by the theologies of the locally relevant Orthodox and Catholic churches to which they belong, their space-making efforts appear to be very terrestrially focused. Given that the heaven/earth map is not equally relevant to all Christians, studying why it is sometimes central and at other times peripheral to their space-making concerns is precisely the kind of comparative question the anthropology of Christianity is well positioned both to uncover and to seek to answer (Robbins 2009).

Christianity and Gender

It is fair to say that with the exception of the pioneering work of the two contributors to this section, the study of gender has not been central to the anthropology of Christianity thus far (Eriksen 2008; Mayblin 2010). This is somewhat unexpected, inasmuch as the relationship between conversion and changing gender roles, particularly in Latin America, was one area in which anthropologists had begun to focus squarely on Pentecostalism before the development of the anthropology of Christianity, making this a particularly rich area for what I referred to in footnote 3 as systematic work on the "prehistory" of the anthropology of Christianity (e.g., Austin-Broos 1997; Brusco 1995; Cucchiari 1990). But regardless of the surprising nature of this neglect, the articles in this section move decisively beyond it.

Both Annelin Eriksen (2014) and Maya Mayblin (2014) characterize much of the earlier literature on Christianity and gender, including that referred to above, as primarily concerned with sociological issues such as the nature of gender identities and the way they determine persons' abilities to assume leadership and public roles within various churches. In their contributions here, Eriksen and Mayblin largely set aside such issues and instead look at how notions of gender difference are fundamental to Pentecostal and Catholic Christian cosmologies. They both consider, that is to say, what Eriksen phrases as "the way Christianity ... itself is gendered."

Eriksen's article is focused on Pentecostal-charismatic churches in urban Vanuatu. The Pentecostal tradition, as she points out, has long been marked by a contradiction between its strenuous affirmation that all believers are equal before God, a point driven home by the fact that all are at least potentially able to receive gifts of the Holy Spirit, and the fact that church leaders tend to be men. More than this, Eriksen argues, Pentecostal moral transformation itself is a practice that is gendered male, not in the sense that only men achieve such transformation but in that working toward it is a male way of behaving regardless of the gender of the person who undertakes such work. Yet despite these gendered distinctions, in normative Pentecostal rhetoric, all such differences are "denied" or "submerged" in favor of egalitarian understandings of Christian belonging. The tension such denials foster often comes to the fore in what Eriksen defines as the "charismatic space" in which Pentecostal men and woman both interact with the Holy Spirit. Men and women, she demonstrates with her Vanuatu material, engage with the Holy Spirit differently: men "encounter" the Spirit in ways that foster their individual capacities for leadership and institution building, while women "mediate" the Spirit's powers in possession episodes that efface their individuality and further embed them in relational networks. But the charismatic space does not just provide a stage on which otherwise denied gendered differences can be expressed through these different kinds of engagement. It also allows the differences themselves to be challenged by those who endeavor to manage the encounters in unusual ways.

To illustrate this point, Eriksen presents the case of Sarah, an excommunicated woman who attempts to fuse male and female aspects of charisma in an attempt to address her situation. That Sarah's efforts to restore herself to church membership ultimately fail indicate the difficulties of challenging the public, normative Pentecostal gender order but also illustrate that there are charismatic resources available for doing so.

Maya Mayblin's (2014) article, based both on fieldwork among Catholics in northeastern Brazil and on the study of Catholic theological and ecclesiological debates, also attests to the fluidity of Christian understandings of gender, though in a church in which such fluidity is publicly important rather than submerged. At the heart of Mayblin's analysis is a consideration of the key problem presented by the fact that the sacred must always be in some proximity to the profane world in order for its influence to be felt, while it must also maintain enough distance from that world to be able to claim a power that is uniquely its own (see Hubert and Mauss 1964 for a classic statement of this problem). In the Catholic tradition, Mayblin demonstrates, proximity tends to be managed in part by stressing the anthropomorphic aspects of divine figures such as Jesus, Mary, and the saints. Such anthropomorphism is present throughout the Christian tradition, she notes, but it is especially well developed in its Catholic branch. Having fostered proximity in this way, the church manages distance through a complicated "gymnastic" play with issues of divine gender that render it always at least potentially different from human forms. Working carefully through such topics as the gender of saints, clerical celibacy, theological arguments over the status of Mary's hymen, and debates about the possibility of allowing women to become deacons, Mayblin demonstrates the ways in which gender ambiguity both helps protect the distinctiveness of the sacred and shapes very concrete earthly struggles over the appropriate ways for human men and women to live.

As both Eriksen and Mayblin note, the two articles in this section are in productive dialogue with each other in ways that open up new possibilities for comparing Pentecostalism and Catholicism as forms of Christianity. To borrow a point Eriksen makes, though phrasing it slightly differently than she does: it is as if the social fluidity of Pentecostalism, allied with its official denial of the importance of gender difference, leads to the use of the charismatic space as a relatively submerged forum for the articulation of different gender values in the pursuit of sacred efficacy, while in the more comfortably hierarchical Catholic case spiritual elaboration tends to work toward forms of androgyny and gender ambiguity in its efforts to produce the power of the divine. More generally, these two very rich articles indicate in compelling terms the promise of moving forward with the project of making the study of gender far more central to the anthropology of Christianity than it has been in the past.

The Anthropology of Christianity on the Boundaries of Christianity and Beyond

Most work in the anthropology of Christianity has focused on Christians. On the face of things, this must appear to be a statement that is too obvious to need making. But in fact it is capable of being nuanced in some interesting ways. To begin with, most work in the anthropology of Christianity has been based on research with people who themselves claim to be Christians rather than with people who are defined as such by anthropologists in the absence of their possession of a self-conscious Christian identity of their own. More than this, this research has been carried out primarily among people who at least in their own terms (which differ quite a bit between various Christian traditions) define themselves as committed Christians rather than simply as people who live in communities in which Christianity is the dominant religion but see themselves as largely indifferent in matters of religion. So much work had to be done early on in the anthropology of Christianity to ward off the claim that this or that group might look Christian in some respects but is best understood as not genuinely Christian, that those wanting to contribute to the development of this area of study tended to pick quite firmly and vocally Christian populations for study (Robbins 2007). But now that the anthropological impulse to analyze away the Christianity of the people anthropologists study has been largely stilled, there is room to ask what the anthropology of Christianity might learn from research on ambivalent or only tenuously committed Christians or on groups of people who are not Christian but define themselves in important respects in relation to Christianity (Robbins 2010). The articles in this section all explore aspects of this kind of project.

In a wide-ranging article that poses Pentecostalism and pilgrimage as contrasting tropes for the anthropology of Christianity, Simon Coleman (2014) focuses his ethnography on pilgrims to the English site of Walsingham. The pilgrim to whom he devotes the most attention is a woman he refers to as Donna, someone who is "a relatively disengaged, agnostic" Anglican and is married to a lapsed Catholic but who still goes on pilgrimages to Walsingham with her extended family. She finds these trips meaningful, both in terms of the familial sociality they foster and because of the relationship of this sociality to forms of ritual that she finds moving, though not necessarily in a religious sense. Donna's form of what Coleman calls "semi-engagement" with "trivial ritual" raises, as he notes, questions not only of who and what is a Christian but also of when and where in social life these kinds of questions might arise. One catches a glimpse here of the way the study of Christians like Donna can help to reframe still unsettled debates within an anthropology of Christianity over how to determine who, for purposes of anthropological study, ought meaningfully to be counted as Christian (Bialecki 2012; Garriott and O'Neill 2008; Robbins 2003c).

In contrast to Coleman's contribution, Matthew Engelke's (2014) article takes up the case of a group that is vocally non-Christian. The British Humanist Association (BHA) is an explicitly secularist group, but inasmuch as it understands its primary religious antagonist to be Christianity, it is profoundly engaged with some of the same issues that preoccupy many of the Christians anthropologists study. For example, the lives of BHA members turn out to raise a host of fascinating questions about continuity, discontinuity, and secularity that Engelke explores in depth, noting how they upend some by now taken for granted assumptions in the anthropology of Christianity. Using the BHA's militant secularity as a mirror, for example, Engelke shows that the assertion made by some anthropologists of Christianity that Christianity must be understood as cultural stands, very much in spite of itself, as itself a strongly secular claim by virtue of its implication that Christianity is something other than a universal truth. BHA practice is also surprising in its members' interest in ritual, a form of social action they work to wedge free from Christianity, and from religion more generally, and to put to their own uses. Like Donna in Coleman's article, ritual holds some attraction for BHA members but only when it is shorn of its theological encumbrances. There is room here to develop in new ways the exploration anthropologists of Christianity have already begun to carry out of the varying attitudes toward ritual that exist within different branches of the Christian tradition (Lindhardt 2011; Pfeil 2011), setting BHA and more gently secularist attitudes such as Donna's within an examination of the way Christianity has historically shaped and continues to influence Western notions of ritual and of religion more generally.

If Donna might be described as sort of Christian, but not very much, while the BHA members that Engelke studies might count as very much not Christian, but in somewhat Christian terms, the practitioners of the Vietnamese religion Caodai that are the focus of Janet Hoskins's (2014) contribution confound completely our usual terms of deciding matters of inclusion in and exclusion from the analytical category "Christian." Caodai is a syncretistic religion that originally arose in conditions of French colonial dominance in Vietnam. Its conditions of origin shaped its religious organization, which is based on a hierarchy of offices modeled on that of the Catholic Church. If one kept rigorously to the suggestion of Barker's article that one should look at church structures as a key variable in defining Christianity for the purpose of compiling sets of comparable cases across social and denominational divides, one would have to consider the possibility of including Caodai churches in such a grouping. And one might be emboldened in the effort to do so by the fact that Caodai also includes Jesus in its pantheon. But on this point, matters immediately become more complex. For most Coadaists, Jesus is a relatively junior member of their pantheon, "placed three levels below Buddha, Lao Tzu, and Confucius" (though he has been moved up somewhat in one North American Caodai temple). Jesus's primary importance appears to be his quality as a nationalist opponent of Roman imperialism, seen as providing a model for Vietnamese resistance to the French, who within the Caodai pantheon finds himself "incorporated into a more encompassing spiritual vision."

A key aspect of Hoskins's article turns on what work in the anthropology of Christianity might offer her in analyzing a religious tradition that is not itself Christian. In this respect, she plays off of various analyses of the Christian contribution to the formation of Western modernity to good effect, and her overall approach to the study of Caodai syncretism bears marks of demands anthropologists of Christianity have made for a more sophisticated handling of this topic. But her work makes contributions to the anthropology of Christianity as well. Not least among these is raising in very direct terms the question of who absolutely cannot be counted as a Christian. As she puts it, the Caodai case indicates that Christians must maintain "an exclusive commitment to keeping Christian figures at the top of the pantheon, not messing things up with other religious teachers." Her article confronts us with the fact that similarities in church institutional structure do not outweigh or obviate this requirement: institutional structure, regardless of "cultural" content, may not be enough to define Christianity as a topic for comparison after all.

During the early years of the anthropology of Christianity, there was some worry that the diversity of the Christian tradition would sink any effort to shape up Christianity as an object of cross-cultural research. Surely there is no such thing as Christianity, many were inclined to argue, but only Christianities. Given this, why compare one form of Christianity with another rather than comparing a Christian case with one involving any other religious tradition and perhaps even with one involving another religious tradition that has the further advantage of being geographically or "socioculturally" nearby to the Christian case under consideration (Robbins 2003c)? The facts that the articles in this issue range widely across the vast and varied landscape of Christian traditions, from Orthodoxy and Catholicism to mainline Protestantism and Pentecostalism, and that the articles in this section turn their attention to cases at or clearly beyond the edges of Christianity itself, indicate that Christian diversity is not, as it turns out, a potentially fatal challenge to the anthropology of Christianity, at least not at its current level of maturity. Learning to make the most of such diversity analytically will be a major challenge for the anthropology of Christianity as it continues to develop.

Reconsidering Key Topics in the Anthropology of Christianity

In designing the conference that produced this issue, I wanted to make space for a number of scholars to address some of the key topics that have marked work in the anthropology of Christianity from its inception. I have saved discussion of the articles that take up such topics for the penultimate section of this introduction first because I worried that addressing them at the beginning might give the impression that in their content the papers were somehow "old fashioned" and as such should be seen as superseded by the articles that would then have followed them. In fact, these papers are as innovative as any in the volume. But more than this, and this is a second reason for saving discussion of them for last, they point to some aspects of the future of the anthropology of Christianity that do not appear as clearly in the articles I have already discussed. Topically, these articles deal with issues of reflexivity, discontinuity and change, materiality, and experience. I had also hoped to include articles on two other topics that had long been central to the anthropology of Christianity. One of these would have been on transcendence, but the scholar invited to address this topic was unable to attend the conference. The other would have been on individualism, a topic for which in the end there was no space to invite someone. I have recently reviewed work on these two topics within the anthropology of Christianity extensively in another place, and I hope that piece might make up somewhat for the absence of articles focused on these two topics here (Robbins 2012). It is clear that both of these subjects, along with those that are discussed in the articles in this section, will continue to be central to the anthropology of Christianity in the future.

From early on, anthropologists of Christianity have explored the extent to which some kinds of Christianity, particularly its Evangelical and Pentecostal branches, promote radical discontinuity in the lives of converts—demanding that they reject their former cultural commitments and ways of living. Work continues in this area and routinely brings the anthropology of Christianity into dialogue with developments elsewhere in the discipline, as is the case in recent discussions of discontinuity in relation to ethics, pedagogy, and state projects of cultural management (Brahinsky 2013; Chua 2012; Daswani 2013). This tradition of work also figures importantly in relation to schism, revolution, and language in Handman's (2014), Humphrey's (2014), and Schieffelin's (2014) contributions to this issue. Aparecida Vilaça's (2014) article in this issue focuses squarely on issues of discontinuity, and she works through a range of issues related to debates on this topic with exemplary analytic care. The Amazonian Wari' with whom Vilaça has carried out long-term fieldwork have been exposed to both Catholic and Evangelical missionization. Vilaça explores not only the differences in how the two missions have approached issues of change, and particularly their views on fostering discontinuity with traditional cultural notions, but also the way in which Catholic approaches to issues of discontinuity have themselves changed in the wake of the Second Vatican Council. Furthermore, she notes that the traditional perspectivism of the Wari', and their allied interest in incorporating the foreign, also outfits them with a complex indigenous model of discontinuous change that shapes their engagement with the varied Christian models they have encountered (Vilaça 2009). Looking at the play of these various models of change over time, and tracking in particular how these models have shaped developing Wari' views of the inner self as well as of culture, Vilaça productively complicates simplistic claims about the effects of Christian discontinuity even as she reaffirms the productivity of research in this area.

From their earliest framings, discussions of discontinuity in the anthropology of Christianity have also had a reflexive component, challenging cultural anthropology as a discipline that has to an important extent been preoccupied with the study of continuity (Robbins 2003*b*, 2007). Ruth Marshall's (2014) contribution also takes up these two issues in tandem. As Marshall notes, she is a political scientist with a strong grounding in political theory rather than an anthropologist. Although she does not state this as explicitly, it is also worth noting that she has carried out extensive fieldwork among Nigerian Pentecostals and has, on the basis of this research, profoundly challenged the ways social scientists, including anthropologists, have thought about Pentecostal politics (Marshall 2009). In her article here, Marshall develops her reflexive interrogation of both political theory and the anthropology of Christianity through a focus on, among other things, the theme of discontinuity. Questioning how an emphasis on the Pentecostal drive for rupture with the past puts currently fashionable notions of ontology to the test, she asks whether the way an anthropological focus on Christianity upends traditional disciplinary investments in studying the other rather than the self, or the different rather than the similar, might also ground a shift from an anthropological politics of self-determination to one of equality. More generally, she insists that anthropologists of Christianity recognize their own attempts to define Christianity as an object of study as being political as well as epistemological practices and ones that potentially have wider disciplinary and broader worldly implications than their reflexive considerations have previously registered.

Like discontinuity and reflexivity, religious understandings of materiality have also been a central topic in the anthropology of Christianity from the beginning. Webb Keane's 2007 book *Christian Moderns: Freedom and Fetish in the Mission Encounter* has been enormously influential in setting the terms of debate in this area. Through a sustained analysis of conflicts between Eastern Indonesian "ancestral ritualists" and Dutch Calvinist missionaries over the status of material items (including institutionalized social forms) in religious practice, in this book Keane develops the important concept of semiotic ideologies and specifies one Protestant version of such an ideology that worked toward the ultimately impossible goal of defining away the material and routinized qualities of signs and their use. In his article here, Keane (2014) revisits the notion of semiotic ideology, cross pollinating it with the notion of material affordances and expanding it through a close analysis of materials from Russian Orthodox and Soviet Atheist materials. The outcome of his argument not only further attests to the value of semiotic ideology as a framework for comparing different kinds of Christianity but also opens up a whole new line of research into the ethical stakes that Keane shows here so often attend debates about the spiritual and the material in the Christian tradition (and by implication in other religious traditions as well). As with recent discussions of discontinuity mentioned above (especially Daswani 2013), his argument successfully joins the anthropology of Christianity to burgeoning anthropological debates about the nature of morality.

Tanya Luhrmann's (2014) article, written with Julia Cassaniti (a psychological anthropologist and scholar of Thai Buddhism), takes up the topic of religious experience, a subject that has received a great deal of attention in the early anthropology of Christianity, particularly from those studying Pentecostal and charismatic Christians (who highly value experiences of encounter with the Holy Spirit). Building on this tradition of work, Luhrmann and Cassaniti go on to ask very general questions about the origin and nature of spiritual experience not only in Christianity but also in all religious traditions. They develop a model of "cultural kindling" in which cultural emphases tied to various religious traditions lead people to attend differently to universally available bodily and psychological phenomena that can be taken as indications of the presence of the supernatural. Primed differently by the traditions in which they participate, people take different (or none) of these stimuli as evidence of supernatural forces and elaborate this evidence into different cosmological models. Comparing charismatic Christians in the United States and Theravada Buddhists in Thailand, they show how this model allows for comparison between religious traditions and sketch how it can provide a basis for comparison between branches of the Christian tradition as well.

Both Keane's and Luhrmann and Cassaniti's articles draw on ideas that have been developed in anthropological work on Christianity and on kinds of data anthropologists have collected or learned to identify through such work.

But both of them develop arguments of very general ambition—aiming to tie together the meaningful, the material, and the ethical in Keane's case and to provide a scientific basis for accounting for religious diversity in Luhrmann's and Cassaniti's. Vilaça similarly demonstrates the sophistication with which anthropologists of Christianity have come to approach issues of continuity and discontinuity that they have shown are of very broad relevance to anthropological theory more generally. By reviving the tie between the anthropology of Christianity's interest in discontinuity and its reflexive impulse, Marshall (2014) is also able to register the potential impact of these features of the field on much broader disciplinary and transdisciplinary debates. All of the articles in this section on "traditional" topics in the anthropology of Christianity thus spill well beyond the limits of the subfield that gave them birth. Of course, the hope has from the outset been that work in the anthropology of Christianity would not be relevant only to the study of Christianity. It is nice to see that ambition so obviously realized in the articles in this section. The fact that the implications of these articles so clearly reach beyond the anthropology of Christianity raises the question of the future of this field—a question I will take up briefly in conclusion.

Conclusion

What, then, should be the future of the anthropology of Christianity? It would of course be an act of tremendous hubris to try to answer this question very directly. But perhaps it makes sense in closing to suggest some ways in which the question might be discussed. One thing that is clear is that Christianity will continue to be a major topic of anthropological research for the foreseeable future and this to an extent it simply was not before. But as ethnographic studies of Christianity continue to appear in ever greater numbers, should the anthropological study of Christianity continue to unfold as part of a self-conscious project of intellectual community building that aims to push anthropologists who study different kinds of Christianity and/or who study Christianity in different regions of the world to see their research as mutually relevant? And should the heightened disciplinary self-consciousness that has been a part of the anthropology of Christianity since its inception remain important no matter what direction it goes next?

In the introduction to this article I suggested that in terms of disciplinary history it might come as a surprise if the answer to either of these questions were to be yes. More often in sociocultural anthropology, new foci of interest arise and generate excitement for a number of years, but by middle age they begin to fade, becoming at best a taken for granted part of the background of anthropological work rather than remaining in the foreground even of their former core supporters' concern. On the evidence of this issue, however, there may well be some cause for keeping the focused conversation that has been the anthropology of Christianity to this point going a little bit longer. So many of the arguments of these articles are decidedly new ones, and they address issues that have been neglected in earlier work in the field. Even the articles that take up longer-standing themes push them in novel directions and draw out their importance for anthropology in general. And part of what makes all of the article distinctive is that they engage with each other and with work that has been done in and around the anthropology of Christianity in the past. Such at least has been the argument of this introduction. It is an argument that drives toward the conclusion that the anthropology of Christianity has good reason, even in academic middle age, to continue to look toward the future.

Acknowledgments

Organizing the conference from which this volume sprang was a very satisfying intellectual experience from start to finish. I want to thank Leslie Aiello for having confidence in this project from the start, for supporting its development, and for remaining highly intellectually involved with it throughout. Laurie Obbink, with her extraordinary gifts of organization and of helping people feel committed to and involved in a major project like this conference, played a large role in making it a success. Together, Leslie and Laurie transformed my sense of how to go about fostering cooperative intellectual work, and the conference itself set a new benchmark for what I have come to hope for from such events. I am very grateful to them both for all their contributions to this project. I also want to thank all the participants for their many contributions at the conference and beyond. Among them, I also need to thank Jon Bialecki, Matthew Engelke, Naomi Haynes, Tanya Luhrmann, and Bambi Schieffelin, along with Rupert Stasch (who was not a conference participant), for many conversations that helped me conceive and plan the conference. Finally, I am very grateful to Naomi Haynes for agreeing to join me in editing this issue. It's been a pleasure working with her on this, and she has continued to be source of steady intellectual inspiration throughout.

THE ANTHROPOLOGY OF CHRISTIANITY 297

References Cited

Anidjar, G. 2009. The idea of an anthropology of Christianity. *Interventions* 11:367–393.

Asad, T. 1993. *Genealogies of religion: discipline and reasons of power in Christianity and Islam*. Baltimore: Johns Hopkins University Press.

Asad, T. 2003. *Formations of the secular: Christianity, Islam, modernity*. Stanford, CA: Stanford University Press.

Austin-Broos, D. J. 1997. *Jamaica genesis: religion and the politics of moral order*. Chicago: University of Chicago Press.

Bandak, A. 2014. Of refrains and rhythms in contemporary Damascus: urban space and Christian-Muslim coexistence. *Current Anthropology* 55(suppl. 10):S248–S261.

Bandak, A., and J. A. Jørgensen. 2012. Foregrounds and backgrounds: ventures in the anthropology of Christianity. *Ethnos* 77:447–458.

Barker, J. 1990. *Christianity in Oceania: ethnographic perspectives*. Lanham, MD: University Press of America.

Barker, J. 2008. Toward an anthropology of Christianity. *American Anthropologist* 110:377–381.

Barker, J. 2014. The One and the Many: church-centered innovations in a Papua New Guinean community. *Current Anthropology* 55(suppl. 10):S172–S181.

Bediako, K. 2011. Conclusion: the emergence of world Christianity and the remaking of theology. In *Understanding world Christianity: the vision and work of Andrew F. Walls*. W. R. Burrows, M. R. Gornick, and J. A. McLean, eds. Pp. 243–255. Maryknoll, NY: Orbis.

Bialecki, J. 2012. Virtual Christianity in an age of nominalist anthropology. *Anthropological Theory* 12:295–319.

Bialecki, J. 2014. After the denominozoic: evolution, differentiation, denominationalism. *Current Anthropology* 55(suppl. 10):S193–S204.

Bialecki, J., N. Haynes, and J. Robbins. 2008. The anthropology of Christianity. *Religion Compass* 2:1139–1158.

Bielo, J. 2009. *Words upon the Word: an ethnography of evangelical group Bible study*. New York: New York University Press.

Borneman, J., and A. Hammoudi. 2009. The fieldwork encounter, experience, and the making of truth: an introduction. In *Being there: the fieldwork encounter and the making of truth*. J. Borneman and A. Hammoudi, eds. Pp. 1–24. Berkeley: University of California Press.

Brahinsky, J. 2013. Cultivating discontinuity: Pentecostal pedagogies of yielding and control. *Anthropology of Education Quarterly* 44:399–422.

Brusco, E. E. 1995. *The reformation of machismo: evangelical conversion and gender in Colombia*. Austin: University of Texas Press.

Cannell, F. 2005. The Christianity of anthropology. *Journal of the Royal Anthropological Institute* 11:335–356.

Cannell, F., ed. 2006a. *The anthropology of Christianity*. Durham, NC: Duke University Press.

Cannell, F. 2006b. Introduction: the anthropology of Christianity. In *The anthropology of Christianity*. F. Cannell, ed. Pp. 1–50. Durham, NC: Duke University Press.

Casanova, José. 1994. *Public religions in the modern world*. Chicago: University of Chicago Press.

Cassaniti, J., and T. M. Luhrmann. 2014. The cultural kindling of spiritual experiences. *Current Anthropology* 55(suppl. 10):S333–S343.

Chua, L. 2012. *The Christianity of culture: conversion, ethnic citizenship, and the matter of religion in Malaysian Borneo*. New York: Palgrave Macmillan.

Coleman, S. 2014. Pilgrimage as trope for an anthropology of Christianity. *Current Anthropology* 55(suppl. 10):S281–S291.

Comaroff, J. 2010. The end of anthropology, again: on the future of an in/discipline. *American Anthropologist* 112:524–538.

Comaroff, J., and J. Comaroff. 1991. *Of revelation and revolution: Christianity, colonialism, and consciousness in South Africa*, vol. 1. Chicago: University of Chicago Press.

Cucchiari, S. 1990. Between shame and sanctification: patriarchy and its transformation in Sicilian Pentecostalism. *American Ethnologist* 17:687–707.

Daswani, G. 2013. On Christianity and ethics: rupture as ethical practice in Ghanaian Pentecostalism. *American Ethnologist* 40:467–479.

de Vries, H., and L. E. Sullivan, eds. 2006. *Political theologies: public religions in a postsecular world*. New York: Fordham University Press.

Douglas, B. 2001. From invisible Christians to Gothic theatre: the romance of the millennial in Melanesian anthropology. *Current Anthropology* 42:615–650.

Engelke, M. 2014. Christianity and the anthropology of secular humanism. *Current Anthropology* 55(suppl. 10):S292–S301.

Engelke, M., and J. Robbins, eds. 2010. *Global Christianity, global critique*. Special issue, *South Atlantic Quarterly* 81(2).

Engelke, M., and M. Tomlinson, eds. 2006. *The limits of meaning: case studies in the anthropology of Christianity*. New York: Berghahn.

Eriksen, A. 2008. *Gender, Christianity and change in Vanuatu: an analysis of social movements in North Ambrym*. Aldershot: Ashgate.

Eriksen, A. 2014. Sarah's sinfulness: egalitarianism, denied difference, and gender in Pentecostal Christianity. *Current Anthropology* 55(suppl. 10): S262–S270.

Fernandez, J. 1978. African religious movements. *Annual Review of Anthropology* 7:195–234.

THE ANTHROPOLOGY OF CHRISTIANITY

Garriott, W., and K. L. O'Neill. 2008. What is a Christian? toward a dialogic approach in the anthropology of Christianity. *Anthropological Theory* 8:381–398.

Handman, C. 2014. Becoming the body of Christ: sacrificing the speaking subject in the making of the colonial Lutheran church in New Guinea. *Current Anthropology* 55(suppl. 10):S205–S215.

Hann, C. 2007. The anthropology of Christianity per se. *Archives Européenns de Sociologie* 48:391–418.

Hann, C. 2014. The heart of the matter: Christianity, materiality, and modernity. *Current Anthropology* 55(suppl. 10):S182–S192.

Harding, S. F. 2000. *The book of Jerry Falwell: fundamentalist language and politics.* Princeton, NJ: Princeton University Press.

Hefner, R. W., ed. 1993. *Conversion to Christianity: historical and anthropological perspectives on a great transformation.* Berkeley: University of California Press.

Hoskins, J. A. 2014. An unjealous God? Christian elements in a Vietnamese syncretistic religion. *Current Anthropology* 55(suppl. 10):S302–S311.

Howell, B. 2003. Practical belief and the localization of Christianity: Pentecostal and denominational Christianity in global/local perspective. *Religion* 33:233–248.

Huang, J. 2014. Being Christians in urbanizing China: the epistemological tensions of the rural churches in the city. *Current Anthropology* 55(suppl. 10):S238–S247.

Hubert, H., and M. Mauss. 1964. *Sacrifice: its nature and function.* Chicago University of Chicago Press.

Humphrey, C. 2014. Schism, event, and revolution the Old Believers of Trans-Baikalia. *Current Anthropology* 55(suppl. 10):S216–S225.

Jacobsen, D. 2011. *The world's Christians: who they are, where they are, and how they got there.* Oxford Wiley-Blackwell.

James, W., ed. 1988. *Vernacular Christianity: essays in the social anthropology of religion presented to Godfrey Lienhardt.* Oxford: JASO.

Jenkins, P. 2002. *The next Christendom: the coming of global Christianity.* Oxford: Oxford University Press.

Jenkins, T. 2012. The anthropology of Christianity: situation and critique. *Ethnos* 77:459–476.

Keane, W. 2007. *Christian moderns: freedom and fetish in the mission encounter.* Berkeley: University of California Press.

Keane, W. 2014. Rotting bodies: the clash of stances toward materiality and its ethical affordances. *Current Anthropology* 55(suppl. 10):S312–S321.

Lindhardt, M., ed. 2011. *Practicing the faith: the ritual life of Pentecostal-charismatic Christians.* New York: Berghahn.

Marshall, R. 2009. *Political spiritualties: the Pentecostal revolution in Nigeria.* Chicago: University of Chicago Press.

Marshall, R. 2014. Christianity, anthropology, politics. *Current Anthropology* 55 (suppl. 10):S344–S356.

Mayblin, M. 2010. *Gender, Catholicism, and morality in Brazil: virtuous husbands, powerful wives*. New York: Palgrave.

Mayblin, M. 2014. People like us: intimacy, distance, and the gender of saints. *Current Anthropology* 55(suppl. 10):S271–S280.

McDougall, D. 2009*a*. Christianity, relationality and the material limits of individualism: reflections on Robbins's *Becoming Sinners. Asia Pacific Journal of Anthropology* 10:1–19.

McDougall, D. 2009*b*. Rethinking Christianity and anthropology: a review article. *Anthropological Forum* 19:185–194.

Niebuhr, H. R. 1957 [1929]. *The social sources of denominationalism*. New York: Meridian.

Pew Forum Religion and Public Life Project. 2011. http://www.pewforum.org/2011/12/19/global-christianity-movements-and-denominations/. Accessed May 28, 2014.

Pfeil, G. 2011. Imperfect vessels: emotion and rituals of anti-ritual in American Pentecostal and charismatic devotional life. In *Practicing the faith: the ritual life of Pentecostal-charismatic Christians*. M. Lindhardt, ed. Pp. 277–306. New York: Berghahn.

Robbins, J. 2001*a*. God is nothing but talk: modernity, language and prayer in a Papua New Guinea society. *American Anthropologist* 103:901–912.

Robbins, J. 2001*b*. Secrecy and the sense of an ending: narrative, time and everyday millenarianism in Papua New Guinea and in Christian fundamentalism. *Comparative Studies in Society and History* 43:525–551.

Robbins, J., ed. 2003*a*. 2003. *The anthropology of Christianity*. Special issue, *Religion* 33(3).

Robbins, J. 2003*b*. On the paradoxes of global Pentecostalism and the perils of continuity thinking. *Religion* 33:221–231.

Robbins, J. 2003*c*. What is a Christian? notes toward and anthropology of Christianity. *Religion* 33:191–199.

Robbins, J. 2004. The globalization of Pentecostal and charismatic Christianity. *Annual Review of Anthropology* 33:117–143.

Robbins, J. 2007. Continuity thinking and the problem of Christian culture: belief, time and the anthropology of Christianity. *Current Anthropology* 48: 5–38.

Robbins, J. 2009. Is the trans- in transnational the trans- in transcendent: on otherness and moral transformation in the age of globalization. In *Transnational transcendence: essays on religion and globalization*. T. J. Csordas, ed. Pp. 55–71. Berkeley: University of California Press.

Robbins, J. 2010. Afterword: ambivalent and resistant Christians and the anthropology of Christianity. *Asia-Pacific Forum* 48:71–96.

Robbins, J. 2012. Transcendence and the anthropology of Christianity: language, change, and individualism. Edward Westermarck Memorial Lecture, October 2011. *Journal of the Finnish Anthropological Society* 37:5–23.

Robbins, J., and M. Engelke. 2010. Introduction to special issue: global Christianity, global critique. *South Atlantic Quarterly* 109:623–631.

Rogers, D. 2009. *The old faith and the Russian land: a historical ethnography of ethics in the Urals*. Ithaca, NY: Cornell University Press.

Saunders, G. R., ed. 1988. *Culture and Christianity: the dialectics of transformation*. New York: Greenwood.

Schieffelin, B. B. 2002. Marking time: the dichotomizing discourse of multiple temporalities. *Current Anthropology* 43(suppl.):S5–S17.

Schieffelin, B. B. 2014. Christianizing language and the dis-placement of culture in Bosavi, Papua New Guinea. *Current Anthropology* 55(suppl. 10): S226–S237.

Shah, A. 2014. "The muck of the past": revolution, social transformation, and the Maoists in India. *Journal of the Royal Anthropological Institute* 20:337–356.

Stanley, B. 2011. Founding the Center for the Study of Christianity in the non-Western world. In *Understanding world Christianity: the vision and work of Andrew F. Walls*. W. R. Burrows, M. R. Gornick, and J. A. McLean, eds. Pp. 51–60. Maryknoll, NY: Orbis.

Synan, V. 1997. *The Holiness-Pentecostal tradition: charismatic movements in the twentieth century*. Grand Rapids, MI: Eerdmans.

Taylor, C. 2007. *A secular age*. Cambridge, MA: Harvard University Press.

Tomlinson, M., and M. Engelke. 2006. Meaning, anthropology, Christianity. In *The limits of meaning: case studies in the anthropology of Christianity*. M. Engelke and M. Tomlinson, eds. Pp. 1–37. New York: Berghahn.

Tomlinson, M., and D. McDougall, eds. 2013. *Christian politics in Oceania*. New York: Berghahn.

Turner, V., and E. Turner. 1978. *Image and pilgrimage in Christian culture*. New York: Columbia University Press.

Vilaça, A. 2009. Conversion, predation and perspective. In *Native Christians: modes and effects of Christianity among indigenous peoples of the Americas*. A. Vilaça and R. M. Wright, eds. Pp. 147–166. Surrey: Ashgate.

Vilaça, A. 2014. Culture and self: the different "gifts" Amerindians receive from Catholics and Evangelicals. *Current Anthropology* 55(suppl. 10): S322–S332.

Expanding Mission Archaeology: A Landscape Approach to Indigenous Autonomy in Colonial California

Lee M. Panich and Tsim D. Schneider

1 Introduction

In California, as elsewhere, the Spanish mission system had far-reaching effects for indigenous autonomy as broadly reflected in the use of space at different points on the landscape. More than 70 years ago, Sherburne Cook (1943:73) underscored this important dimension of the Spanish missionary program, writing, "The initial act of contact between the mission organization and the Indian was one involving spatial relationships." We contend that the crucial role of spatial relationships in structuring colonial encounters extended far beyond the missions themselves and the initial act of contact. Instead, the colonial entanglements that missionization set in motion unfolded in distinct ways across the landscape and over the course of the colonial period and its aftermath. This paper examines the relationship between indigenous autonomy and spatial organization within the context of Spanish colonialism in central California (Fig. 1). We suggest that by broadening the scope of mission archaeology to include not just mission settlements but also more distant areas where the colonial presence was impermanent, archaeologists can provide new insight into native autonomy under colonialism. Given the wide geographic range of Spanish missionization in the Americas—and the use of missions as part of colonial strategies worldwide—our findings point to avenues of future research that may be applied to other missionized regions.

Source: Panich, L. and T. D. Schneider, "Expanding Mission Archeology: A Landscape Approach to Indigenous Autonomy in Colonial California," *Journal of Anthropological Archeology* 40 (2015): pp. 48–58. Reprinted with permission from Elsevier.
The original article holds an illustration, (Fig. 5), which is not included here. The location of this illustration is marked with an * in the text.

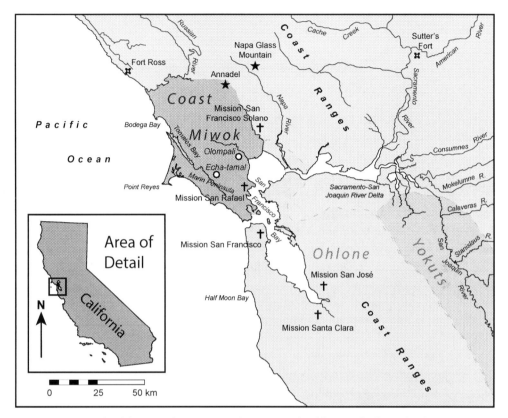

FIGURE 1   Central California, with reconstructed Coast Miwok, Ohlone, and Yokuts ethnolinguistic boundaries (after Milliken, 1995), colonial settlements, and other places discussed in text

Through three brief case studies, we examine how indigenous people organized and used space at mission establishments, along the shifting frontiers between native homelands and colonial hinterlands, and in areas outside of direct colonial control. Traditional scholarship positions the Spanish colonial missions of California as tightly controlled social spaces to which native people were inextricably bound. Yet recent archaeological and ethnohistorical research indicates that Spanish spatial hegemony was far from complete, nor was it negotiated in a uniform manner by the region's inhabitants. Based on our research in central California, we argue that native people living in the Spanish mission era exercised a considerable, if differential, degree of control over their organization and use of space at different locales on the landscape. These practices complicate traditional understandings of the spatial relationships of missionization, and further demonstrate the importance of empirically grounded archaeological research to counter the seeming disappearance of indigenous people in colonial California.

2   Colonialism, Landscapes, and Autonomy

The fundamental questions of many archaeological approaches to colonialism center on the dichotomy of continuity and change within native societies. Recently, the pendulum has swung from archaeological concerns with demographic decline and acculturation to approaches that seek to understand indigenous persistence in spite of far-reaching changes wrought by colonialism (Jordan, 2008; Mitchell and Scheiber, 2010; Panich, 2013; Silliman, 2009). Within these latter studies, many recognize the intertwined nature of continuity and change, which is perhaps better modeled as "changing continuities" (Ferris, 2009). Indeed, careful reading of the archaeological and ethnohistorical records shows that even seeming discontinuities in categories such as settlement patterns or resource exploitation were structured by the internal dynamics of native societies. Archaeologists are thus poised to move beyond decades-old questions about continuity and change to consider indigenous agency and autonomy in the colonial period. As used here, autonomy refers to freedom of action within situational constraints (Jordan, 2013; Schwartz and Green, 2013). When applied to the archaeology of colonialism, an examination of autonomy de-centers static, trait-based approaches to native cultures and the concomitant scholarly focus on externally-imposed change. By countering the myth of the vanishing Indian, such studies also offer opportunities for collaboration between archaeologists and indigenous communities (Cipolla, 2013; Mrozowski et al., 2009).

A landscape approach intersects these debates by providing a venue for exploring not only the intended spatial structures of colonialism but also how native people actually experienced and used space in different contexts (Lightfoot and Martinez, 1995; Mann, 2012). Within such approaches, it is largely taken as a given that the landscape is both reflective and constitutive of environmental adaptations, social relationships, and individual and collective agency. The various ways that people construct, organize, and inhabit space thus offer multiple perspectives on lived experience in colonial settings, including the (re)production of cultural values and social identities, as well as the negotiation of colonial power structures, enculturation programs, and labor regimes (Lightfoot et al., 1998; Panich and Schneider, 2014; Wernke, 2013).

Spatially, native autonomy ranged from intra-site organization to regional settlement patterns and economic connections, to the maintenance of sites of cultural importance and commemoration (Rodning, 2009; Rubertone, 2000). At these different places in the landscape, however, agents may have pursued different strategies based on their age, gender, ethnolinguistic affiliation, or relative social status (Rodríguez-Alegría, 2010). Archaeologists therefore must be attentive to how native people exercised autonomy differentially even within one ethnolinguistic or political group. Such an approach articulates with broad developments in the archaeology of colonialism in the Americas (Cobb and De Pratter, 2012; Funari and Senatore, 2015; Hauser and Armstrong, 2012; Van Buren, 2010), and counters the traditional view of colonialism as a "static and monolithic" imposition on indigenous societies (Gosden, 2000).

2.1 Mission Archaeology in North America

Where employed by European powers, missions were typically designed to be the central institution through which indigenous people would enter civilized society. Accordingly, much scholarship on the social aspects of missionization in the Spanish Borderlands of North America winds around a common interpretive thread: the notion that mission communities were "carceral" institutions. In this viewpoint, native people subject to missionization were inevitably caught up in a European colonial program designed to efficiently strip them of their cultural practices (Lydon, 2009:248). Missions, then, outwardly resemble other institutions in their attempted regulation of behavior and movement through the design and control of space (De Cunzo, 2006; Voss, 2008:148; Wade, 2008:142). Scholarly focus on the California missions, for example, often invokes the use of corporal punishment, control of native social practices, and restrictions on use of space within and beyond the mission walls. Decades of archaeological research on native acculturation at mission sites in California and elsewhere (e.g., Cheek, 1974; Deetz, 1963; Hoover, 1992) has buttressed this understanding of missions as anchoring normative landscapes where strict social controls dominated all aspects of the lives of indigenous people.

While missions and other colonial sites may have constrained native use of particular places, a careful reading of mission archaeology and ethnohistory reveals patterns of landscape use that may inform a new approach to native autonomy under missionization (Panich and Schneider, 2014). Across the North American Borderlands, important differences existed between how Spanish missionaries dealt with mobile hunter–gatherers versus sedentary agriculturalists, suggesting that native political economies were a key structuring principle in the process of missionization (Lightfoot et al., 2013; Thomas, 2014; and see Spicer, 1962:287–288). These dynamic missionary strategies can be seen in regional differences in mission spatial organization and variation in the degree of control missionaries held over particular establishments (Graham, 1998).

Among agriculturalists, such as in the Spanish colony of La Florida, missions were incorporated into existing indigenous communities. This process resulted in a relative balance of power in which mission churches were often placed opposite native council houses in town plazas and native people retained control over the organization of their domestic space (McEwan, 1991; Saunders, 1998; Scarry and McEwan, 1995). Similarly, missions to the Pueblo communities of New Mexico were constructed within existing native settlements (Lycett, 2014). In contrast, missionaries working in regions where native people were seasonally mobile, such as California or Texas, typically attempted to concentrate dispersed indigenous communities at newly built mission establishments (Lightfoot, 2005; Wade, 2008). As noted by Spicer (1962:288–298), however, the fundamental "blueprint" for Spanish missions revolved around the interrelated policies of *reducción* (relocation) and *congregación* (congregation). Native communities, regardless of existing settlement patterns, were to be centered on a mission church.

The results of these practices, however, varied across space and through time. In La Florida, Franciscan padres usually ignored outlying hamlets and instead channeled their energy into erecting missions within principal towns. Out of this practice formed "a reservoir of villages outside of Spanish control to which the disaffected could flee" (Saunders, 1998:405). In Texas, native groups such as the Aranama and Karankawa incorporated Spanish mission outposts into their seasonal schedules, at least during the initial decades of the colonial period (Ricklis, 1996; Walter and Hester, 2014). Missions established in the American Southwest were usually attached to the most densely populated Pueblos, but the Franciscan project was frustrated by seasonal patterns of dispersal, as well as broad demographic changes. The status of these joint colonial-indigenous projects often shifted from *cabecera* (head mission) to *visita* and back again, with implications for how native people engaged with the broader landscape over time (Lycett, 2004, 2014). The Pueblo Revolt of 1680 and ensuing decades ushered in further spatial transformations in the region (Liebmann, 2012; Liebmann et al., 2005). Along the far western margins of New Spain, Jesuit missionaries in the arid deserts of Baja California could not support large populations at the *caberceras* and instead allowed hunting and gathering groups to remain in their ancestral villages (Crosby, 1994:197–199).

In sum, the intended spatial re-organization of native communities around particular Spanish mission sites had far-reaching but variable consequences for native autonomy. To be sure, many native people moved to mission establishments, but once there, domestic spaces and work areas were structured in part by their own dynamic cultural practices. The effects of missionization also rippled outward to regions where the colonial presence was impermanent, represented by *visitas* or occasional visits by traveling missionaries. Across the landscape, native people adapted their settlement patterns and economic activities to accommodate, coopt, or resist efforts at missionization. Each of these processes was the result not simply of Euroamerican domination, but rather the interested action—the agency—of native individuals and groups. To account for this relative degree of autonomy, however, archaeologists must look anew at the relationships between mission sites, outlying areas, and regions beyond the control of any one colonial power.

3 Developing a Spatial Model

To address the landscape-level dimensions of indigenous autonomy under missionization, we build on the model developed by Lightfoot et al. (2009) to describe the range of spatial relationships between native people and colonists in the northern San Francisco Bay region. This model conceptualizes native engagement with colonial institutions across four broad spatial categories: colonial settlements, proximal zones, hinterlands, and the interspaces of colonial regimes. Such categories are useful for understanding the spatial dimension of colonial entanglements, but they pose two problems when applied to the contextual examination of native autonomy. First, these zones could be read as being mutually exclusive or applicable to all colonial contexts. They are not. Diachronic changes in the scale and intensity of native engagement with colonial institutions, in particular, preclude a static application of these categories, which shifted along with the ebb and flow of colonial entanglements. Second, the zones demarcated by Lightfoot et al. (2009) are conceptualized in reference to their proximity to colonial establishments. While an expedient way of demarcating space, this view of colonial-era landscapes could serve to subtly perpetuate outdated core-periphery models of European expansion. Instead, archaeological approaches to colonialism should examine the structuring qualities of the indigenous landscape as well as the multisited nature of colonial encounters (Lightfoot, 2006).

To augment these spatial zones for our examination of indigenous autonomy in the colonial era, we recast them in the following way: (1) colonial settlements as native places, a category that collapses colonial settlements and proximal zones, (2) native homelands/colonial hinterlands, and (3) interior worlds and interspaces. This approach explicitly underscores the complex nature of space as experienced by different actors (Robinson, 2013). Indeed, we envision these spatial zones not simply as representing immutable and dichotomous categories of native or colonizer, but rather as porous and often fleeting social spaces in which people of diverse backgrounds actively engaged in processes of accommodation and negotiation.

Within these zones, native people lived and worked at multiple sites across the landscape, some of which are characterized by high archaeological visibility while others may require more systematic approaches to discovery and artifact identification (Sayers, 2014:109; Seymour, 2014:99–104). We see the value of defining the range of spatial zones as expanding the purview of "mission archaeology." This broader approach includes the examination of materials and people that flowed back and forth across colonial frontiers, between native villages, and within and beyond the walls of particular mission establishments.

3.1 Colonial Settlements as Native Places

Missions were, at a fundamental demographic level, as much native places as they were colonial settlements. Mission sites are a common focus of research throughout the Americas, and this immense dataset offers diverse perspectives on native autonomy under missionization. The empirical evidence amply demonstrates wide variation in intrasite spatial patterning both within specific mission provinces and across the Borderlands (Allen, 2010; Costello, 1989; Saunders, 1996). We argue that such variation is not simply the result of Euroamerican institutional protocols or personal preferences, but rather an expression of the complex negotiations that unfolded between missionaries,

EXPANDING MISSION ARCHAEOLOGY

secular colonists, and native people. As we discuss elsewhere (Panich, 2010; Schneider and Panich, 2014), the archaeological and ethnohistorical records for mission sites can also hold clues to how native neophytes interacted with people and places beyond the mission walls. For example, archaeological remains such as lithics, marine shell, animal bone, and botanical remains can often be effectively linked to particular places on the landscape. Properly contextualized, these materials offer insights into native mobility and economic connections under missionization. We also note that colonial settlements need not be missions at all to be included in an examination of native autonomy under missionization. Secular and military interests offered a distinct alternative to life under the bell, and laboring (as opposed to converting) thus can be examined as yet another angle for understanding native autonomy (Van Buren, 2010). For this reason, we combine the original categories of colonial settlements and proximal zones, as proposed by Lightfoot et al. (2009), to include a broader array of native involvement in colonial institutions.

3.2   *Native Homelands/Colonial Hinterlands*

Colonial hinterlands are often imagined as the vanguard of European influence, but may be better understood in reference to the native societies who already lived there. In these areas, native people maintained connections to ancestral sites while often simultaneously rearticulating group structure and economic relationships. The Chumash world of south-central California provides contrasting examples of how hunter–gatherers dealt with colonial intrusions. Some Emigdiano Chumash sought refuge in relatively inaccessible interior regions where they may have been joined by members of neighboring groups (Bernard et al., 2014). Others, such as those living at the autonomous coastal Chumash village of *Humaliwo*, labored at secular *ranchos* giving some individuals new pathways to status and an alternative to mission life (Gamble, 2008:202–206). Further south in the Los Angeles Basin, Gabrieliño/Tongva living at one coastal village continued many ceremonial traditions into the colonial period even as they incorporated domesticated plants into feasts and their everyday diet (Reddy, 2015). These examples attest to how native people drew on their home territories to forge different strategies of persistence. Indeed, the overlapping fringes between native homelands and colonial frontiers provided native people with a familiar home ground from which to negotiate Euroamerican colonialism.

3.3   *Interior Worlds and Interspaces*

The third zone comprises the "interior worlds" described by Zappia (2014) in his study of indigenous autonomy in the Colorado River Basin, or what

Lightfoot et al. (2009:6) referred to as the interspaces between colonial regimes. These zones, which were situated between two or more colonial powers, were much more than simply places of evasion and resistance—they were in many cases transformative (Hämäläinen, 2008). Indeed, the very autonomy of the often multiethnic indigenous groups living in interior worlds subverted colonial cultural hegemony and ultimately "shaped the larger designs of state power" (Zappia, 2012:194). We see these interspaces as fluid regions continually remade by competing interests, not just those of colonists. Within interior worlds, native people were free to pursue diverse social, economic, and political options. In this sense, individuals and groups within these zones acted back upon Euroamerican institutions, as seen in colonial policies (e.g., military expeditions or the administration of *paseos*) implemented to define and control unknown areas beyond the walls of missions and other colonial establishments.

4   Contested Landscapes in Central California

In the late precontact period, California was home to hundreds of small, hunter–gatherer–fisher societies who spoke a variety of languages, employed intensive landscape management practices, and participated in far-flung exchange relationships (Lightfoot and Parrish, 2009). The first sustained encounters between Native Californians and Euroamerican colonists came in the late eighteenth century. Between 1769 and the 1830s, Franciscan missionaries founded a chain of 21 missions along the coast from San Diego to Sonoma. The Franciscans who entered the colonial province of Alta (Upper) California in 1769 were part of a long lineage of Spanish missionaries from Franciscan, Dominican, and Jesuit orders with a 200-year record of establishing missions within the borderland provinces of Florida, Texas, Arizona, New Mexico, Northern Mexico, and Baja California (Thomas, 2014; Wade, 2008).

The core of the regional plan for California was the relocation, or *reducción*, of the region's indigenous peoples from their home villages to the head mission establishments. There, native peoples could be closely monitored during their conversion to Catholicism and Euroamerican lifeways, without interference from Indians living outside of colonial control or neighboring *gente de razón* (Lightfoot, 2005:63). The experience of missionization for native peoples in California was thus closely tied to the organization and use of space: as neophytes, native people were bound to the mission and expected to reside within its confines unless explicitly granted leave by the Franciscans.

EXPANDING MISSION ARCHAEOLOGY   311

Yet the social worlds of native people in Spanish California extended beyond the mission walls. As part of the widespread economic and social connections linking the missions and autonomous communities, native people manipulated a system of temporary leaves, called *paseo*, to achieve a degree of autonomy and flexibility in the face of *reducción* (Arkush, 2011; Newell, 2009; Schneider, 2010, in press-a). These permitted furloughs—in addition to rampant fugitivism—created opportunities for some native people to return to home villages for short durations, to give birth, to die, or to disappear entirely. As reflected by the policy of *paseo*, places within indigenous homelands also retained importance throughout the mission period. Many Native Californians lived along the colonial frontier and evaded missionization, while others selectively engaged with different Euroamerican institutions in regions where missionaries competed with other colonial powers for native labor and allegiance. Below, we examine the evidence for native autonomy across each of the three spatial zones.

4.1   *Colonial Settlements as Native Places: Mission Santa Clara de Asís*

Mission Santa Clara, near the southern extent of San Francisco Bay, operated from 1777 until the 1840s. The mission drew native people from throughout central California, including local Ohlone (Costanoan) groups as well as Yokuts speakers from the San Joaquin Valley (Milliken, 2002). At the local level, Mission Santa Clara incorporated most of the basic spatial attributes of the Franciscan missions of California, although it is unique in that the mission itself had five different locations during the colonial period (Skowronek and Wizorek, 1997). Archaeological investigations on and around the modern Santa Clara University (SCU) campus have revealed the spatial organization of the mission, reflecting the Franciscans' power to dictate the use of space, but also how native people exercised a degree of autonomy within those parameters (Fig. 2).

Neophyte housing offers a clear picture of the intended process of spatial control. As at other California mission sites, three discrete residential areas were established: separate dormitories for unmarried men and women, as well as a larger neighborhood for neophyte families and married couples. Although the *monjerio* and separate quarters for young men have not been studied archaeologically at Santa Clara, such practices no doubt fractured families and likely complicated traditional courtship practices (Voss, 2000). Despite the multiple shifts in the location of the mission church, the *ranchería* for married neophytes appears to have remained in the same place—within earshot of the bell—from the early 1780s to the 1840s. Within these residential spaces,

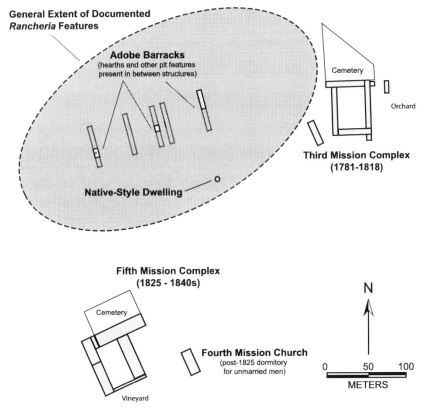

FIGURE 2   Mission Santa Clara, with areas discussed in text

the native population was decidedly diverse, and there is no indication that missionaries paid any particular attention to the linguistic barriers or animosities that existed among neophytes at Santa Clara. Instead, the segregation of the indigenous *ranchería* reflects the racialized caste system that reified native identity in colonial New Spain (Voss, 2008).

Despite the control that the Franciscans sought to implement over the daily activities of neophytes at Mission Santa Clara, recent research demonstrates that native people did maintain some autonomy over domestic space within the mission. Archaeological mitigation associated with several major SCU construction projects has revealed large portions of the native *ranchería*, including numerous pit features as well as the remnants of adobe barracks and a native-style thatched house (Allen, 2010). One of the most significant findings is that native people adapted the *ranchería* to their own needs. Dozens of pit features of different forms—including storage pits, hearths, and possible wells—dotted the open spaces (Allen et al., 2010; Garlinghouse et al., 2015; Panich et al., 2014).

EXPANDING MISSION ARCHAEOLOGY

Some large pits may have served ceremonial purposes, and three in particular appear to have been filled with materials that were ritually destroyed in accordance with well-documented Native Californian mourning practices (Panich, 2014, in press). With regard to domestic architecture, the presence of native-style dwellings offers the opportunity to see how native people organized domestic space in different areas of their neighborhood. Indeed, the comparison of materials associated with different domestic structures and related features within the mission *ranchería* indicates differential access to certain materials or exchange networks (Panich et al., 2014; Panich, 2014).

Importantly, many of the archaeological finds point to enduring connections between neophytes and people and places beyond the mission walls. Thousands of shell beads, for example, have been recovered from multiple spatial contexts (Panich, 2014). These shell beads include types manufactured in two distinct regions within coastal California: clamshell disk beads produced north of San Francisco Bay and small disk beads made from the shells of olive snails (*Olivella* sp.) and red abalones (*Haliotis rufescens*), likely created in workshops along the Santa Barbara Channel (Fig. 3). Hundreds of obsidian artifacts have also been recovered in excavations. Of 136 samples recently analyzed, the majority were from sources north of San Francisco Bay, including 105 from Napa Glass Mountain and 18 from the Annadel source. Smaller quantities of artifacts were manufactured from obsidian obtained further north in the Coast Ranges and in the eastern Sierra Nevada (Garlinghouse et al., 2015; Panich et al., 2014, 2015). In aggregate, it appears that most of the shell beads and all of the raw obsidian material originated in regions outside the ancestral homelands of the Ohlone and Yokuts neophytes who joined Mission Santa Clara, offering insight into the broader regional networks in which mission neophytes were enmeshed. A systematic review of available data is underway, but the evidence from Santa Clara suggests that neophytes also continued to practice some hunting of wild animals and gathering of wild plants (Allen et al., 2010).

The documentary record offers additional glimpses into the varied possibilities for autonomy under missionization. For example, missionaries at Santa Clara, writing in 1814, stated that neophytes maintained their own garden plots, and that native people also persisted in many so-called vices, such as gambling, dances, and abortions (Geiger and Meighan, 1976:106, 111). Analysis of the death records contained in Santa Clara's sacramental registers suggests that a significant portion of neophyte deaths occurred outside of the mission (Panich, in press). Of the approximately 7670 deaths of native individuals recorded for Santa Clara, roughly nine percent took place beyond the mission walls. This tally contains individuals who died at other missions or nearby

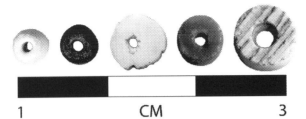

FIGURE 3   Beads collected from Mission Santa Clara, including (left to right) glass beads, *Olivella* disk bead, *Haliotis rufescens* disk bead, and clamshell disk bead. Similar beads have been noted in assemblages from throughout central California

FIGURE 4
Phoenix button collected from Mission Santa Clara. Similar buttons have been recovered from sites in the San Joaquin Valley and the Marin Peninsula

colonial establishments, but it also includes more than 430 neophytes who died and were buried in their ancestral homelands. Several individuals in this latter group were listed as being fugitives or on *paseo*, suggesting that, as Newell (2009) shows for Mission San Francisco, native neophytes in the San Francisco Bay region actively manipulated the missionaries' intended control of space. The wealth of documentary information regarding fugitivism and *paseo*, combined with the quantity of non-local materials found at missions like Santa Clara, points toward possible mechanisms by which introduced goods such as phoenix buttons and glass beads were conveyed outward to distant native villages (Figs. 3 and 4).

These diverse lines of evidence shed new light on the autonomy of native people in the heart of the mission system. On the whole, the analysis of materials from the Santa Clara *ranchería* confirms earlier indications that native

EXPANDING MISSION ARCHAEOLOGY

people maintained and rearticulated several important cultural traditions within their own neighborhood, away from the watchful eyes of the Franciscans and colonial soldiers (Lightfoot, 2005). At Mission Santa Clara, these included intra-settlement organization of domestic space, the perpetuation of certain mourning ceremonies, technological practices such as flint-knapping, and the hunting and gathering of wild species. These findings also demonstrate that native people were not totally confined to mission establishments or nearby proximal zones. Instead, neophytes at Santa Clara created a native space within the mission while simultaneously keeping ties to neophyte communities at other missions, to far-flung indigenous economic networks, and to their ancestral homelands and other areas outside of direct colonial control.

4.2 *Native Homelands/Colonial Hinterlands: The San Joaquin Valley*

As evidenced by the materials recovered from Mission Santa Clara and other colonial sites, native people continued to participate in far-reaching social and economic relationships under missionization. In central California, however, the complexities of native landscape use outside of the Spanish missions and other colonial establishments are not fully understood. This situation is due in part to assumed Spanish hegemony during the colonial period but also to prevailing research frameworks within mission archaeology, which tend to focus on mission sites themselves rather than on native homelands (Lightfoot et al., 2009; Schneider and Panich, 2014; Schneider, in press-b). Here, we focus on the once-extensive *tulares* (tule marshes) of the San Joaquin Valley, a region which included the traditional homelands of multiple Yokuts-speaking groups and their neighbors.

   To the Franciscans and other Spanish authorities, the San Joaquin Valley was seen simultaneously as a source of new mission converts and a troubling hotbed of indigenous independence. Neophytes fleeing or on leave from missions brought knowledge of horse handling to native people who already had well developed economic relationships linking the Pacific Coast to the Sierra Nevada and beyond. These groups integrated the horse into their economic repertoire,* which quickly expanded to include frequent raiding of coastal missions and other colonial establishments (Arkush, 1993; Phillips, 1993). Fearing that the region would become another "*Apachería*" where mounted native raiders could flourish outside of colonial control, many Franciscans advocated for the founding of additional missions in San Joaquin Valley (Cutter, 1995:171; Hackel, 2005:338–339). Although the valley missions were never constructed, many native people from the *tulares* did join missions closer to the coast, prompting Milliken (2002:59) to state that nearly "all of the San Joaquin River people were at the missions by the end of 1820."

Several lines of evidence complicate this picture of a vast valley entirely drained of its indigenous inhabitants. Ethnohistorical research, for example, provides insight into the native people who created dynamic communities in the tule marshlands. Some were Yokuts speakers who refused to join the missions, while others were mission neophytes who returned to their homelands either on leave or as fugitives (Cook, 1960, 1962; Phillips, 1993:32–64). Many of the death records from Mission Santa Clara, for instance, indicate that neophytes of Yokuts ancestry returned often to the *tulares*, where no small number of them perished and were laid to rest (Panich, in press). In this milieu, the native groups of the San Joaquin Valley enjoyed a period of relative autonomy—even using their intimate knowledge of their surroundings to successfully repel punitive expeditions seeking fugitive neophytes—during which they rearticulated social and economic practices within their own ancestral homelands.

One of the best examples of the complexity of the spatial and social relationships that structured life in the *tulares* comes from an account written by Father Narciso Durán, of Mission San José, detailing a 14-day expedition in 1817. Traveling by boat down the San Joaquin River, Durán (in Cook, 1960:275) reported:

> We went all night, except for a while during which we stopped in the boat itself, and at eight o'clock [in the morning] we arrived near the village of the Passasimas. During the night we passed on our right the village of the Nototemnes, who are already Christians in San José and who were living almost in the middle of the tule swamps ... some of the Passasimas came out to greet us in peace. This is not strange because they have been many times in the mission [San José] and several of them have been baptized.

Fifty miles from the closest mission, this eye-witness account details the complicated social settings that unfolded within California's interior. In thinking beyond impermeable missions and distant hinterlands, the account of Father Durán and others like it point to the complex and shifting spatial relationships of colonialism and their concomitant implications for native autonomy.

To date, the archaeological evidence for these relationships is most visible in large-scale excavations of villages and associated cemeteries. In the northern San Joaquin Valley, for example, archaeologists focused on glass beads that could be used to essentially ground-truth the place names in Durán's diary (Schenck, 1926; Schenck and Dawson, 1929). Glass bead assemblages from particular sites ranged in number from 15,000 to 85—the latter of which was

EXPANDING MISSION ARCHAEOLOGY   317

found in association with *Olivella* shell beads "with edges chipped instead of ground" (Schenck and Dawson, 1929:357). These *Olivella* beads are indicative of the late mission period, and are found at mission sites and native villages throughout southern and central California (Bennyhoff and Hughes, 1987). In his work in the nearby Sacramento-San Joaquin River Delta, Bennyhoff (1977) outlined several historic-era "bead complexes" developed through the seriation of glass and shell beads from hundreds of grave lots and which point toward temporally distinct regional interaction spheres. Viewed together with more recent archaeological studies in the broader region (e.g., Wiberg, 2005), two noteworthy patterns emerge. First, glass beads were spread far afield from the coastal missions, into areas only intermittently visited by Euroamericans prior to the mid-nineteenth century. Second, different types of shell beads produced in distant coastal regions also circulated throughout California's vast interior during the mission period. The large quantity of historic-era beads (both glass and shell) in the Central Valley suggests that Yokuts raiders and traders served to convey diverse materials along the length of their valley homelands and back and forth across the colonial frontier (Arkush, 1993).

Further evidence for the dynamic social worlds of the mission-era comes from the valley's southern reaches. At one site in Kern County (CA-KER-64), early archaeological work documented a cemetery that appears to have been used from precontact times into the 1860s (Walker, 1947). Out of 99 burials, 46 contained goods of Euroamerican origin, including thousands of glass beads as well as phoenix buttons, crucifixes, and ceramic artifacts. Many of the historic-era burials also contained *Olivella* and/or clamshell beads, stone beads, stone bowls, or basketry remnants (Walker, 1947:13). The site may represent the village of Tulamniu, which was known for harboring large numbers of neophytes fleeing Mission La Purísima in the early nineteenth century (Bernard et al., 2014:157; Honig, 2003:56; Phillips, 1993:59–60). Another site in the area, CA-KER-74, yielded similar materials from nine burials from the same general time range (Riddell, 1951). There, religious medallions from the missions were found not just with glass beads, but also *Olivella* and clamshell beads as well as numerous *Haliotis* pendants. While the Catholic religious objects from these sites no doubt reflect direct or indirect contact with missionaries, the burial of such objects in independent villages speaks to how native people contextualized such objects within familiar frames of reference. Viewed this way, such practices indicate native autonomy rather than acculturation. Indeed, Father President Mariano Payeras likely expressed the thoughts of many Franciscans when he characterized the region's mixture of free Indians and fugitive neophytes as "a republic of Hell and a diabolical union" (Cutter, 1995:149).

In his seminal essay on the direct historical approach in California archaeology, Heizer (1941:120) noted that the colonial-era *tulares* were home to dynamic native communities "led by former neophytes who had renounced Christianity and returned to their old homes, consolidated with other similar remnants and withdrew beyond the reach of the Spanish military to defensible, inaccessible retreats." In this region, ethnohistorical records indicate fugitive neophytes found safe harbor in their natal villages, while others manipulated mission furloughs to die and be mourned in culturally appropriate ways. Still others visited with family and friends before returning to the lives they had created anew at the missions. Archaeologically, the importance of these native homelands is seen most readily in the persistence of particular village sites well into the nineteenth century, although data from smaller, more ephemeral sites would likely further illuminate how Yokuts groups drew on familiar places to retain autonomy under missionization (cf. Schneider, in press-b). Together, the existing ethnohistorical and archaeological data point toward the importance of landscapes beyond the missions, as well as the frequent passing of people and things across the porous frontiers between indigenous homelands and Euroamerican colonies.

4.3 Interior Worlds and Interspaces: Native Refugia on the Marin Peninsula

Often missions bordered regions where no one colonial system dominated or where multiple powers sought to extract labor, tribute, or resources from local native people. Such was the case north of San Francisco Bay, along the Marin Peninsula where local Coast Miwok groups found themselves along the frontier between the far northern reaches of New Spain and the eastern expansion of imperial Russia (Lightfoot, 2005). This coastal region was also plied by American and British trading vessels, and was home to several Mexican ranching establishments after the 1820s. The complex mix of colonial interests in this region created an interspace that paradoxically allowed native people to participate in Euroamerican colonialism largely on their own terms.

We are currently working with the Federated Indians of Graton Rancheria (FIGR) to understand the range of strategies employed by native people to create and maintain interior worlds away from the multiple colonial incursions that cross-cut coastal California. While evolving ties to Euroamerican colonial enterprises upended traditional political economies based on hunting and gathering, the spatial organization of such relationships may have nonetheless offered opportunities for differential autonomy across the region. In the Coast Miwok world, our research suggests that broad changes in political organization, economic production, and landscape use were internally structured

EXPANDING MISSION ARCHAEOLOGY

during the colonial period at different points across the landscape. We note two complementary processes as evidenced by the archaeological and ethnohistorical records. First, particular sites and familiar landscapes beyond colonial control held lasting significance as sites of refuge and relief from the colonial presence in the neighboring regions. Second, the Marin Peninsula and nearby areas on the Pacific Coast provided opportunities for Coast Miwok villages to openly endure throughout the mission period and beyond.

The first pattern involves landscapes of refuge, which are by their very nature difficult to see archaeologically or in the documentary record. Nevertheless, new approaches are illuminating continuities of seasonally structured landscapes as well as the continued use of particular sites over time. In the Marin Peninsula, the examination of long-term seasonality trends through stable isotope analysis of archaeological mussel shell corresponds to documented seasonal shifts in Coast Miwok participation in the Spanish mission system (Schneider, in press-a). Similarly, a reappraisal of regional archaeology suggests that many sites thought to have been abandoned at the onset of Euroamerican colonialism may have in fact remained important places on the landscape, perhaps as clandestine sites of refuge (Schneider, in press-b).

One such site in our study area is known as Cotomko'tca (CA-MRN-138), a prominent Coast Miwok village on the eastern side of the Marin Peninsula (Barrett, 1908; Kroeber, 1925). Forty-two people from the village were baptized at Mission San Francisco in 1808, and one joined Mission San Rafael in 1821 (Milliken, 2009). Archaeological excavations at the site produced few materials that speak directly to the use of the site in the colonial era, but the assemblage did include a phoenix button as well as a chipped obsidian cross (Slaymaker, 1977). Together, the archaeological and ethnohistoric evidence place native people at sites like Cotomko'tca into the 1820s. While past researchers largely considered such sites "prehistoric" in nature, an expanded approach to mission archaeology encourages the interrogation of such temporal placements and may therefore better capture the way native people used ancestral landscapes as they regrouped beyond shifting colonial frontiers.

The second pattern, that of enduring village settlements, is best characterized by Echa-tamal (CA-MRN-402). Located in the western portion of the Marin Peninsula, Echa-tamal was occupied more or less continuously from precontact times through the late nineteenth century. Some Coast Miwok people from around Echa-tamal were baptized at Mission San Francisco in 1808–1809, while others joined Mission San Rafael a decade later (Milliken, 2009). The use of the site during the height of missionary activity in the Marin Peninsula (ca. 1817–1833) is not well understood, but the village and roughly 22,600 hectares of surrounding lands were granted to the "Christianized Indians" of

Mission San Rafael in 1835 at the petition of five Coast Miwok men. Significant portions of the site were excavated in the 1970s, revealing materials that date from the waning years of the mission era into American period (ca. 1830s–1880s) (Dietz, 1976). Of particular interest are large quantities of clamshell disk beads, glass beads, phoenix buttons, and other items of personal adornment. Some materials reflect connections to other native communities, while many objects—such as vaquero gear and mass-produced consumer goods—speak to Coast Miwok engagement with the changing regional economy.

Similar processes unfolded at Olompali, another large Coast Miwok village that existed from precontact times into the mid-nineteenth century (Barrett, 1908; Kroeber, 1925). Coast Miwok from Olompali appear on baptismal registers for Mission San Francisco (1814–1817), Mission San José (1816–1817), and Mission San Rafael (1817–1822) (Milliken, 2009). However, the site remained in use throughout the Spanish period, inhabited by a community of baptized and unbaptized native people who likely provisioned local missions (Carlson and Parkman, 1986). Archaeological excavation at the site (CA-MRN-193/H) has documented numerous cultural features, including house pits and the floor of a possible dance structure, although temporal placement and associations are not well documented (Slaymaker, 1972). After the missions were secularized in the 1830s, Camillo Ynitia, a Native Californian, gained title to the 3560-hectare Rancho Olompali where he constructed an adobe structure. Excavations of the floor of Ynitia's home revealed quantities of ground and flaked stone tools, bone and shell implements, and glass beads (Wegars, 1974).

Together, places like Cotomko'tca, Echa-tamal, and Olompali suggest that the interior world of the Marin Peninsula was not simply a landscape of isolation, but rather a venue of ingenuity and autonomy. People from many native villages joined mission communities, but they did not all join the same mission at the same time. Instead, some individuals and families stayed in and around their ancestral villages even during the peak years of missionization. To date, the archaeological investigation of many of these sites has focused on their precontact components, overlooking or not fully examining the potential use of materials such as shell beads and obsidian during colonial times. As discussed above, both categories of material continued to be conveyed along indigenous networks throughout the colonial period, providing insight into adjustments to inter-community relationships. Further, ethnohistorical evidence demonstrates that Native Californians actively engaged with different colonial systems to retain control of salient places in the landscape. For both Olompali and Echa-tamal, native people used the courts to petition colonial governments for title to lands occupied for generations. As these examples demonstrate, the archaeology and ethnohistory of interspaces can illuminate

EXPANDING MISSION ARCHAEOLOGY

native autonomy in multiple ways, ranging from clandestine sites of refuge, to tenaciously defended villages, to regional interaction that crosscut indigenous and colonial boundaries.

5 Conclusion

Through the policies of *reducción* and *congregación*, spatial organization provided the foundation of the Spanish missionary program across the North American Borderlands. In California, the intended spatial relationships of missionization amounted to an imposed and radical reorganization of space to control social relationships and to thwart hunter–gatherer mobility. While the efficacy of the missionary program is often assumed in scholarly research and popular understandings of colonial California, a reexamination of the evidence suggests subtle and overt ways that Native Californians exercised autonomy at multiple places on the landscape. To understand better the situational agency of native people in mission contexts, we outlined three zones that reflect dynamic spatial relationships throughout the colonial period.

First, we examined colonial settlements as native places, focusing on indigenous life at Mission Santa Clara. Within the Native American *ranchería*, neophytes appear to have organized exterior space largely as they saw fit. In these areas, they were also relatively free to maintain aspects of traditional technologies and cultural practices, although these may have differed along the lines of status and ethnolinguistic affiliation. The second zone is comprised of native homelands on the colonial margins. In California, the vast marshlands of the San Joaquin Valley were home to Yokuts speaking people who formed new kinds of social groups and economic practices through the integration of horses and fugitive neophytes. The third zone includes interior worlds, or interspaces where no one colonial power was dominant and where native people enjoyed diverse forms of autonomy. In central California, this kind of zone developed on the Marin Peninsula and adjacent areas of the Pacific Coast. There, Coast Miwok people lived between the Spanish/Mexican, Russian, and American frontiers, enabling them to interact with colonial institutions—and other native groups—on a differential basis.

In contrast to the unidirectional movement from homeland to mission that characterizes much early acculturation-based research, our case studies demonstrate that native people and the materials they used often crossed back and forth from one zone to another. Through the policy of *paseo*, for example, mission neophytes in central California moved from the missions to their ancestral homelands and back again on a regular basis. Further, the spatial relationships of colonialism often changed even within a particular geographic area. While the Franciscans never extended the mission chain to the San Joaquin Valley, they did eventually establish two missions north of San Francisco Bay, simultaneously reacting to and changing the social and physical shape of the Coast Miwok refugium.

We propose these spatial zones not as universal categories that apply in all colonial contexts but as a conceptual model from which to expand mission archaeology. These zones do not represent bounded social fields nor are they mutually exclusive. Rather, this broader view of native autonomy in missionized regions draws upon recent methodological and theoretical advances to reveal persistent and, at times, unobtrusive social, economic, and political linkages that crosscut the physical and metaphorical walls of colonial institutions. These complex connections were not limited to colonial California, and can be explored in a range of mission settings, as demonstrated by numerous studies that include a landscape approach to colonialism across the North American Borderlands and beyond. By examining the possibilities for native autonomy at different points across the colonial-era landscape, archaeologists may better view indigenous action against the formidable interpretive backdrop of colonial domination.

Acknowledgments

We thank the Federated Indians of Graton Rancheria for supporting our work in Marin County. We also acknowledge the efforts of the many Santa Clara University students who participated in research at Mission Santa Clara, as well as the assistance of the staff at the Northwest Information Center, Sonoma State University. The comments of Rebecca Allen, Seetha Reddy, and an anonymous reviewer greatly enhanced the argument presented here.

References

Allen, R., 2010. Rethinking mission land use and the archaeological record in California: an example from Santa Clara. Hist. Archaeol. 44 (2), 72–96.

Allen, R., Baxter, R. S., Hylkema, L., Blount, C., D'Oro, S., 2010. Uncovering and Interpreting History and Archaeology at Mission Santa Clara. Report to Santa Clara University, Santa Clara, California.

Arkush, B. S., 1993. Yokuts trade networks and native culture change in central and eastern California. Ethnohistory 40 (4), 619–640.

Arkush, B. S., 2011. Native responses to European intrusion: cultural persistence and agency among mission neophytes in Spanish colonial California. Hist. Archaeol. 45 (4), 62–90.

Barrett, S. A., 1908. The Ethno-Geography of the Pomo and Neighboring Indians. University of California Publications in American Archaeology and Ethnology, vol. 6. University of California, Berkeley.

Bennyhoff, J. A., 1977. Ethnogeography of the Plains Miwok. Center for Archaeological Research at Davis Publication Number 5. Davis, California.

Bennyhoff, J. A., Hughes, R. E., 1987. Shell Bead Ornament Exchange Networks Between California and the Western Great Basin. Anthropol. Pap. Am. Mus. Nat. Hist. 64 (2). American Museum of Natural History, New York.

Bernard, J., Robinson, D., Sturt, F., 2014. Points of refuge in the south central California hinterlands. In: Panich, L. M., Schneider, T. D. (Eds.), Indigenous Landscapes and Spanish Missions: New Perspectives from Archaeology and Ethnohistory. University of Arizona Press, Tucson, pp. 154–171.

Carlson, P. M., Parkman, E. B., 1986. An exceptional adaptation: Camillo Ynitia the last headman of the Olompalis. Calif. Hist. 65 (4), 238–310.

Cheek, A., 1974. The Evidence for Acculturation in Artifacts: Indians and Non-Indians at San Xavier de Bac, Arizona. Ph.D. Dissertation. University of Arizona, Tucson.

Cipolla, C. N., 2013. Native American historical archaeology and the trope of authenticity. Hist. Archaeol. 47 (3), 12–22.

Cobb, C. R., De Pratter, C. B., 2012. Multisited research on colonowares and the paradox of globalization. Am. Anthropol. 114 (3), 446–461.

Cook, S. F., 1943. The conflict between the California Indian and white civilization: I. The Indian versus the Spanish mission. Ibero-Americana 21, 1–194.

Cook, S. F., 1960. Colonial expeditions to the interior of California: central valley, 1800–1820. Univ. Calif. Anthropol. Rec. 16, 239–292.

Cook, S. F., 1962. Expeditions to the interior of California: central valley, 1820–1840. Univ. Calif. Anthropol. Rec. 20, 151–213.

Costello, J. G., 1989. Variability among the Alta California missions: the economics of agricultural production. In: Thomas, D. H. (Ed.), Columbian Consequences, Archaeological and Historical Perspectives on the Spanish Borderlands West, vol. 1. Smithsonian Institution Press, Washington, D.C., pp. 435–450.

Crosby, H. W., 1994. Antigua California: Mission and Colony on the Peninsular Frontier, 1697–1768. University of New Mexico Press, Albuquerque.

Cutter, D. (Trans., Ed.), 1995. Writings of Mariano Payeras. Bellerophon Books for the Academy of American Franciscan History, Santa Barbara, California.

De Cunzo, L. A., 2006. Exploring the institution: reform, confinement, social change. In: Hall, M., Silliman, S. W. (Eds.), Historical Archaeology. Blackwell, Malden, Massachusetts, pp. 167–189.

Deetz, J. F., 1963. Archaeological investigations at La Purisima mission. Archaeol. Surv. Annu. Rep. 5, 161–241.

Dietz, S. A., 1976. Echa-Tamal: A Study of Coast Miwok Acculturation. M.A. Thesis. San Francisco State University, San Francisco.

Ferris, N., 2009. The Archaeology of Native-Lived Colonialism: Challenging History in the Great Lakes. University of Arizona Press, Tucson.

Funari, P. P. A., Senatore, M. X., 2015. Archaeology of Culture Contact and Colonialism in Spanish and Portuguese America. Springer, Heidelberg.

Gamble, L. H., 2008. The Chumash World at European Contact: Power, Trade, and Feasting among Complex Hunter-Gatherers. University of California Press, Berkeley.

Garlinghouse, T. S., Peelo, S., D'Oro, S., Ellison, J., Brady, R. T., Blount, C. M., Hylkema, L., 2015. Archaeological Data Recovery for the St. Clare Residence Hall Storm Drain Project. Report Prepared for Santa Clara University. Albion Environmental Inc., Santa Cruz, California.

Geiger, M. J., Meighan, C. W. (Eds.), 1976. As the Padres Saw Them: California Indian Life and Customs as Reported by the Franciscan Missionaries, 1813–1815. Santa Barbara Mission Archive Library, Santa Barbara.

Gosden, C., 2000. Postcolonial archaeology: issues of culture, identity and knowledge. In: Hodder, I. (Ed.), Archaeological Theory Today. Polity Press, Cambridge, pp. 241–261.

Graham, E., 1998. Mission archaeology. Annu. Rev. Anthropol. 27, 25–62.

Hackel, S. W., 2005. Children of Coyote. Missionaries of Saint Francis: Indian-Spanish Relations in Colonial California. University of North Carolina Press for the Omohundro Institute of Early American History and Culture, Chapel Hill, pp. 1769–1850.

Hämäläinen, P., 2008. The Comanche Empire. Yale University Press, New Haven.

Hauser, M. W., Armstrong, D. V., 2012. The archaeology of not being governed: a counterpoint to a history of settlement of two colonies in the Eastern Caribbean. J. Soc. Archaeol. 12 (3), 310–333.

Heizer, R. F., 1941. The direct-historical approach in California archaeology. Am. Antiq. 7 (2), 98–122.

Honig, S., 2003. Yokuts, Spaniards, and Californios in the southern San Joaquin Valley, 1772–1824. Boletín: J. Calif. Mission Stud. Assoc. 20 (1), 50–62.

Hoover, R. L., 1992. Some models for Spanish colonial archaeology in California. Hist. Archaeol. 26 (1), 37–44.

Jordan, K. A., 2008. The Seneca Restoration, 1715–1754: An Iroquois Local Political Economy. University Press of Florida, Gainesville.

Jordan, K. A., 2013. Incorporation and colonization: postcolumbian Iroquois satellite communities and processes of indigenous autonomy. Am. Anthropol. 115 (1), 29–43.

Kroeber, A. L., 1925. Handbook of the Indians of California. Bureau of American Ethnology Bulletin, vol. 78. Washington, D.C.

Liebmann, M., 2012. Revolt: An Archaeological History of Pueblo Resistance and Revitalization in 17th Century New Mexico. University of Arizona Press, Tucson.

Liebmann, M., Ferguson, T. J., Preucel, R. W., 2005. Pueblo settlement, architecture, and social change in the Pueblo Revolt era, A.D. 1680 to 1696. J. Field Archaeol. 30 (1), 45–60.

Lightfoot, K. G., 2005. Indians, Missionaries, and Merchants: The Legacy of Colonial Encounters on the California Frontiers. University of California Press, Berkeley.

Lightfoot, K. G., 2006. Missions, furs, gold, and manifest destiny: rethinking an archaeology of colonialism for western North America. In: Hall, M., Silliman, S. W. (Eds.), Historical Archaeology. Blackwell, Malden, Massachusetts, pp. 272–292.

Lightfoot, K. G., Gonzalez, S. L., Schneider, T. D., 2009. Refugees and interethnic residences: examples of colonial entanglements in the north San Francisco Bay area. Pacific Coast Archaeol. Soc. Quart. 42 (1), 1–21.

Lightfoot, K. G., Martinez, A., 1995. Frontiers and boundaries in archaeological perspective. Annu. Rev. Anthropol. 24, 471–492.

Lightfoot, K. G., Martinez, A., Schiff, A. M., 1998. Daily practice and material culture in pluralistic social settings: an archaeological study of culture change and persistence from Fort Ross, California. Am. Antiq. 63 (2), 199–222.

Lightfoot, K. G., Panich, L. M., Schneider, T. D., Gonzalez, S. L., Russell, M. A., Molino, T., Blair, E. H., 2013. The study of political economies and colonialism in native California: implications for contemporary tribal groups and federal recognition. Am. Antiq. 78 (1), 89–104.

Lightfoot, K. G., Parrish, O., 2009. California Indians and Their Environment: An Introduction. University of California Press, Berkeley.

Lycett, M. T., 2004. Archaeology under the bell: the mission as situated history in 17th century New Mexico. Missionalia 32, 357–379.

Lycett, M. T., 2014. Toward a historical ecology of the mission in seventeenth-century New Mexico. In: Panich, L. M., Schneider, T. D. (Eds.), Indigenous Landscapes and Spanish Missions: New Perspectives from Archaeology and Ethnohistory. University of Arizona Press, Tucson, pp. 172–187.

Lydon, J., 2009. Fantastic Dreaming: The Archaeology of An Aboriginal Mission. AltaMira Press, Lanham, Maryland.

Mann, R., 2012. Plazas and power: Canary Islanders at Galveztown, an eighteenth-century Spanish colonial outpost in Louisiana. Hist. Archaeol. 46 (1), 49–61.

McEwan, B. G., 1991. San Luis de Talimali: the archaeology of Spanish-Indian relations at a Florida mission. Hist. Archaeol. 25 (3), 36–60.

Milliken, R., 1995. A Time of Little Choice: The Disintegration of Tribal Culture in the San Francisco Bay Area, 1769–1810. Ballena Press, Menlo Park, California.

Milliken, R., 2002. The Indians of mission Santa Clara. In: Skowronek, R. K. (Ed.), Telling the Santa Clara Story: Sesquicentennial Voices. Santa Clara University and City of Santa Clara, California, pp. 45–63.

Milliken, R., 2009. Ethnohistory and Ethnogeography of the Coast Miwok and Their Neighbors, 1783–1840. Archaeological/Historical Consultants, Oakland, California. Report Prepared for the National Park Service, Golden Gate National Recreational Area, Cultural Resources and Museum Management Division, San Francisco.

Mitchell, M. D., Scheiber, L. L., 2010. Crossing divides: archaeology as long-term history. In: Scheiber, L. L., Mitchell, M. D. (Eds.), Across a Great Divide: Continuity and Change in Native North American Societies, 1400–1900. University of Arizona Press, Tucson, pp. 1–22.

Mrozowski, S. A., Herbster, H., Brown, D., Priddy, K. L., 2009. Magunkaquog materiality, federal recognition, and the search for a deeper history. Int. J. Hist. Archaeol. 13, 430–463.

Newell, Q. D., 2009. Constructing Lives at Mission San Francisco: Native Californians and Hispanic Colonists, 1776–1821. University of New Mexico Press, Albuquerque.

Panich, L. M., 2010. Spanish missions in the indigenous landscape: a view from Mission Santa Catalina, Baja California. J. Calif. Great Basin Anthropol. 30 (1), 69–86.

Panich, L. M., 2013. Archaeologies of persistence: reconsidering the legacies of colonialism in native North America. Am. Antiq. 78 (1), 105–122.

Panich, L. M., 2014. Native American consumption of shell and glass beads at Mission Santa Clara de Asís. Am. Antiq. 79 (4), 730–748.

Panich, L. M., 2015. "Sometimes they bury the deceased's clothes and trinkets:" indigenous mortuary practices at Mission Santa Clara de Asís. Hist. Archaeol. (in press).

Panich, L. M., Afaghani, H., Mathwich, N., 2014. Assessing the diversity of mission populations through the comparison of Native American residences at Mission Santa Clara de Asís. Int. J. Hist. Archaeol. 18 (3), 467–488.

Panich, L. M., Daly, R., Hiatt, A., Mathews, D., Moreno, F., McDougall, J., Ross, A., 2015. XRF Analysis of Obsidian Artifacts from the North Campus Parking Structure Project, Santa Clara University, California. Report on file, Curation and Conservation Facility, Santa Clara University, Santa Clara, California.

Panich, L. M., Schneider, T. D. (Eds.), 2014. Indigenous Landscapes and Spanish Missions: New Perspectives from Archaeology and Ethnohistory. University of Arizona Press, Tucson.

Phillips, G. H., 1993. Indians and Intruders in Central California, 1769–1849. University of Oklahoma Press, Norman.

Reddy, S. N., 2015. Feeding family and ancestors: persistence of traditional Native American lifeways during the mission period in Coastal Southern California. J. Anthropol. Archaeol. 37, 48–66.

Ricklis, R. A., 1996. The Karankawa Indians of Texas: An Ecological Study of Cultural Tradition and Change. University of Texas Press, Austin.

Riddell, F. A., 1951. The archaeology of site Ker-74. Univ. Calif. Archaeol. Surv. Rep. 10, 1–28.

Robinson, D., 2013. Polyvalent metaphors in south-central California missionary processes. Am. Antiq. 78 (2), 302–321.

Rodning, C. B., 2009. Mounds, myths, and Cherokee townhouses in southwestern North Carolina. Am. Antiq. 74 (4), 627–663.

Rodríguez-Alegría, E., 2010. Incumbents and challengers: indigenous politics and the adoption of Spanish material culture in colonial Xaltocan, Mexico. Hist. Archaeol. 44 (2), 51–71.

Rubertone, P. E., 2000. The historical archaeology of Native Americans. Annu. Rev. Anthropol. 29, 425–446.

Saunders, R., 1996. Mission period settlement structure: a test of the model at San Martin de Timucua. Hist. Archaeol. 30 (4), 24–36.

Saunders, R., 1998. Forced relocation, power relations, and culture contact in the missions of La Florida. In: Cusick, J. G. (Ed.), Studies in Culture Contact: Interaction, Culture Change, and Archaeology. Center for Archaeological Investigations, Occasional Paper 25. Southern Illinois University, Carbondale, pp. 402–429.

Sayers, D. O., 2014. A Desolate Place for a Defiant People: The Archaeology of Maroons, Indigenous Americans, and Enslaved Laborers in the Great Dismal Swamp. University Press of Florida, Gainesville.

Scarry, J. F., McEwan, B. G., 1995. Domestic architecture in Apalachee Province: Apalachee and Spanish residential styles in the late prehistoric and early historic period southeast. Am. Antiq. 60 (3), 482–495.

Schenck, W. E., 1926. Historic aboriginal groups of the California delta region. Univ. Calif. Publ. Am. Archaeol. Ethnol. 23 (2), 123–146.

Schenck, W. E., Dawson, E. J., 1929. Archaeology of the Northern San Joaquin Valley. Univ. Calif. Publ. Am. Archaeol. Ethnol. 25 (4), 289–413.

Schneider, T. D., 2010. Placing Refuge: Shell Mounds and the Archaeology of Colonial Encounters in the San Francisco Bay Area, California. Ph.D. Dissertation. University of California, Berkeley.

Schneider, T. D., 2015a. Envisioning colonial landscapes using mission registers, radiocarbon, and stable isotopes: an experimental approach from San Francisco Bay. Am. Antiq. (in press-a).

Schneider, T. D., 2015b. Placing refuge and the archaeology indigenous hinterlands in colonial California. Am. Antiq. (in press-b).

Schneider, T. D., Panich, L. M., 2014. Native agency at the margins of empire: indigenous landscapes, Spanish missions, and contested histories. In: Panich, L. M., Schneider,

T. D. (Eds.), Indigenous Landscapes and Spanish Missions: New Perspectives from Archaeology and Ethnohistory. University of Arizona Press, Tucson, pp. 5–22.

Schwartz, S., Green, W., 2013. Middle ground or native ground? Material culture at Iowaville. Ethnohistory 60, 537–565.

Seymour, D. J., 2014. A Fateful Day in 1698: The Remarkable Sobaipuri-O'odham Victory over the Apaches and Their Allies. The University of Utah Press, Salt Lake City.

Silliman, S. W., 2009. Change and continuity, practice and memory: Native American persistence in colonial New England. Am. Antiq. 74 (2), 211–230.

Skowronek, R. K., Wizorek, J. C., 1997. Archaeology at Santa Clara de Asís: the slow rediscovery of a moveable mission. Pacific Coast Archaeol. Soc. Quart. 33 (3), 54–92.

Slaymaker, C. M., 1972. Cry for Olompali. Privately Printed. Bancroft Library, University of California, Berkeley.

Slaymaker, C. M., 1977. The Material Culture of Cotomko'tca: A Coast Miwok Tribelet in Marin County, California. Miwok Archaeological Preserve of Marin Occasional Paper, No. 3. Miwok Archaeological Preserve of Marin, San Rafael, California.

Spicer, E. H., 1962. Cycles of Conquest: The Impact of Spain, Mexico, and the United States on the Indians of the Southwest, 1533–1960. University of Arizona Press, Tucson.

Thomas, D. H., 2014. The life and times of Fr. Junípero Serra: a pan-borderlands perspective. Americas 71 (2), 185–225.

Van Buren, M., 2010. The archaeological study of Spanish colonialism in the Americas. J. Archaeol. Res. 18 (2), 151–201.

Voss, B. L., 2000. Colonial sex: archaeology, structured space, and sexuality in Alta California's Spanish-Colonial missions. In: Schmidt, R. A., Voss, B. L. (Eds.), Archaeologies of Sexuality. Routledge, London, pp. 35–61.

Voss, B. L., 2008. The Archaeology of Ethnogenesis: Race and Sexuality in Colonial San Francisco. University of California Press, Berkeley.

Wade, M. F., 2008. Missions, Missionaries, and Native Americans: Long-Term Processes and Daily Practices. University Press of Florida, Gainesville.

Walker, E. F., 1947. Excavation of a Yokuts Indian Cemetery: Elk Hills, Kern County, California. Kern County Historical Society, Bakersfield, California.

Walter, T. L., Hester, T. R., 2014. "Countless heathens": Native Americans and the Spanish missions of Southern Texas and Northeastern Coahuila. In: Panich, L. M., Schneider, T. D. (Eds.), Indigenous Landscapes and Spanish Missions: New Perspectives from Archaeology and Ethnohistory. University of Arizona Press, Tucson, pp. 93–113.

Wegars, P., 1974. The last survivor: a preliminary archaeological report on Marin County's Camillo Ynitia Adobe. In: Paper Presented at the 7th Annual Meeting of the Society for Historical Archaeology, Berkeley.

Wernke, S. A., 2013. Negotiated Settlements: Andean Communities and Landscapes under Inka and Spanish Colonialism. University Press of Florida, Gainesville.

Wiberg, R. S., 2005. Final Report: Archaeological Evaluation and Mitigative Data Recovery at CA-YOL-69, Madison Aggregate Plant, Yolo County, California. Report Prepared for Solano Concrete Company, Inc. Holman and Associates, Archaeological Consultants, San Francisco, California.

Zappia, N. A., 2012. Indigenous borderlands: livestock, captivity, and power in the far West. Pacific Hist. Rev. 81 (2), 193–220.

Zappia, N. A., 2014. Traders and Raiders: The Indigenous World of the Colorado Basin, 1540–1859. The University of North Carolina Press, Chapel Hill.

Schooling on the Missionary Frontier: The Hohi Mission Station, New Zealand

Ian W. G. Smith

Introduction

Teaching played an integral part in the process of missionization virtually everywhere that it occurred throughout the world. Whether it was confined to religious instruction, or encompassed broader training in literacy, economic skills and social behaviors, educational training was almost by definition a part of the missionary toolkit, and central to the cultural interactions that they engaged in. The extent to which these took place in institutional settings that we might call schools is somewhat difficult to judge, as the historical literature is often opaque in this regard.

Archaeology has documented teaching-related material assemblages in settings from monastic teaching of literacy in seventh-century CE Inchmarnock, Scotland (Lowe 2008), to nineteenth-century domestic training of Maori girls at Te Puna, New Zealand (Middleton 2008) and institutional education of aboriginal children at Ebenezer mission, Australia (Lydon 2009). Beyond these published descriptions of missionary educational contexts are scarce.

Just as missions themselves varied from small household operations to large institutions (Middleton 2013a), it seems likely that teaching varied from one-on-one instruction to classroom-style schooling, in contexts that range from casual encounters to incarcerative institutions. Historical analysis has pointed to the importance of teaching in a wide range of missionary settings, including the monasteries of the early Christian world (Hanson 1972), during Buddhist

---

Source: Smith, I. W. G., "Schooling on the Missionary Frontier: The Hohi Mission Station, New Zealand," *International Journal of Historical Archaeology* 18.4 (2014): pp. 612–628. Reprinted by permission from Springer Nature, Copyright © (2014).

The original article holds an illustration, (fig. 5), which is not included here. The location of this illustration is marked with an * in the text.

SCHOOLING ON THE MISSIONARY FRONTIER 331

infiltration of China (Zurcher 1972) and on the African fringes of the Islamic world (Keddie 1972). The success of sixteenth-century Spanish colonization of the Philippines has been attributed in large part to the organized schooling system established by missionaries there (Kane 1982, p. 62), and the economic systems of North America's Spanish borderlands during the seventeenth-century and later depended at least in part upon labor inducted through schooling (Weber 1992, pp. 105–106). However there are few detailed accounts of the ways in which schooling was conducted.

Outside the missionary world archaeological examination of schooling has also been limited. Baugher's (2009) overview of North American work points to several studies of dormitories from seventeenth- and nineteenth-century universities, as well as artifact assemblages and structural features from junior schools, but the most extensive study is Gibb and Beisaw's (2000) analysis of nineteenth- and twentieth-century rural schools in the northeastern United States which emphasizes the importance of the material record from these sites in reconstructing the attitudes and actions of the communities that they served. The only detailed study of schooling in a cross-cultural setting that might parallel the missionary context is Lindauer's (2009) analysis of the Phoenix Indian School. This late nineteenth/twentieth-century boarding school was a federal institution that sought to assimilate primary and secondary aged American Indian children into the Anglo-American world through training boys in productive trades and girls in housekeeping skills. All instruction was conducted in English. Indian languages, dress, and religious observance were forbidden, enforced through a repressive punishment regime. Lindauer's archaeological investigations disclosed material evidence of resistance through small items that were covert expressions of traditional cultural practices and individual identity, highlighting the struggle between accommodation and resistance for students in this cross-cultural setting.

This paper describes a very different kind of educational context at the early nineteenth-century Hohi mission in New Zealand, where the power balance favored the indigenous Maori population and coercion was not an option in the achievement of educational objectives. Schooling at Hohi involved both formal lessons in a schoolhouse and training through work experience in missionary households. It is proposed that in this frontier setting indigenous agency, coupled with the ambitions of individuals on both sides of the cross-cultural encounter, played a central part in the origins and progress of this educational endeavor.

The Hohi Mission, New Zealand

The Hohi mission station (Fig. 1) was established in late December 1814 by the Church Missionary Society (CMS), a London-based evangelical organisation associated with the Church of England. Three "artisan missionary" families and their retinue were sent via Sydney, Australia, as the first permanent European settlers of New Zealand, almost three decades before the imposition of European law and beginnings of formal colonization in 1840 (Smith 2013). This mission was founded on the belief that conversion to Christianity would best be achieved through first "civilizing" the indigenous population. The priority given to "conversion" or "civilizing" was widely debated within the evangelical missionary movement (Porter 1985; Walls 1975; Woolmington 1986). Samuel Marsden, Anglican chaplain to the colony of New South Wales, Australia, and instigator of the New Zealand mission was among the foremost advocates of the latter. As he explained to the Secretary of the CMS: "The attention of the Heathens can only be gained and their vagrant Habits corrected by the Arts. Till their attention is gained, and moral and industrious Habits are induced, little or no progress can be made in teaching them the Gospel" (Havard-Williams 1961, p. 15). The three men chosen to pursue this task were Thomas Kendall, formerly a draper and Sunday school teacher, John King, a shoemaker and twine spinner, and William Hall, carpenter (Binney 2005, pp. 23–33; McLennan and McLennan 2012, pp. 2–3; Middleton 2008, pp. 51–52). All three were married with children; the CMS expected its missionaries to "model the Christian monogamous family life that it was hoped could bring about a transformation of societies not yet influenced by the gospel" (Murray 2000, p. 69). None were ordained ministers. Teaching was central in their instructions from Marsden; "Mr. Kendall was to devote himself to the school. Messrs. Hall and King were also to instruct the natives in agriculture or anything for their general improvement" (Elder 1932, p. 224). Their wives were expected to provide training in household skills (Middleton 2007, 2013a). The missionary party of 25 also included sawyers, a brickmaker and blacksmith to assist in the construction of buildings (Smith et al. 2012).

Hohi was located adjacent to Rangihoua Pa, a fortified Maori village in the Bay of Islands, and one of the major settlements of Ruatara, an important chief of the Ngapuhi *iwi* (tribe). Ruatara's late father-in-law, Te Pahi, had been amongst the first *rangatira* (chiefs) to travel beyond New Zealand, visiting Sydney in 1805 where he met Marsden, inspiring the latter to work towards establishing a mission in New Zealand (Middleton 2008). Te Pahi's Australian

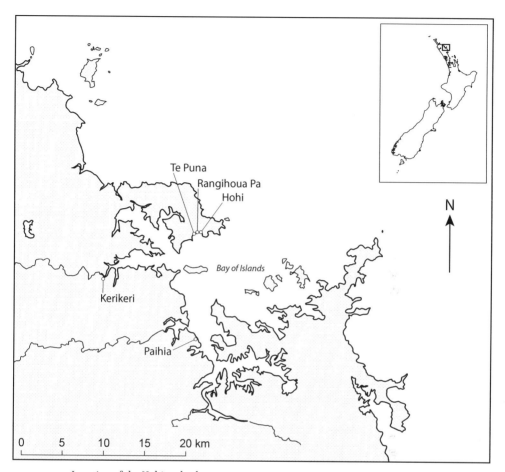

FIGURE 1   Location of the Hohi and subsequent CMS mission stations in the Bay of Islands

visit was focused on studying European gardening, carpentry, spinning and weaving, and the acquisition of seeds and fruit trees. Even before this trip Te Pahi had begun producing European-derived pigs and potatoes for trade with visiting whale ships. He further extended his interest in cultural and technological exchange by sending one of his sons, Matara, to England in 1807 "to see the King and obtain from his Majesty and the English nation axes, iron and musquets in order that they may be enabled to live as English men do" (Banks n.d.). Ruatara was also a cross-cultural traveler, working on whaling ships between 1805 and 1809 and visiting both England and Australia. In the latter place he lived for eight months with Marsden, studying agriculture and carpentry, and renewing Te Pahi's invitation to bring a mission to the Bay of Islands. Ruatara was especially keen for it to include a teacher to instruct his people in reading and writing; Marsden reported that Ruatara "was very urgent with me to send him a man to teach his boys and girls to read and write" (McNab 1908, p. 320).

For both missionary and Maori, a school was central to their vision of what was to happen at Hohi. Within a few weeks of arrival there Thomas Kendall began teaching reading and writing to a small number of pupils in his home (Elder 1932, p. 222), and each of the missionary families took in one or more Maori girls for training in domestic arts (King n.d.b). However cramped conditions made Kendall's teaching impossible to continue with (Binney 2005, p. 57) and formal schooling did not recommence until the building of a schoolhouse was completed in August 1816 (Elder 1934, p. 127).

Archaeology of the Hohi School House

The site of the Hohi mission comprises a series of terraces cut into a steep hillside rising above Rangihoua Bay on the northwestern shore of the Bay of Islands (Fig. 2). Prior to archaeological investigations commencing in February 2012 it was not known where the school house had stood on the site (Smith et al. 2012). Area 1 was selected for excavation in anticipation that it had been the location of one of the missionary houses. While two super-imposed structures were located here, neither yielded the food refuse nor diverse range of household goods that might be expected of a domestic structure, and one disclosed artifacts suggestive of a school.

The earliest structure in Area 1 was represented by the stone and brick base of a chimney, and foundation trenches defining part of its perimeter. The latter were shallow cuts into the yellow clay substrate containing remnants of wood indicating that ground plates for the walls had been laid within the trenches. These defined one corner and most of the length of one wall; the trench was not discernible at the western end of the area where the substrate changed to a gritty brown clay, although charred remnants of the ground plate indicated its minimum extent. This indicates a minimum length for the structure of 10.36m (34ft), although if the chimney was centered, the length of the north wall would have been 10.82m (35.5ft). Postholes and shallow depressions downslope from this wall indicate that the rest of the structure was supported on wooden piles and large stone foundation blocks. The southernmost posthole suggests that

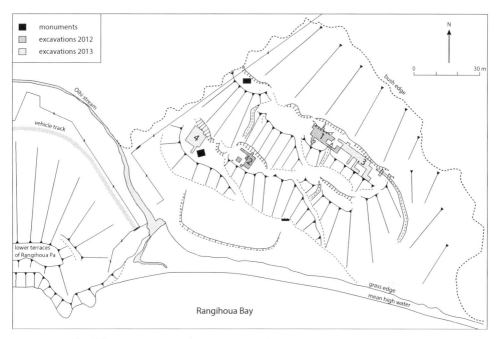

FIGURE 2   The Hohi mission station showing excavated areas

the width of the building was 6.1m (20ft). Pebbles had been laid to form a path along its northern side, which also had a drain that extended around the eastern end. The second structure was also centered on the fireplace, but much smaller at about 4.88m (16ft) square. Its perimeter was defined by a dense layer of pebble paving that overlaid the foundation trenches and other features associated with the earlier structure.

Artifacts were recovered from three stratigraphically defined contexts in Area 1; the soil above the dense pebble paving (layer 1), the pebble layer and associated features including fill of the fireplace (layer 2), and surfaces and features below the pebble paving (layer 3). These included a range of domestic, personal, and architectural items, most of which (91.4%) can be grouped into seven classes (Table 1). Joining or matching sherds from six ceramic vessels were distributed through all three assemblages indicating that there was some mixing between the deposits. Nonetheless there was a clear stratigraphic pattern to the distribution of artifacts. Slate pencils, metal fasteners, window glass, and personal items were all more common within and beneath the pebble layer, indicating that they were associated primarily with the first building

TABLE 1   Numbers of Identified Specimens (NISP) of selected artifact classes in area 1

Class	NISP	%NISP		
		Layer 1	Layer 2	Layer 3
clay pipes	149	59.7	38.9	1.3
ceramic vessels	482	56.4	37.6	0.6
glass vessels	821	54.3	40.9	4.8
personal items	36	46.2	46.2	7.6
window glass	1043	42.9	49.9	7.2
metal fasteners	1755	37.1	56.4	6.5
slate pencils	142	33.8	52.1	14.1

constructed in this area, while glass and ceramic vessels and clay pipes were most common in layer 1.

The architectural items provide some indications of the likely form of the original building in Area 1. The fasteners were predominantly wrought iron nails of sizes and forms commonly associated with the construction of wooden buildings (Middleton 2005). While they were found most abundantly along the lines of the building's perimeter walls, their widespread presence within this footprint indicate that the structure had a nailed wooden floor. Most (72%) of the items showing modification through use were bent in the manner that usually occurs when nails are removed from timbers. The building clearly had windows, and the glass from these was highly fragmented and worn, with micro-chipping and rounding on broken edges, as would be expected of fragments that were scuffed around in pebble paving or lay on the surface for some time before being buried. Reasons for the breakage of glass will be considered further below.

Slate pencils were the artifact class most strongly represented at the base of the site. The 142 items recovered represent a minimum number of 90 pencils, based on the number of points present. All had parallel flat facets on their shafts indicating that they had been manufactured by the reduction method (Davies 2005, p. 64). All were relatively short, most had blunted or unevenly sharpened points, with eleven pointed at both ends, indicating that these pencils were well used (Fig. 3). Five had marks scratched into the surface of the shaft, presumably for personal identification. There were also 17 fragments of flat slate averaging ca. 2.0mm in thickness, which is close to the standard

FIGURE 3
Slate pencil and tablet fragments

measurement (ca. 2.5mm) for writing, rather than roofing slates (Davies 2005, p. 63). Ten of these were inscribed with lines and three had faint traces of writing, unfortunately no longer legible.

The spatial distribution of slate pencil and tablet fragments is closely associated with the earlier of the two structures in Area 1 (Fig. 4). Almost half (48%) were recovered from within the footprint of the building, presumably having fallen through gaps in the floor boards, while another 41% were concentrated within and around the chimney and just outside the rear wall. Reasons for the absence of items from the western end of the building are considered below.

The 90 pencils recovered at Hohi is considerably more than has been reported from any other site in New Zealand, and exceeds the numbers from all but two of the sites from Australia reported by Davies (2005). The exceptions include an extensive investigation of a densely settled urban block (Porter and Ferrier 2006), and a smaller excavation on the site of a late nineteenth/ early twentieth-century school, the latter yielding 182 fragments of pencil and 72 from writing tablets (Davies 2005, p. 65). There can be little doubt that in the remote context of the Hohi mission station, the abundance of pencil and tablet fragments located beneath and around the first building in Area 1 indicate that this was the mission school.

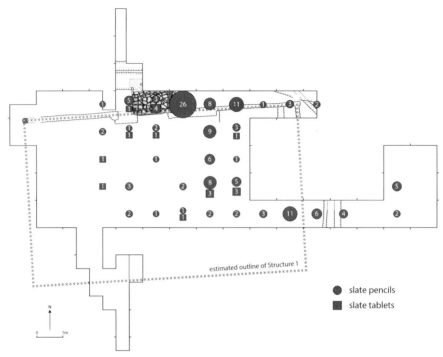

FIGURE 4   The distribution of slate fragments (NISP/m^2) in Area 1 in relation to the outline of the school

Schooling at Hohi

Missionary carpenter William Hall noted in his journal that on April 29, 1816 that he "laid the foundations of the School-house," and over the next few weeks raised the roof, constructed a wooden chimney lined with bricks, prepared openings for windows and clad the building in weatherboards (McLennan and McLennan 2012, pp. 13–16). In August he described the building as "thirty feet by eighteen, with a small apartment raised seven inches above the floor intended for the teachers and the European children, divided off by a low partition about brest [sic] high" (Elder 1932, p. 222). The archaeological observations show that the building was slightly larger than Hall reported, and suggest that the "raised apartment" is likely to have been at its western end, the second layer of flooring there preventing slate pencils from slipping through to the subfloor space.

The school opened on August 12, 1816. The attendance roll records five male and 19 female students in attendance that day, their ages calculated "by

SCHOOLING ON THE MISSIONARY FRONTIER

computation" ranged from seven to 20 years of age*. A total of 33 students attended during the remainder of August, and 76 were present for at least one day
during four of the following five months for which rolls have survived (Jones
and Jenkins 2011, pp. 108, 212, n189). These rolls were an account of the attendance of "native children" (Kendall and Carlisle n.d.); there is no comparable
data for European children. Thomas Kendall reported that "the children of settlers [i.e. the missionary community] are also instructed" (Elder 1934, p. 138),
but the numbers must have been low. During 1816–17 there were no more than
nine European children at Hohi, the oldest four of whom were between five
and nine years old. It is unclear, therefore, to what extent the racial segregation
implicit in the school house design was put into practice.

Teaching at the school was based around learning the alphabet, syllables,
and catechisms, with the pupils being taught to read and write in their native Maori language. They used a book of lessons, *A Korao no New Zealand;
or the New Zealander's First Book; being An Attempt to Compose some Lessons
for the Instruction of the Natives*, which Kendall had written in 1815, the first
printed representation of the Maori language in written form (Binney 2005,
pp. 175–176; Jones and Jenkins 2011, pp. 119–129). Kendall had an assistant teacher in the recently arrived missionary, William Carlisle. He also employed Bell's
(1813) monitorial system, using older pupils who had already mastered some
skills to teach younger pupils by rote. One such monitor was the first named
pupil on the school roll, "A Towha" (Towai), 17 year-old son of the late chief
Te Pahi, who had first visited Sydney in 1805 (Salmond 1997, p. 351) and knew
the basics of reading and writing (Jones and Jenkins 2011, p. 106). Kendall described the daily routine they attempted to follow. The children, who slept in
the loft of the school house, "rise at daylight, according to the custom of the
natives in general, and repeat their lessons to me. After breakfast several of the
boys write a copy. The girls are employed in making their raiment the whole of
the day. After dinner the native children repeat their lessons to my colleague
Mr. Carlisle. The boys learn to write on every day of the week except Sunday"
(Elder 1934, p. 138). Establishing this pattern had been difficult:

> My little wild pupils were all noise and play during the first four months.
> We could scarcely hear them read for their incessant shouting, singing
> and dancing. The first month they attempted to repeat their lessons in
> the schoolhouse very well, but we soon had to follow them to a short
> distance into the bushes. I had no command over them, having at that
> time neither provisions or rewards to give them. Since I received these,
> my authority and influence have been greatly augmented amongst them.
>
> ELDER 1934, p. 138

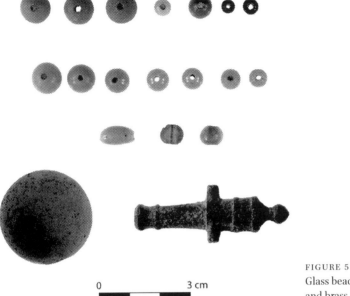

FIGURE 5
Glass beads, clay marble, and brass toy cannon

Bell's teaching system relied upon the distribution of rewards (Bell 1813, pp. 45–49), and a list of items that Kendall requested for this purpose included fish hooks, beads, colored ribbons, rings and ear rings, clasps, knives, scissors, needles, knitting needles, thimbles, various metal tools, whistles, birdcalls "or any other toys that will take little room (made of iron)" (Elder 1934, p. 130). Colored glass beads were recovered archaeologically from beneath the schoolhouse floor and from the fill of the drains around its perimeter (Fig. 5). A clay marble and the barrel of a miniature brass cannon may be toys that were distributed in a similar way.

More important to the success of the school than the distribution of rewards was the provision of food for the pupils. During the initial months, before supplies for the school arrived from Sydney, the pupils generally spent the period between morning and evening lessons in "the rivers or bush in pursuit of fish, fern-root, cockles, etc." (Elder 1934, p. 129). Further details were recorded in the school roll for September 1816: "Purchased fern root and distributed it amongst the scholars / Gave one fish to each scholar / No victuals for Scholars / A party of scholars absent procuring cockles / Served out one pound of pork to each scholar which I purchased upon credit of the Natives" (Kendall and Carlisle n.d.). Food supply was a problem for the whole community, which was unable to produce sufficient food for itself and was awaiting further supplies

SCHOOLING ON THE MISSIONARY FRONTIER 341

from Sydney; during October 1816 the sawyers stopped work "on account of the scarcity of provisions" (McLennan and McLennan 2012, p. 21) and, along with the blacksmith and brickmaker, they departed Hohi in November (Smith et al. 2012, p. 11). Not surprisingly, student attendance declined.

Once a shipment of food supplies arrived in December 1816, pupils returned to the school, and its peak attendance of 70 was achieved in April 1817 (Missionary Register 1819, p. 464). Nonetheless, provisioning remained a vexed issue. Marsden and the CMS had intended that the Hohi community were to quickly make themselves self-sufficient in food supply, and that all goods acquired by their own labor or trade with visiting ships or Maori were to be deposited into a communal store and distributed to those engaged in the mission according to need (Middleton 2006, p. 53). Although Maori had productive gardens nearby and produced surplus potatoes and pigs for trade, the soils at Hohi were steep and infertile, precluding successful cultivation or stockraising by the mission community (Elder 1934, p. 131), who appear not to have engaged seriously in fishing, fowling, or gathering the wild foods that formed significant components of Maori subsistence. Acquisition of pork and potatoes from Maori became increasingly difficult as the quality of their iron trade goods, locally made and from New South Wales, was soon recognized as inferior to English items brought in by overseas shipping (Binney 2005, p. 53). Perhaps most importantly, Marsden's prohibition on the use of muskets and gunpowder for trade made it impossible for the missionaries to compete with less scrupulous captains of whaling ships who each summer were purchasing large quantities of pork and potatoes (Binney 2005, p. 59).

The demands placed on the community's food supplies by the school created divisions; both King and Hall considered that it absorbed resources that were necessary for their families (Binney 2005, p. 58). Relationships between the principal missionaries, which had never been easy, became increasingly tense; each accused the others of conducting "private trade," and dealing in muskets (Elder 1932, pp. 232–236, 1934, pp. 142–148). In December 1818 Kendall wrote "I have endeavoured to keep the School together for as long as I could, and I have spent for this purpose some of my own private property. I can now do no more" (Kendall n.d.a). By the end of that year the school was closed, although the building continued to serve as a chapel for Sunday worship, as it had since its opening (McLennan and McLennan 2012, p. 52)

Marsden returned to New Zealand in August 1819, bringing a new contingent of missionaries to establish a second mission station in the Bay of Islands (Elder 1932, p. 143). The new residents were housed temporarily at Hohi, and their goods were stored in the schoolhouse until January 1820 (King n.d.a,

August 13, 1819; McLennan and McLennan 2012, p. 61). Soon after this Kendall departed on an unauthorized voyage to England with two chiefs to assist Professor Samuel Lee of Cambridge University on the compilation of the first Maori grammar (Binney 2005, pp. 67–73). Even after his return in July 1821, the Hohi school remained closed. Kendall's relationships with his colleagues worsened, in part due to continued arguments about trading in muskets, but also because of his adulterous affair with the daughter of a chief. Journal entries and correspondence from all the leading members of the mission show that both these matter deepened the existing rifts, even after Kendall ended the affair and expressed remorse for his sins (Binney 2005, pp. 92–103). By August 1822 he had been suspended from missionary activities, and in February 1823 moved with his family to a Maori settlement across the Bay before his formal dismissal from the CMS on August 9, 1823 (Binney 2005, pp. 112–119). Kendall and family departed the Bay of Islands for Valparaiso, Chile, in January 1825, and two years later settled in New South Wales, Australia (Binney 2005, pp. 162–163).

Within a month of Kendall's dismissal schooling was resumed, with seven boys under the tutelage of John King (n.d.a, September 7, 1823). Initially this took place in one of the empty houses as the school building was in poor condition, but repairs were conducted and it was restored to use by the end of the year (McLennan and McLennan 2012, pp. 87–89). However, this was to be short-lived. In November 1823 and April 1824 Maori parties, seeking to avenge the expulsion of Kendall from the mission (Binney 2005, pp. 18–19), inflicted damage to his former house, and on the second occasion also to the school; "they tore off the weatherboards, of the back of the ... School-house and went in through the Wall, and tore the lock off the Closet with the expectation of getting the Children's Cloathing [sic], but Mr. King had removed them before; they took away the Alphabets that were hanging against the wall, tore the fastening off the Reading Desk, and broke the Windows" (McLennan and McLennan 2012, p. 92). The CMS committee immediately resolved to demolish Kendall's house and the school, and this was carried out within a week (McLennan and McLennan 2012, pp. 92–93; Middleton 2014, p. 55). Both the vandalism and the demolition are likely to have contributed to the concentrations of window glass fragments and iron nails recovered archaeologically from the schoolhouse.

Before the end of 1824 William Hall built a second school house "convenient to Mr King's dwelling" (McLennan and McLennan 2012, p. 96) on a lower terrace of the mission. This operated in a similar manner to Kendall's earlier school, with rote learning of the alphabet, syllables, and catechisms between 6 and 8 AM and again from 4 to 6 PM (Elder 1934, pp. 258–259). Between the

SCHOOLING ON THE MISSIONARY FRONTIER

two sessions most pupils were supervised in agricultural, manual or domestic tasks. Although King's school had initially taught only boys, girls and adult pupils were included from 1826 (Table 2). Numbers in attendance varied, due mostly, it would seem, to seasonal demands for men and boys in other activities, but the fluctuations were less dramatic than during Kendall's tenure. This can be attributed primarily to greater security of food supply with more reliable access to imported goods after the Bay of Islands mission community launched their own ship in 1826 (Purchas 1914, pp. 43–44). In addition, a fund to support the school had been instituted in 1824, and subscriptions to this were forthcoming from captains of several visiting ships (McLennan and McLennan 2012, pp. 98, 100). King also noted educational successes, reporting in 1825 that he had "taught eight boys to read: they are capable of reading the Bible, were it translated into their tongue. Some of them can read with ease all the Dialogues contained in the Grammar of their language: they are also learning to spell, and write, and form sentences on their slates: they are taught from time to time the way of death by sin, and the way of life by Jesus Christ" (Missionary Register 1827, p. 123).

TABLE 2   Reported attendance at John King's School, 1823–32

Year	Attendance	Reference
1823	7 boys	King n.d.a, September 7, 1823
	10 to 15 boys from 6 to 9 years of age	Missionary Register 1825, p. 101
1824	14 children	Missionary Register 1826, p. 159
1825	"I have taught eight boys to read"	Missionary Register 1827, p. 123
1826	7–10 boys, 7 girls, 3 adults	Missionary Register 1828, p. 128
1827	8 boys, 9 girls, 3 adults	CMS n.d., July 3, 1827
1828	23 males, 10 females	CMS n.d., October 7, 1828
1829	16 men & boys, 12 girls	CMS n.d., January 6, 1829
	24 men & boys, 11 girls	CMS n.d., October 5, 1829
1830	17 men & boys, 10 girls	CMS n.d., March 17, 1830
	27 men & boys, 11 girls	CMS n.d., December 27, 1830
1831	20–24 natives	CMS n.d., July 4, 1831
	19 men & boys, 10 girls	CMS n.d., October 4, 1831
1832	19 male natives, 12 female	CMS n.d., April 9, 1832
	15 men & boys, 9 girls	CMS n.d., July 2, 1832

For the missionaries at Hohi, schooling was seen primarily as means to "civilize" Maori to prepare them for conversion to Christianity. In terms of this ultimate goal of the mission, success was realized very slowly. It was not until almost 15 years after the first school opened that King was able to report that "two of the natives belonging to the school have been baptized" (CMS n.d., July 4, 1831). This achievement came as the last of the missionaries at Hohi were preparing to shift their operations to a more fertile location ca. 1km to the west. In September 1832 John King and James Shepherd moved their families into new houses at Te Puna where their work in schooling, domestic, and agricultural training and missionizing continued (Middleton 2008).

Discussion

Hohi operated on the frontier of cultural engagement in New Zealand. When the 25 Europeans founded the settlement in 1814 they were the only Europeans residents in a country with an indigenous population estimated at ca. 100,000 (Pool 1991, p. 57). By the time it was abandoned in 1832, the European population in the Bay of Islands had grown to just over 100, with perhaps 300 in the whole of the country (Adams 1977, pp. 22–25). The missionary venture operated in a Maori world, beyond the rule of European law or military strength. The Hohi settlement was under the protection of the chiefs at Rangihoua pa, and for most of its existence was dependent upon them for a significant part of its food supply. It was also subject to the cultural and political precepts that governed the Maori world (Middleton 2003).

The school at Hohi can be viewed as a microcosm of the broader missionary endeavor there. From both sides of the cultural frontier on which it operated, schooling was seen as central to the engagement taking place, although in each case for reasons that went beyond its immediate purpose. For the missionaries, schooling was a Trojan horse for their ultimate goal of Christian conversion. For Maori, literacy and artisanal skills were seen as pathways to power in the European world. Kendall noted that "none of the grown up people are averse to having their children instructed; they believe that education is valuable as it bears upon the temporal interests of mankind. Their commercial disposition induces them to believe this" (Elder 1934, p. 134). The competition between Bay of Island chiefs to secure first Hohi, then subsequent missions on their lands, although often expressed as a desire for someone to "preach, teach little children to read and write, administer medicine when they are sick, and show them how to cultivate the land" (Elder 1932, p. 206), was equally focused on the imperative of controlling access to, and trade in, European goods (Urlich Cloher 2003, pp. 95–117).

Despite, or perhaps because of these ulterior motives, the school and its associated training activities became one of the primary venues for interactions that served to both inform and modify the daily practices of the participants, and more broadly their cultures. Among the missionaries attempts to intervene in Maori cultural practices were their efforts to impose regular hours of attendance, clothe their pupils in the European style, and structure their learning according to European perceptions of gender-appropriate tasks. Likewise, some Maori tried to modify the activities of the missionaries, John King noting: "They want to instruct us how to treat our children, to cook, and many other things" (Elder 1934, p. 111). Other interactions reflect contrasting views of social order. The missionaries happily accommodated commoners, orphans and slaves alongside chiefly offspring in the school, despite the objections of at least two chiefs that there was no point in teaching common people (Elder 1932, p. 118). This stands in marked contrast to the missionaries treatment of the children of the Hansen family, European settlers who from 1817 lived adjacent to the mission and pa. Although Thomas Hansen was brother of missionary John King's wife, his family were considered to be of a lower class, and prohibited from attending school—a slight still remembered today by their descendants (Martin 1990, p. 53).

It is noteworthy that the indigenous language was chosen as the medium for instruction, and the learning of this was one of the key ways in which the missionaries were drawn into the Maori world. While they had learned rudiments of the language from Maori who travelled with them from England to Australia and while residing there before arriving in New Zealand, it was through the intensive engagement of teaching in the school, home, farm and workshop that they gained proficiency and began to develop understanding of concepts such as *mana* (prestige, efficacy), *tapu* (sacred, set apart) and *utu* (compensation, revenge) which pervaded the Maori world (Hohepa 1999; Middleton 2003). Kendall sought knowledge of the language more than any of the others in his quest to develop effective tools for teaching, to the extent that Jones and Jenkins (2011, p. 118) have described him as the "star graduate" of the Hohi school. However, his quest to understand the cosmological underpinnings of the language was deeply challenging to his own beliefs (Binney 2005, pp. 10–19), leading him to write "I have been almost completely turned from a Christian to a Heathen" (Kendall n.d.b).

The response to Kendall's dismissal from the CMS illustrates one of the many ways in which the mission was operating in a Maori world. When Marsden arrived on his fourth visit to the Bay, bearing Kendall's formal letter of dismissal, he discussed reasons for this with the chiefly families at Rangihoua. While they acknowledged that Kendall had done wrong, they contended that as he was no longer living with the young woman, his conduct should be forgotten.

The Maori community still respected their first teacher, and Marsden was informed that they would pull down the house that he had formerly lived in because "they were very angry on account of Mr. Kendall's dismissal" (Elder 1932, p. 351). Elsewhere in the Bay there was also discontent (Urlich Cloher 2003, pp. 205–213). Although Marsden could not believe such violence would take place, there were, as already noted, two attacks on Kendall's house and school in the ensuing months. In Maori terms this was *utu*, which provided a balanced redress to restore equilibrium (Hohepa 1999, p. 196). The means used to achieve this at Hohi was *muru*, sometimes translated as "plunder" but more accurately "compensation," and usually refers to the taking of goods to redress an affront or offence, either deliberate or unintentional (Ministry of Justice 2001, pp. 75–79). For Maori, muru provided closure as it restored the *mana* of those who had been affronted while the initial transgressors would accept the blame apportioned to them. In the cross-cultural context at Hohi it seems unlikely that the missionaries accepted responsibility for the offence they had caused.

In the same way that the initial growth then demise of the school reflected the broader trajectory of mission activity, so too did its subsequent rebirth and steady success. It is no surprise that the revival of schooling at Hohi was coincident with the departure of Kendall, whose behavior toward his colleagues and challenges to missionary propriety were significant contributors to the troubles that beset the first nine years of the mission. The more settled community in which the second school flourished was also influenced by the emergence of more authoritative leadership of the CMS in New Zealand with the arrival of Henry Williams in 1823. This not only led to resolution of the internal tensions that had blighted the mission's progress, but also presented Maori with a recognizably "chiefly" figure as a focal point for engagement (Middleton 2014). In parallel with this, the CMS missions were achieving increasing economic independence from Maori through the expansion of their agricultural base and development of their own shipping (Binney 1969, pp. 146–147). The late 1820s and early 1830s saw expansions of missionary efforts beyond their initial confinement within the Bay of Islands (Middleton 2013b) and as part of this a renewed emphasis on schooling (Binney 1969, p. 148).

There were also changes in Maori attitudes to and engagement with missionaries and their schools. While their initial interest was focused primarily on the desire to gain access to and control trade in European goods, it turned increasingly towards acquisition of literacy "to comprehend and command the system of meanings that determined European technological superiority" (Jackson 1975, p. 31). The growth in school attendance by adults as well as children seen at Hohi was paralleled in other mission schools (Binney 1969, table 2). Maori who had learned to read were active in passing on this knowledge to others, both in mission schools and in Maori-run village schools (Parr 1963, pp. 211–212).

Conclusion

The school at Hohi provides some important insights into the nature of cultural encounters on the missionary frontier in the South Pacific during the early nineteenth century. Both historical contingencies and broader cultural processes are reflected in its origins and erratic progress. Among the former were the coincidence of divergent but overlapping ambitions of key individuals in bringing the mission into existence and placing schooling at the centre of its activities, and the ambiguous consequences of the cross-cultural explorations by the school's first teacher. While it can be anticipated that similarly unique circumstances will have arisen elsewhere on the missionary frontier, it is the broader processes that are of greater significance when looking outwards from this specific case. Foremost amongst these is the role of indigenous agency in the formation and progress of the mission. Maori were active players in bringing this new institution into their midst and utilized it in an attempt to participate in the modern world on their own terms. The slow progress towards the missionary objective of conversion to Christianity can be attributed, for the most part, to Maori disinterest; for them the missionaries represented a source of foreign goods and, through control of these, a monopoly on power within the Maori world. Only when trade goods were more widely available and the negative consequences of more widespread European presence began to be apparent did Maori seek out the Christian message in the hope that it would provide access to the knowledge behind European culture.

The extent to which factors such as these may be paralleled in the early phases of missionization in the South Pacific is difficult to judge at present because, outside New Zealand, there are few published archaeological investigations of mission sites (for an exception see Flexner 2013). Equally, the scarcity of archaeologically based studies of mission schools globally precludes broader comparison of the role of schooling in the process of missionization. What the analysis of Hohi suggests is that this should be a fruitful focus for further study.

Acknowledgments

I am grateful to Hugh Rihari of Ngati Torehina for insights into his ancestors who attended the Hohi school, Jessie Garland and Naomi Woods who undertook the artifact analysis, and Angela Middleton and two anonymous referees for comments on the text. The research was funded by a University of Otago Research Grant and the New Zealand Department of Conservation.

References

Adams, P. (1977). *Fatal Necessity: British Intervention in New Zealand, 1830–1847*, Auckland University Press, Auckland.

Banks, J. (n.d.). Note describing "The New Zealand Boy" [undated, 1807?]. Ms 9/139, National Library of Australia, Auckland.

Baugher, S. (2009). Historical overview of the archaeology of institutional life. In Beisaw, A. M., and Gibb, J. G. (eds.), *The Archaeology of Institutional Life*, University of Alabama Press, Tuscaloosa, pp. 5–13.

Bell, A. (1813). *Instructions for Conducting a School Through the Agency of the Scholars Themselves: Comprising the Analysis of an Experiment in Education made at the Male Asylum, Madras, 1789–1796*, John Murray, London.

Binney, J. (1969). Christianity and the Maoris to 1840: a comment. *New Zealand Journal of History* 3: 143–65.

Binney, J. (2005). *The Legacy of Guilt: A Life of Thomas Kendall*, Bridget Williams, Wellington.

CMS (n.d.). Minutes of Missionary Meetings. CN/O4, Hocken Library, Dunedin.

Davies, P. (2005). Writing slates and schooling. *Australasian Historical Archaeology* 23: 63–69.

Elder, J. R. (1932). *The Letters and Journals of Samuel Marsden 1765–1838*, Coulls Sommerville Wilkie and A. H. Reed, Dunedin.

Elder, J. R. (1934). *Marsden's Lieutenants*, Coulls Somerville Wilkie and A. H. Reed, Dunedin.

Flexner, J. (2013). Mission archaeology in Vanuatu: preliminary findings, problems and prospects. *Australasian Historical Archaeology* 31: 14–24.

Gibb, J. G., and Beisaw, A. M. (2000). Learning cast up from the mire: archaeological investigations of schoolhouses in northeastern United States. *Northeast Historical Archaeology* 29: 107–29.

Hanson, W. G. (1972). *The Early Monastic Schools of Ireland: Their Missionaries, Saints and Scholars*, B. Franklin, New York.

SCHOOLING ON THE MISSIONARY FRONTIER

Havard-Williams, P. (1961). *Marsden and the New Zealand Mission; Sixteen Letters*, University of Otago Press in association with Reed, Dunedin.

Hohepa, P. (1999). My musket, my missionary, my mana. In Calder, A., Lamb, J., and Orr, B. (eds.), *Voyages and Beaches: Pacific Encounters 1769–1840*, University of Hawaii Press, Honolulu, pp. 180–201.

Jackson, M. D. (1975). Literacy, communications and social change: a study of the meaning and effect of literacy in early nineteenth century Maori society. In Kawharu, I. H. (ed.), *Conflict and Compromise: Essays on the Maori since Colonisation*, A. H. and A. W. Reed, Wellington, pp. 27–54.

Jones, A., and Jenkins, K. (2011). *Words Between Us—He Korero: First Maori-Pakeha Conversations on Paper*, Huia, Wellington.

Kane, J. H. (1982). *A Concise History of the Christian World Mission*, Baker Book House, Grand Rapids, MI.

Keddie, N. R. (1972). *Scholars, Saints and Sufis: Muslim Religious Institutions in the Middle East since 1500*, University of California Press, Berkeley.

Kendall, T. (n.d.a). Letter to Reverend Josiah Pratt, 8 December 1818. MS-0056/210, Hocken Library, Dunedin.

Kendall, T. (n.d.b). Letter to Reverend John Eyre, 27 December 1822. MS-0071/040, Hocken Library, Dunedin.

Kendall, T. and Carlisle, W. (n.d). Monthly account of the attendance of the native children at the Church Missionary Society's School, Bay of Islands, New Zealand, commencing 12 August 1816. MS-0056/003, Hocken Library, Dunedin.

King, J. (n.d.a). Letters and Journals 1819–1853. MS-0073, Hocken Library, Dunedin.

King, J. (n.d.b). Letter to CMS, 10 May 1852. MS-0073, Hocken Library, Dunedin.

Lindauer, O. (2009). Individual struggles and institutional goals: small voices from the Phoenix Indian School track site. In Beisaw, A. M., and Gibb, J. G. (eds.), *The Archaeology of Institutional Life*, University of Alabama Press, Tuscaloosa.

Lowe, C. (2008). *Inchmarnock: An Early Historical Island Monastery and its Archaeological Landscape*, Society of Antiquaries, Edinburgh.

Lydon, J. (2009). *Fantastic Dreaming: The Archaeology of an Aboriginal Mission*, Altamira, Lanham, MD.

Martin, R. (1990). *The First Family: Captain Thomas and Hannah Hansen and their Children*, Hansen Celebration Committee, Auckland.

McLennan, M. M., and McLennan, P. R. (2012). *Son of Carlisle—Maori Missionary: The Diary of CMS Missionary William Hall, 1816–1838*, Privately Published, Kellyville, NSW.

McNab, R. (1908). *Historical Records of New Zealand, Volume 1*, John Mckay Government Printer, Wellington.

Middleton, A. (2003). Maori and European landscapes at Te Puna, Bay of Islands, New Zealand, 1805–1850. *Archaeology in Oceania* 38: 110–124.

Middleton, A. (2005). Nail chronology: the case of Te Puna mission station. *Australasian Historical Archaeology* 23: 55–62.

Middleton, A. (2006). Mission station as trading post: the economy of the Church Missionary Society in the Bay of Islands, New Zealand. *New Zealand Journal of Archaeology* 28: 51–81.

Middleton, A. (2007). Silent voices, hidden lives: archaeology, class and gender in the CMS mission, Bay of Islands, New Zealand, 1814–1845. *International Journal of Historical Archaeology* 11: 1–31.

Middleton, A. (2008). *Te Puna: A New Zealand Mission Station*, Springer, New York.

Middleton, A. (2013a). Missionization and the cult of domesticity: local investigation of a global process. In Spencer-Wood, S. (ed.), *Historical and Archaeological Perspectives on Gender Transformations: From Private to Public*, Springer, New York, pp. 149–170.

Middleton, A. (2013b). Mission archaeology in New Zealand. In Campbell, M., Holdaway, S. J., and Macready, S. (eds.), *Finding our Recent Past: Historical Archaeology in New Zealand*, New Zealand Archaeological Association, Auckland, pp. 33–58.

Middleton, A. (2014). *Pēwhairangi: Bay of Islands Missions and Maori, 1814–1845*, University of Otago Press, Dunedin.

Ministry of Justice (2001). *He Hinatore ki te Ao Maori: A Glimpse into the Maori World. Maori Perspectives on Justice*, New Zealand Ministry of Justice, Wellington.

Missionary Register (1813–55). *Missionary Register. Containing an Abstract of the Principal Missionary and Bible Societies Throughout The World*, L. B. Seeley and Sons, London.

Murray, J. (2000). The role of women in the CMS, 1799–1917. In Ward, K., and Stanley, B. (eds.), *The Church Missionary Society and World Christianity 1799–1999*, W. B. Eerdmans, Grand Rapids, MI, pp. 67–90.

Parr, C. J. (1963). Maori literacy 1843–1867. *Journal of the Polynesian Society* 72: 211–34.

Pool, I. (1991). *Te Iwi Maori: A New Zealand Population, Past, Present and Future*, Auckland University Press, Auckland.

Porter, A. (1985). "Commerce and Christianity": the rise and fall of a nineteenth-century missionary slogan. *The Historical Journal* 28: 597–621.

Porter, J., and Ferrier, A. (2006). Miscellaneous artifacts from Casselden Place, Melbourne. *International Journal of Historical Archaeology* 10: 375–393.

Purchas, H. T. (1914). *A History of the English Church in New Zealand*, Simpson and Williams, Christchurch.

Salmond, A. (1997). *Between Worlds Early Exchanges between Maori and Europeans 1773–1815*, Viking, Auckland.

Smith, I. W. G. (2013). Ephemeral foundations: early European settlement of the Tasman frontier. In Campbell, M., Holdaway, S. J., and Macready, S. (eds.), *Finding our Recent Past: Historical Archaeology in New Zealand*, New Zealand Archaeological Association, Auckland, pp. 9–32.

Smith, I. W. G., Middleton, A., Garland, J., and Woods, N. (2012). *Archaeology of the Hohi Mission Station, Volume 1: The 2012 Excavations*, University of Otago Studies in Archaeology, Dunedin.

Urlich Cloher, D. (2003). *Hongi Hika: Warrior Chief*, Viking, Auckland.

Walls, A. F. (1975). A colonial concordat: two views of christianity and civilisation. In Baker, D. (ed.), *Church, Society and Politics*, Basil Blackwell, Oxford, pp. 293–302.

Weber, D. J. (1992). *The Spanish Frontier in North America*, Yale University Press, New Haven.

Woolmington, J. (1986). The civilisation/christianisation debate and the Australian aborigines. *Aboriginal History* 10: 90–98.

Zurcher, E. (1972). *The Buddhist Conquest of China: The Spread and Adaptation of Buddhism in Early Medieval China*, E. J. Brill, Leiden.

Objects of Expert Knowledge: On Time and the Materialities of Conversion to Christianity in the Southern New Hebrides

Jean Mitchell

In a letter dated 8 November 1859 to a member of his first congregation in Cavendish, Prince Edward Island, John Geddie describes the activities of the Presbyterian mission he established in Aneityum, an island in southern New Hebrides (now Vanuatu). The letter, written just a decade after his arrival in Aneityum, notes:

> there are over 50 schools in operation attended by persons of both sexes and every age.... We have lately completed the translation of the New Testament.... The Natives are at present employed in building a new stone church. Some of the larger stones required 60 men to carry them. This has been a great undertaking.[1]

Reported to accommodate up to 1,000 people, the church would become one of the largest in the southern hemisphere. These extraordinary activities marked the rapid conversion to Christianity in Aneityum. Even more remarkable is that the Aneityumese were simultaneously negotiating the demands of the sandalwood trade, its violence and new technologies. Still more remarkable is that the ambitious projects of conversion were undertaken as the islanders endured epidemics from exogenous causes that were exacting tragic tolls on people and their knowledge. During Geddie's tenure, more than half of the population died as islanders came to terms with spiritual and material upheavals. Geddie's letter highlights aspects of temporality and expert knowledge thus underlining that becoming Christian entailed "doing" material things or

---

Source: Mitchell, J., "Objects of Expert Knowledge: On Time and the Materialities of Conversion to Christianity in the Southern New Hebrides," *Anthropologica* 55.2 (2013): pp. 291–302. Reprinted with permission from University of Toronto Press (https://utpjournals.press).

---

1 I was told about this letter to John Lockerby by his descendant Earl Lockerby. There are also several letters from Charlotte Geddie to Mrs. Lockerby, one of which is referred to later in this article.

OBJECTS OF EXPERT KNOWLEDGE 353

"undertakings." Expertise, evident in the letter, is, according to E. Summerson Carr, "inherently interactional, invoking the participation of objects, producers and consumers of knowledge and inescapably ideologically implicated in the evolving hierarchies of value" (2010:17). Carr's conceptualization of expertise is a useful way in which to consider Geddie's project of conversion, for expertise "is also fundamentally a process of becoming" (Carr 2010:19).

Conversion to Christianity in Melanesia has been the subject of significant ethnographic analyses driven, in no small part, by Barker's (1990, 1992) insistence that Christianity is a cultural phenomenon that demands an anti-essentialist framing. While the introduction of Christianity in Melanesia unfolded in different ways, the relationship between indigenous and Christian temporalities and knowledge are often foregrounded. There has been a tendency to move between an emphasis on continuity and discontinuity in understanding the complex processes of conversion to Christianity and colonialism in the Pacific Islands. Anthropologists, Joel Robbins (2007) contends, have been attached to a temporal framework that privileges continuities underplaying the ruptures with the past that are central to conversion. In her early analysis of conversion to Christianity in Aneityum, Bronwen Douglas argues that it entailed a dialectic of "reciprocal processes of incorporation and transformation of new concepts and rituals in terms of local cosmology and cultural assumptions" (1989:11). In his ethnographic work in northern Vanuatu, John Taylor (2010:423) crafted the term "crossing" to convey "the simultaneous convergence and contradictions among indigenous and exogenous religious paradigms that have guided the transformative dialogues of religious colonialism." The idea that conversion is a complex and ongoing process is evident in Michael Scott's (2005:102) ethnographic work in the Solomon Islands, where he argues islanders continuously "engage and re-engage with Christianity" and its "multiple interlocking macro and micro Christian logics." This perspective suggests that conversion is not comprised of a singular cultural logic; rather, becoming Christian is a fraught ontological project in which temporalities and knowledge are continuously reworked.

Temporalities, according to Munn "are lived or apprehended concretely via the various meaningful connectivities, among persons, objects, and space continually being made in and through the everyday world" (1992:116). In this article, I am interested in the ways in which objects help to "apprehend" the "connectivities" that are made and remade in the context of conversion. I was alerted to the power of objects connected to conversion while visiting Aneityum in 2008, where I had discussed Geddie's mission with James and

John, two elderly deacons in the Presbyterian Church. Just before leaving Aneityum, they showed me John Geddie's eye-glasses, which they explained, had been in the possession of islanders since his departure from the island in 1872. The eyeglasses conjure the technologies of reading and writing connected to new sources of authoritative knowledge encompassed by the introduction of the Bible that, as Anna Johnston argues, has its own "conflicted temporality" (2001:34). The eyeglasses suggest the social life of an object (Appadurai 1988) and its various trajectories and valuations. They also underline the temporal relationships between Geddie and the descendants of the early converts. Missionaries were attentive to indigenous objects which they collected, preserved and sent back to their countries. However, objects connected to religious rites and beliefs regarded as idols in the new Christian contexts were frequently destroyed or discarded (Colley 2003; Lawson 1994, 2005; Manning and Meneley 2008).

Objects, both mundane and sacred, focus attention on the "messy materiality of things" connected to cosmological worlds (Manning and Meneley 2008:287). Geddie's letter points to the materiality of conversion to Christianity by way of schools, the work of Bible translation and the heavy stones that were converted into the large church that made Christianity manifest and material. These objects make visible the pedagogical, cosmological and temporal commitments that were at the heart of becoming Christian in Aneityum. The materiality of conversion in Aneityum is underlined by Douglas who states that "sacred ground was rendered mundane, foods previously prohibited were ingested safely and sacred stones thrown away" (1989:20). By drawing on the technology of introduced cloth in Tahiti and Samoa, Nicholas Thomas described how it "made the conversion to Christianity visible as a feature of people's behaviour and domestic life" (1999:6). Special clothes dedicated to the Sabbath marked profound changes in reckoning time (Bolton 2003; Jolly 1991; Thomas 1999:6). Objects may be seen as bridges between "incompatible systems" (Thomas 1991:206) where time and knowledge are given to shifting meanings and practices. Objects mediate across contexts and the "material qualities of objects can be mobilized dynamically to reposition objects rhetorically as contested grounds between different fields of meaning" (Manning and Meneley 2008: 288). Attending to objects "makes matter matter" in cosmological worlds and underlines that objects do not passively await meaning but are intertwined with practices of knowing, doing and becoming (Barad 2008:130).

Here, I explore how objects and expert knowledge illuminate the temporal dislocations and the "connectivities" of conversion to Christianity in Aneityum. In *Entangled Objects* (1991), Thomas has discussed the ways in which seemingly

OBJECTS OF EXPERT KNOWLEDGE

passive objects introduced to Pacific Island societies are "recontextualized." He later extended his argument by demonstrating how "things" also "actively constitute new social contexts" (1999:18). Introduced objects have the capacity to preserve "a prior order" and to "create a novel one" (Thomas 1999:18), affirming their capacities to produce cultural continuities and discontinuities with the past. Time, knowledge and objects are central to conversion that "literally refers to the act of turning a thing into something else" (Jolly 1996:231). Aneityumese sacred stones that made visible their cosmologies and connections to ancestors were "thrown away," while new stones were sanctified in an extravagant church. The Bible, translated word by word, circulated as an enchanted object among converts. Its circulation was made possible by the sale of arrowroot, which was converted from an ordinary plant. Arrowroot acquired new material-spiritual qualities, facilitating the circulation of thousands of Aneityumese Bibles that materialized new cosmological commitments to Christianity. Attending to these objects allows us to understand how knowledge and time are enmeshed in particular, material ways creating or affirming cosmologies and ontologies. Expert knowledge coincided with new temporal economies where objects constituted social contexts for enactments of the sacred and mundane.

I begin by introducing Geddie, the evangelist and clockmaker, and his acquisition of expert knowledge of the Aneityumese cosmology and its materiality. It is important to contextualize the ways in which he both privileged and disparaged indigenous knowledge and its objects. The changes already underway before the Geddies' arrival in 1848, including the introduction of new objects, technologies and pathologies are noted. A discussion of the *naroko*, a ritual centred on competitive feasting, offers insight into Aneityumese conceptions of time and how its cessation reallocated time enabling a new productive regime for the projects and objects of conversion. Finally, I discuss the translation of the Bible and the construction of the stone church as such "undertakings" suggest how material objects connect "prior" and "novel" orders. Through my consideration of the temporal lives of these objects, I show how conversion encompasses continuities and discontinuities.

Clockmaker and Evangelist: Christian Expert Knowledge and Practices

Early attempts at Christian conversion in southern New Hebrides had ended in the violent death of John Williams from the London Missionary Society (LMS) on the shores of Erromango, an island located near Aneityum. The legendary missionary of the South Seas, Williams was clubbed to death while attempting to extend his mission to the southern islands of New Hebrides. His death was a galvanizing moment for the young John Geddie, a newly ordained Presbyterian minister serving in Prince Edward Island. Geddie had grown up in Nova Scotia reading LMS reports of heathenism and evangelical triumphs. Haunted by William's death and drawn by resistance to Christianity, Geddie spent seven years in Prince Edward Island travelling to his rural congregations in snow, sleet and sun proclaiming the need to launch an overseas Presbyterian mission. He eventually persuaded his Prince Edward Island congregations and the Maritime Presbyterian Synod that, despite their lack of funds and their own marginalized colonial status, they could initiate and support a foreign mission. His persuasive effort and relentless advocacy were effective and, by 1848, John Geddie, together with his wife, Charlotte, and children had travelled 20,000 miles to Aneityum and set about establishing "the first successfully missionized island in Melanesia" (Linnekin 1997; Spriggs 1985:24). Geddie's bold effort to establish a Presbyterian mission in Aneityum attracted missionaries to the southern New Hebrides from Scotland (Proctor 1999), Nova Scotia as well as two brothers from Prince Edward Island who also died violently in Erromango during Geddie's tenure in the Pacific.

John Geddie was not one of the "godly mechanics" (Gunson 1978:32), those earliest of missionaries sent to the South Pacific selected on the basis of faith and practical skills, both of which they were expected to pass on to Pacific Islanders. Geddie was a trained and practicing church minister; however, he was also the son of a clockmaker from Scotland who had immigrated to Nova Scotia. Geddie was himself an accomplished clockmaker having worked with his father as a youth (Patterson 1946:14). Well versed in the mechanics of time, he recalibrated notions of time and its rhythm in Aneityum by introducing new measures of time tied to teleological practices of progress (Dening 1980). Drawing on the expert knowledge of John Williams, Geddie set out to reconfigure calendars, the cyclical experience of time and to challenge the chiefly and ancestral authority that underwrote the making of time in Aneityum. Indeed, Williams had long identified the link between refashioning temporalities and "raising up" the "heathen" through material projects (Dening 1980; Johnston 2001:34; Munn 1992). Before leaving colonial Canada, Geddie had taken time to learn new skills, such as printing and medicine, considered crucial to "raising up" the Aneityumese. En route to Aneityum, the Geddies stopped in Hawai'i, Samoa and New Zealand, where they learned about LMS mission practices and

OBJECTS OF EXPERT KNOWLEDGE 357

techniques of translation. Samoan teachers had been placed in Aneityum by the LMS around the time of William's death, and they were essential to Geddie's mission. Their geopolitical knowledge of the island facilitated the rapid establishment of evangelical outposts throughout the island (Spriggs 1985:26). John and Jessie Inglis from Scotland joined the Mission in 1852, and they were instrumental in the "undertakings" of conversion.

Europeans in search of sandalwood arrived in the 1830s, but sustained influence only began in the early 1840s. After a regional sandalwood and trading depot was established in 1844, Aneityum became a frequent port of call for sandalwood traders and whalers (Spriggs 1985:25). The sandalwood trade, which ended in the mid-1860s, was followed by a demand for plantation labourers in Australia and other Pacific regions. When Geddie arrived in 1848, the metal axes introduced by the sandalwood trade had replaced stone tools for food cultivation, freeing male labour for work at the sandalwood depot in exchange for food and cloth. Women's sexual services were also exchanged for material goods (Spriggs 1985:33). The trade with foreigners primarily involved those inhabitants of Anelcauhat where Geddie set up his mission and where he soon came to blows with the traders. The missionaries' "desire to raise islanders to 'moral and useful lives,' inevitably clashed with the desire of most Europeans to find pleasure and profit in islander bodies and resources" (Barker 2008:101).

Epidemics

The epidemics that followed foreign incursions resulted in enormous losses in Aneityum and many other Pacific Islands (Douglas 1989, 1994). In Aneityum there had been epidemics in the 1830s and in 1842, causing considerable mortality. Estimates of the population in the 1830s vary but, according to Spriggs, it was between 4,600 and 5,800 (1985:25). Epidemics continued to kill islanders and, according to Norma McArthur (1978), the population was halved between 1848 and 1867, a period that spanned most of Geddie's stay in Aneityum. He reported that the 1861 measles epidemic killed one-third of the population and all but "suspended" Church work (Geddie 1861b:246). Ten years earlier, the 1851 epidemic was considered a turning point for the mission, precipitating the conversion of villagers who had strongly opposed the mission (Douglas 1989). It appeared that converts under the care of the mission were benefitting from the mission's medical knowledge. There was increasing demand for medicine from those who had earlier identified Christianity as the source of such terrible illnesses (Douglas 1989; Spriggs 1985:35). Medicine positioned missionaries as ritual specialists (Lawson 1994:72; Spriggs 1985:33). The epidemics not only eroded the efficacy of local knowledge but also inflated the potential value of the Geddies' medical knowledge and authority. The deaths, due to epidemics, did not just affect individuals and clans in devastating ways but also resulted in the loss of knowledge that perished with its owners before it was transmitted. According to Thomas (2012), the population losses due to epidemics were political and not simply demographic. Knowledge connected to agricultural, maritime, medical, artistic and cosmological domains was decimated. Drawing on the experience of Marquesas, Thomas argues that it was "not just the passing of individual chiefs but more or less the end to ritual and social life, of everything they had created and struggled for" (2012:23). The catastrophic epidemics also represented enormous losses in Aneityum and forced new understandings of such events that undermined the efficacy of indigenous healing and its cosmological basis. This may well have facilitated the rapid conversion to Christianity (Douglas 1989, 1994). However, Lindstrom (2011:143) has argued that, "expectations of historical transformation ... are not necessarily exogenous" in places such as Aneityum. The epidemics along with the advent of traders and missionaries represented such a historical transformation.

Sacred Stones: Objects of Knowledge and Temporalities

While much expert knowledge was being eroded through epidemics, Geddie was acquiring knowledge about the spiritual and material world of the Aneityumese. It was an exercise considered essential to the establishment of missions in many places (Gardner 2006:296; Taylor 2010:430). Keenly interested in understanding the islanders he was dedicated to changing, Geddie quickly recognized that religion and its enactments of faith in Aneityum were woven into the practices of daily life and were, as Talal Asad has argued, "inseparable from the particularities of the temporal world and the traditions that inhabit it" (2001:139). Geddie's journal entries suggest that he was compelled to learn and to respect the system of laws (*itap*) that linked humans and ancestral spirits (*natmass*). In the early days of establishing the mission, Geddie in his journal (Miller 1975:53)[2] describes his practice of "itinerating" or walking around preaching the message of Christianity to those whom he met by

---

2   R. S. Miller's book is a collection of John Geddie's journal entries from his years in Aneityum.

OBJECTS OF EXPERT KNOWLEDGE
359

chance. It was during these times that Geddie would inadvertently interrupt the activities of chiefs and ritual specialists or violate the restrictions set by itap. His transgressions resulted in insults and these public displays of Geddie's ignorance jeopardized his capacity to assert his expertise and authority. He was issued warnings about his transgressions, including cutting down coconut trees that were reserved for the upcoming *nakaro*, an important ritual; taking coral from the reef to make lime for his building which disturbed the natmass; and closing the roads to natmass (Miller 1975:35–36). Natmass, as Douglas explained, were ancestral spirits of chiefs, which could and did intervene autonomously in human affairs and might reward or punish human actions" (1989:16). In Aneityum, natmass were approached through rituals, but their actions were unpredictable and could be precipitated by transgressive human activities (Douglas 1989). The *natimarid* or hereditary chiefs were also unsafe "if natmass wrath was incurred through the breaking of restrictions considered to be itap" (Gardner 2006:302). Understanding the nature of itap and the action of natmass became essential to all aspects of mission endeavours, including translation of the Bible and its production and circulation.

Reports from several generations of missionaries, including Geddie, described "the destruction of idols and documented [missionary] successes in creating a void then filled with their own structures and institutions" (Colley 2003:406; Lawson 1994:78, 2005). During my 2008 visit to Aneityum, James described how Geddie demobilized the *kastom* (custom) stones, integral to the Aneityumese cosmological system. James further explained: "The stone for pigs, the stone for taro, and the stone for yam and on and on were all gone." Geddie recognized the power of the ancestral spirits and sacred stones. The regenerative capacity of stones was affiliated with the production and reproduction of the essentials of daily life. Geddie noted that there is "one said to be a maker of pigs, another of fish, another of coconuts, another of taro, another of bananas. As nearly as I can learn, every division of the island has its *natmasses* of this class" (Patterson 1882:128). Geddie's efforts to eliminate the use of sacred stones and other ritual objects were so successful that he could not find a single "idol" to bring home to Maritime Canada in 1865 (Lawson 1994:78). Stones linked humans to sacred power in material ways that, as discussed below, reshaped new temporal narratives.

Recalibrating Aneityumese Temporalities

Chiefly and ancestral authority and knowledge were enacted in narrations of myth and ritual performances that underwrote the making and marking of time in Aneityum. Efforts to recalibrate the organization of time were central to the reordering of social and political life anchored by cosmological beliefs. Greg Dening observed that Christian missions did so by "making seven days in a week and one of them a sabbath, making mealtimes in a day, making work-time and leisure-time, making sacred time and profane time laid out time in a line, as it were" (1980:264). The introduction of the sabbath in Aneityum, for example, was accompanied by a set pattern wherein islanders, as Geddie noted in his journal, were summoned to the 8:30 morning church service by the beating of a piece of hollowed out log, and later a bell. During the service, Geddie preached for 30 minutes, followed by a sabbath school. In the afternoon, at 4:00, a divine service was held and included another short sermon, short addresses given by "natives" followed by a "family devotion" (Miller 1975:75–76). Dening (1980:264) argues that the new sense of time shaped by evangelical Christianity was tethered to a notion of progress and represented "a break-out from the present. A notion of progress called for a self and social discipline informed by an image of the future." Geddie's mission also recalibrated time through its measured attachment to projects such as Bible translation (which was translated one chapter per week), its printing, arrowroot production and church building, all of which were material, spiritual and temporal. These projects and the objects that defined them, along with new knowledge practices, reconfigured but did not replace indigenous time. Drawing on his work in the Solomon Islands, Geoffrey White has argued that the "locally produced histories" of Solomon Islanders are "reflexive," privileging ancestors and communities (1991:9). In this context the "hegemony of the mission rhetoric" and its practices are "incomplete" (White 1991:9).

Aneityumese temporalities embedded in the nakaro ritual were dynamic and material. On the nearby island of Tanna, time is "centered" (Lindstrom 2011), rather than measured, taking account of nights, moons, yams and, with Christianity, prayers. Lunar months are marked by practical and cosmological associations to food production, consumption and exchange. Time, in important ways, is materialized through food. Charting lunar time, according to Alfred Gell, "means attending to life in an organized, structured way" and keeping "track of time is part of keeping up with events" (1999:251–252). In Aneityum the nakaro was a cyclical exchange ritual where large quantities of food were given and received by chiefs. It was a central feature of social and political life and, as Spriggs argued, it provided a time and space where Aneityumese social organization, the position of chiefs and relationships to ancestors were made visible (1985:32). The central role of the chiefs in the

OBJECTS OF EXPERT KNOWLEDGE

nakaro involved the appropriation and circulation of surplus food production in their own areas and its redistribution across these boundaries. The quantity of food commanded by a particular chief could indicate that he was, for example, especially knowledgeable or favoured by ancestral spirits (1985:32). Natmass, involved in every action and phenomenon on the island, were the "power behind the success of crops" (Gardner 2006:302).

While regularizing everyday life and separating the sacred and mundane were important, it was even more important to remove "the cyclical time of rituals in which a legendary past was re-enacted to legitimate and prolong the present" (Dening 1980:264). Drawing on Alfred Gell's (1992:314) insight that temporal cycles such as the nakaro are better conceptualized as "lineal spirals of progressive time," Lindstrom notes "one never swings back around to the same moment twice" (2011:143). The indigenous system of time "pretends to eternal stasis and continual social reproduction while at another level history may rewrite eternity" (2011:150). The contrast between linear and cyclical time does not adequately capture the differences between Aneityumese and Christian practices of time. The nakaro was instrumental in the "making" and "remaking" of time. It demonstrated how natmass and mortals were "enmeshed through reciprocity in a relationship" with porous boundaries (Gardner 2006:302). Food, a key object of sociality and propitiation in Oceana, was at the core of the nakora, linking production and consumption to sacred power.

Geddie depicted the nakaro exchange as a wasteful and exploitative endeavour rather than a complex temporal enactment of knowledge and power linking islanders to ancestral spirits (natmass). Geddie, quoted in Spriggs, further explained in 1852 "that as the importance of a chief is judged by the quantity of food collected on such occasions, the common people are most heavily taxed in order to support his dignity" (Spriggs 1985:28). Paul, a young man from Aneityum whom I interviewed, explained that the Presbyterian mission was so intent on ending the elaborate food exchanges and chiefly displays of power and knowledge because "the missionaries needed to end such kastoms for they were time-consuming and the missionaries wanted the time of the Aneityumese. Feasting was a waste of time." Time, as Paul suggests, was diverted to new undertakings such as the production of arrowroot. LMS missionaries in Polynesia had taught converts to make arrowroot from the readily available "potato-like tuber" (Miller 1981:153). There was an international market for the arrowroot, considered an excellent food for invalids, and it had a variety of uses both in Europe and the Pacific. Christian converts produced countless tons of arrowroot throughout the island Pacific.[3] In Aneityum, Jessie Inglis learned to make arrowroot from a Rarotongan teacher and his wife, Tutan (Paton 1907). She then introduced the idea of using arrowroot as a source of income for the mission in Aneityum. Arrowroot exports covered the entire and considerable costs of printing the translated Bibles and a range of other texts needed for church and schools. The arrowroot, which was of superior quality, was sold through missionary networks in Australia and Scotland (Paton 1907:126). The new object of arrowroot transited from the mundane into a thing "too sacred to be used for daily food" and "was set apart as the Lord's portion" (Paton 1907:126). Arrowroot separated from the everyday was instrumental in creating novel contexts for enactments of the sacred.

The cessation of competitive food exchanges also freed women's time heretofore absorbed by the production and processing of ceremonial food and pigs for feasting. There was, then, competition for women's time with the establishment of the mission. Charlotte Geddie had started a school for women and recognized that feasts prevented women from attending school (Spriggs 1985:32). Margaret Jolly (1991) has described the way in which women's time and knowledge were reoriented through schools for women that targeted domestic practices associated with food production for ritual events and familial relationships. Missionaries, according to Jolly (1991:36), redirected women's energies away from work outside the home to work within it and from raising food and ceremonial crops to raising Christian families. For the Presbyterian mission, the new domestic domain became "that place where difference must be inclined toward time in certain ways" (Patel 2000:59). Women who were taught to read, for example, could organize the household into "the proper temporality" (Patel 2000:59). Gender was a crucial site for remaking time in Aneityum and for the process of conversion to Christianity in New Hebrides (Douglas 1999; Eriksen 2008; Jolly 1991). The conversion of women in Aneityum, according to Douglas, "provided the perfect before and after scenarios depicting the power of Christianity" (1999:13). This temporal framing made visible

---

3   Arrow root, (*tacca leontopelaloides*) "was a pan-pacific cultigen," locally known as tacca, island arrowroot, Polynesian arrowroot, Tahiti arrowroot or Fiji arrowroot (Spennemann 1994:215). The plants were self-propagating and easily grown. J. G. Miller describes arrowroot "as a new and easy source of cash" to pay for the costly production of print materials at a time when there were no other readily available cash crops to pay for mission activities (1981:153). The production of arrowroot predated the introduction of copra, and cotton had proven difficult to establish as a cash crop (Miller 1981). Arrowroot preparation was a time-consuming process (Spennemann 1994:215). It was grated, washed several times, dried and sifted through a "long and careful process" (Miller 1981:153).

OBJECTS OF EXPERT KNOWLEDGE   363

the contrast of the brutality of the "heathen" past that had been indexed by the condition of women. From the mission's viewpoint, women who were among the earliest converts, received Christianity "as the means of their deliverance from temporal and spiritual degradation and misery" (Douglas 1999:113; Jolly 1991).[4]

Temporalities of Expert Texts and Their Objects

When the 2,000 leather-bound copies of the Aneityumese New Testament arrived from England where they had been printed, Reverend John Inglis (1864:261) writes, "we lost no time in letting the natives have access to the Testaments; upwards of a thousand copies are already in their hands and they are reading them with great interest." Putting Bibles into the hands of Aneityumese was a laborious process that entailed the translation of "nearly a million words" (Inglis 1877:280). A full translation of the New Testament was made available in 1860, produced from the mission's own small printing press, and three years later the entire New Testament had been revised to meet the stringent standards of the British and Foreign Bible Society (Gardner 2006). The Bible could not have been translated without indigenous scholars (Gardner 2006; Taylor 2010:431). The printing of the Bible entailed a journey from Aneityum to England where Reverend Inglis and Willamu, an Aneityumese scholar, assiduously checked the translation en route (Gardner 2006:301). Its printing in England, as noted, was made possible by income from arrowroot. Writing down the language for the first time enabled conversion by localizing the text (Johnston 2001:17), making it available to everyone to hold, which was undoubtedly, a larger number than those who could read it. The Bible, with its authoritative presence accessible through reading, allowed "the radical individualism of the Protestants," who were dependent upon the "immediate relationship between the individual and God" (Johnston 2001:24). However, the materialization of the Aneityumese Bible, as an individually

---

4   Douglas argues that, in contrast to depictions of women's conversion in Aneityum, men's "embrace" of Christianity was represented as an engaged process that considered indigenous and Christian cosmologies and debated the nature of local and foreign spirits (1999:118). Eriksen (2008), who has considered gender differences in the Presbyterian Church in North Ambrym, Vanuatu, states that gender is fundamental to understanding Christianity and change. In North Ambrym, she argues, there is a contrast between male personified forms and female communal forms of structure. The Presbyterian Church builds on the communal principle, and the church "comes to stand for social wholes" (2008:158).

owned object of faith, comprised a series of collective commitments of time and expert knowledge.

Geddie's printing press, which locally produced the first copies of the complete New Testament, was fundamental to the pedagogical and religious mandates attached to conversion. Since 1816, printing presses had been affiliated with evangelical efforts in the Pacific region (Gunson 1978; Johnston 2001). The Geddies carried a printing press to Aneityum and quickly produced an alphabet, and within six weeks he was able to preach a rudimentary sermon in the Aneityumese language. Believing that objects such as print materials were essential to the mission's success, Geddie produced elementary school books, scripture portions and hymns before undertaking the full translation of the Bible. The work of bookmaking is evident in a letter written in 1853 by Charlotte Geddie, in which she describes being interrupted by "Mr. G [who] has just come in from the printing and says that two of our boys have already struck off 900 copies of the second edition of the Catechism.... You can have no idea of the demand there is for books" (Geddie 1908:30). John Geddie noted that in Aneityum, books that had formerly been objects of fear were increasingly regarded as enchanted objects that protected people from harm (Lawson 1994:78).

The proliferation of texts was accompanied by the simultaneous teaching of all the islanders to read, a project that engaged Samoan teachers, missionaries and Aneityumese catechists (Gardner 2006:296). Young women were also engaged in teaching as well as learning (Douglas 1999). Within a very short time, a network of schools and churches throughout the island (Spriggs 1985) were provided books from Geddie's printing operation such that, as John Inglis states, "no scholar was more than a mile from a school" (Gardner 2006:300). Books in the local language make visible the process of becoming Christian and the complex technologies of translation that encompassed both competing and convergent readings of the sacred and mundane. The schools scattered throughout the island acted as nodes in the networks that comprised conversion.

Anna Johnston argues that the texts—only enabled by the material presence of books—"could produce social change" and transform notions of indigenous time (2001:24). The Bible, according to Johnston, authored a kind of "doubled discursive time" that signified the modern dissemination of the Bible while, at the same time, affirmed its universal and eternal status (2001:17). The introduction of the Bible also "opens up a doubled place for the text—a place in Imperial British culture and a place in indigenous culture" (2001:17).

OBJECTS OF EXPERT KNOWLEDGE   365

Among the missionaries, the translation of the Bible into Aneityumese also prompted new insights into their own as well as indigenous beliefs. Translations of the Bible into indigenous languages represent "the discursive (if not fully cosmo-ontological) inevitable crossing" (Taylor 2010:434) between the Christian and indigenous understandings of sacred categories and power. In her close reading of the translation of the Bible in Aneityum, Gardner also contends that "both missionary and local cosmologies and cultural assumptions were challenged and changed through the on-going dialogues between missionaries and Islanders" (2006:302).[5] The translation of the Bible demanded a deep knowledge of Aneityumese cosmology and an acknowledgement of the complexity of Aneityumese languages (Gardner 2006:296).

The epidemics that swept through the island also ensured that death was the subject of both "contest and negotiation between missionary and indigenous understandings of scared power" (Jolly 1996:24). Such discussions were central to the translation and the search "for understandings that would convey both the same and different meanings" (Gardner 2006:303). Debates between missionaries and islanders showed "respective understandings of sacred power overlapped in crucial areas" (Taylor 2010:434). This perspective, which attends to similarities as well as differences, complicates Anna Johnston's contention that the Bible created a rupture with the past by introducing the break that enables cultural and temporal transformations in indigenous cultures (2001:34).

Immersion in the project of translation and conversion was so thorough that the Geddies often expressed concern that their facility in English was diminishing. And even more interestingly, as Charlotte Geddie states, "native words" were considered "more expressive than English" (1908:30). The missionaries who had first translated the word *itap* as "forbidden" came to understand it as "sacred" and used itap as the title for the Old and New Testaments (Gardner 2006:302). The discursive and material qualities of the objects of conversion are evident in Charlotte Geddie's letter and in the translation and printing of biblical texts. The Bible or itap that took the form of leather-bound books suggests the "connectivities" and materialities of conversion in Aneityum.

---

5   Margaret Jolly (1996:24) cautions that the tropes of conversation, debates and dialogue used to characterize conversion can obscure the power inequities embedded in conversion between males and females and between indigenous islanders and foreign missionaries.

Converting Stones and Temporalities

Translating and printing the Bible and establishing a system of schools were enormous tasks but so too were the 18 months of hard labour dedicated to building the stone church. Geddie noted (Patterson 1882:402) that such activities "occupy the minds of people to such an extent that they have neither the time nor inclination for feasting and other usages common in the days of heathenism." Time allocated to new objects of Christianity meant that, by 1859, the church in Aneityum was paying for itself without support from overseas funding. However, the church and the schools, signifying the success of conversion, were centres of deadly contagions fuelling the epidemics among islanders, who did not have immunity to the newly introduced diseases (Gardner 2006:299).

The large church built stone b-stone suggests how islanders "used things to change contexts" (Thomas 1999:19). The location of the new stone church was a practical decision based on proximity to large stones, rather than a consideration of sacred spaces and spirits in Aneityum. Geddie was clearly confident that he no longer needed to consider indigenous sacred power or the action of the natmass. Geddie describes the building of the church as follows:

> To natives who have been accustomed only to build small grass houses, it has been a great undertaking. The amount of labour expended on it can hardly be conceived by persons at home where every facility for such an undertaking is enjoyed. The stones were all carried by the natives, and some of them were so large that it required 60 men to remove them to their destination. The stones were so large they were quarried near the building, otherwise we could not have undertaken it. [1861a:40]

The heavy stones sanctified in the large new church made tangible new enactments of sacred power. In addition to quarrying the stones, islanders cut down large trees in the interior and carried them for miles to make the beams for the church. According to one account, hundreds of people carried the main beam on their shoulders and "Chief Nohoat stood on the log, with his plumes in his hair, and the best ornaments on his arms. Natives headed the procession blowing conches" (Steel 1880:102). The church was constructed without using any nails, held together by local technologies and expert knowledge. It was also intricately ornamented with decorative figures painted with various colours from dyes made with roots and "a million yards of fine plaiting" (Johnston 1861:74). Food was central to marking the opening of the new church. There was "a large

OBJECTS OF EXPERT KNOWLEDGE

collection of food which was cooked and distributed among the people of the different villages ... according to their usual custom" (Geddie 1861a:41).

While condemning the extravagance and wastefulness of competitive exchanges of food in the naroko ritual, Geddie also embarked on a taxing and competitive project of church-building. He declared, "With the exception of the King's church at Honolulu, Sandwich Islands, I have not seen any equal to it in the islands which I have visited" (Geddie 1861a:40). Competition was also extended to the hard-won Bibles, as the new "Bibles like all other books were distributed by merit: we have given them to the best readers first and only to those who can read tolerably well; we make them prizes to be contended for, but prizes which every one may obtain" (Inglis 1864:261). The arrowroot, too, was noted for its superior quality. The objects of conversion embodied a competitive spirit that resonated within the Aneityumese context, displaying the "overlapping" of exogenous and indigenous valuations of sacred and mundane.

Conclusion

I have explored how objects such as stones, books and food materialized temporalities and expert knowledge in the context of the Presbyterian mission in Aneityum in the mid-19th century. Attention to objects emphasizes the materiality of conversion to Christianity that links becoming, doing and knowing. Following objects complicates the understanding of conversion by defying static conceptions of indigenous time and querying the irretrievable loss or inevitable gains at stake in becoming Christian. Discussions of conversion to Christianity often hinge on the separation of spirit and matter, the sacred and mundane, the mind and body, the past and present. These oppositions are themselves "artefactual" (Manning and Meneley 2008:291), concealing the fragmentation of knowledge and the ephemeral nature of its expertise.

Objects such as leather-bound Bibles were essential to Aneityumese strategies of conversion, offering a hands-on context for enchantment or re-enchantment. The Bibles were distributed as a "prize" that all could obtain, and the production of thousands of Bibles (and the enormous church) side-stepped the tragedy of death and depopulation, where the numbers of Bibles could conceivably exceed the numbers of Aneityumese. Death was a sombre marker of time and epidemics were part of the new temporal regimes introduced by traders in search of whales, sandalwood and labour, as well as missionaries in search of converts. Epidemics in Aneityum eroded the expert knowledge that anchored indigenous temporal frameworks and undermined the efficacy of indigenous deities and rituals. While intent on challenging the chiefly institution of natimarid and ending rituals that enacted sacred power and its temporalities, Geddie was compelled to recognize the power of indigenous cosmologies and to understand how objects connected material and spiritual realms. I have discussed the notion that Aneityumese time was atemporal or "timelessly" reproduced through myth and ritual, in contrast to modern Christian time depicted as transformative and dynamic. "Expectations of historical transformation," as Lindstrom (2011:143) reminds us, are integral to indigenous temporalities. Attending to similarity and difference are essential to understanding "the structural dialectics of history" (Douglas 1989; Taylor 2010:423). While Geddie recalibrated time in Aneityum by measuring and organizing it in new ways and banning rituals such as the nakaro, the mission project was also the object of temporal, discursive and material reconfigurations.

Approaching Aneityum by boat in 2008, I saw the traces of the first Presbyterian mission: the landscape shelters the ruins of the stone church, some rusted metal near the beach, possibly the printing press and the foundation of the missionary's house. Geddie's church built stone by stone has now been replaced by a more modest Church. In 1861, while an epidemic raged, the newly completed church was deliberately set afire: only the stone walls remained (Geddie 1861b:246). The fire, in Geddie's view, represented the collusion of a small group of "natives" and sandalwood traders who opposed the mission (1861b:247). The fire was soon followed by a hurricane, leading Geddie to remark, "The church was not taken from us without a reason. Perhaps we have been devoting too much attention to externals" (1861b:248).

The church has been transmuted into impressive and haunting ruins where saplings erupt through the remaining stonewalls. Another generation of children plays in the ruins of the church that their ancestors built. In contrast to the ruins, Geddie's eyeglasses, safeguarded by islanders since his departure, are a more intimate object of conversion that renders time and expert knowledge tactile and personal. They, like the stone ruins, point to the complex history between Geddie's Christian mission and Aneityumese islanders and between the temporalities of past and present.

While Geddie was intent on the temporal transformation of the Aneityumese, he was himself bound by the past and haunted by his missionary ancestors. Geddie drew on the expertise of missionary John Williams, who emphasized that conversion to Christianity was yoked to "material undertakings." Geddie's expert knowledge was also tempered by experience in the art of persuasion acquired in Prince Edward Island along with the powerful insight that expert knowledge materialized in objects is essential to recalibrating temporalities.

OBJECTS OF EXPERT KNOWLEDGE 369

Acknowledgments

Research in Vanuatu was made possible from funding from the Social Sciences and Humanities Research Council of Canada. For invaluable help, I am indebted to Jim Rodd, Emily Niras, Alexandra Widmer and Naomi McPherson.

References

Appadurai, Arjun (1988). Introduction: Commodities and the Politics of Value. *In* The Social Life of Things Commodities in Cultural Perspective. Arjun Appadurai, ed. Pp. 3–36. Cambridge: Cambridge University Press.

Asad, Talal (2001). Reading a Modern Classic: W. C. Smith's The Meaning and End of Religion. *In* Religion and Media. H. de Vries and S. Weber, eds. Pp. 131–147. Stanford: Stanford University Press.

Barad, Karen (2008). Posthumanist Performativity: Toward an Understanding of How Matter Comes to Matter. *In* Material Feminisms. Stacy Aliaimo and Susan Hekman, eds. Pp. 120–156. Bloomington: Indiana University Press.

Barker, John (1990). Introduction. Ethnographic Perspectives on Christianity in Oceanic Societies. *In* Christianity in Oceania: Ethnographic Perspectives. John Barker, ed. Pp. 1–24. London: University Press of America.

Barker, John (1992). Christianity in Western Melanesian Ethnography. *In* History and Tradition in Melanesian Society. James G. Carrier, ed. Pp. 144–173. Berkeley: University of California Press.

Barker, John (2008). Where the Missionary Frontier Ran Ahead of Empire. *In* Missions and Empire. Norman Etherington, ed. Pp. 86–106. Oxford: Oxford University Press. http://dx.doi.org/10.1093/acprof:oso/9780199253487.003.0005.

Bolton, Lissant (2003). Gender, Status and Introduced Clothing in Vanuatu. *In* Clothing the Pacific. Chloë Colchester, ed. Pp. 118–139. Oxford: Berg.

Carr, E. Summerton (2010). Enactments of Expertise. Annual Review of Anthropology 39(1):17–32. http://dx.doi.org/10.1146/annurev.anthro.012809.104948.

Colley, Ann C. (2003). Colonies of Memory. Victorian Literature and Culture 31(2): 405–427. http://dx.doi.org/10.1017/S1060150303000214.

Dening, Greg (1980). Islands and Beaches: Discourse on a Silent Land; Marquesas, 1774–1880. Chicago: Dorsey.

Douglas, Bronwen (1989). Autonomous and Controlled Spirits: Traditional Ritual and Early Interpretations of Christianity on Tanna, Aneityum and the Isle of Pines in Perspective. Journal of the Polynesian Society (N. Z.) 98(1):7–48.

Douglas, Bronwen (1994). Discourses of Death in A Melanesian World. *In* Dangerous Liaisons: Essays in Honour of Greg Dening. Donna Merwick, ed. Pp. 353–378. Melbourne: University of Melbourne.

Douglas, Bronwen (1999). Provocative Readings in Intransigent Archives: Finding Aneityumese Women. Oceania 70:111–128.

Eriksen, Annelin (2008). Gender, Christianity and Change in Vanuatu: An Analysis of Social Movement in North Ambryn. Aldershot: Ashgate.

Gardner, Helen Bethea (2006). New Heaven and New Earth: Translation and Conversion on Aneityum. Journal of Pacific History 41(3):293–311. http://dx.doi.org/10.1080/00223340600984778.

Geddie, Charlotte (1853). Letter to Mrs John Lockerby, 15 February 1853. Accession No. 2974. Public Archives of Prince Edward Island.

Geddie, Charlotte (1908). Letter to Mrs James Waddell, 18 February 1853. *In* The Letters of Charlotte Geddie and Charlotte Geddie Harrington. Truro, Nova Scotia: News Publishing Company.

Geddie, John (1859). Letter to Mr John Lockerby, 8 November 1859. Accession No. 2974. Public Archives of Prince Edward Island.

Geddie, John (1861a). Letter to Rev James Bayne. The Home and Foreign Record of the Presbyterian Church of the Lower Provinces of British North America. 1(January):39–41.

Geddie, John (1861b). Letter to Rev James Bayne. The Home and Foreign Record of the Presbyterian Church of the Lower Provinces of British North America. 1 (September): 246–249.

Gell, Alfred (1992). The Anthropology of Time: Cultural Constructions of Temporal Maps and Images. Oxford: Berg.

Gell, Alfred (1999). Time and Social Anthropology. *In* Time and Contemporary Intellectual Life. Patrick Baert, ed. Pp. 251–268. Cambridge: Elsevier.

Gunson, Niel (1978). Messengers of Grace: Evangelical Missionaries in the South Seas, 1797–1860. Oxford: Oxford University Press.

Inglis, John (1864). The New Hebrides Mission Report. The Home and Foreign Record of the Presbyterian Church of the Lower Provinces of British North America 4(October):259–262.

Inglis, John (1877). In the New Hebrides: Reminiscences of Missionary Life and Work Especially on the Island of Aneityum from 1850 till 1877. London: Nelson & Sons.

Johnston, Anna (2001). The Book Eaters: Textuality, Modernity, and the London Missionary Society. Semeia 88:13–40.

Johnston, Bessie (1861). Letter 16 June 1860: Rev. and Dear Sir. The Home and Foreign Record of the Presbyterian Church of the Lower Provinces of British North America 1(March):73–75.

Jolly, Margaret (1991). "To Save the Girls for Brighter and Better Lives": Presbyterian Missions and Women in Southern Vanuatu, 1848–1870. Journal of Pacific History 26(1):27–48. http://dx.doi.org/10.1080/00223349108572645.

OBJECTS OF EXPERT KNOWLEDGE

Jolly, Margaret (1996). Devils, Holy Spirits, and the Swollen God: Translation, Conversion and Colonial Power in the Marist Mission, Vanuatu, 1887–1934. *In* Conversion to Modernities: The Globalization of Christianity. Peter Van der Veer, ed. Pp. 231–262. London: Routledge.

Lawson, Barbara (1994). Collected Curios: Missionary Tales from the South Pacific. Fontanus Monograph Series No. 3. Montreal: McGill University Libraries.

Lawson, Barbara (2005). Collecting Cultures: Canadian Missionaries, Pacific Islanders and Museums. *In* Canadian Mission, Indigenous People, Representing Religion at Home and Abroad. Scott James and Austin Alvyn, eds. Pp. 235–261. Toronto: University of Toronto Press.

Lindstrom, Lamont (2011). Naming and Memory on Tanna, Vanuatu. *In* Changing Contexts, Shifting Meanings: Transformations of Cultural Traditions in Oceania. Elfriede Hermann, ed. Pp. 141–156. Honolulu: University of Hawai'i Press.

Linnekin, Jocelyn (1997). New Political Orders. *In* The Cambridge History of the Pacific Islanders. Donald DeNoon, ed. Pp. 185–217. Cambridge: Cambridge University Press. http://dx.doi.org/10.1017/CHOL9780521441957.007.

Manning, Paul, and Anne Meneley (2008). Material Objects in Cosmological Worlds: An Introduction. Ethnos 73(3):285–302. http://dx.doi.org/10.1080/00141840802323997.

McArthur, Norma (1978). And Behold, the Plague Was Begun among the People. *In* The Changing Pacific: Essays in Honour of H. E. Maude. Niel Gunson, ed. Pp. 273–284. Melbourne: Oxford University Press.

Miller, G. J. (1981). Live: A History of Church Planting in the New Hebrides, to 1880. Book One. Sydney: Committees on Christian Education and Overseas Missions of the Central Assembly of the Presbyterian Church of Australia.

Miller, R. S., ed. (1975). *Misi Gete*: John Geddie, Pioneer Missionary to the New Hebrides. Launceston: Presbyterian Church of Tasmania.

Munn, Nancy D. (1992). The Cultural Anthropology of Time: A Critical Essay. Annual Review of Anthropology 21(1):93–123. http://dx.doi.org/10.1146/annurev.an.21.100192.000521.

Patel, Geeta (2000). Ghostly Appearances: Time Tales Tallied Up. Social Text 18(3):47–66. http://dx.doi.org/10.1215/01642472-18-3_64-47.

Paton, John G. (1907). Missionary to the New Hebrides. New York: Fleming H. Revell Company.

Patterson, George Geddie (1946). Geddie's Earlier Life and Work. *In* The Geddie Centennial Addresses. Pictou, Nova Scotia. October 1–3. Pp. 12–28. Box No. FRA-1, Atlantic School of Theology Library. Halifax Nova Scotia.

Patterson, George (1882). Missionary Life Among the Cannibals: Being the Life of Rev John Geddie, First Missionary to the New Hebrides, With a History of the Nova Scotian Missions on that Group. Toronto: Campbell, Bain and Hart.

Proctor, J. H. (1999). Scottish Missionaries and the Governance of the New Hebrides. A Journal of Church and State 41(2):349–372. http://dx.doi.org/10.1093/jcs/41.2.349.

Robbins, J. (2007). Continuity Thinking and the Problem of Christian Culture: Belief, Time and the Anthropology of Christianity. Current Anthropology 48(1):5–38. http://dx.doi.org/10.1086/508690.

Scott, Michael W. (2005). "I Was Like Abraham": Notes on the Anthropology of Christianity from the Solomon Islands. Ethnos 70(1):101–125. http://dx.doi.org/10.1080/00141840500048565.

Spennemann, Dirk H. R. (1994). Traditional Arrowroot Production and Utilization in the Marshall Islands. Journal of Ethnobiology 14(2):211–234.

Spriggs, Matthew (1985). "A School in Every District": The Cultural Geography of Conversion on Aneityum, Southern Vanuatu. Journal of Pacific History 20(1):23–41. http://dx.doi.org/10.1080/00223348508572503.

Steel, Robert (1880). The New Hebrides and Christian Missions. London: James Nisbet & Co.

Taylor, John (2010). The Troubled Histories of a Stranger God: Religious Crossing, Sacred Power, and Anglican Colonialism in Vanuatu. Comparative Studies in Society and History 52(2):418–446. http://dx.doi.org/10.1017/S0010417510000095.

Thomas, Nicholas (1991). Entangled Objects: Exchange, Material Culture, and Colonialism in the Pacific. Cambridge, MA: Harvard University.

Thomas, Nicholas (1999). The Case of the Misplaced Ponchos: Speculations Concerning the History of Cloth in Polynesia. Journal of Material Culture 4(1):5–20. http://dx.doi.org/10.1177/135918359900400101.

Thomas, Nicholas (2012). Islanders: The Pacific in the Age of Conquest. New Haven, CT: Yale University Press.

White, Geoffrey M. (1991). Identity Through History: Living Stories in a Solomon Islands Society. Cambridge: Cambridge University Press. http://dx.doi.org/10.1017/CBO9780511621895.